general editor John M. MacKenzie

When the 'Studies in Imperialism' series was founded more than twenty years ago, emphasis was laid upon the conviction that 'imperialism as a cultural phenomenon had as significant an effect on the dominant as on the subordinate societies'. With more than sixty books published, this remains the prime concern of the series. Cross-disciplinary work has indeed appeared covering the full spectrum of cultural phenomena, as well as examining aspects of gender and sex, frontiers and law, science and the environment, language and literature, migration and patriotic societies, and much else. Moreover, the series has always wished to present comparative work on European and American imperialism, and particularly welcomes the submission of books in these areas. The fascination with imperialism, in all its aspects, shows no sign of abating, and this series will continue to lead the way in encouraging the widest possible range of studies in the field. 'Studies in Imperialism' is fully organic in its development, always seeking to be at the cutting edge, responding to the latest interests of scholars and the needs of this ever-expanding area of scholarship.

The Scots in South Africa

The Scots in South Africa

ETHNICITY, IDENTITY, GENDER
AND RACE, 1772–1914

John M. MacKenzie
with Nigel R. Dalziel

MANCHESTER
UNIVERSITY PRESS
Manchester and New York

distributed exclusively in the USA by
PALGRAVE

Copyright © John M. MacKenzie 2007

The right of John M. MacKenzie to be identified as the author of this work has been asserted by him in accordance with the Copyright, Designs and Patents Act 1988.

Published by Manchester University Press
Oxford Road, Manchester M13 9NR, UK
and Room 400, 175 Fifth Avenue, New York, NY 10010, USA
www.manchesteruniversitypress.co.uk

Distributed in the United States exclusively by
Palgrave Macmillan, 175 Fifth Avenue,
New York, NY 10010, USA

Distributed in Canada exclusively by
UBC Press, University of British Columbia, 2029 West Mall,
Vancouver, BC, Canada V6T 1Z2

British Library Cataloguing-in-Publication Data is available

Library of Congress Cataloging-in-Publication Data is available

ISBN 978 0 7190 8783 7 paperback

First published by Manchester University Press in hardback 2007

This paperback edition first published 2012

The publisher has no responsibility for the persistence or accuracy of URLs for any external or third-party internet websites referred to in this book, and does not guarantee that any content on such websites is, or will remain, accurate or appropriate.

Printed by Lightning Source

CONTENTS

Foreword by T. M. Devine — page vii
Acknowledgements — page ix
List of abbreviations — page xii

1	**Introduction: imperialism and identities**	*page* 1
	Scots and empire	4
	Scots, Scottish identity, Scotland and southern Africa	9
2	**The Scots presence at the Cape**	29
	The travelling Scot	29
	Prominent Scots in the British occupations	37
	The Moodie settlement	39
	The 1820 settlement	48
3	**Radicals, evangelicals, the Scottish Enlightenment and Cape Colonial autocracy**	64
	How many Scots?	65
	Somerset and the 'Scotch Independents'	66
	Greig and the dissemination of the press	74
	Reform and Emancipation	76
	Fairbairn: commerce, finance and education	79
	Representative government	81
	Intellectual and scientific institutions	84
	Conclusion	88
4	**Scots missions and the frontier**	94
	The military frontier	96
	The missionary frontier	99
	Scots missionaries: politics, land and war	106
	Mission education: the Lovedale and Blythswood Institutions	109
	Lovedale and medical mission	115
	African ministers	116
	Scots women on the frontier	118
	Natal and the Gordon Memorial Mission	120
	Conclusion	121

5	**Continuing migration to Natal, the Cape and the Transvaal**	135
	Migration to Natal	135
	Byrne and other settlements	138
	Success stories	144
	Ne'er-do-wells	148
	Women and entrepreneurship	149
	White population and later settlements	149
	Immigration to the Cape	156
	New Scotland	157
	South Africa and the migration boom	161
6	**Professionals: the Church and education**	169
	The Church	170
	Education	183
7	**The professionals: the environment, medicine, business and radicals**	204
	Scots and the environment	204
	Medicine	216
	Business	223
	Radicals	228
8	**Maintaining Scots identity**	240
	Caledonian and other Scottish societies	242
	The South African Scot	248
	The South African 'Scottish' regiments	252
	Scotland and South African 'Scottishness'	258
9	**Conclusion**	267

Index — 276

FOREWORD

This important book is one product of an innovative academic development in diaspora studies sponsored by the UK Arts and Humanities Research Council (AHRC) from 2001. In that year the AHRC provided substantial funding for a Research Centre in Irish and Scottish Studies hosted by the University of Aberdeen but also consisting of scholars drawn from its partner institutions of Queen's University, Belfast, and Trinity College, Dublin. Both the Irish and Scots contributed disproportionately to emigration from the British Isles and so intrinsic to the venture, in addition to research programmes in languages and literatures, were several projects on the nature, origins and impact of the mobility of these two ethnic groups at the global level from the seventeenth century to the present.

John MacKenzie's fine book on the Scots in South Africa is one of the first of these studies to appear in print. Previous works have considered the role of the Scots in Canada, the United States and Australasia but never before has the Scottish community in South Africa been considered in such systematic fashion. This, then, is a truly pioneering volume thoroughly based on archival work on Southern Africa together with a comprehensive reading of the secondary literature. The Scottish contribution to missionary activity in Africa and particularly the role of the legendary David Livingstone are reasonably familiar areas. But MacKenzie breaks much new ground in his examination of such key themes as identity, ethnicity, politics, education, science, intellectual developments and much else. The result is a wonderfully rich and textured evaluation of the impact of the Scots on the history of nineteenth-century South Africa which helps to fill a yawning gap in the study of the Scottish diaspora.

But John MacKenzie's volume is not simply a major contribution to Scottish emigration history. As a master historian of empire he is also deeply familiar with the current issues of debate in British imperial history. Thus at every point MacKenzie seeks to integrate into his narrative such vital topics as 'Anglicisation' in the colonial context, 'whiteness' and cultural transfers and their longevity. This, then, is a book which will appeal well beyond the ranks of historians of Scotland and its remarkable influence on the making of British Empire. It can also be guaranteed an appreciative readership among those intrigued

FOREWORD

by the complex nature of the imperial project, the story of South Africa and European migration history in general.

T. M. Devine
Sir William Fraser Professor of Scottish History and Palaeography, University of Edinburgh, and Director of the AHRC Centre for Irish and Scottish Studies, University of Aberdeen, 2000–05

ACKNOWLEDGEMENTS

My first expression of appreciation must go to the Arts and Humanities Research Board (now Council) of the United Kingdom. The Board placed such faith in the Research Institute of Irish and Scottish Studies (RIISS) at the University of Aberdeen as to fund it exceptionally generously. My research trips to South Africa were made possible as a result of a grant from the AHRB funds of the Institute. RIISS was founded and expertly developed by Tom Devine, and I am grateful to him as colleague and friend for much support and stimulation. Among the other members of RIISS and the Department of History at Aberdeen (past and present) I must also acknowledge the warmly affectionate help of Roy Bridges, John Hargreaves, Marjory Harper, Alan Macinnes, Angela McCarthy, Steve Murdoch, Andrew Mackillop, Nick Evans and the many participants, too numerous to mention (but many appear in endnotes), at lively Aberdeen conferences and symposia.

In South Africa and elsewhere in Africa I must thank the following for friendship, hospitality and help with bibliographies and ideas: Vivian and Claudia Bickford Smith, Nigel Worden, the Rev. James Patrick, John and Barbara Lambert, Jane and Vincent Carruthers, Jonathan Hyslop, Natasha Erlank, Donal McCracken, Peter Merrington, Gordon Pirie, Julian Cobbing, Christopher Saunders, Greg Cuthbertson, Bridget Theron and Reuben Matheka. In Britain I have long been indebted to William Beinart, Saul Dubow, Douglas Hamilton, Richard Grove, Richard Rathbone, David Anderson, Avril Powell, Frank Dikotter, Stephen Constantine, Jeffrey Richards, Shula Marks, Tom Tomlinson, Ian Brown, Wayne Dooling, Justin Willis, Cherry Leonardi, Peter Marshall, Nigel Rigby, Aubrey Newman, Gareth Griffiths, Elizabeth Buettner, Miles Taylor and others interested in questions of ethnicity, identity and empire. I have been fortunate in developing considerable scholarly networks through the Studies in Imperialism series, which I have edited for more than twenty years. In Europe colleagues such as Robert Ross, Nicola Labanca, Sandrine Lemaire, Joachim Miggelbrink, Giuseppe Finaldi (now in Australia), Hermann Hiery, Vincent Kuitenbrewer, Klaus Bade, Bernhard Gissibl, Jürgen Osterhammel and Stig Forster helped even when they were unaware of doing so.

Broader issues of Scots and the empire have been debated with Jenni Calder, David Forsyth, Michael Fry, Angus Calder, Chandrika Kaul, Bruce Lenman, Michael Bentley, Christopher Smout, Eliza Riedi,

ACKNOWLEDGEMENTS

Elizabeth Buettner and Esther Breitenbach. In the missionary historians' network I have been fortunate to work with Brian Stanley, Andrew Porter, Andrew Walls, Jed Brown, Andrew Ross and others. Overseas, David McNab, Chris Youé, Peter Henshaw and Robert Kubicek have always been supportive in Canada, as have Eric Richards, Jim Hammerton, Norman Etherington, Derek Schreuder, Patricia Grimshaw, Kirsten McKenzie and others in Australia, as well as James Belich, John Cookson, Tom Brooking, Katie Pickles and Jennie Coleman in New Zealand.

Archivists and librarians in Britain, Canada, Australia, New Zealand and above all in South Africa have contributed in some shape or form to this work. In the latter, the staffs of the following have been particularly helpful: the Archives of the Western Cape (particularly Jacob van der Merwe), the South African Library, the library of the University of Cape Town, the National Archives in Pretoria, the superb Archives and Africana collection of the University of South Africa (where Marié Coetzee knew her collection so well that she spent a day pulling out sources for us), the National Library in Pretoria (undergoing some much needed refurbishment), the Archives of KwaZulu Natal in Pietermaritzburg, the library of the University of KwaZulu Natal (particularly the excellent support of Margaret Bass), the Natal Society Library (now the copyright library of KZN) and the Cory Library in Grahamstown. The Cory has now emerged as my favourite library. There the head librarian, Shirley Stewart, the User Services librarian, Zweliyanyikima Jackson Vena and the librarians Shirley Kabwato and Victor Velile Gacula were unstinting in finding material from its rich collections.

Richard Price (working on the history of British Kaffraria) helped to make a period of work in the Western Cape archives interesting and pleasurable, as did Elizabeth van Heyningen in both Pretoria and Pietermaritzburg while pursuing her research on the medical aspects of the Anglo-Boer War concentration camps. My old friend Terry Barringer, formerly librarian of the wonderful library of the Royal Commonwealth Society (for long my favourite library), so sadly moved from its great location in Northumberland Avenue, London, to the Cambridge University Library, has been an indefatigable correspondent, bibliographer and supplier of review copies. Her knowledge of missionary history, among much else, has been invaluable. Our friends and neighbours Tam and Morag Thomson kindly provided the use of their Edinburgh flat while we worked at the National Library of Scotland. Our other friends and neighbours, Rob and Margaret Kidd, kindly collected us from stations and airports. Thomsons and Kidds provided much agreeable hospitality, as did Sir William Macpherson

ACKNOWLEDGEMENTS

of Cluny, whose family archive located at Newton Castle is unrivalled. Another neighbour, Donald MacLeod, provided Gaelic translations. The minister of Alyth, the Rev. Neil Gardner, has become an inspirational friend and supporter. Nigel Dalziel, who accompanied me on visits to South Africa and was a devoted fellow researcher in building up the materials on which this book is based, rightly takes his place on the title page. However, the book was written by J. M. M. and any errors are his alone.

J. M. M.

LIST OF ABBREVIATIONS

AWC	Archives of the Western Cape
AYBSAH	*Archives Year Book of South African History*
CLG	Cory Library, Grahamstown
CO	Colonial Office
DRC	Dutch Reformed Church
DSAB	*Dictionary of South African Biography*
EIC	East India Company
EMS	Edinburgh Missionary Society
FMC	Foreign Missions Committee (Free Church)
GAMS	Glasgow African Missionary Society
GMS	Glasgow Missionary Society
GMSPCS	Glasgow Missionary Society according to the Principles of the Church of Scotland
HMG	Her Majesty's Government
KZNA	KwaZulu Natal Archives
LMS	London Missionary Society
MLA	Member of the Legislative Assembly
NAP	National Archives, Pretoria
NGR	Natal Government Railways
NLSA	National Library of South Africa
OFS	Orange Free State
SAS	*South African Scot*
SED	Scottish Education Department
SESA	*Standard Encyclopaedia of South Africa*
UP	United Presbyterian
VOC	Vereenigde Oostindische Compagnie

CHAPTER ONE

Introduction: imperialism and identities

When Archbishop Desmond Tutu coined the phrase 'the rainbow nation' for post-apartheid South Africa he was no doubt thinking of varying shades of black, brown and white. But within each of those categories there are of course further ethnic subdivisions, identifiable through language, history, cultural traditions and religious forms. Africans are mainly divided into different branches of the Nguni and the Sotho–Tswana peoples, as well as migrants (and sometimes refugees) from adjacent states. People of Asian descent have migrated, or been brought as slaves and indentured labourers, from parts of the Indian subcontinent and South East Asia. The Cape Coloured people are extraordinarily diverse in their genetic make-up, incorporating some of the original Khoisan (hunter-gatherers and pastoralists) inhabitants of the region, the so-called Malays, as well as many mixed-race groupings. Yet they have a sense of identity and pride in their cultural forms that are second to none. So far as the whites are concerned, it has long been customary to divide them simply into Afrikaans- and English-speakers. Yet the first are made up of an amalgamation of at least Dutch, French, German and even Scots forebears (the latter will be explained below), while the second include those who owe their descent to English, Welsh, Irish, Scots, as well as European migrants who adopted the English language and at least some elements of English cultural norms.

Of course South Africa is far from unique in this respect. Most modern nations are made up of complex amalgams of various ethnicities. The nineteenth-century notion of the ideal coherence of state and ethnic nation, so strongly propagated by Germany, but also the ambition of other Europeans, including the English, was always an impossible dream. It is ironic that this vision of nationalism helped to produce the imperial expansion which was to prove its nemesis. Imperialism created 'colonies of white settlement', all of them with dispossessed indigenous populations, which briefly clung to a notion of globalised nationalisms retaining some semblance of linguistic, cultural, religious, if not ethnic, purity. From the eighteenth century at least, the Dutch, French and British all vainly assumed that empires could envisage such an expansion of a European national ideal. It was of course a chimera, doomed to what might be described (in both older and more modern formulations) as dilution, contamination, reordering and cultural drift. Empires went further: in Asia, Africa and the Americas they created wholly artificial borders, incorporating multiple ethnicities, and called them territories, colonies, or in the Indian case a separate 'empire'. These were destined though not necessarily designed to become multi-ethnic states, often riven by the tensions and potential conflicts of such a condition.

In the territories of white settlement, the increase in ethnic complexity became part of the process of migration and population growth. Of course, as we shall see in the case of the Cape (and later South Africa), some diversity in European origins was always characteristic of the white population. A degree of polyglot migration was necessary not only to the yearning for power and dominion which developed among such populations but also to the growth and extension of exploitative forces and economic diversity. Efforts at overwhelming indigenous populations, through a high degree of violence (intentional) as well as the spread of destructive disease (largely unintentional), required infusions of population that were not always available within the parent imperial society. Imperial expansion in that period often had a curiously international flavour, but usually such additions to the white population were sufficiently small that they could be assimilated into the majority group. By the nineteenth century, however, these multiple migrations were accelerating, largely as a result of the pull of mineral discoveries. As ever, gold proved a powerful lure in North America, Australia, New Zealand, and South Africa. Reversing the alchemist's dream, golden opportunity invariably turned to dross, but the migratory deeds had been done, aided by many other 'push' and 'pull' factors. United States society turned this diversification of its immigrants into a virtue, part of its professed national mission to be a melting pot of (mainly white) peoples, although it was quick to raise the barriers in the twentieth century when it faced economic recession or feared particular forms of migration.

The melting pot was the perceived ideal, creating a wholly new and supposedly enlightened society, but the reality was that assimilation was often hindered by the scale of migration of particular ethnicities, providing them with the opportunity to survive as separate cultural forces, sometimes living in the same regions or neighbourhoods, dominating particular jobs, or adhering to specific religious or national institutions. Sometimes, degrees of assimilation could be reversed, as when new generations rediscovered cultural 'roots' and found comfort in emphasising difference, in identifying themselves as representatives of a national, or indeed international, ethnicity which distinguished them from the common herd. Blood lines (however 'contaminated') offered opportunities to mark themselves out as belonging to different 'stock'. For some, this is no more than a folkloric residue; for others it represents cultural affiliations of significant psychological value. For many it offers the chance to participate in attractive cultural expressions – music, dance, dress, games, processions and the like – forms that connect them with others exhibiting similar predilections across the globe, all supposedly tying them into a European 'Ur' culture. Such ethnic identity seldom disrupts national affiliation, but it provides an appealing alternative layer.

Canada, Australia and New Zealand have all exhibited similarly complex migratory patterns, ethnic constructions and layers of identity. In the case of these former British 'dominions' there has been a striking range of studies of these phenomena in recent years. Among these, perhaps the Irish and the Scots have received most attention. Apart from the obvious fact that these two nationalities contributed a high proportion of their populations to international migration, the reasons for this renewed interest are complex. Ireland's economic miracle, largely resulting from membership of the European Union, has turned the country into a sophisticated and affluent society. Despite the continuing difficulties in Ulster, though now much ameliorated, older nationalist and religious hang-ups have been put to rest. Restoration and modernisation have proceeded apace, and in parallel with this the writing of Hibernian history has also been refurbished. As the nationalist 'master narrative' has to a certain extent receded the strength of cultural affiliation seems to have survived or even advanced.

In the case of Scotland, devolution has produced greater interest in bilateral cultural, educational and political relations with Ireland. An Irish consular representative came to reside in Edinburgh. There is renewed concern with aspects of a common Celtic inheritance, in language, literature, music and sport. Universities sought research partnerships, and scholars, notably historians, linguists and literary critics, came to collaborate on what they perceived to be parallel patterns and common interests both within the history of the United Kingdom and in the British Empire beyond.[1] It was not, of course, always so. Although there have been, since the Elizabethan settlements, close relations between Scotland and Northern Ireland (creating the category of the

Ulster Scots or the 'Scotch Irish'), the Scots in the nineteenth century largely sought to distance themselves from the Catholic Irish. The Scots had a domestic and international reputation to uphold. The English had a tendency to emphasise their supposed virtues in contrast to the alleged disabilities of the Irish. Nineteenth-century imperial travellers like Sir Charles Dilke and J. A. Froude extolled the Scots, even in comparison with the English, while Anthony Trollope compared the Irish unfavourably with Scots, revealing a biased ethnic preference of the day.[2] Quite apart from the prejudice, we now know this to be often false in economic terms. The Irish were much more successful economically and socially in many parts of the British Empire than they were given credit for.[3] They also came to dominate (often together with the Scots) certain professions, including surveying and medicine, and they played a striking role in the creation of complex identities.[4] The recent historiography of the Irish diaspora has been subtle, suggestive and sophisticated. No one concerned with Scottish migration and activities in the former imperial territories can ignore it.

Scots and empire

Sir Charles Lucas,[5] writing in his *Historical Geography of the British Colonies* in 1897, pointed out that 'the annals of the dark continent are rich with Scotch names'. Having listed many missionaries and explorers, he noted that 'the first British commandant of the Cape was General Craig, his successor in command of the forces was General Dundas. The second and final expedition against the colony was led by Sir David Baird. All three were Scotchmen.' He also considered that:

> the strength of the missionary movement was in great measure due to the infusion of Scotch blood and to the effects of Scotch training. We trace to this source enterprise and tenacity, endurance and shrewdness, capacity for hard practical work, zeal in controversy. Difficulties, whether physical, social, or intellectual, have always acted as a stimulus to the northern character, and the qualities which are inherent in Scotchmen were tested and strengthened by the trials and dangers of missionary enterprise. Men of this type put their hands to the plough and looked not back.[6]

Earlier in the century, Sir Joseph Banks, the great scientist and President of the Royal Society, had written, 'So well does the serious mind of a Scotch education fit Scotsmen to the habits of industry, and frugality, that they rarely abandon them at any time of life, and I may say never while they are young.'[7]

Both of these were non-partisan commentators, but their views reflect the nineteenth-century admiration for imperial Scots, noted for their military and business capacity, as well as their educational attainment. Moreover, such views of the distinctive character of the Scots were apparently shared by the functionaries of other empires. A German traveller, Tom von Prince, a *Schutztruppe* lieutenant travelling to Lake Nyasa, found himself in Blantyre in about 1893. Under the heading 'African Scotland', he noted the cold and un-African fog, and went on, 'all around was the unmistakable accent of that kind of Englishmen. What is more, Livingston[8] [sic], who discovered that area, was a Scotsman. Almost all inhabitants there seem to be Scottish, a breed of men which is very clever in monetary affairs. They combine the pleasant with the useful, are the best soldiers of England, and are very precise as businessmen.'[9] In a sense, the Scots have almost had to live down this inflated reputation, but in recent years there has been a positive spate of studies of their roles in the original American colonies, the United States and the British imperial territories throughout the world.[10] There have also been exhibitions and museum displays, with associated publications.[11]

Some of this work has assumed the character of 'celebration', but most has been concerned with much more hard-headed interests. Among the earliest works devoted to the Scots in the United States and the British Empire, such as W. J. Rattray's four-volume *The Scots in British North America* (1880) and J. H. Brander's *The Scot Abroad* (1881), the principal concern seems to have been with the identification of significant migrations and key individuals.[12] From the 1880s, the decade of the first act in the process of devolution, the founding of a Scottish Office and the ministerial post of Secretary of State for Scotland (1885) to the 1930s and beyond, there was a disposition to view the overseas activities of the Scots as a source of national pride, even as an indicator that they were perfectly capable of running their own affairs. Andrew Dewar Gibb, a professor of law and member of the imperial faction of Scottish nationalism, published his *Scottish Empire* in 1937. Gibb framed his imperial ideas with two books whose titles tell all, *Scotland in Eclipse* (1930) and *Scotland Resurgent* (1950).[13] He seemed to be suggesting that a greater awareness of Scottish activities (he would certainly have called them 'achievements') in the British Empire and beyond would lead to a renewal of national pride, even to a new national determination. The same sentiments emerged at the British Empire Exhibition in Glasgow in 1938, encapsulated in a specific appeal to history. The distinguished Tudor historian J. D. Mackie wrote in one of the exhibition publications that 'in the far-flung outposts of Empire' Scots 'never lose their identity'. They were bound by 'traditions and customs which, while their outward forms may change with the passing of centuries, their inward and spiritual significance remain rooted in the heart'.[14] At the same exhibition, the Church of Scotland even dared to have a mural depicting the failed Darien scheme between 1695 and 1700.[15]

Almost inevitably, a contrary tendency saw Scots' exploits overseas as a badge of shame, evidence of their subservient status to the English, of their complicity in an English project of power and domination.[16] Others saw Scottish involvement in the British Empire as evidence of a shared experience of subordination and exploitation with the indigenous peoples of other continents.[17] They too were a colonised people, albeit in different ways from the Irish. They were the dispossessed victims of extreme forms of landlordism (the Highland Clearances), of a cyclically fragile and socially disruptive capitalism (the periodic exigencies of the heavy industrial complex of the central belt), of an excessively rapid and destructive urbanism (the horrors of the slums of Glasgow, Dundee and elsewhere), not to mention the displacement of rural workers and small tenants from the richer agricultural lands of eastern Scotland and the Borders as a result of the development of new, more highly capitalised, technologically advanced and latifundian agricultural practices.

In examining Scots in the empire we should, however, remember that the Scots also migrated in large numbers to England and that this most obvious and nearest migration has, perhaps, been the least studied.[18] The Scots 'colonised' the professions in England. Working-class Scots created whole new communities in the nineteenth and twentieth centuries, in places such as Barrow-in-Furness and Corby. The Scots population has been long in decline and, uniquely in Europe, continues to be so. Dr Johnson's celebrated canard about Scots and the high road to England has remained true for more than 250 years. The same economic and social forces were at work here, but at the elite end of society it is also possible that Scotland seemed to be just too small a stage upon which to act out ambition. The number of Scots Prime Ministers since Gladstone (genetically a full Scot, though born in England) has been out of proportion to the respective populations. Even in the twenty-first century, the predominance of Scots in British public life has been much commented upon. In 2005 the celebrated television journalist Jeremy Paxman suggested that England was labouring under a 'Scottish Raj'.[19] Since the artist William Hogarth and others satirised the Scots in British public life in the eighteenth century they have paradoxically been seen as both perpetrators and victims, driven from their own country by a powerful range of forces.

In recent years, this 'victimhood complex' has been displaced by a realisation that the activities of Scots need to be examined in much

INTRODUCTION

more independent and instrumental ways. Of course some were involuntary migrants (and they make good copy for sentimental depictions in paintings and in literature), but the vast majority made elective decisions to try their fortunes elsewhere. Once there, the Scots seized the opportunities afforded by colonisation with an eagerness which belies any sense of being in some kind of slavish relationship with English political masters or a dominant landlord class. Scots migrants came from all the social strata and brought their cultural, religious, educational and social experiences to bear upon new environments. In all these ways a new degree of sophistication has developed in considering the manner in which the domestic affairs and predilections of Scots interacted with those peoples (fellow white settlers and indigenous inhabitants) and places (fresh climatic, social, economic and environmental contexts) to be found in their new locations elsewhere in the world.[20]

Sceptics suggest that none of this matters. Irish, Scots, English and Welsh soon adopt another identity in their new social and environmental context. Patrick O'Farrell has forcefully argued this, quoting his father, an Irish immigrant to New Zealand, as saying, 'What has Ireland ever done for me?'[21] Another notable sceptic is Eric Richards, who, despite (or maybe because of) his studies of the distinctive character of Highland land owning, believes that the strongly assimilative and integrative forces in Australian society obliterate ethnic origins fairly rapidly.[22] Intermarriage accelerates these processes, soon diluting such identities. Thus it does not ultimately matter whether economic enterprise, acts of oppression or political dispensations (to use just three examples) prompt the migration of one ethnicity or another. If migrants do cling to some cultural forms, this is no more than adherence to a kind of comforting residuum, a relatively minor social arabesque, which ultimately has little effect upon their actions or upon the structural character of the society and state to which they now offer allegiance.

This book is dedicated to the overturning of this proposition. Even if the contemporary situation suggests that ethnic identities are in retreat (and even this proposition is debatable, given the survival and even development of cultural and clan societies around the world), such a sense of allegiance to 'home' is significant and instrumental in the historical period covered by this book.[23] This may constitute a phenomenon continuing into the twenty-first century which may be described as the homeland remembered, reimagined and reinvoked.[24] There is plenty of evidence to suggest that migrants retained not only an awareness of layered or multiple identities, but also in many cases a sense of plural domicile. The more distant identity, from the migrant's or ancestor's place of cultural origins, does not necessarily experience a linear decline. Even after generational 'dilution' through intermarriage, such identities can experience surprising revivals. To a certain extent, this runs contrary to the notion of a homogeneous *British* approach to empire which was of long standing, had a clearly propagandist purpose and has always been deeply embedded in an imperial historiography. Sir John Seeley entitled his lectures of 1883 *The Expansion of England* because he saw the English conquest or assimilation of the other nations of the British Isles as a necessary prerequisite of global dominion. This was, in other words, an English-led and English-dominated imperial project. At the other end of an imperial historiography, Sir Reginald Coupland, who was himself involved in the constitutional debates surrounding the progressive decolonisation of the twentieth century, notably in Ireland and India, worried that the logical extension of such a decline of empire might indeed be the contraction of Britain. His last and posthumously published book, *Welsh and Scottish Nationalism* (1954), was devoted precisely to this proposition. The greater part of Ireland might have gone, but the other components of Union had to survive to maintain national self-respect. With the sinking over the horizon of such an imperial historiography, at precisely the time that the sun was setting on the British Empire, we now take an entirely different approach to imperialism. The fact of the matter is that the creation of a supposedly English dominion equally involved the Expansion of Scotland, the Expansion of Wales and the Expansion of Ireland.

Perhaps the extreme form of expressing this notion lies in the title of Donald Akenson's book *If the Irish ran the World*.[25] In this latter-day series of lectures, a distinguished historian of migration has charted the Irish effect upon the island of Montserrat, the Irish contribution to its genetic code, as he puts it, despite the fact that there are no people who could be identified as Irish left. Their significance as planters and slave owners in the past left place and personal names. Even more significantly, they contributed various aspects of the culture of the island (though he is sceptical of overplaying this, as some have done). But, whereas the Irish in Montserrat have been assimilated or have departed, the inheritors of the Scots and Irish mantle are an identifiable and sometimes all too visible strand in the populations of Canada, Australia and New Zealand, where they constituted, in the nineteenth and early twentieth centuries, a considerably higher proportion of the population than their numbers in Britain warranted. In the Cape and the other South African territories which combined in the Union in 1910 they were never so prominent numerically. But their influence was out of proportion to their numbers.

INTRODUCTION

Scots, Scottish identity, Scotland and southern Africa

There was no truly large-scale Scots migration to the Cape, although the gold mines of the Transvaal sucked in a surprising number at the end of the nineteenth century. (These figures are examined in Chapters 3 and 5.) But before that the Scots at the Cape and in the other territories were largely (though not exclusively) members of a commercial and intellectual elite. As merchants and shipowners they seized the opportunities available at the Cape after the colony was first taken from the Dutch in 1795. Scottish regiments were prominent in the garrison (and some soldiers stayed). But, above all, the intellectual and religious life of the colony was indelibly marked by Scots (or people trained in Scotland) and their activities. Scots were active in the establishment of the intellectual institutions of the Cape from the 1820s. They were central to the development of printing and a free press. They were key figures in the creation of educational and medical services. They were prominent in all the infrastructural and environmental professions, as surveyors, engineers, builders, botanists, foresters. They were significant in the transfer of the concept of the museum, in the study of natural history, geology, fossils, and in astronomical research. Later, they were active as trade union leaders. They virtually saved the Dutch Reformed Church from decline and they established their own forms of Presbyterianism almost everywhere. Above all, they constituted, through various societies and denominations, a highly significant band of missionaries. As such, they developed important connections with the frontier (as well as with the heartland of the colony) and consequently with African societies.

To produce this list is not to suggest that the Scots were uniquely enlightened, humanitarian or politically and culturally radical. They were just as capable of being reactionary, as brutal in the carving out of their settlements and involvement in warfare, as any other whites. But this book is not designed either to celebrate or to pass moral judgements – except in so far as these are unavoidably entwined in the meanings of words as they have mutated in contemporary times. Far too many recent histories have fallen into E. P. Thompson's well expressed trap of looking at the past with the 'enormous condescension of posterity'.[26] Rather, the argument will suggest that the Scots brought a particular set of experiences of cultural and religious institutions, of an intellectual background with a severely practical bent, and of the social relations of both urban and rural life, to bear upon the region, and that their world view was so formed by these sets of influences that they operated in significantly different and clearly identifiable ways from, say, the English, the Welsh or the Irish.

This raises the whole question of whether there was a distinct Scottish identity which was maintained, promoted or even developed at the so-called periphery of empire. This is the corollary of the notion that an overall Scottish identity after the Union of 1707 was specifically related to the Scots participation in the opportunities of the British Empire (so called precisely to embrace the Scots and other ethnicities within the British Isles).[27] There has been a very considerable debate about these complex questions of identity, not least from the point of view of the relationship between a new sense of 'Scottishness' in the era and the nature of 'Britishness' as developed in the late eighteenth and early nineteenth centuries.[28] I have myself argued that some of the regional differences among Scots were broken down overseas, where a stronger sense of a distinct Scots ethnicity based upon a range of cultural, religious, military and historical signifiers came into play.[29] It may even be the case that the British Empire was actually the milieu for the cultural survival of the various ethnicities of the British union.[30] But all identities are dynamic and fluid. They can be multiple and complex, shifting according to sets of relationships connected with gender, generation, class and occupation, all modified by geographical and historical context. They change over time and space, through individual and group experience, and with the evolution of each individual generation and its successors. The metaphor of strata or layers has been used, but that is perhaps too mechanistically archaeological.[31] The process is much more like a compound which changes both its composition and its overall characteristics as new elements are added.

Moreover, identities are made up of internal and external perceptions. We each of us have some sense of our identity, complex or simple as it may be. We are also aware of how others perceive us, and that external perception interacts with and modifies our own self-construction. The Cape produced its own diverse set of identities, framed in both interior and exterior forms, among White, Black and Coloured peoples deeply embedded within their economic, social and spatial relations. And yet, within the ethnic complexities of the Colony, and the other territories that eventually made up the Union of South Africa, there emerged a continuing and changing sense of being both Scottish and colonial in the nineteenth century. The Southern African experience, for example, significantly modified and enhanced the military and religious components of the emerging identity of the Scots.[32] But as these latter examples illustrate, we should remember that expressions of these identities, particularly in the nineteenth century, were invariably generated by, and mainly applied to, males. Women were just as active in their identity formation and may well have influenced that of males in the process.

I have also argued that, although the British Empire was English in its administrative and legal forms (as it happens in the latter case less so in South Africa), it was strongly influenced by the Scots in most other respects.[33] The reservations of the Act of Union of 1707 preserved Scottish religious, educational, legal and financial systems, and this meant that Scottish civil society survived. Indeed, it was the continuing existence of such a distinct civil society which constituted one of the strongest arguments for devolution, namely that this civil apparatus should be regulated in the place where it was best understood, in the Scottish capital, Edinburgh. By extension characteristics of the Scottish civil experience can be identified clearly surviving throughout the former British Empire in a range of educational, religious and other institutions. To this we may add the specific contribution of the Scottish Enlightenment, notably the manner in which it created new disciplines. These included political economy, comparative social study constituting a proto-anthropology, early forms of geography, a scientific tradition that was connected to European networks, as well as social, legal and political ideas that were national in some of their forms but international in their connections and significance.[34]

Moreover, the Scottish universities (generally numbered as four, but by some calculations there were six) were grossly over-producing graduates in the late eighteenth and nineteenth centuries.[35] Greater social mobility could be exercised through education in Scotland than elsewhere in the United Kingdom, and Scots were often forced to seek career opportunities overseas. Such graduates came from a relatively sophisticated urban society where powerful economic and social forces, related to the early phases of the industrial revolution, were at work. While some doubt has been cast on such high figures, it is possible that literacy (at least in basic forms) in Scotland was as high as 75 per cent in 1750. Scots were also surrounded by examples of new technology and their capacity to produce dramatic transformations in economic forms, affording fresh opportunities for power in every sense. These produced, and were backed up by, the provision of infrastructure and the creation of new or renewed built environments. Even in rural areas, technical change was frequently apparent. On the great Scottish estates landowners exerted considerable power, and each estate was a minor polity and community in its own right. Each had its great house and economically active outbuildings, decorative and productive gardens and woodland, its home farm, residences for a hierarchy of workers from factor to labourer, with central institutions like church, mill, sawmill and school.

Another key influence in the framing of a distinct Scotland was the fact that it was one of the centres of the Romantic movement, both in terms of its own writers and artists, and also in respect of the manner in which it was regarded by Europeans. The faked Ossian sagas of James Macpherson and the novels of Sir Walter Scott were celebrated and highly influential throughout Europe. Constructions of landscape, appreciation of its natural historical, geological and fossil forms, became central characteristics of Scottish attitudes to the environment. As is well known, Johnson and Boswell, despite their rather hostile account of the Highlands, were travelling at a time when new forms of exploratory, scientific, quantitative and aesthetic travel were beginning to be fashionable. The attitudes of the English Tory Johnson can be contrasted with those of the Welsh Whig Thomas Pennant, who had influenced Johnson in his desire to travel to Scotland in the first place.[36] As the revolts of the eighteenth century – notably the Jacobite rebellion of 1745–46 – retreated into history the land came to be mapped. The Statistical Accounts of Scotland first mooted in 1790 and which came to be known as the Old, were published in twenty-one volumes between 1791 and 1799. These were followed by the New, compiled between 1831 and 1845 and the whole enterprise impressively charted the population, settlements and economic activities of the country. Even these were based upon earlier proposals for the surveying of Scotland parish by parish dating from the 1760s and 1770s, an early manifestation of a fascination with statistics that was to become so significant in the early nineteenth century. Antiquarian, archaeological, historical, naturalist and scientific societies as well as field clubs were springing up everywhere between the 1780s and the middle of the following century, mirroring the grander societies of Edinburgh, like the Royal Society of 1783 and the Wernerian Natural History Society of 1814. Thus, virtually for the first time, the wildness was tamed and both wilderness and population patterns and occupations came to be understood. As Charles Withers has forcefully argued, Scottish identity was defined by science, societies and surveys of all sorts.[37] And the membership of these societies reflects a striking degree of social mobility.[38]

The yearning to chart and survey everything to do with Scotland came partly from its diversity, partly from its relatively small size. The first made the project apparently necessary, but also intriguing and possible. The second ensured that the country could be conveniently swept up into research and publication projects on which professionals, members of the elite and amateurs, often drawn from a variety of social classes, could work. All this activity emphasised the notion that Scotland was a country of distinct geographical, geological, botanical, zoological, ornithological, and in some ways ethnographic regions. It was a land where there was strong awareness of the significance of frontiers – Highland, Lowland, Borders, western and northern islands. Occasionally these frontiers were religious in form, as in the remaining Catholic parts of the Hebrides and the Highlands. It was also a land which was trilingual. As well as Gaelic and English, most of the Scottish population spoke dialects of the Scots tongue which, though linguistically related, were more or less impenetrable to the English. Burns, after all, wrote in both Scots and standard English. Many ministers were accustomed to delivering sermons in both Gaelic and English, or at times with Scots variants. Scottish culture was thus thoroughly hybrid and this was to be highly significant in its colonial manifestations.

Although the founding of societies, scientific study and literary and philosophical movements were similarly occurring in other parts of the British Isles, the Scottish examples had a degree of intensity and comprehensiveness that contributed to this sense of Scots distinctness. The conviction that Scotland was different was also derived from its educational system of parish schools associated with the Church and from its universities. These both mirrored and created sets of social and economic characteristics that offered an awareness of forms of cohesiveness and potentiality for achievement arising out of this very sense of supposedly unique diversity. Meanwhile, processes of rural change and economic structural weaknesses, invariably noticed by contemporary observers, were to contribute greatly to the force of the Scottish diaspora. Thus, on the one hand, these very studies threw up evidence of the dislocations which were to affect the Scottish economy and society down to the end of the twentieth century, and which were to influence Scottish migration, not least to the Cape and elsewhere in South Africa. On the other, the notion of the strengths to be derived from statistical and qualitative forms of knowledge was to be transferred to other parts of the globe.[39] Information systems and the data they provided were not only a prerequisite of power; they also offered a means to self-knowledge and a definition of ethnic identity.[40]

In some respects, this identity was made up of a sense of being a marginal people, marginal in terms of Europe, marginal in respect of the larger British state. And there were degrees of marginality within Scotland itself. As we shall see, there were those in South Africa who thought that Highland Scots in particular were better able to cope with the harsh conditions of the Cape frontier because of the nature of the lands and climate which were their lot beyond the Highland frontier. Even those who migrated from Scots cities and towns or from more favourable land in the east and central areas of Scotland were not unused to hardship. Their living conditions were generally far from luxurious and some of them at least put up with the rigours of a supposedly primitive frontier existence. They also indulged in forms of clannishness and mutual help that were also observed in other parts of the nineteenth-century Empire.

All these characteristics were to be powerfully influential in southern Africa. Just as in Europe Scots migrants and traders had formed connections between the worlds of the Baltic and the Low Countries,[41] and then effectively created a seagoing bridge to North America, so, at the Cape, Scots discovered a port which linked the Atlantic to the Indian Ocean and Pacific worlds, a key link between Europe, the Americas, South Asia, the Far East and Australasia. It also constituted the major jumping-off point to an extensive interior. Yet this port largely lacked the infrastructure and the intellectual, scientific and literary institutions which its importance warranted. Like Scotland, South Africa was a land of geographical, environmental, and climatic frontiers, though they were grander and more extreme in their forms. The societies of southern Africa, white and black, were complex and polyglot. As in Scotland, they ranged from the comparative sophistication of the town (at this stage only Cape Town and a few much smaller outriders like Stellenbosch, Swellendam and Graaff Reinet) to remote and, to European eyes, 'primitive' settlements, whether white, black or those of mixed race like the Griqua. It seemed obvious to the influential Scots who arrived in the early years of British rule that the techniques and institutions that had so transformed Scotland were eminently exportable and could be equally effective in a seemingly alien land.

Hence, for good or ill, Scots contributed more powerfully than their numbers would suggest to the processes of westernisation and modernisation in the region. Through their linguistic and ethnographic activities, particularly in the context of the frontier missions, they had a considerable influence upon attitudes to African peoples, to the classic nineteenth-century activity, derived from the Enlightenment, of creating taxonomies and stereotypes for humans as much as for the phenomena of the natural world. Such activities led to strong, though inevitably diverse, ideas about the frontier, African administration, labour policy, and much else. These views invariably made some missionaries and 'intellectuals' distinctly unpopular with settler farmers (of whom some were of course Scots) and other exploiters of the land and environment. Moreover, they were seldom popular with colonial administrations. But they had a tendency to be 'noisy'. That

INTRODUCTION

is, they entered vigorously into controversy, made their views known through the press and any other media available to them. They published books, and they set out to activate their contacts and networks at home in order to influence religious, administrative and political policy makers.[42]

Through all this activity, they imprinted themselves on the landscape. Perhaps more than any other group, they set out to establish a taxonomy of southern African plants, to systematise the geology of the region, to create lexicographies and orthographies (however flawed) for African languages, as well as to produce literary accounts of land and peoples.[43] They would have seen this as an essential prerequisite in the creation of forms of Calvinist theocracy as mediated through the Scottish and Dutch variants. Meanwhile, Scots ministers gave their names to subdivided parishes. Other settlers named farms and geographical features. This was part of the international process of founding miniature Caledonias in unlikely places. Missionaries attempted to recreate what were in effect Scottish estates on their mission stations.[44] They saw newly planted gardens and woodland as evidence of the redemptive power of a recreated environment.[45] As we shall see, Scots surveyed roads and alarming routes over *kloofs*, or passes. They were involved in the building of railways and harbours. Later in the nineteenth century, a fresh wave of Scots brought with them some knowledge of mining techniques. Experimental chemists in Glasgow were also to produce the methods by which the low-grade gold of the Witwatersrand could be extracted.

But some sceptics would enquire whether this overall designation of 'Scots' really works. It has sometimes been argued that Scots were more conscious of their local than of their supposedly national origins. It has been suggested that migrating Scots thought of themselves much more as Highlanders, Islanders, residents, for example, of Aberdeenshire, Fife, the central Lowlands or the Borders. Although the Declaration of Arbroath of 1320 offers evidence of a sense of Scottish national identity much earlier than was envisaged by Benedict Anderson's 'imagined community',[46] this sense of nationhood may have been largely restricted to an elite. Yet, as suggested above, the evidence seems to suggest that migratory Scots did identify themselves as belonging to some national identity larger than the purely local. In 1825 a party of people from the Borders and Dumfries and Galloway left Leith for Argentina. A shipboard diary kept by a Dumfriesshire farmer, William Grierson, indicates just such a sense of national origins. He waxed lyrical about the land that was left behind, declaring that 'our present children will prattle your names, and our future offspring shall learn your songs', all demonstrating that 'our reciprocal *Love* [emphasis in the original] is immortal'. He described the nostalgia of hearing bagpipes played on board (although bagpipes do of course have a wider incidence than the Highlands) and he described the party as indulging themselves in Highland reels (or 'flings') on deck on fine tropical evenings.[47] This also suggests that the adoption of Highland symbols as signifiers for the whole of Scotland, long attributed to the visit of George IV to Edinburgh in 1822, so carefully choreographed by Sir Walter Scott, had already percolated through both the geographical regions and the social classes.

But a more general sense of Scotland was also invoked. 'Fiddle, flute and bagpipe ... showed that 8,000 miles of Sea had not cooled their Scottish blood' and 'an hour or two was dedicated to some of Burns' most Patriotic lays'.[48] On arrival in Buenos Aires the existence of a Scottish network there was demonstrated by the way in which Grierson passed from one 'Scotchman' to another, organising the details of the settlement.[49] A memoir written in old age by another member of this party, Jane Robson, reveals her clinging to her Scottishness in the southern hemisphere into the twentieth century, and demonstrating the manner in which members of the Scots community held together in an alien environment, complete with weddings, dances, church dedications and funerals. In a politically disturbed Argentina, she found it a 'wild uncertain life after leaving our peaceful Scottish home'.[50] The younger generation retained their Scottish identities despite the changes wrought in their countenances by a different climate. Jane was much disgusted when a visitor remarked that 'No one would think you girls were Scottish with your white heads and black faces'.[51]

Maybe Argentina, outside the formal British Empire and much racked by civil strife, invoked different and mutually protective emotions, but some of the reactions of Grierson and Robson must have been matched by migrants across the South Atlantic in another part of the southern hemisphere. The evidence from South Africa also indicates that, however Scots characterised themselves at the point of departure, there can be little doubt that once in the territories of formal and informal empire (as in Argentina) they were quite clear that they were distinguished from the English, Welsh or Irish by their overall Scottishness. The notable historian W. M. Macmillan suggested in his autobiography that, although he was only five years old when his parents migrated from Aberdeen to the Cape, he was 'already old enough to consider myself a good Scot'.[52] At the Cape, his family joined the 'strong Scotch colony' at Stellenbosch, and maintained their links with home through correspondence (Wednesday mail day was the key point in the week) and the arrival of the weekly editions of the *Free Press* (of Aberdeen) and *The Scotsman* (of Edinburgh). By his own admission, Macmillan's identity as a Scot influenced his thinking and his publications throughout his time in South Africa.[53]

Macmillan also indicates the extent to which, in southern Africa, Scots were powerfully aware of the Presbyterian culture shared by the majority of them, a Calvinist character which they felt (and repeatedly uttered as a propagandist device, often against the English) drew them closer to the Dutch or Afrikaners.[54] The 'Scotch' community in Stellenbosch had easy-going relations with the Afrikaners (at least before the Anglo-Boer War), involved as they were in what seemed like a joint educational and religious project. The Scots even conducted their services for a time in the Dutch Church, accepting Dutch Reformed pastors as much as their own.[55] Moreover, the nineteenth-century tendency to schism in the Scottish Church often had the effect of stimulating renewed energy in missionary and other religious activities elsewhere in the world, including South Africa. But, given the lack of ministers and the vast areas to be covered, this schismatic character was sometimes ironed out there. Scots were of course also active in other denominations, notably the Congregationalists, Methodists and Baptists.

As Macmillan and others demonstrate, this sense of identity enabled them to establish networks, religious and social groupings, as well as self-help organisations, through which they consciously interacted with fellow Scots. Whether they did so or not depended, of course, on 'critical mass'. If there were too few of them, they were much more likely to assimilate to their surroundings. But as we shall see from the example of the Western Cape, if there was an opportunity to form a separate, though not necessarily exclusive, community they generally did so. It was a community that was articulated not only by the economic and professional activities of the men, but also by the social and literary pursuits of the women. In the missions, missionary wives constituted a vital, and insufficiently recognised, force within the Christian settlements. Later, as women sought to develop their own professional roles, they often emphasised the religious and cultural forms which marked out their identities. Thus, identities are made up of aspects of gender, class and race, as well as of ethnicity.

These characteristics are probably to be found in Scots communities wherever they settled. If intermarriage and the passage of the generations allegedly tend to cause 'dilution', nonetheless we do not have a linear progression here. Later generations, particularly after a fresh infusion of population, can rediscover 'roots' and can re-emphasise supposed cultural origins. This has been a feature of populations claiming Scots descent in many territories, not least in South Africa. This offers a reminder that in writing about the Scots in the territories of southern

Africa, later the Union, one is dealing with what is essentially an international phenomenon, with undoubted variants, but also with recognisable similarities.[56] To take but one example, Scots heroes like Wallace, Bruce or Burns were used as totems everywhere. It also offers clear recognition of the fact that the record of the Scots in southern Africa is made up of elements of international intellectual, religious, scientific, environmental, social and cultural histories. In excavating the 'archaeology' of a self-identified Scottish community at the southern end of the African continent the historian has to bear in mind the existence of many parallel 'sites' elsewhere in the world.

These comparative studies are already well advanced in the case of Canada, the United States, Australia,[57] New Zealand,[58] India[59] and the dependent territories of the former British Empire, but generally South Africa has been left out of account in these respects.[60] Although South Africa has been cited as a key exemplar in aspects of comparative environmental history,[61] in the consideration of frontiers,[62] of so-called 'native administration',[63] land laws, political rights[64] and the like, it has seldom entered into discussion of British ethnicities in the colonial context. Meanwhile, within an exceptionally sophisticated South African historiography, the role of the Scots has been frequently noted, but not always fully understood. The work of Natasha Erlank on Scottish missionaries on the Eastern Cape frontier[65] and of Jonathan Hyslop in respect of Scottish trade union activists and South African 'Scottish' regiments has been more sophisticated than that of any of their predecessors.[66] But so far there has been no study of the Scots as a community.

One reason is that, with the exception of one distinctive period, there was apparently no large-scale migration to South Africa of the sort experienced by North America and Australasia. It has been conventional to say that Scots at the Cape and in the other territories constituted mainly a professional elite. Thus you can find a good deal on notable individuals, but less on the larger numbers further down the social scale. It is not just that the latter leave less visible trace, there were simply fewer of them. This is indeed only partly true. The cadre of Scots professionals in South Africa was indeed remarkable, but the history of the many other Scots who joined the societies of the four territories of the Cape, Natal, the Transvaal and the Orange Free State can still be retrieved, at least in part. Moreover, in one key period, driven by that great migratory engine, gold, Scots migrants to South Africa may have actually exceeded those going to other imperial territories. More Scots went to southern Africa than to Australia and New Zealand in the years 1893 to 1907, and, even more surprisingly, between 1895 and 1898 more migrated there than to Canada.[67]

INTRODUCTION

Another reason for the failure to consider Scots in South Africa lies in an apparent paucity of sources. The National Library of Scotland in Edinburgh maintains data bases of Scots abroad. These contain a great deal of material on Scots in North America, Scots in Australia and New Zealand, and even a section on Scots in Russia. There are many emigrant guides, as well as collections of emigrants' correspondence. But there seems to be nothing on southern Africa. Entering Cape Colony, Cape Town, South Africa, Natal, etc., in the computer produces no 'hits' of any sort. The major works of Fry and Devine are weaker on South Africa than on any other part of the former British Empire. Yet there are many other means of tracking down Scots in South Africa, in the archives of the Western Cape in Cape Town, of the (former) Transvaal in Pretoria, and of Kwazulu Natal in Pietermaritzburg, as well as in notable libraries such as the South African Library and the Cory Library in Grahamstown. Moreover, missionary records and published works, some of them relatively obscure, contain a great deal. Even a survey of the *South African Dictionary of Biography* or the *Standard Encyclopaedia of South Africa* turns up a rich collection of Scots.[68] One of the twentieth-century historians of Natal, Alan F. Hattersley, included a complete chapter on Scots in a book on migration to the colony published in 1950.[69] Many other sources are to be found in the footnotes of his book.

For comparative purposes, there has been some parallel work on the Irish and the English. Donal McCracken has written about Irish identity, but his studies of the Irish in South Africa have mainly been directed to specific ends, such as the Irish Pro-Boers and McBride's Brigade, the Irish Commandos who fought on the Afrikaner side in the Anglo-Boer War.[70] Interestingly, by the time of that war, the proportion of Irish in the region was in any case declining, at a time when that of the Scots was increasing (see Chapter 5 below). As it happens, there were some Scottish pro-Boers, and probably a few Scots who had been integrated into the Afrikaner community fought against the British, but they have been much less noticed (except for Hyslop's work on J. T. Bain[71]). In any case, whether dealing with the Irish or the Scots, we have to remember that we are considering communities that ultimately became part of a political minority, in the Union, Afrikaner nationalist and post-apartheid eras. In Canada, Australia and New Zealand people claiming Irish or Scottish descent have always been part of a ruling majority, divided like any other group into different political parties and factions. In South Africa the English were also part of a white minority, one which is the subject of a study currently in progress by John Lambert.[72]

The dissection of such colonial ethnicities inevitably confronts some of the major anatomical issues of all imperial history. For a start, all acts of migration also constitute forms of dispossession.[73] In Canada, Australia and New Zealand, though in varying ways, the Scots contributed to the marginalisation (and sometimes brutalisation) of indigenous peoples, as well as to their partial reinstatement in the political process in recent times. In the case of South Africa, indigenous peoples were indeed brutalised, but they were never fully marginalised, except in many respects in a geographical sense. Scots played their part in this, but they also helped to bring to Africans some of the essential means by which they could respond to white power. Nevertheless, Scots were inevitably complicit in the programme of racial domination. This was closely bound up with the manner in which the Scots positioned themselves as intermediaries between the Afrikaners and the English. By stressing their affinities with Afrikaans people and by participating in the central notion that the prime 'racial' problem was this relationship among the whites they contributed to the suppression of African interests and concerns.

But, as we shall see, Scots were always to be found on different sides of all political, economic and racial debates. In all these respects, the period in which Scots were visible and influential was essentially (though not exclusively) that of the imperial period, from the intermittent start of British rule in 1795 and again in 1806 up to Union. That is why this book concentrates in this southern African version of the 'long nineteenth century'. The conventional end point of 1914 is adopted in order to include some of the major arrangements, including the census, of the early years of Union. It also marks a point from which Scottish migration to the region steeply declined. Moreover, if the racial order hardened into increasing segregation and ultimately grand apartheid in the succeeding decades, this helped to mark the decline of Scots as a separate ethnic influence. Of course many of them were implicated in these developments in one way or another, but their specific role was now subordinated to that of the dominant majority within a minority. It is thus more difficult to disentangle. Scottish cultural institutions survived and conformed to segregationist norms; Scottish professionals and businessmen continued to be prominent and equally conformist; but now they generally danced to an Afrikaans nationalist tune. The history of Scots dissidence in this period (and it is certainly the case that the anti-apartheid organisation was particularly strong in Scotland itself) would have to be a separate study.

Despite the growing international notoriety of the region, Scots migration never fully faded and some Scots responded to invitations to head for southern Africa right down to the 1950s. Some may well

INTRODUCTION

have returned. (They are generally less visible, though some can be identified.[74]) But most such movement was at least intended to be permanent. In India and elsewhere in Africa – with the marginal exceptions of Kenya, Malawi (Nyasaland), Zambia (Northern Rhodesia) and Zimbabwe (Southern Rhodesia), Scots were primarily sojourners, temporary visitors of the 'expatriate' type, as we would call them today, a fact which, slightly paradoxically, ensures that their influence extended over a longer period in the twentieth century.[75] In South Africa there were some such sojourners.[76] Others stopped off temporarily, and a few stayed on, while journeying to India, Australia or New Zealand, particularly before the opening of the Suez Canal. Some intended to settle in southern Africa, but disappointments and the news of gold strikes in Australasia often encouraged them to move on round the southern hemisphere.[77] A few braved the Atlantic again – and often a drastic change in climate – to go to North America.[78] And occasionally migrants were so taken aback by the Canadian climate that they moved to southern Africa in search of warmth and (often) cheap labour.[79] Such were, however, a relatively small minority. Most of those who arrived in South Africa stayed. Even missionaries settled for the greater part, if not the whole, of their lives. Yet, while South Africa shares aspects of the experience of the other so-called white dominions, white supremacy ultimately did not prevail. Scots did not necessarily anticipate this, but some, in common with other acute observers, must have recognised that the numbers and tenacity of the black population would eventually render white dominance untenable.

As has often been pointed out, we write history backwards. A study of the Scots in South Africa would have seemed like a redundant luxury during the apartheid period. At that time, and given the development of an Africanist historiography from at least the 1960s, the various forms of resistance of black peoples and their search for the overthrow of white rule had to maintain centre stage in the writing of history. Since 1994 subjects that had long waited in the wings of a southern African historiography have been able to emerge. The study of a specific white ethnicity presents a major opportunity in southern African history. It creates a strand through which a whole range of topics can be integrated in ways that have not been attempted before. Under this banner it is possible to consider questions of identity, issues of migration, as well as aspects of political and social, cultural and intellectual, environmental and economic history. Important themes of missionary activity, so often separated out into a distinct historical category, can be revealed through this focus. Most significantly, the important influence of Scots missions upon Africans can be placed in wider contexts. All these will be considered in the chapters that follow.

The work cannot, however, be comprehensive. While many Scots are mentioned and some attempt is made at multiple biographies, many byways – and some highways – remain unexplored through sheer lack of space. The chapter on missions (4) could easily have become an entire book. One major omission is much consideration of the Boer War, though Scots involvement in its origins and its results inevitably receive some mention. While many Scots and Scots regiments were involved in this warfare, space constraints preclude any consideration of the theme that would do it full justice. Some may argue that, in any case, this is overwhelmingly about imperial power and not the operations of a specific ethnicity (except perhaps in terms of post-war settlement). In any event, it will have to await a further study. Overall the book is intended to occupy the space which lies at the margins of 'public' and 'academic' history.[80] On the one hand, it is intended to be of interest to general readers (hopefully both black and white) concerned with Scots and Scots identities around the Commonwealth. On the other, it is hoped that it takes sufficient notice of current scholarly debates to give it a degree of academic respectability. But, above all, it addresses the Scots' interaction with other ethnicities, and their contribution to the institutional and intellectual forms of South Africa as a whole, and by extension with parallel examples of Scots settlement. Such ethnic studies have now become not only possible but in some ways necessary. To use an image from which many Scots may recoil, the rainbow has a tartan tinge and it is an element of the spectrum which needs to be understood.

Notes

1 The University of Aberdeen Research Institute of Irish and Scottish Studies, munificently funded by the Arts and Humanities Research Board (now Council) of the United Kingdom, is one important manifestation of this multi-disciplinary and multi-ethnic research.
2 Sir Charles Dilke, *Greater Britain* (London 1872), pp. 373–4 and 533; J. A. Froude, *Oceana, or, England and her Colonies* (London 1886), p. 116; Anthony Trollope, *Australia* (London 1873), p. 420.
3 Lyndon Fraser, 'Irish migration to the west coast, 1884–1900', *New Zealand Journal of History*, 34: 2 (2000), pp. 197–225, and subsequent papers given by Fraser in Dunedin in November 2003 (New Zealand Historical Association conference) and in Aberdeen in April 2004 ('Europeans on the Move' conference). See also Brad Patterson (ed.), *The Irish in New Zealand: Historical Context and Perspectives* (Wellington 2002). For wider treatment see Keith Jeffery (ed.), *An Irish Empire? Aspects of Ireland and the British Empire* (Manchester 1996), and Patrick Bishop, *Irish Empire: the Story of the Irish Abroad* (London 1999).
4 The research of Barry Crosbie at the University of Cambridge has been revealing the extent of this professionalisation: Crosbie, 'Irishmen, the Professions and India during the Nineteenth Century', 'Scotland, Ireland and India' symposium, Aberdeen, September 2003. The work of Andrew Mackillop has also revealed the extent of Scottish and Irish medical participation in the activities of the East India Company

INTRODUCTION

in the eighteenth century. A paper on this was given to the 'Scottish Diaspora' conference at Aberdeen in January 2003.
5 Lucas was a Colonial Office official as well as writing histories and geographies of the British Empire.
6 C. P. Lucas, *A Historical Geography of the British Colonies*, IV, *South and East Africa*, Part 1, 'Historical'
7 Quoted in Trevor Clark, *Good Second Class* (Stanhope, Co. Durham, 2004), p. xiii.
8 David Livingstone's father adopted the final 'e' for their name.
9 Tom von Prince, *Gegen Araber und Wahebe. Erinnerungen aus meiner ostafrikanischen Leutnantszeit 1890–1895* (Berlin 1914), pp. 238 ff. I am grateful to Bernhard Gissibl for this intriguing reference and the translation.
10 Michael Fry, *The Scottish Empire* (Phantassie and Edinburgh 2001); Arthur Herman, *The Scottish Enlightenment: the Scots' Invention of the Modern World* (London 2002); T. M. Devine, *Scotland's Empire, 1600–1815* (London 2003); Michael Fry, *'Bold, Independent, Unconquer'd and Free': How the Scots made America safe for Liberty, Democracy and Capitalism* (Ayr 2003); T. M. Devine, *Scotland's Empire and the Shaping of the Americas* (London 2004). As this list makes clear, there has been something of a scramble for titles going on.
11 For some reason there was a spate of such exhibitions in the 1980s. See: *Clyde Men of the World*, an exhibition of archives at Kelvingrove Museum and Art Gallery, November 1979; Helen Smailes, *Scottish Empire: Scots in Pursuit of Hope and Glory*, National Portrait Gallery of Scotland (Edinburgh 1981); Smailes, *Scotland and Africa*, National Library of Scotland (Edinburgh 1982); Smailes, *The Scots and the Commonwealth*, National Book League, Scotland, Exhibition (Edinburgh 1986); Alex M. Cain, *The Cornchest for Scotland: Scots in India*, National Library of Scotland (Edinburgh 1986); Cain, *That Land of Exile: Scots in Australia*, National Library of Scotland (Edinburgh 1988). When the new National Museum of Scotland opened in Edinburgh it had a significant section on Scots overseas and ran temporary exhibitions on Scots in New Zealand and in Canada. This work was developed by Jenni Calder and David Forsyth, but their department, Museum of Scotland International, was subsequently closed down in a short-sighted decision by the museum after its first director, Mark Jones, had moved on to the V&A in London. There have also been a number of conferences on Scots in the empire at the Universities of Strathclyde, Edinburgh, Aberdeen and Otago (the latter to celebrate the 150th anniversary of the Otago Settlement in 1848).
12 Both these works were published in Edinburgh.
13 *Scottish Empire* and *Scotland in Eclipse* were both published in London but *Scotland Resurgent*, interestingly, was published in Stirling.
14 J. D. Mackie, 'The building of the Empire: great part played by Scotsmen' in *The Glasgow Herald, Empire Exhibition, Special Number*, 28 April 1938, pp. 59–61. See also G. F. Maine, *Scotland's Welcome, 1938* (Glasgow and London 1938).
15 'Glasgow Empire Exhibition, 1938: Official Guide'; 'Guide to the Scottish Pavilion, Empire Exhibition, Glasgow 1938'. One of the objects of the exhibition was to encourage dominions tourism of people of Scottish extraction back to Scotland, and various programmes were arranged for them: John M. MacKenzie, '"The Second City of the Empire": Glasgow – imperial municipality' in Felix Driver and David Gilbert (eds), *Imperial Cities: Landscape, Display and Identity* (Manchester 1999), pp. 215–37.
16 See, for example, Tom Nairn, *The Break-up of Britain* (London 1977). In a postscript to the second edition of 1981 Nairn described the dispute he had with his publisher as to whether the title should have a question mark.
17 Michael Hechter, *Internal Colonialism: the Celtic Fringe in British National Development, 1536–1966* (London 1975). It is noticeable that while Ireland was treated as a separate imperial entity in the five-volume *Oxford History of the British Empire* (Oxford, 1998–99) Scotland did not secure such a status, although I proposed the writing of an article on Scotland and the Empire to the editor-in-chief, Roger Louis. For 'Ireland and the Empire' by David Fitzpatrick see Andrew

Porter (ed.), *OHBE*, III, *The Nineteenth Century* (Oxford 1999), pp. 494–521.
18 A project at Aberdeen University, led by Angela McCarthy, is seeking to redress the balance.
19 This remark came after a hostile television interview with the Scots-born Minister of Health (later Defence Secretary), John Reid. The number of Scots in Tony Blair's government received much negative comment. In 1997 the holders of four of the five major offices of state, the Prime Minister, the Chancellor of the Exchequer, the Foreign Secretary and the Lord Chancellor, were held by Scottish-born politicians. Even the Cabinets of Margaret Thatcher were disproportionately skewed in the direction of Scots and the lord chancellorship had become virtually a Scots preserve, despite the fact that Scotland had its own legal system. After the 2001 election the leaders of the three major political parties – Tony Blair, Charles Kennedy and Iain Duncan Smith – were all Scots-born. *The Guardian*, 18 March 2005, carried an article on the phenomenon, though it was not always accurate.
20 The modern historiography had firm foundations. Since Andrew Gibb's works of propaganda there has been a considerable flow of more scholarly books: Gordon Donaldson, *The Scots Overseas* (London 1966); David S. Macmillan, *Scotland and Australia, 1788–1850: Emigration, Commerce and Investment* (Oxford 1967); G. L. Pearce, *The Scots of New Zealand* (Dundee 1976); W. Stamford Reid, *The Scottish Tradition in Canada* (Toronto 1976); J. M. Bumstead, *The People's Clearance, 1770–1815: Highland Emigration to British North America* (Edinburgh 1982), Malcolm D. Prentis, *The Scots in Australia: a Study of New South Wales, Victoria and Queensland, 1788–1900* (Sydney 1983); Don Watson, *Caledonia Australis: Scottish Highlands on the Frontier of Australia* (Sydney 1984); R. A. Cage (ed.), *The Scots Abroad* (London 1985), and, as an early example of the considerable literature of migration, Marjory Harper, *Emigration from North East Scotland* (two volumes, Aberdeen 1988).
21 Patrick O'Farrell, 'On being New Zealand Irish', in Patterson, *The Irish in New Zealand*, p. 1.
22 Eric Richards, 'Scottish Australia, 1788–1914' in *That Land of Exile: Scots in Australia*, and 'Australia and the Scottish Connection, 1788–1914' in Cage, *Scots Abroad*. Richards's most recent work on emigration (dealing with Britain as a whole) is *Britannia's Children* (London 2004). But it is a curious fact that Scottish identity often comes through such intermarriage. This is well expressed by Alexandra Fuller. When her mother proclaimed her Scottishness, Alexandra taxed her with the fact that her father was English. She replied, 'It doesn't count. Scottish blood cancels out English blood.' Alexandra Fuller, *An African Childhood* (London 2002), p. 10.
23 In a series of television programmes on Scotland and the Empire, broadcast on BBC 2 in 2004, one scene featured a Caledonian Society dance in Australia. Participants with broad Australian accents made several references to 'home', meaning Scotland. One speaker had not been there but felt an affinity through the dancing. Another who had visited declared that it had been exactly as expected. In the 2004 Edinburgh military tattoo one dance troupe portrayed emigration from Scotland to New Zealand and the cultural efforts there to maintain a connection with Scottish origins.
24 The Clan MacKenzie annual publications chart the continuing activities of clan associations throughout the United States and former dominions. Similarly, Sir William Macpherson of Cluny has told me of the international operations of the Macpherson clan association of which he is chief.
25 Donald Harman Akenson, *If the Irish ran the World: Montserrat, 1630–1730* (Montreal, Kingston and Liverpool 1997). This was based on a series of lectures delivered at the University of Western Ontario.
26 E. P. Thompson, *The Making of the English Working Class* (Harmondsworth 1968), p. 13.
27 Michael Lynch, *Scotland: a New History* (London 1991); Linda Colley, *Britons:*

INTRODUCTION

Forging the Nation, 1707–1837 (London 1992). See also Callum G. Brown, *Religion and Society in Scotland since 1707* (Edinburgh 1997).

28   Murray G. H. Pittock, *Celtic Identity and the British Image* (Manchester 1999) and also his *Scottish Nationality* (Basingstoke 2001); David McCrone, Stephen Kendrick and Pat Straw (eds), *The Making of Scotland: Nation, Culture and Social Change* (Edinburgh 1989); Michael Lynch (ed.), *Scotland, 1850–1979: Society, Politics and the Union* (London 1993), particularly the chapter by R. J. Morris and G. Morton, 'The re-making of Scotland: a nation within a nation, 1850–1920'; T. C. Smout, 'Perspectives on the Scottish identity', *Scottish Affairs*, 6 (1994), pp. 101–13; Dauvit Broun, R. J. Finlay and Michael Lynch (eds), *Image and Identity: the Making and Re-making of Scotland through the Ages* (Edinburgh 1998); for the later period, Richard Finlay, *A Partnership for Good? Scottish Politics and the Union since 1880* (Edinburgh 1997) and 'The rise and fall of popular imperialism in Scotland, 1850–1959', *Scottish Geographical Magazine*, 113: 1 (1997), pp. 13–21, and David McCrone, 'Unmasking Britannia: the rise and fall of British national identity', *Nations and Nationalism*, 3: 4 (1997), pp. 579–96. See also W. Ferguson, *The Identity of the Scottish Nation* (Edinburgh 1998); Neal Ascherson, *Stone Voices: the Search for Scotland* (London 2003); Ian Donnachie and Christopher Whatley, *The Manufacture of Scottish History* (Edinburgh 1992); and T. M. Devine, *Exploring the Scottish Past: Themes in the History of Scottish Society* (Phantassie 1995).

29   John M. MacKenzie, *Scotland and the Empire*, an inaugural lecture delivered at Lancaster University, May 1992 (Lancaster 1992); also 'Essay and reflection: on Scotland and the empire', *International History Review*, 15: 4 (1993), pp. 714–39. See also Angus Calder, *Revolving Culture: Notes from the Scottish Republic* (London 1994), pp. 32–7, 46, 50. Jenni Calder has written, 'You could argue that there is nothing more authentically Scottish than a community built by emigrant Scots', *Not Nebuchadnezzar* (Edinburgh 2005), p. 128.

30   John M. MacKenzie, 'Empire and national identities: the case of Scotland', *Transactions of the Royal Historical Society*, sixth series, VIII (Cambridge 1998), pp. 215–31.

31   Calder, *Not Nebuchadnezzar*, p. 39.

32   Military (and related) aspects of Scottish identity have been discussed in Steve Murdoch and A. Mackillop (eds), *Fighting for Identity: Scottish Military Experience, c. 1550–1900* (Leiden 2002), particularly the chapters by Dauvit Horsbroch, Andrew Mackillop and Heather Streets; A. Mackillop and Steve Murdoch (eds), *Military Governors and Imperial Frontiers, c. 1600–1800: a Study of Scotland and Empires* (Leiden 2003); Stephen Wood, *The Scottish Soldier* (Edinburgh 1987); Stuart Allan and Allan Carswell, *The Thin Red Line: War, Empire and Visions of Scotland* (Edinburgh 2004). For religious identities see below. For the manner in which Highland Scots were later incorporated into martial race theory see Heather Streets, *Martial Races: the Military, Race and Masculinity in British Imperial Culture, 1857–1914* (Manchester 2004).

33   In the articles cited in notes 19 and 20. This idea is based upon George Elder Davie's influential *The Democratic Intellect: Scotland and her Universities in the Nineteenth Century* (Edinburgh 1961).

34   Herman, *The Scottish Enlightenment*, is mainly interested in the effects of the Enlightenment on American politics, economics and culture. Although there has been some consideration of the influence of the Enlightenment upon Scottish administrators in India, much work remains to be done on its wider international dimensions.

35   As well as St Andrews, Glasgow and Edinburgh, Aberdeen had King's and Marischal Colleges, independent institutions until the later nineteenth century. In Glasgow, the Andersonian Institution was a university in all but name (it was the forerunner of the University of Strathclyde) and was, for example, the source of David Livingstone's medical qualifications.

36   Pennant toured in Scotland in 1769 and 1772. He followed the publication of his first journey by publishing a two-volume work between 1774 and 1776, dedicated

to Sir Joseph Banks, *A Tour in Scotland and Voyage to the Hebrides in 1772* (ed. Andrew Simmons, Edinburgh 1998). See also Pat Rogers, *Johnson and Boswell in Scotland: a Journey to the Hebrides* (New Haven CT and London 1993). In his account of his 1773 journey Johnson made allusions to the Cape by using, in common with many contemporaries, abusive references to 'Hottentots'. He referred to Scots houses as being as 'filthy as the cottages of Hottentots'. When he disputed with a Scottish minister about the virtues or iniquities of the Church of England he charged, 'Sir, you know no more of our Church than a Hottentot.'

37 Charles W. J. Withers, *Geography, Science and National Identity: Scotland since 1520* (Cambridge 2001), particularly sections 4, 5 and 6.

38 D. E. Allen, *The Naturalist in Britain: a Social History* (London 1976); N. Jardine, J. A. Secord and E. C. Spary (eds), *Cultures of Natural History* (Cambridge 1996). See also Christine E. Jackson and Peter Davis, *Sir William Jardine: a Life in Natural History* (Leicester 2001), which reveals the range of Jardine's contacts within the naturalist network throughout Britain and the British Empire.

39 Zöe Caldwell, *Colonial Connections* (Manchester 2005), chapter 7, has an excellent analysis of the interweaving of the domestic and colonial information revolutions.

40 An extreme statement of this phenomenon is to be found in Thomas Richards, *The Imperial Archive* (London 1993).

41 T. C. Smout (ed.), *Scotland and Europe, 1200–1850* (Edinburgh 1986); Smout (ed.), *Scotland and the Sea* (Edinburgh 1992); T. A. Fischer, *The Scots in Germany, being a Contribution to the History of the Scot Abroad* (Edinburgh 1902). Christopher Harvie, *Travelling Scot* (Glendaruel 1999) has chapters on Scots and England, Europe and the Atlantic.

42 For a comprehensive account of West Indian/English religious and humanitarian networks see Catherine Hall, *Civilising Subjects: Colony and Metropole in the English Imagination, 1830–1867* (Cambridge 2002). See also Esther Breitenbach, 'Empire, Religion and National Identity: Scottish Christian Imperialism in the Nineteenth and early Twentieth Centuries', Ph.D., University of Edinburgh (2005).

43 See below, Chapter 6. Also William Beinart, *The Rise of Conservation in South Africa: Settlers, Livestock and the Environment, 1770–1950* (Oxford 2003).

44 John M. MacKenzie, 'Missionaries, science and the environment in nineteenth-century Africa' in Andrew Porter (ed.), *The Imperial Horizons of British Protestant Missions, 1880–1914* (Grand Rapids MI and Cambridge 2003), pp. 106–30.

45 Robert Moffat, *Missionary Labours and Scenes in Southern Africa* (London 1846), p. 66; Richard H. Grove, 'Scottish missionaries, evangelical discourses and the origins of conservation thinking in southern Africa, 1820–1900', *Journal of Southern African Studies*, 15: 2 (1989), pp. 163–87; also Grove, *Ecology, Climate and Empire: Colonialism and Environmental History, 1400–1940* (Cambridge 1997), pp. 89–91.

46 Benedict Anderson, *Imagined Communities* (London 1983).

47 Iain A. D. Stewart (ed.), *From Caledonia to the Pampas: Two Accounts by early Scottish Emigrants to the Argentine* (Phantassie 2000), 'The Voyage of the *Symmetry*' by William Grierson, pp. 43, 61.

48 Ibid., p. 62.

49 Ibid., pp. 68–9.

50 Ibid., 'The Memoir of Jane Robson', p. 76. See also p. 89.

51 Ibid., p. 79. Jane Robson's father called his land 'New Caledonia' and she included descriptions of their building of a church and Presbyterian religious observance in a Catholic society.

52 W. M. Macmillan, *My South African Years: an Autobiography* (Cape Town 1975), p. 1.

53 Ibid., p. 9. These connections are extensively explored in Hugh Macmillan and Shula Marks (eds), *Africa and Empire: W. M. Macmillan, Historian and Social Critic* (London 1989), particularly in the introduction by Hugh Macmillan. In this and other contributions Macmillan's attitudes to the land, the environment, the working class, the Scottishness of Dr John Philip and much else were influenced

INTRODUCTION

by his upbringing and partial education in Aberdeen. But Macmillan never resolved the tension between his social radicalism and his political liberalism. Scottish origins were also influential, if to a lesser extent, in the work of another major historian of southern Africa in the twentieth century, Eric A. Walker.

54 The reality is of course that there are significant theological differences between Scottish Calvinism and Dutch Protestantism, often pietist in form. But the alleged affinities were so often repeated as to take on a life of their own.
55 Ibid., pp. 2–7, 57 and *passim*.
56 For parallel, but somewhat different, cases see Marjory Harper and Michael E. Vance (eds), *Myth, Migration and the Making of Memory: Scotia and Nova Scotia, c. 1700–1990* (Halifax NS and Edinburgh 1999).
57 See, *inter alia*, the works listed in notes 5, 6 and 11 above.
58 Tom Brooking and Jennie Coleman (eds), *The Heather and the Fern: Scottish Migration and New Zealand Settlement* (Dunedin 2003).
59 Martha McLaren, *British India and British Scotland, 1780–1830* (Akron OH 2001); George Kirk McGilvary, 'East India Patronage and the Political Management of Scotland, 1720–1774', Ph.D., Open University in Scotland (1989). See also John Riddy, 'Warren Hastings: Scotland's benefactor?' in Geoffrey Carnall and Colin Nicholson (eds), *The Impeachment of Warren Hastings* (Edinburgh 1989), pp. 30–57, and Jane Rendall, 'Scottish orientalism: from Robertson to James Mill', *Historical Journal*, 25 (1982), pp. 43–69.
60 J. D. Hargreaves has written of Africa more generally in *Aberdeenshire to Africa: North-east Scots and British Expansion Overseas* (Aberdeen 1981) and also in *Academe and Empire: Some Overseas Connections of Aberdeen University, 1860–1970* (Aberdeen 1994), particularly pp. 78–85. See also W. Thompson, 'Glasgow and Africa: Connections and Attitudes', Ph.D., University of Strathclyde (Glasgow 1970).
61 William Beinart and Peter Coates, *Environment and History: the Taming of Nature in the USA and South Africa* (London 1995).
62 Howard Lamar and Leonard Thompson (eds), *The Frontier in History: North America and Southern Africa Compared* (New Haven CT and London 1981); Lynette Russell (ed.), *Colonial Frontiers: Indigenous–European Encounters in Settler Societies* (Manchester 2001).
63 This started with Lord Hailey's *Native Administration in the British African Territories* (five volumes, London 1951–53).
64 Julie Evans, Patricia Grimshaw, David Philips and Shurlee Swain, *Equal Subjects, Unequal Rights: Indigenous Peoples in British Settler Colonies, 1830s–1910* (Manchester 2003); Diane Kirkby and Catherine Coleborne, *Law, History, Colonialism: the Reach of Empire* (Manchester 2001).
65 Natasha Erlank, 'Kilts for Loincloths: Scottishness in the Eastern Cape in the Nineteenth Century'; Erlank, 'Re-examining Initial Encounters between Christian Missionaries and the Xhosa, 1820–1850: The Scottish Case'. I am grateful to Natasha Erlank for supplying me with copies of these papers, based upon her Ph.D. thesis. See also Peter Hinchliff, 'Whatever happened to the Glasgow Missionary Society?' *Studia Historiae Ecclesiasticae*, 18: 2 (1992), pp. 104–20, and J. H. Proctor, 'The Church of Scotland and British colonialism in Africa', *Journal of Church and State*, 29 (1987), pp. 475–93.
66 Jonathan Hyslop, *The Notorious Syndicalist: J. T. Bain, a Scottish Rebel in Colonial South Africa* (Johannesburg 2004); Hyslop, 'Cape Town Highlanders, Transvaal Scottish: military Scottishness and social power in nineteenth and twentieth-century South Africa', *South African Historical Journal*, 47 (2002), pp. 96–114; Hyslop, 'A Scottish socialist reads Carlyle in Johannesburg Prison, June 1900: reflections on the literary culture of the imperial working class', *Journal of Southern African Studies*, 29: 3 (2003), pp. 639–55.
67 Donaldson, *The Scots Overseas*, pp. 187–8.
68 Among reference works see also Michael Rosenthal, *Encyclopaedia of Southern Africa* (fifth edition, London 1970).

69 Alan F. Hattersley, *The British Settlement of Natal: a Study in Imperial Migration* (Cambridge 1950), chapter VII.
70 Donal P. McCracken, 'Irish settlement and identity in South Africa before 1910', *Irish Historical Studies*, 28: 110 (1992), pp. 134–49; McCracken, *The Irish pro-Boers, 1877–1902* (Johannesburg 1989); McCracken, *MacBride's Brigade: Irish Commandos in the Anglo-Boer War* (Dublin 1999). See also the series of occasional papers 'Southern African–Irish Studies', edited by Donal P. McCracken and published by the History Department at the University of Durban, Westville: for the twentieth century volume 3, *Ireland and South Africa in Modern Times* (1996), is useful. D. H. Akenson, *The Irish in South Africa* (Grahamstown 1991), remains an informative source. Other useful, if a little antiquarian, articles include Andrew Cook, 'Irish settlers in the eastern Cape in the early nineteenth century', *The Annals*, 24 (1994), pp. 17–28, and Chris Hummel, 'The Irish in Kimberley', *The Annals*, 22 (1992), pp. 5–10.
71 See note 53.
72 John Lambert, 'South African British? Or dominion South Africans? The evolution of an identity in the 1910s and 1920s', *South African Historical Journal*, 43 (2000), pp. 197–222; Lambert, 'Britishness, South Africanism and the First World War', conference paper at the 'British World' conference, Calgary, July 2003; Lambert, '"Munitions factories . . . turning out a constant supply of living material": White South African elite Boys' Schools and the First World War', paper at the 'British World' conference, Melbourne, July 2004. I am grateful to John Lambert for supplying me with copies of these papers.
73 It is interesting that the Voortrekker Monument in Pretoria has redesigned displays – now in English, Afrikaans and Sotho – in which the Great Trek of the Afrikaners is placed in the context of worldwide migrations, including those of the Mongols, the Chinese and Indians. The uniqueness formerly claimed by the Trekkers is now blunted by anxiety to demonstrate that their movement was little different from that of other peoples in various parts of the world. But the tensions were reinvoked by an April Fool's joke in a local paper which announced that the monument was to be renamed 'the Monument of Oppression'. Local Afrikaners almost reached for their weapons until the date was pointed out to them.
74 Hattersley recounts the story of a young Clydeside joiner, Henry Johnston, who returned to Scotland as a 'conquering hero': Hattersley, *British Settlement of Natal*, p. 219. In the village of Alyth, Perthshire, a house named 'Natal' was built by a Scottish migrant to that colony who returned and put his small fortune into a fine Victorian Scottish villa. See also Marjory Harper (ed.), *Emigrant Homecomings* (Manchester 2005).
75 Marjory Harper, *Adventurers and Exiles: the Scottish Exodus* (London 2003), deals with sojourners as well as emigrants. See also her forthcoming joint work with Stephen Constantine in the *Oxford History of the British Empire* series.
76 The existence of such sojourners, returning 'home laden with wealth' and 'forgetting the duties and responsibilities they owe to the country of their adoption', was lamented by the *South African Scot* in 1905, quoted in Harper, *Adventurers and Exiles*, pp. 324–5.
77 Such inter-colonial movements have been too little studied, although they turn up very frequently in the records of individual migratory stories.
78 The historian Douglas Lorimer tells me of an uncle of his who migrated from Scotland to South Africa but later moved on to join a brother in Canada.
79 See the example in Chapter 5.
80 A plea for just such an approach can be found in an address by Paul Maylam, 'The frontiers of Eastern Cape history', *The Annals*, 28 (1998), pp. 8–17.

CHAPTER TWO

The Scots presence at the Cape

The travelling Scot

The modern visitor to Cape Town may notice on the map an area known as Schotsche Kloof, a key route between Table Mountain and the Lion's Head connecting the city with the southern part of the Cape peninsula. No one seems quite clear how it acquired its name, or when. It may have run over land owned by a Scot or it may commemorate the presence of the Scots Brigade as the garrison at the Cape for a substantial period in the eighteenth century. At any rate, it symbolises a Scots presence which is of long standing. Indeed, Scots did not wait until the first British capture of the Cape in 1795 to be engaged in the establishment of a white community at the southern tip of Africa. In this respect they were following a long-standing propensity to be involved in commercial ventures throughout the North Sea and Baltic regions. Thus when such ventures reached out into the South Atlantic they were soon there too. It should also be remembered that there were considerable Scots communities in Amsterdam, Rotterdam and other Dutch towns in the early modern period.[1] In common with several of these, Rotterdam boasted a Scots kirk in the seventeenth century and it has remained active until the present day.[2]

It is therefore not surprising to find that there were Scots at the Cape from the earliest days of the Dutch East India Company (VOC) settlement following the arrival of Jan van Riebeeck's party in 1652. Moreover, they had also become celebrated mercenaries, selling their military services in many parts of Europe. This almost inevitably developed an overseas dimension. In common with other early imperial systems, the VOC had manpower problems, and these were partially solved by the arrival of Scots soldiers in Dutch employ.[3] Their presence may also be reflected in the fact that one of the notorious taverns of the Cape, which often doubled up as brothels, was known as the Schotsche Tempel. But there were civilians too. Before 1660 one William Robbertson (*sic*), of Dundee, formerly surgeon on the ship *Fort William*, is described as *opper chirurgen* (senior surgeon) at the Fort of Good Hope.[4] Others sneaked ashore as deserters. Two men with the slightly strange names of Patrick Jock and Jacob Born (Burn or Burns?) turn up in early records. They were described as shepherds from Glasgow, presumably meaning that that was their jumping-off point in leaving on their ocean journey.[5] Other deserters, Colin Lawson, Alexander Crawford, John Brown and John Beck from Dundee and Jacob Bain of Glasgow turn up in a court case in 1659. They conspired to steal a yacht named *Erasmus* then lying in Table Bay (perhaps to try to return home?). But surgeon Robertson got to hear of the idea and warned its captain. The plotters were arrested and punished.[6] An early burgher, Sergius Swellengrebel, had a wife called Anna Fothergill, who may well have been a member of the Scots community in the Netherlands. The situation was reversed when a George Gunn was said to be married to Maria Krynauw. Again, this may have been a union contracted in Holland. The combined effects of the migration of some Scots from the Netherlands, of the operations of the Scots Brigade and of desertion from ships sailing to India and the East must have ensured a steady, if relatively slight, feed of Scots into the Cape in the course of the eighteenth century.

The significance of the Scots community in the Netherlands is well represented by Robert Jacob Gordon, who was born in 1743, probably of a family long settled there. He was the second son of Major General Jacob Gordon, of the Scottish Regiment, and a Dutch mother, Johanna Maria Heydenrijk.[7] He himself joined the regiment in 1758, having studied natural sciences. He went to the Cape in 1773 as an officer in the garrison. He seems to have maintained a sense of his ethnic origins on his father's side that gave him a fellow feeling with two important Scottish travellers and plant hunters, Francis Masson and William Paterson. On his first journey to the interior, partly with Masson, he saw and named the Orange River, and he further honoured his ruler by taking a springbok back as a present for him in 1777.[8] In 1779 and 1785–86 he made further journeys into the interior, collecting plants and fossils, keeping diaries and making maps which were filled with a good deal of carefully observed detail.[9] As with most early travellers, he was interested in climatology, zoology and ethnography as well as botany. He was also concerned with 'acclimatisation'. He took some merino sheep from Spain to the Cape, where they were later to become a significant component of the colonial economy. Some of his early observations were sent back to Professor J. Allamand of Leiden University, who published articles using Gordon as his source. He conducted a correspondence on natural history in Dutch, French and English, and he provided information to the great French naturalist the Comte de Buffon, the director of the Jardin du Roi in Paris. He also encountered the French *philosophe* Denis Diderot and enlightened him on aspects of the Cape. These travellers at the Cape were very much involved in an Enlightenment project which was international in its character.

Gordon has had a good press: he has been characterised as a 'humane and civilised man, a paragon of the Age of Enlightenment',[10] whose 'personal acquaintance with the interior of the colony probably exceeded by far that of any other well educated man of his day'.[11] His travels into the interior and his many geographical insights, recorded in his drawings and meticulous travel narratives, have been described as the 'crowning achievement of the eighteenth century'.[12] He was also described as having a remarkable facility for learning languages, as well as for absorbing the musical forms of indigenous peoples. Lachlan Macquarie (later Governor of New South Wales) attended an occasion on board a ship anchored in Simon's Bay when Gordon entertained the company by singing Gaelic songs as well as with some music of the Khoi, whose language he had learned.[13] Gordon seems to represent a striking combination of Scots, Dutch and Cape colonial identities which is going to be a feature of this book. Yet his wife, who was Swiss, writing to a Mr Pinkerton in 1803, announced that she was always willing to give her confidence 'to a gentleman who is a native of Scotland: it was to that country that my late husband belonged; and to the last hour of his life he always cherished feelings of warm attachment towards it'.[14]

Gordonskop,[15] Gordonsfontein and Gordon's Bay were all called after him. Here was a form of symbolic possession through naming, an imprinting of an individual presence upon the landscape. This was a geographical prize to be secured by many, not least Scots, after him. In 1785 the newly promoted Colonel Gordon became the commander of the garrison, which still had members of the VOC Scots brigade even though it had been officially laid down at the time of the War of American Independence. When, ten years later, British forces landed at False Bay, he advised the Dutch to surrender without resistance.[16] He probably correctly assessed that putting up a fight was hopeless, particularly given the quality of his troops, but he had another motive. He was a royalist and the Netherlands had fallen to the French. Ensuring the loss of the Cape seemed to him to be a way of striking a blow against Napoleon. But other senior administrators and burghers were less convinced. He was subjected to so much hostility for what was judged to be a treasonous act that he committed suicide.

Partly because of the disappearance of Gordon's records, only recently rediscovered, the activities of Francis Masson (1741–1805) and William Paterson (1755–1810) have in some respects been more enduring. These were among the earliest travellers into the interior of the Cape, and, together with the Swede Carl Peter Thunberg and the Dutchman Anders Sparrman, they did most to make the unique flora of the Cape familiar in Europe.[17] Masson went further into the interior than any other Briton and was the first to publish a personal travel narrative on the region in English.[18] Born in Aberdeen, he was apprenticed there as a garden boy, and his botanical and horticultural abilities earned him a post as under-gardener at Kew under the superintendent, William Aiton. He was fortunate in his timing, for this was precisely the period when Joseph Banks and Aiton judged that it was necessary to place plant hunting on a more systematic and professional basis. Banks persuaded George III to make money available for this enterprise, clearly designed to fulfil national ambitions in various ways. Banks selected Masson to go to the Cape, under royal patronage, to collect botanical specimens. He joined Captain James Cook when he departed on his second voyage on the *Resolution*. Cook's expedition naturalists, Johann Reinhold Forster and his son Johann George Adam Forster, were highly patronising about Masson and dismissed him as nothing more than a 'Scots garden hand'.[19] Strictly speaking, that was true, but once Masson reached Cape Town in October 1772 he was soon to move into a wholly different league. He was fortunate to fall in with a Scandinavian mercenary, Franz Pehr Oldenburg, in the employ of the VOC, and the Swedish botanist Thunberg. Oldenburg provided the practical knowledge of exploration while Thunberg contributed greater scientific sophistication. Masson brought considerable horticultural skill together with talent as draughtsman and artist. He also had Khoi associates and may well have benefited from their knowledge of the natural environment. Because he was in the King's employ he seems to have done well financially out of his botanical journeys.[20]

He remained at the Cape for two and half years, completing three journeys to the interior, sometimes joining up with Thunberg, sometimes with Gordon. He travelled north as far as St Helena Bay and east to the Little Karoo, Mossel Bay and Algoa Bay (where the modern city of Port Elizabeth stands). He took back to Kew what has been described as a 'unique hoard' of 400 specimens, including a collection of pelargoniums, later to be common garden and greenhouse plants in Britain and elsewhere in Europe.[21] He also brought back a plant which was named *Strelitzia* to honour George III's wife, Charlotte of Mecklenburg-Strelitz. Its exotic appearance has made it something of a cliché in the world of artificial restaurant plants. A number of the new botanical finds were named after him, a botanical prize which more than matched the geographical equivalents. He published accounts of his travels in the *Philosophical Transactions* of the Royal Society in 1776, but his only other publication was a series of botanical plates, *Stepeliae Novae*, which appeared in 1796. Nevertheless, it is clear from his journals that he was interested in more than simply botanical observation: he was, for example, dismayed by the attacks upon the Khoisan people and the destruction of wildlife attendant upon the spread of Dutch farmers into the interior.

Masson returned to the Cape in 1785 and embarked on further collecting, though nothing on the scale of his earlier journeys. Coming as he did from humble origins, he represents the extraordinary social mobility that was open to capable Scots in the period. He also illustrates the manner in which Enlightenment efforts to create a taxonomy of the globe led to the creation of international intellectual networks. He maintained an extensive correspondence with both Thunberg in Sweden and with Banks, and he also had connections with Carl Linnaeus, the greatest botanist of the age. Banks considered that through his and other labours Kew had become the world leader in botanical science, exceeding the scope and range of rivals in France and Sweden. The 'garden hand' had achieved considerable scientific status.

His successor, William Paterson, from Kinettles, in Angus, also came from a relatively lowly position in the social scale. Another talented botanist, he secured a post at the Chelsea Physic Garden. In 1777 he was sent to the Cape under the patronage of the highly intelligent Countess of Strathmore, whose extraordinary independence of mind and complexity of personal relations is strikingly revealed in her *Confessions*.[22] Lady Strathmore also had a garden in Chelsea, and the castle of her first husband, Glamis, was only a few miles from Paterson's birthplace. He spent almost three years at the Cape and travelled farther into the interior than Masson, reaching Little Namaqualand and the mouth of the Orange River to the north and the Keiskamma River to the east, sometimes travelling with Gordon and at other times with Sebastiaan van Reenan and the latter's brother. He covered some 5,000 miles in all.[23] After his return Paterson prepared and published in 1789 a major work, *A Narrative of Four Journeys into the Country of the Hottentots and Caffraria in the Years 1777–78–79*. A second, corrected, edition appeared in 1790. The book was dedicated to Sir Joseph Banks, 'the Patron of Natural History', and in his preface Paterson asserted that this was no work on the romance of travel: it was devoted to facts. 'No part of the world is so little known,' he proclaimed, 'as those regions of Africa, which lie south of the equinoctial line.'[24] He paid handsome tributes to Gordon and his other companions, describing fauna and flora in some detail, as well as the hunting methods of the Khoi. The majority of the nineteen copper plates were devoted to botanical illustrations. Despite his lowly social origins and his plain and untutored manner, he was elected a Fellow of the Royal Society. Like Masson, he received his share of abuse. Thunberg considered him to be a 'mere gardener' and the French naturalist Le Vaillant thought that he enjoyed smoking and drinking too much![25]

He reproduced Sparrman's map of the region, a detailed and beautifully produced piece of cartography, while adding additional features of his own (and failing to correct errors that he knew were wrong). In addition, he appended tables of weather information collected over a six-month period, including temperatures at four times of the day, wind strength and direction, and remarks on daily climatic conditions. He also showed considerable interest in poisons, both animal and vegetable, detailing their use by indigenous people, as well as in the manner in which channa (or mesambryanthemum) was combined with dacka (or dacha, dagga) to produce an intoxicating drug. Paterson, in other words, displayed concerns with scientific observation which were to become standard in the nineteenth-century works of travel. Apart from Masson's articles, this was the first major work published in English relating to the southern African interior. The work of the Dutch traveller Anders Sparrman was published earlier, in 1785, but Thunberg's even more detailed three-volume work did not appear until 1795.[26]

There is some evidence that botanical travellers were acting as 'spies', reconnaissance agents for European imperial ambitions, in the last decades of the eighteenth and the early years of the nineteenth centuries. For this reason VOC officials viewed Masson with great distrust on his second arrival at the Cape in 1785, partly because Paterson had been suspected of being a spy.[27] Limits were placed on where he could travel, particularly forbidding him from reaching the coasts within thirty miles from Cape Town. The VOC had good reason to be suspicious. A British expeditionary force had set out to take the Cape in 1781 (because the Dutch had allied themselves with the Americans in the War of Independence) and knowledge of the coast would of course be vital strategic information in any landing. Yet, despite Dutch suspicions, Paterson had no difficulty in travelling even greater distances than Masson into a relatively little known interior. In some respects, Paterson was indeed laying the groundwork for further white expansion from the Cape, although the Afrikaner travellers who continued to push further north and east were unlikely to have encountered his work or been influenced by it. But, since

Paterson's companions were necessarily Dutch (apart from the ethnically ambiguous Gordon), he also demonstrated a degree of cooperation between Scot and Afrikaner which was to become standard after the establishment of British rule. Although his botanical achievement was a good deal less significant than that of Masson, his book helped to bring greater understanding of the Cape to the attention of a British scientific, military and administrative elite, thereby helping to facilitate the subsequent extension of British power. But the initial energy in plant hunting was later dissipated. In 1816 Allan Cunningham, the son of a Scot, arrived at the Cape en route to New South Wales. James Bowie, a gardener at Kew of Scots extraction, was charged with collecting at the Cape, but he was soon dismissed because of Treasury parsimony and the lack of interest of George IV. It had also been discovered that he was trading privately in Cape plants.

If Masson and Paterson were indulging in imperial espionage under the guise of botanical collecting they give little impression of being aware of this role.[28] They were, perhaps, more concerned with international scientific activity, and the position of British science in relation to it, than with national political ambitions. Nevertheless, they were followed by surprising numbers of their countrymen after Britain's first capture of the Cape in 1795. In many respects that was a Scottish exploit. The Secretary of State for War, Henry Dundas, was keen to take the Cape from the Dutch and regarded it as his 'favourite child'.[29] The expeditionary fleet was commanded by Admiral George Keith Elphinstone, born in Stirling the fifth son of Lord Elphinstone, who had served in China, in the War of American Independence and in the Mediterranean. The invading army was under the command of General James Henry Craig, who though born in Gibraltar has been described as being 'from a respectable Scottish family'.[30] Craig became the acting Governor of the Cape and was later Governor General of Canada.[31] He was succeeded in 1796 by General Francis Dundas, a nephew of the great Henry, who became acting Governor after the recall of Sir George Yonge in 1801. Dundas was greatly disliked by Lady Anne Barnard, who described him as 'quick-tempered, arrogant, tactless and high-handed'. Lady Anne, the daughter of the Earl of Balcarres and brought up in Fife and Edinburgh, kept Henry Dundas fully informed of all developments at the Cape during her residence there as wife of Andrew Barnard, the colonial secretary. She also kept lively and vivid diaries, full of sketches of personalities at the Cape, of social and political life there, and of the many passing dignitaries heading for India or New South Wales.[32]

The Cape was returned to the Dutch under the Treaty of Amiens in 1802. After the brief period of the Batavian Republic, it was taken again by the British in 1806 – when a largely Scots expeditionary force, commanded by General Sir David Baird (better known for his imprisonment by, and subsequent victory over, the Sultan of Mysore, known to the British as Tippoo Sahib), landed at Blaauberg strand, at the north end of Table Bay. It was confirmed as a British possession at Vienna in 1815. Many Scots had now arrived in British regiments. Between 1795 and 1803 the Seaforth Highlanders, the Argyll and Sutherland Highlanders and the Scotch Brigade[33] all served at the Cape. After 1806 the Seaforths and Argyll and Sutherland Highlanders returned, preceded by the Highland Light Infantry.[34] These troops occupied the castle and drilled on the parade ground in front of it. They became a familiar sight in Cape Town and had some influence (as will be recounted in later chapters) upon the establishment of both Presbyterianism and Freemasonry at the Cape.

An examination of the lists of British civilian residents at the Cape between 1795 and 1819 compiled by Peter Philip reveals a large number of Scottish names.[35] The evidence of names is, however, very slippery. Some of them may be Irish or 'Scotch Irish' (though in religious and cultural terms they would in any case have had an affinity with the Scots). Some may have been born in England, in the Netherlands, or in other parts of the British Empire. However, the presence of twenty-eight Macdonalds, twenty-five Mackenzies, forty-eight Campbells, seventeen MacLeans, fifteen MacKays and multiple examples of Chisholm, Cameron, Ogilvie and other 'Macs' seems significant. Moreover, many names shared by Scots and English cannot be pinned down to any specific ethnicity. We can certainly identify key individual figures, particularly merchants and shipowners, whose origins in Scotland are known.

In 1819 a census indicated that the total white population of the Cape numbered 42,000.[36] The great majority of these were Dutch. Philip identified 4,800 English-speaking residents during the years he studied, but some of them were temporary visitors. Some simply spent time there on the way to India. The Scots proportion would have been relatively tiny, not more than a few hundred, though it had been slightly inflated by the Moodie settlement of 1817 and would be further augmented by the Scots component of the 1820 settlement in the following year (see below). It is also apparent that economic advantage, or maybe financial constraints upon departing, influenced some of the British residents (among whom there would inevitably have been a few Scots) to sign the oaths of submission to the Batavian Republic in 1803. A hundred and forty-five male British signatories (the figure should perhaps be multiplied by at least three to include women and children, who were regarded as dependants) took the oath.³⁷ They were not to know that the Dutch republic would be short-lived, so their willingness to do so offers a throw-back to the search for international opportunities which was so significant in the earlier days of imperialism. Economic advantage invariably took precedence over national loyalty.

The number of English-speaking settlers, including Scots, was increased by the discharged soldiers and sailors who were permitted to settle. This was probably a phenomenon throughout the Napoleonic War period (and there would also have been deserters), but we know more about those who settled through this method between 1815 and 1824.³⁸ Once more, some were certainly Scots, particularly as Scots regiments were so prominent in the garrison, although it will never be possible to estimate the precise number.

Prominent Scots in the British occupations

If the military commands of the Cape in the two occupations were largely in the hands of Scots, so were many of the significant mercantile positions. One of the most influential was John Pringle (1769–1815), who was born in Selkirk, the grandson of Lord Haining and the illegitimate son of a wealthy merchant.³⁹ He was apprenticed in the East India Company in London and spent time in Bombay, 1790–93. In 1794, at the age of twenty-four, he was appointed Agent to the East India Company (EIC) in Cape Town, arriving fourteen months before the invasion. He soon knew enough about the marine characteristics and the defences of the Cape to be able to offer a good deal of advice to Craig and Elphinstone, though he withdrew to St Helena at the crucial period. He served in the EIC office in Cape Town during both occupations, supported by two other Scottish clerks, Thomas Maxwell and Joseph Gibson. Pringle's position was not an enviable one. He was charged with attempting to maintain the monopoly of the Company and with dealing with so-called interlopers. So many of the Scots at the Cape were free traders eager to destroy the vestiges of the EIC monopoly that it is instructive to remember that, as always, they were to be found on both sides. Pringle served a monopoly. But it was a monopoly whose power was declining rapidly. General Craig even issued a proclamation that trading with the East would be free, but when Pringle arrived from St Helena he was able to persuade him that this was illegal and it was rescinded. But he was fighting a losing battle. Company ships were greatly outnumbered by private vessels.⁴⁰ Moreover, Pringle had an astonishing range of duties. He was concerned with the refitting and revictualling of EIC ships, with supplying St Helena, as well as with trade with Mauritius, Ceylon, India, the Far

East and New South Wales. He was also commissary-general, assisted in the management of the experimental farm at Groenekloof, had to deal with EIC personnel and passengers in transit, not to mention maintain diplomatic relations with the directors in London, the officials in the East and the Governors at the Cape. He was also an amateur botanist and maintained interests in farming and 'acclimatisation'. We know from the correspondence of the Barnards that he led a lively social life and mixed with the most senior figures at the Cape.

Pringle inherited money from his father and made a fair amount at the Cape, enough to buy an estate there. But he had an unhappy private life (his son and his wife both died) and his own health cracked under the strain of attempting to reconcile so many concerns. His timing was bad, for he was clinging to the tail end of monopoly just when monopolies were being overwhelmed by a rival economic theory. And, among a number of Scottish merchants who worked to overturn the Company's interests, several stand out. Alex MacDonald was born in Sutherland in 1771 and arrived at the Cape as a seafarer in 1798. He stayed and swiftly became a merchant and entrepreneur of some significance. In 1800 he bought premises on the Keizergracht (later Darling Street) and built up an extensive import/export business trading with the Far East, India (including rice and piece goods), Mauritius, St Helena and South America. He also imported specie and acted as agent for visiting British ships. Throughout he struggled with the EIC monopoly, but became influential enough to give testimony to the Council of Advice on Cape trade in 1827. He was active in the Cape Trade Society and the Commercial Exchange, dying at the Cape in 1848.

Henry Murray was born in Edinburgh and arrived in Cape Town in 1810. He stayed only until 1817, but in that period he succeeded in making a fortune. He returned to Scotland, where he died in 1845. Thus he was a sojourner who achieved every temporary migrant's dream – to make a pile and return with a higher social status. But he never forgot the source of his wealth and he clearly followed educational and social developments at the Cape. In his will he bequeathed £5,000 for South African College bursaries and £3,000 to the Cape Orphan House.[41] Another Murray who arrived even earlier was John, born in 1749 and married to Jane Mitchell, both of them Aberdonians.[42] He arrived at the beginning of the first occupation and developed a whale fishery and the coastal trade to Mossel Bay, where he owned a loan farm and established a trading station. He bought out a Dutch merchant business and dealt in cloth, hats, silk, glass, ironware and timber. He enterprisingly leased his two brigs to the administration during the Batavian period (1803–06). With the return of the British, acting Governor Sir David Baird granted him whaling rights once more, with a station and other buildings, including his home, on Robben Island. He exported large quantities of whale oil and bone to London. After his death in 1815 his son took over the business. Other Scots merchants of this early period included Alex Aitchison (1781–1825); Kenneth Duncan (1786–1815), who arrived in 1806; Henry Home (1777–1853); W. A. B. Rowan, who arrived in 1809 and conveniently combined mercantile activity with work as a land surveyor; and Alex Tennant (1772–1814). As can be seen from these dates, some of their lives were cut short. Nor were they uniformly successful. As Peter Philip has shown, business at the Cape was precarious and there were large numbers of insolvencies, though some picked themselves up again.[43]

Some of these insolvencies, in this period and in depression in the early 1830s, led to suicides, suicides which are chronicled in the letters of the daughters of another maritime figure of the second occupation. Captain John Findlay, the son of a boatbuilder from Cullen, arrived at the Cape in 1810. He had been pressed into the navy but had managed to do sufficiently well from prize money to buy himself a brig. He was frequently at the Cape, and delivered stores to the 1820 settlers. He settled in Cape Town in 1821 and developed a coastal business to Algoa Bay which made him influential in many of the developments of the period. The reason we know a good deal about Findlay is that his two daughters corresponded regularly with their brother, who went to live in Tasmania (though he subsequently returned to the Cape) and other members of the family. Their letters provide fascinating insights into the life and role of women at the Cape in the period, but they also offer a great deal of evidence of the existence of a Scottish network. Their father was closely connected with a web of shipping, military and administrative personnel and the daughters, Ann and Margaret, socialised extensively with these figures, as well as with their womenfolk. But what comes out most strikingly from their letters is the manner in which they interacted socially with the leading Scottish figures, merchants, doctors, even the Rev. James Adamson, the rather formidable Presbyterian divine who arrived in 1829. The Findlay letters make it clear that the Scots at the Cape in the period of the 1820s and early 1830s constituted a critical mass sufficiently large to be able to influence each other and offer much mutual help and support.[44]

The Moodie settlement

With the Moodie settlement of 1817 we move into a well documented field, with a range of sources offering considerable detail on the settlers, their origins, occupations and in some cases their fortunes at the Cape. Although it involved a relatively small number of people, it is worth dwelling on this settlement because of the insights it provides into conditions both in Scotland and at the Cape in this period. It neatly reveals the interconnected histories of the two ends of the emigration process. The Moodie project arose out of a number of economic and social conditions of the post-Napoleonic War period. Benjamin Moodie (1789–1856), the leader of the settlement, came from the lands of Melsetter on the Orkney island of Hoy. This estate, which had been in the Moodie family for generations, had fallen on hard times and was seriously in debt to the tune of over £23,000. The crisis was exacerbated by the fact that the kelp harvests were poor in those years (it was later sold for a sum which barely covered the indebtedness).[45] Moreover, both Benjamin and his younger brothers Donald and John were half-pay officers desperately looking for new opportunities now that their chance of further employment in the military or navy seemed to be at an end. In a book published two decades later John wrote of the 'irksome and cheerless' condition of being a half-pay officer, 'regarded as useless by society', 'ignorant of the usual occupations of life' and consequently sunk in a 'gloomy despondency' or in 'dissipation'. He was clearly articulating a common sentiment of his class when he wrote:

> It often happens that people suffering under some recent infliction of that capricious dame, Fortune, hastily determine on emigrating to some one of our colonies, in the confident expectation that there, as a matter of course, all their difficulties will cease, and that they will forthwith enter on the enjoyment of all the independence and luxuries which in England are usually the fruit of long and persevering industry, or superior sagacity and success in business.[46]

The Moodies, he went on, were hated on the Orkneys and there was some satisfaction at their decline. The reason for this dislike was that they had traditionally supported the Hanoverians. The brothers' great-grandfather had been murdered by a Jacobite and their grandfather had sought his revenge in the '45.

The condition of the Moodies was therefore deeply embedded in eighteenth-century Scottish history, in the fact that their generation was ripe for employment in the Napoleonic Wars, and in the economic difficulties that followed. Facing ruin and a drastic decline in social status, Benjamin hoped that, by paying for the transport of the settlers, and by entering into a form of indenture with them, he would recreate quasi-feudal relations with a tenantry on land which he hoped would be granted to him by the colonial authorities. As John put it, it was a commonly held belief that they could 'hardly fail to better their condition [than] by emigrating to one of our colonies'. Surveying the imperial field, Benjamin decided that the Cape was the most hopeful, both to recoup his status and fortune and for providing a 'livelihood with a less violent alteration in his habits than might be expected of most persons'.[47] That probably means that he imagined he would be more likely to have servants and followers there.

The Cape was seen by a number of figures as ripe for colonisation. An increase in the numbers of 'English' settlers would help to protect this vital staging post on the route to India (and increasingly to Australia too). Second, the Eastern Cape frontier was frequently in turmoil and required settlers to stabilise it. Third, such a settlement would help to redress the balance of population in respect of the Dutch. Finally, it would relieve social distress at home and alleviate the potential for revolutionary activity. In 1808 Colonel Collins had advised that the immigration of Highland Scots would help to consolidate the frontier. In his view they had made the transition from a clan society involved in endemic raiding into a more civilised and commercial state over the past century and could help the Xhosa to do the same.[48] In 1813 Colonel John Graham of the 93rd Highlanders had taken up the same theme. While on leave he had pressed the Colonial Secretary Lord Bathurst to permit the colonising of the Zuurveld (land nearer the frontier thought to be fertile and seasonally suitable for the running of stock) by Highlanders, not least those wishing to escape from the lands of the Marquess of Stafford (otherwise the Duke of Sutherland, whose notorious Clearances were proceeding at this period). But Whitehall officials did nothing to encourage Graham. Donald McLean of Oban proposed a similar scheme and received no more joy.[49]

Moodie tried again in 1816, memorialising Bathurst on the efficacy of sending Highlanders to settle the frontier. He appealed to the national interest, that this was about the maintenance of sea power and the diversion of emigrants away from America. He suggested that 'the Agricultural Classes are the only part of our population fit for colonisation, and of them the Scotch Highlanders, from being the least useful in this country and the most inured to hardship, are the fittest'. His own leadership of such a group would be greatly helped by the fact that 'Proprietors who inherit lands from their ancestors in that Country still however retain an influence over the minds of the lower Classes quite unexampled in the Southern parts of the Kingdom'. His own 'agricultural habits' rendered him a suitable leader, while the state owed the Moodies gratitude (and indeed compensation) for the stand they had taken in favour of the Hanoverians.[50] He also sought the help of a friend, Alexander McLeay, Secretary of the Transport

Board, in furthering his cause. He subsequently claimed that McLeay had led him to believe that, if emigration to the Cape was subsequently encouraged, he could expect to receive the same benefits, since his 'enterprise had anticipated HMG'. This alleged promise was to remain a bone of contention throughout Moodie's life.[51]

However, Moodie was also to receive little encouragement,[52] although Bathurst later sent a letter of introduction to Lord Charles Somerset, the Governor of the Cape, proposing that Moodie might be given a land grant consistent with the regulations of the colony.[53] As Moodie set about recruiting his emigrants, he fell in with a Cape merchant and adventurer called Hamilton Ross.[54] Ross was born in Ireland and proposed a grossly inflated emigration scheme involving as many as 10,000 Scots. But gradually he reined back his enthusiasm. Having agreed to take half the liability for a more modest figure of 200, he withdrew after helping only with the first fifty.

In the event Moodie's settlers had generally very slight connection with the Highlands, little or nothing to do with the Sutherland clearances, and were by and large not agriculturalists. In fact he set out to recruit in Edinburgh and some other places on the east coast and the Borders. The potential emigrants were also experiencing hard times in the post-war slump. This is well represented by the manner in which, when they came to give their occupation, a large majority entered 'labourer' but also (no doubt out of self respect and a desire to promote their suitability as settlers) indicated previous occupations which included tailors, painters, printers, shoemakers, upholsterers, cabinetmakers, bookbinders and others. These were people who had come down in the world. Quite a number indicated 'unemployed'. So far as Moodie's extolling of agricultural workers was concerned, only a small minority identified themselves as cattlemen, farm stewards or farmers. Most of them came from Edinburgh, Leith and Dalkeith, with handfuls from Glasgow, Dundee, Perth, Haddington and Glamis. Almost fifty other places of origin were represented by just two or three individuals. Only five came from the Highlands (one from Golspie and four from Dornoch). This was essentially a Lowland migration, with only a few Highland names suggesting step migration. Most of them were in their twenties and generally single, although there were the occasional teenager and a few in their thirties. A minority were married, with children. The great majority were literate enough to sign their name, only a few affirming their agreement with a cross. All of them had to submit character references from former employers and their parish ministers.[55]

Moodie's master plan was that the emigrants would sign letters of agreement with him that he would pay for their transport to South

Africa in exchange for offering him labour to the amount of twice his costs. The cost of the passages was to be £30 each and in Cape Town he would expect recompense of £60 in either cash or labour. (This was calculated to mean eighteen months' service.) In other words, he hoped to recoup a minimum of almost £12,000 in cash or labour. (Arrangements for paying for wives and children are more obscure, but presumably the labour time required to redeem the debt was increased *pro rata*.)[56] He was confident that he was legally covered, but events were to confound him. He was impossibly sanguine about conditions at the Cape and, in effect, much of the rest of his life was devoted to the working out of his grievances.[57] But in early 1817 everything seemed to be set fair, although Moodie had incurred a further initial debt of £3,750 in order to help finance the passages. The first party of just over fifty hand-picked emigrants, led by Moodie himself, left London (having sailed down from Leith) on the brig *Brilliant* in March 1817, arriving at the Cape in June. They were described in the *Cape Town Gazette* as being 'English mechanics and labourers', neatly reflecting the imprecision in ethnic identity of the period. The naval lieutenant (and younger brother) Donald Moodie supervised further departures. The second group, numbering about forty-nine, sailed on the *Garland* and reached the Cape in late August, while the third (probably over ninety) arrived on the *Clyde* towards the end of September, 'under charge of surgeon Abercrombie'.[58] These figures refer only to the men and differ from source to source. Altogether almost 200 men migrated, and when women and children are included the number comes closer to 300. Some of the men subsequently applied for wives to follow them out.

Somerset granted them permission to remain in the colony, although once again the documents are imprecise. Moodie bought, for 8,000 rixdollars, or £600, land at Groot Vaders Bosch on the Brede River near Swellendam (a considerable distance from the frontier). It already had an old dwelling house on it. He subsequently secured further estates. The settlers were a diverse group. Moodie's assistant, John Hay, was described as a 'gentleman' (probably another half-pay officer) and secured land adjacent to Groot Vaders Bosch on what was known as 'Arichees Land'. There were three surgeons, and several others were described as being superior men of good appearance and character. Another was described as having 'reluctantly engaged' (on the recommendation of General Johnstone), having been to the Cape before in the 93rd Regiment. Several found work on the government Experimental Station at Groote Post. Some later worked for the government on building the road to French Hoek (now Franschhoek). A number of others were still working for Moodie on land at Long Hope, near Bushman's River, or at his estate, Groot Vaders Bosch, in the 1820s. One of the surgeons, John Laing, became second district surgeon of Cape Town, working at the Somerset Hospital. Another surgeon, James Abercrombie, who sailed with the third party, also became a surgeon at the Somerset Hospital before developing a private practice. He later became prominent in the public life of Cape Town and was a member of the Legislative Council after the granting of representative government.

There were some other success stories. One did well making furniture. Two brothers, James and Alexander McPhail, became notable building contractors at Uitenhage. Another, George Nicol, won the tender for building a new Leper Hospital (which the Edinburgh-trained Dr James Barry was instrumental in founding). Alex Reid became a prosperous millwright at Swellendam. James Scoon, who had been in Moodie's first party, was said to have led trading expeditions to the northern Transvaal, reaching farther north than any other white before him. At least one other can be identified as working on the Cape Town–Simonstown road. Moodie had received the contract for this, although it turned out to be one of his less successful exploits, partly because his techniques were inappropriate (he cannot have been experienced in road building, let alone in the conditions of the Cape), partly because his workers were pressed into the navy as they reached the Simonstown end. One went to live in the distant and relatively remote Namaqualand, where he was effectively unreachable when Moodie tried to secure his debt. Some absconded. One, Colin Bain, reached Ascension Island, where he worked as a cooper in the naval establishment. Attempts to have him returned failed, presumably because he was far too useful to the Royal Navy. Another, Archibald Dodds, was enterprising enough to forge the fiscal's name on a passport, but he was arrested trying to take passage on a ship in Table Bay and was duly punished. He was recorded in the lists as travelling with his wife, but there is no indication of what was to happen to her.[59]

In 1835, in a memorial to the Governor trying to recoup some of the expenses, Moodie proclaimed that his 'mechanicks and labourers' had formed the 'best emigration in point of character and qualifications that ever left England', that 'the individuals composing it would have been a valuable acquisition to any country'.[60] On another occasion he wrote that five were on their way to making their fortunes. He extolled the quality of his settlers when it suited him and castigated them when he could not secure his debts. Thomas Pringle, of the 1820 settlement, who would no doubt have admired such independence, complimented the Moodie settlement as an example of what could be done. In his propaganda to secure help for the 1820 settlers he pointed out that some of the Moodie settlers had contrived to make fortunes varying from £500 to £2,000.[61] But obviously only a tiny majority were successful on that scale.

John Moodie, who sailed for the Cape in 1819, offers an intriguing picture of some of the settlers who remained in the employ of his elder brother. When he reached Groot Vaders Bosch he found two Scots carpenters employed to make furniture for sale to other farmers. They also made coffins (and he relates a story in which one forced an extremely corpulent Afrikaner neighbour called Botha, who was ordering his own coffin, to lie down so that measurements could be taken, knowing that he would be unable to get up again unaided). There were several other settlers working on the farm, and some had openly formed liaisons with 'Hottentot' or Khoi women. John suggested that the Dutch were outraged by this, but in fact they did exactly the same thing, but with greater discretion. The Scots workers indulged in wild parties and drinking bouts, much appreciated by the local Khoi, who evinced a passion for music, shared by the Scots' love of melody. The Khoi women, he suggested, had sweet voices and a better sense of harmony. They were also strikingly elegant in their proportions, exhibiting a lightness and ease in their motion which was much preferable to the 'clumsy, torpid, insensible Dutch women'. He provides an engaging picture of this social life, and of the Scots' dependence on the Khoi in performing some farm functions (for example, in yoking the half-wild oxen). He describes a gardener, John Weir, as an eccentric who lived like a hermit in an old mill. But he had a passion for astronomy and covered bits of wood with complex calculations. He was, wrote Moodie, 'a true philosopher' with considerable independence of mind who talked to the Moodie brothers on a basis of equality. He also loved dancing and chased the Khoi girls, but they fled, calling him wild boar or porcupine because of his beard. 'The Scots,' he wrote, 'have a large share of national pride and self-conceit' and, 'like the thistle for their country, their prejudices are stiff and unbending', but this obviously did not prevent them from pursuing the Khoi women. They regarded themselves as superior to the Dutch yet invariably established good relations with them. There is a very definite flavour of an early nineteenth-century frontier existence in all of this.[62] We also see evidence of a cross-racial rural 'canteen culture'.[63]

But, so far as Benjamin Moodie was concerned, the whole project became something of a financial and legal nightmare. As we have seen, he discovered that the indentures meant very little at the Cape, and that many of the men flouted them with impunity. The colonists regarded the members of the settlement as 'white slaves' who should be helped to avoid Moodie at all costs. There was method in this:

there was a shortage of labour for construction, for the making of barrels for the booming wine trade, and for other employment. Moodie's settlers were generally in possession of valuable craft skills and had every incentive to seek to escape from the irksome indentures. He was reduced to lamenting the fact that men who had seemed to be of good character in Scotland took on a very different demeanour in the colony, indulging in conduct scarcely credible to anyone who had known them at home.[64] His brother John wrote that the lower classes, so moral in Scotland, yet broke their engagements at the Cape. Whereas bad conduct in Scotland brought its punishments (presumably as much from the Church as from the courts) there were no constraints at the Cape.[65] Thus the place of opportunity for the landed gentry was an unacceptably free and open society for their supposed dependants. Moodie settlers created their own routes to respectability while losing it in the eyes of their Scots social superiors.

Moodie also became embroiled in official animosities at the Cape, notably between Colonel Bird, the colonial secretary, who had helped to facilitate the scheme, and Judge Truter, Bird's sworn enemy, who seemed determined to 'liberate' the settlers. Moodie embarked on a series of legal actions which gave him a taste for litigation and infighting, sometimes with fellow members of the Cape Scots elite such as John Fairbairn and Charles Davidson Bell.[66] Bell was the surveyor-general of the colony, who surveyed Moodie's land to his apparent disadvantage. There was a long and acrimonious court case, which Moodie lost. He also fell out with William Douglas Bell,[67] the first harbourmaster and pilot of Port Natal (Durban). He was deprived of his office but later reinstated. In 1827 Moodie was still trying to secure the settlers' debts through an agent and at a considerable discount. His efforts to secure official indemnity for his original costs were also unsuccessful. The one portrait of Moodie, not surprisingly, gives him a rather pugnacious, even cantankerous appearance.

Yet, despite all his disappointments with the 1817 settlement, Moodie continued to be involved in other migration schemes. In 1840 the South African Association, modelled on the ideas of Edward Gibbon Wakefield, set about buying up land in the Cape and proposed using Moodie as its agent. He offered some of his own land for settlement, no doubt in an attempt to recreate the feudal dream of his original plan. The project failed. In 1841 the Eastern Province Loan Fund Emigration Society was formed in Grahamstown, with similar ambitions, but it too never got off the ground. However, Moodie did bring out some twenty-one boys and girls under the auspices of the Children's Friendly Society. Who these children were and what happened to them do not seem to have been recorded.

Moodie had an extraordinary capacity to alienate those whom he needed as his supporters. He infuriated Somerset by attacking the latter's principal recreational activity, horse breeding and racing. And Somerset was not a man to be crossed. He also succeeded in offending Sir Rufane Donkin, who acted for Somerset for twenty-one months at the time of the 1820 settlement. Moodie and his two brothers, John and Donald (another brother, Thomas, joined them at the Cape), attempted to establish a frontier settlement with ex-soldiers. The idea turned out to be a disaster, particularly when Somerset reversed Donkin's frontier policy. In compensation Moodie was granted a large tract of land on the Bushman's River: he called it 'Long Hope', after a place in the Orkneys. John and Donald also secured extensive tracts of land and named a nearby valley 'Hoy'. Donald ended with a moderately distinguished career. He became government resident and magistrate at Kowie River, later resident magistrate at Grahamstown. In 1842 he moved to Natal, just in time for its annexation by the British. He was colonial secretary of Natal from 1845 to 1849 and in 1857 became speaker of the colony's legislative assembly.[68] He became a major propagandist for the settler cause, and a founder of a white historiography, generally unsympathetic to indigenous rights.[69]

Long Hope was a failure, despite having reputedly fertile soil and lots of game, and was soon sold. As well as failing as a road contractor, Benjamin Moodie was unsuccessful as a merchant and trader. He was involved in the development of Port Beaufort (on the coast, south of Swellendam and Heidelberg) and opened a store there, but it failed to make money. However, Somerset's successor, Sir Lowry Cole, granted him another large estate, more than 10,000 acres in extent, which was named Westfield after Scottish land in Moray that had come to the Moodies through marriage. He started wool farming in 1825 and his flocks grew to a tremendous extent, creating the fortune which he would pass on to some of his sons (who by the late 1850s were the largest producers of wool in the district). He bought up adjacent land, and both Groot Vaders Bosch and Westfield remained in the Moodie family until at least the 1950s. One son, James, later mysteriously disinherited, had a farm called Dundonald near Swellendam and later trekked to the Orange Free State, acquiring land in the Bethlehem area, which he called Melsetter. A nephew, George Pigott Moodie, was involved in the gold discoveries in the Transvaal. A grandson, George Dunbar Moodie, led a settlement *trek*, encouraged by Cecil Rhodes, to Mashonaland in Rhodesia in 1891 and also called the area Melsetter. There was a Moodie's Pass, and 'Moodie's Drift' commemorated their crossing of the Sabi River on the way.

Moodie always maintained that he had been tricked, although he died a substantial landowner and the founder of a major southern African farming dynasty. But there was always an extraordinary degree of cultural ambivalence about the Moodie settlement. Although they were dubbed 'English' on arrival, in fact some of the settlers maintained a degree of Scottishness and also assimilated, in places where it mattered, like Swellendam, into the Afrikaans community. Moodie himself became a reasonably fluent speaker of the language. When the architect John Wilson (an 1820 settler) was commissioned to build Westfield, Moodie started off by wanting it built in Palladian style (intriguingly, he had brought the works of Palladio out with him), but it was eventually constructed in the Cape Dutch manner. He joined the Dutch Reformed Church (as a member of the Church of Scotland he secured immediate communion) and he became an *ouderling*, or elder. Yet he maintained contacts with Scottish missionaries, such as the celebrated superintendent of the London Missionary Society, Dr John Philip, who visited him at Groot Vaders Bosch in 1830, though he vigorously attacked the humanitarianism of Philip, Fairbairn and Pringle.[70] He also filled his homes with the family heirlooms brought from the Orkneys. Land was repeatedly named after Scottish precedents, and it has been said that his descendants were always aware of their Orcadian inheritance.

The 1820 settlement

If the Moodie settlement seemed chaotic, the 1820 scheme to 'plant' settlers on the eastern frontier was even more so. Few settlements produced so much tragedy and so much controversy. Few were more instrumental in the dispossession of African peoples: it served to produce endemic and brutal violence where it was supposed to bring peace. But because of its heroic status in the history of English-speakers in South Africa it has been subjected to intense scrutiny by family historians seeking to trace their origins among the several thousand people who participated. Societies, memorials, museums and a small publishing industry have grown up, and the names of settlers have been listed despite considerable complexities in retrieving them. It has been suggested that about 10 per cent of the settlers were Scots, but the figure is hard to verify. The total figure has been variously given as between 4,000 and 5,000 people.[71] Relatively tiny as it was, Alan Lester has seen this settlement as a key location for the intersection of settler, official and humanitarian discourses in the period. It introduced to South Africa many British social perceptions of the time, but it resulted in the creation of a settler order which would serve to overwhelm humanitarian ideas and form the strongly racialised ideology which prevailed at least from the 1850s.⁷² But Lester is less clear on the ways in which distinct white ethnicities were worked out through it.

In July 1819 the British government decided to vote £50,000 to help finance a settlement whose arrangements are redolent of the social and economic character of the age. This was something of a turn-round, since the government had been resisting such public support for more than ten years. The reasons given were the usual threefold ones: consolidate the frontier and consequently produce more strategic security at the Cape; redress the balance of the white population in favour of the English; help to alleviate social distress in Britain. Of these, perhaps the third was the most pressing. The post-war slump and the dislocations of industrialism had produced extensive unemployment, not least of soldiers and sailors thrown out of work and of the hand-loom weavers, who were experiencing considerable distress. This seemed to be building up social pressures that might transform agitations into revolutionary activity. Yet the people who actually participated in the settlement were seldom drawn from such groups. The basic structure of the settlement was that 'proprietors' would put together parties of followers who would be supervised by them. The option in the scheme whereby parishes could pay the deposits of indigent people was seldom taken up. Better-off migrants could pay for themselves, but they banded together into parties. In other words, there was to be little in the way of anarchic individualism. The proprietorial system would maintain discipline by transplanting the stabilising hierarchies and obligations of home. A deposit of £10 for each settler, to include a wife and two children where applicable, plus additional bonds of £5 for more children (£2 10s for those under fourteen), was to be left with the government agents. Single women over eighteen years of age would also deposit £10. The money would be repaid by instalments, ensuring that the settlers fulfilled their obligations. (Was the government mindful of the problems Moodie had experienced?)⁷³ In return, each settler would receive a grant of land of 100 acres (on land arranged by the Government Land Surveyor), relatively generous when placed against the average size of a smallholding in the United Kingdom at the period, although, as the settlers were to discover by bitter experience, the environmental conditions at the Cape frontier were very different.

If a party of more than 100 people was put together, they could appoint an approved minister, of their chosen denomination, and his salary would be paid for by the government. When the government advertised its scheme, there was an immediate and dramatic response. It has been said that there were no fewer than 90,000 applicants, many of them from people of lower middle-class standing. Meetings took place in London and elsewhere, clubs were formed and groups set about fulfilling the terms of the plan. Proprietors emerged from the ranks of half-pay officers, as well as from the gentry and a few middle-class professional and mercantile figures. But there were delays. Some who had seemed to commit themselves proceeded to renew engagements with employers or continue their leases upon the land. Parties were invariably made up of family members and friends, through word-of-mouth recruitment. But there were repeated substitutions, some people even adding to the confusion by adopting the names of those whom they were replacing. The popularity of the scheme is illustrated by the eagerness of substitutes to take up places abandoned by others; it is even said that they hung around the docks hoping for a last-minute chance to go.[74] Some of these substitutions were highly unsuitable for the agricultural settlement envisaged. One source suggests that clerks, confectioners and piano tuners signed up; another that there were 'manufacturers, jam makers and fringe embroiderers' among those who took ship.[75] Given the pricing structure of the deposits, the ages of children were often misrepresented. In addition, some of the parties went on a self-financing basis, making their own arrangements for shipping, and thus avoiding the deposits. They were given the 100 acre grant for each able-bodied man along with those who were funded. In the event, less than a third of the parties were of the proprietorial type originally envisaged. Many of the others, ranging in size from ten to 100 families, were essentially self-help groups with a nominated leader.[76] Of the planned 10,000 settlers, roughly 4,000 landed at the Cape, followed by another 1,000 soon afterwards.[77] Emigration schemes had a habit of turning out differently from the plans of their begetters.

In the end some seventeen ships sailed for the Cape, the first parties departing in December 1819 on the *Chapman, Nautilus, Ocean* and *Northampton*, all from Gravesend. Other vessels left from Portsmouth, Bristol, Liverpool, Cork and Greenock. Tragedy was to strike the latter party, made up of Scots artisans under the leadership of William Russell of Glasgow. They sailed on a ship called the *Abeona* in October 1820. Six weeks into the voyage the ship caught fire and was totally destroyed. Sixteen of the crew, twenty-seven of the emigrants and nine other passengers were saved, while nine of the crew, 100 emigrants and five other passengers went down with the ship. A few of the survivors eventually reached the Cape and applied for a grant of land.[78] Another large Highland party, to have been led by Captain Grant, and made up of almost 500 emigrants, withdrew from the scheme even though land had been allocated to them on the Mancazana River.[79] They left for North America instead. General Charles Campbell led a small party of about fifty from Argyllshire. They sailed on three vessels, the *Mary Ann Sophia*, the *Dowson* and the *Salisbury*, the third in 1821, accompanied by Campbell himself. He died a year after his arrival and the land was inherited by his widow.[80] Peter Tait had already brought out small groups of Scots, on two occasions, in 1819, but these were not part of the formal settlement scheme and dispersed in the colony. Another sizeable emigrant party from Invernessshire, led by Finlay Matheson, was intended for America but was advised to go to the Cape. It is not clear whether they ever arrived.[81]

The other – and most famous – Scottish party comprised some twelve men and their families from Roxburghshire and East Lothian, the majority of whom were employed in agriculture. This group had been put together under the patronage of Sir Walter Scott, who had used his influence to have them accepted. Their leader was the unlikely figure of Thomas Pringle (1789–1834), a disabled writer and journalist, poet and campaigner, a sensitive figure in appearance and character, who was to become the leading publicist for the settlers' plight on the frontier. The Pringle family seem to have lost the farm which they had occupied as tenants for half a century. Moreover, one of Thomas's brothers had emigrated to the United States, and one of the objects of migrating to the Cape was to attempt to keep the family unit together.[82] They sailed from Leith to the Thames and left Gravesend on the *Brilliant* (presumably the same brig as had conveyed Benjamin Moodie and members of his party to the Cape almost three years earlier) in February 1820. Pringle left the frontier in 1822 for Cape Town and his position as leader was taken over by his brother William. (Their father, Robert, a farmer, was also a member of the group, despite being sixty-five years of age at the time of the voyage.) As we shall see in Chapter 3, Thomas Pringle was to become a leading member of the highly literate and tempestuous Scottish group which opposed Governor Lord Charles Somerset in Cape Town.

Although the Scottish component of the settlement seemed singularly ill starred, there were certainly Scots in some of the parties, as a fair number of Scottish names can be identified on the frontier, some of them intermarrying with members of other groups. Among these parties, which totalled fifty-seven in all, there were a fair number of Irish people, mainly from the south of the island and embarking on two ships from Cork, some Welsh, while many of the English came from distressed areas of Nottinghamshire and London. Interestingly, Lord Bathurst, the Colonial Secretary, decreed that they should be settled in distinct ethnic groups, with English, Scots, Welsh and Irish geographically separated. Given the mixed nature of many parties, this cannot have been carried out to the letter, although the order does cast an interesting sidelight on 'Anglicisation'. The acting Governor, Rufane Donkin, sent the Scots north to the Baviaans River, thirty miles from Cradock, in the area of the Winterberg Mountains, to form a shield to protect Graaff Reinet.[83] The Welsh and some English went initially to the upper Zonder Eind River near Caledon and the Irish to the Olifants River valley near Clanwilliam. But some of this land, notably that allocated to the Welsh and the Irish, was unsuitable and the settlers retreated to Albany.[84] They duly received their grants of land and were settled in blocks on the colonial side of the Great Fish River in the region of Grahamstown and Bathurst, the latter settlement encouraged by Donkin, for the support of the settlers. It was later said that the Scots' land was better in quality than that of other parties. And, because Grant's Highland party never arrived, there was plenty of it.[85]

Pringle was clearly the most literate of all the settlers, and it is thanks to him that we have graphic descriptions of the landing of the parties on the beach at Algoa Bay, the future Port Elizabeth, as well as much on their subsequent fate. Pringle's group on the *Brilliant* landed at the same time as a notable, and well documented Wesleyan Methodist party under the leadership of Hezekiah Sephton.[86] The township at Algoa Bay was tiny, but the Scots must have been a little reassured by the fact that the 72nd Highland Regiment was the garrison at Fort Frederick, which commanded the anchorage. Pringle's descriptions of the southern African environment were romantic and lyrical. He brought an eye and a pen which had been trained on the romantic appreciation of Scottish landscape, seeing 'mountains and glens' in the region where they had settled.[87] Moreover, he was quite convinced that it was a landscape more suited to Scots than to the English.

> The sublimely stern aspect of the country so different from the rich tameness of ordinary English scenery, seemed to strike many of the Southron [English] with a degree of care approaching to consternation. The Scotch, on the contrary, as the stirring recollections of their native land were vividly called up by the rugged peaks and shaggy declivities of this wild coast, were strongly affected, like all true mountaineers on such occasions. Some were excited to extravagant spirits, others silently shed tears.[88]

But if the landscape was reasonably appealing, more practical considerations were pressing. They had to build shelters (usually wattle-and-daub huts more akin to African habitations than European, though they were usually rectangular rather than round[89]), sow crops, and acquire stock as quickly as they could in order to survive.

But they soon found themselves on an edge in which survival was at a premium. Disaster struck the settlements almost immediately. They had been encouraged to grow Bengal wheat, together with other crops, and this was unsuitable for the Cape environment. Their crops were also attacked by rust, over five or six seasons, and they suffered from extreme weather conditions. In 1823 drought was broken by downpours of torrential rain, flooding and high winds, destroying many farms and their insubstantial residences. The first two harvests failed, and the third nearly so. Even if a surplus was produced, the settlers were too far from markets to be able to sell it. For much of the early years of the settlement the settlers were also not permitted to trade with the Africans across the colonial frontier. A number of settlers left for Grahamstown and other centres, where some of them prospered. It was also apparent that the original vision of closely settled small farms was entirely impracticable. Hundred-acre farms were not nearly large enough to support a family. Commissioners were appointed to investigate the 'distressed state of the Cape of Good Hope' in 1825 and reported in 1826–27.[90] The problems of the Cape settlement were compounded by the poor state of the colonial economy. The wine trade was in decline and the death of Napoleon on St Helena in 1821 had led to a dramatic drop in exports to the garrison and court there.

To add to all their other troubles, the settlements had been consciously located in the region where the frontier wars with the southern Nguni had been occurring intermittently since the 1770s. The land on which they settled had been cleared of the southern Nguni Xhosa people on the orders of Governor Sir John Cradock, carried out by John Graham. It is hardly surprising that the Xhosa were bitter about imperial actions on the frontier and the brutality to which they had been subjected. The most recent 'Kaffir War' had taken place in 1818–19, and another was to break out in 1834. The settlers were not only located in a difficult environment; they were also in a former and potential war zone. Initially they were only dimly aware of this. They were, moreover, trapped in the fierce wrangles of the Cape Town administrative elite. During the period of Donkin's governorship the settlers were partially protected by his desire to see them succeed. He remitted some of their expenses and saw to it that they received relief rations. He also permitted some trading on the frontier. But when Somerset returned he was outraged at what he saw as the overturning of his frontier policy; he immediately reversed many of Donkin's provisions and resumed for a period his autocratic and seemingly uncaring approach.

A committee for the relief of the settlers was established in Cape Town, with Pringle as its secretary, together with another in London.

Pringle was the leading publicist, writing extensively on the hardships they were encountering.[91] In his relatively short life Pringle was an intriguing and ambivalent figure. He was steeped in the lore of the Scottish Borders, including the cattle-raiding propensities of the Reivers, but also in other aspects of Scottish history and literature. His interest in Africa was inspired by reading the fellow Borderer Mungo Park's *Travels*. He regarded himself as a follower of Sir Walter Scott, whom he visited and with whom he corresponded. Yet Scott was a Tory and he was a liberal Whig. His radicalism and his realistic descriptions of life on an African frontier were tempered by 'gentility', an anxiety apparently to please the more refined sensitivities of the English. Hence, perhaps in order to reach the widest audience, he wrote very little in Scots. He admired the poetry of the Scottish writer Thomas Campbell (1777–1844) and Scott, but was anxious about the supposed crudity of James Hogg, the 'Ettrick Shepherd'. As a poet he has been described as 'the father of South African poetry' (at least as written by whites), but he has also been reclaimed by Scotland. He was admired (if in a somewhat backhanded way) by Coleridge, but his poetry was highly derivative, reflecting the influence of Scott, Byron, Campbell, Keats and others.[92]

He was sympathetic to the Khoi and San people whom he encountered on the frontier, and was perceptive enough to work out that they were 'peoples' who were closely connected, differentiated only by a dynamic pattern of modes of subsistence. He also pointed out that the name 'Hottentot' was an abusive one. He regarded the San as living a natural life, but saw them as fallen noble savages. But he referred to them in one poem as South African 'Children of the Mist', a clear reference to Scott's characterisation of Highlanders in *Rob Roy*. Yet he was prepared to react like any settler when his stock were attacked by a San band, and called out a commando. But he insisted that the San should not be killed and he was sensitive enough to remark that he and his companions had in effect been brutalised by the harsh and confrontational conditions of the frontier. As for the Xhosa, he encountered several individuals after the first landing at Algoa Bay and was impressed by their dignity and fine physique. He extolled the manner in which they showed loyalty to their chiefs, perhaps an echo of an ideal Scottish social condition, but one which seems scarcely liberal or radical. Indeed, a number of tensions revealed themselves in Pringle's thought, action and writings. In 1830 he wrote to Scott that he regarded himself as a South African patriarch with his flocks, followers and thousand acres of rock and forest. Yet he was described as a 'Utopian Philanthropist' by one contemporary and, after his return to London, he became secretary of the Anti-slavery Society, and often sheltered abused blacks in his home. He has been described as combining Enlightenment rationalism with Romantic enthusiasm.[93] For him the Khoisan were degraded but redeemable; the Xhosa were not unlike Scots raiders. But the other settlers had a high regard for him and he was also admired by the Boers, not least for his feats of horsemanship, achieved despite his disability.[94]

For his part he respected the Boers but attacked the commando system and slavery. Above all, he was an evangelical, and argued passionately, contrary to many settlers, for the efficacy of missionaries on the frontier. Despite his disability, he was an accomplished horseman and hunter. His principal book on the settlement is filled with descriptions of animals and of the hunt.[95] He wrote of the exuberance of animal life, in a natural theological phrase that anticipates similar remarks of David Livingstone. When a marauding lion was killed, he sent the head and skin to Scott to join other trophies at Abbotsford. His radicalism was tempered by the manner in which he fulfilled the classic characteristics of the settler. He was a man on horseback, flourishing his gun as well as his crutches, his Bible as well as his limited socially radical views.

It must be partly because we see the 1820 settlement through the eyes of key Scots that the Scottish settlers are given such a good press by contemporaries. Pringle himself argued that Scots made the best settlers, used as they were to working marginal land and enduring harsh conditions.[96] They were also highly adaptable: for example, they soon abandoned the seeds they had brought with them and acquired seeds, plants and techniques from their Boer neighbours.[97] The English, on the other hand, were lacking in the necessary natural skills, no doubt because they were so often drawn from non-agricultural sectors of society. One individual (identified only by initials, J.H.R.) wrote a letter to the *Morning Chronicle* in July 1823 urging that more 'Scotch (and especially Highlanders)' should be sent to the frontier.[98] Certainly, the (non-Highland) Scots group at Glen Lynden, as Pringle called their valley, flourished more than the others farther east and south.[99] Their flocks and herds of sheep, goats and horned cattle prospered. A church was founded.[100] Relatives joined them from Scotland[101] and new land was opened up.[102] But the Scots also owed a great deal to their willingness to learn from the Boers and the Khoi. As well as living in dwellings that were essentially of the country, they picked up a good deal about the natural environment from those who had inhabited the land before them. For example, they learned how to deal with snake bites and used Khoi techniques for curing them.[103] These efforts at adaptation helped to ensure that a significant Scots component remained on the frontier, even although the 1820 settlement was largely a failure. There was an upturn in their fortunes from about 1825 and larger grants of land were given to those who had survived, starting with the Scots settlement near Cradock. As we have seen, many of the settlers became town dwellers and the closer settlement of the frontier was prosecuted again only after the foundation of mission stations (many of them Scots) and the further frontier violence of white expansion and more so-called 'Kaffir Wars'. Scots settlers were duly swept up in these frontier wars and participated as commandos and volunteers in the mix of settler, Boer and imperial actions which set about suppressing the Xhosa and denying them access to land which, in some cases, had originally been theirs.[104] The 1820 settlers created more problems than they solved.

These early Scottish connections with the Cape introduce a number of themes which are to be significant in the future. Efforts to maintain the social relations of home were entirely disrupted. Individuals set out on their own routes to respectability, occasionally succeeding in securing higher status. Many revealed an intense interest in the environment, in scientific activity and in its representation in various forms, as well as a fascination with observational studies, including the ethnographic. The Scots connection with the Dutch is also a recurrent theme, not only through the Scots communities in the Netherlands but also in shared interests at the frontier. Yet another is propaganda that Scots were particularly suited to migration and settlement. They were allegedly more practical, more inured to hardship, more capable of coping with the environment than other settlers. There can be no doubt at all that contemporaries singled out the Scots. This was sometimes self-generated propaganda, but others also promoted this set of ideas. And although the Scots were sometimes lumped together with the English, they were often identified as a separate ethnic identity, and settled as such. The notion that there was a Teutonic race connection between the English and the Lowland and Borders Scots, allegedly so beloved of writers and intellectuals in the nineteenth century, does not appear to have entered into popular consciousness.[105] Such racial preoccupations were no doubt a convenient piece of Unionist propaganda, as well as a means of obscuring difference at a time when it was convenient to both Scots and English to do so, but in the colonial setting difference could be significant and instrumental, not least in forming social, religious and cultural alliances with other colonial peoples like the Dutch. That was particularly important when figures like Pringle carried a portfolio of Scottish ideas to southern Africa and allowed them to be both re-emphasised and modified in this different environment. Moreover, the Scots usually carried their badge of Presbyterianism: it distinguished them from the English and inspired sympathy and confidence in fellow Calvinists. In the next chapter these connections will also be seen working themselves out in Cape Town itself.

Notes

1 There were Scots communities in Veere, Middelberg and Bergen-op-Zoom, partly commercial and partly associated with the families of the officers and men of the Scots brigade. Joachim Middelbrink, 'The end of the Scots–Dutch Brigade' in Steve Murdoch and A. Mackillop (eds), *Fighting for Identity: Scots Military Experience, c. 1550–1900* (Leiden 2002), p. 98.
2 For a detailed examination of the Scots community of Rotterdam in the seventeenth century see D. Catterall, 'Community without Borders: Scots Migrants and the Changing Face of Power in the Dutch Republic, 1600–1690', Ph.D., University of Minnesota (Minneapolis MN 1998).
3 A Scottish brigade had been in the employ of the Dutch since 1572 and became celebrated, at least by repute, as the finest soldiers in the Dutch army. In the late seventeenth and eighteenth centuries they maintained aspects of Scots identity in their uniform, their flag, emblems and music – they drilled to the 'Scots March'. Although other nationalities were enlisted, the majority of officers and men were Scottish. They were temporarily disbanded (along with English regiments in Dutch employ) in 1665 during the second Anglo-Dutch War, but were soon recreated. They established a particularly notable reputation during the wars of the eighteenth century until the War of American Independence caused new alignments to be formed. Middelbrink, 'The end of the Scots–Dutch Brigade'.
4 Esmé Bull, *Aided Immigration from Britain to South Africa, 1857–1867*, ed. J. L. Barron (Pretoria 1991), p. 1.
5 Ibid.
6 This incident is recorded in Theal's *Records of the Cape* and is quoted in Frank Quinn and Greg Cuthbertson, *Presbyterianism in Cape Town: the History of St Andrew's Church, 1829–1979* (Cape Town 1979), p. 3. Since all these figures were apparently Presbyterian, Quinn and Cuthbertson date the origins of the Presbyterian Church in South Africa to this incident.
7 Patrick Cullinan, *Robert Jacob Gordon, 1743–1795: the Man and his Travels at the Cape* (Winchester, Cape 1993).
8 This royal connection may have helped him to get leave of absence from his duties in the garrison for his travels, or it may be that the Dutch East India Company authorities saw his knowledge of the interior as potentially useful to them.
9 After his death, his wife attempted to sell many of his maps and journals. They were ultimately dispersed and came to light again only in the course of the twentieth century. Cullinan, *Gordon*, p. 9.
10 Ibid.
11 Vernon S. Forbes, *Pioneer Travellers of South Africa: a Geographical Commentary on Routes, Records, Observations and Opinions of Travellers at the Cape, 1750–1800* (Cape Town 1965), p. 93.
12 Forbes, *Pioneer Travellers*, p. 116.
13 Ibid.
14 Cullinan, *Gordon*, p. 12.
15 Gordonskop, or Gordon's Kop, near the town of Aberdeen, was declared a national monument in 1955 at the time of the celebrations of Aberdeen's centennial. Eily Gledhill, 'Robert Gordon and the Sneeuwberg farmers', *The Annals*, 4: 3 (1985), pp. 65–71.
16 P. W. Marnitz and H. D. Campagne, *The Dutch Surrender of the Cape of Good Hope, 1795* (Cape Town 2002), provide a detailed account of these events.

17 For accounts of the activities and publications of Thunberg and Sparrmann see William Beinart, *The Rise of Conservation in South Africa* (Oxford 2003), chapter 1.
18 Forbes, *Pioneer Travellers*, pp. 37 ff.
19 Quoted in ibid., p. 38.
20 Richard Drayton, *Nature's Government: Science, Imperial Britain and the 'Improvement' of the World* (New Haven CT and London 2000), pp. 46-7 and 127; Charles Lyte, *The Plant Hunters* (London 1983), pp. 23-35.
21 Drayton, *Nature's Government*, p. 46. Lyte, *Plant Hunters*, lists the plants collected by Masson on p. 182.
22 *The Confessions of the Countess of Strathmore, Mary Eleanour Bowes, written by herself* (London 1793). Her husband, the Earl of Strathmore, joined his name to hers and ever since the family has been known as the Bowes Lyons.
23 Forbes, *Pioneer Travellers*, p. 91.
24 Lieutenant William Paterson, *A Narrative of Four Journeys into the Country of the Hottentots and Caffraria in the Years 1777-1778-1779, illustrated with a Map and seventeen Copper Plates* (London 1789), pp. 1-4. Paterson misspelt Masson's name as Mason. Second edition, corrected (London 1790).
25 Forbes, *Pioneer Travellers*, p. 92.
26 Sparrman, Andrew (sic), *A Voyage to the Cape of Good Hope from the Year 1772-1776* (London 1785). Beinart has detected some copying of Sparrman by Paterson: *The Rise of Conservation*, p. 35; Carl Peter Thunberg, *Travels in Europe, Africa and Asia performed between the Years 1770 and 1779* (three volumes, London 1795).
27 Drayton. *Nature's Government*, p. 111 and p. 298n.174.
28 It has been suggested that Masson and Paterson could not have been spies because they ended up in financial difficulties. The turbulent private life of Lady Strathmore meant that she could not honour the bills drawn on her by Paterson for his travelling expenses. The nabob William Hickey stepped in and paid up £900 despite not knowing the characters involved. Forbes connects these financial problems with Masson, but it surely refers to Paterson, who was financed by Strathmore. Forbes, *Pioneer Travellers*, p. 82.
29 H. E. Wilkins (ed.), *South Africa a Century Ago: Letters written from the Cape of Good Hope (1797-1801) by Lady Anne Barnard* (London 1901), p. viii. Robert Temple later dedicated his *Walks and Sketches at the Cape of Good Hope* (London 1803) to Dundas on the grounds that 'no one has paid so much attention' to the Cape or 'has so intimate an acquaintanceship with every subject relative to that Colony as your lordship'. Dundas carefully kept all her letters, tied them together and placed them in the library at Arniston House.
30 *Dictionary of Canadian Biography.*
31 In a letter to Dundas, Lady Anne Barnard described Craig as 'very fat and lives very high'. Wilkins, *a Century Ago*, p. 105.
32 Margaret Lenta and Basil le Cordeur (eds), *The Cape Diaries of Lady Anne Barnard, 1799-1800* (two volumes, Cape Town 1999). In these, and in the Dundas, letters Lady Anne displays her extraordinary range of acquaintanceship among leading figures of the Scottish Enlightenment (including Hume and Monboddo), in London (politicians and directors of the East India Company such as the Dundonian George Dempster, 1732-1818) and at the Cape. She reveals herself to be well read, to have an intelligent and informed interest in the issues and ideas of the day, as well as commenting on events in the Napoleonic Wars, such as Admiral Adam Duncan's victory at Camperdown in 1797 and Nelson's triumph at the Nile the following year.
33 By this time the Scotch Brigade was a British line regiment, but its name may imply some pride in the Dutch brigade, in which some of its officers may have served.
34 K. J. Wilson, 'To Buenos Aires via Melkbosstrand, Blouberg and Cape Town with the Highland Light Infantry in 1806', *Quarterly Bulletin of the South African*

Library, 40: 4 (1986), pp. 148–55, provides an account of the exploits of the HLI in the South Atlantic in 1805–06.
35 Peter Philip, *British Residents at the Cape, 1795–1819: Biographical Records of 4,800 Pioneers* (Cape Town 1981). Philip also listed the Scottish regiments present at the Cape. They included the 71st Foot (Highland Light Infantry), January to April 1806; the 72nd Foot (Seaforth Highlanders), January 1806 to October 1810, and the first battalion, February 1816 to March 1822; the 78th Foot (Seaforth Highlanders), first and second battalions, June 1795 to November 1796; the 91st Foot (Argyll and Sutherland Highlanders), September 1795 to October 1798 (then known as the 98th Foot) and as the 91st, October 1798 to March 1803; the 93rd Foot (Argyll and Sutherland Highlanders), January 1806 to May 1814; the Scotch Brigade, September 1796 to November 1798 and January 1799.
36 Ibid., p. vii.
37 Ibid., p. ix.
38 The Register of Permissions to remain in the Cape Colony, including those granted to discharged soldiers, can be found at the Western Cape Archives (WCA): CO 6055. See Wilfred Brinton, *The Story of the British Regiments in South Africa, 1795–1895* (Cape Town n.d.); also 'Catalogue of British Regimental Histories', South African Library: A 355 0942 JOH.
39 M. Arkin, 'John Company at the Cape: a history of the agency under Pringle (1794–1815), based on a study of the Cape of Good Hope Factory Records', *Archives Year Book for South African History (AYBSAH)* (1960, II), pp. 177–332.
40 Between 1795 and early 1803 1,095 merchant ships called at the Cape, 271of which belonged to the East India Company and 302 were private British vessels. The rest were foreign. Arkin, 'John Company', p. 201.
41 Entry in the *Dictionary of South African Biography*.
42 Lady Anne Barnard encountered them as fellow Scots. Lenta and le Cordeur, *Cape Diaries*, I, p. 235. She also commented on the preposterous wig worn by another Scots merchant, John Duncan Lowrie, whom she likened to the parakeet, the lourie. *Cape Diaries* II, p. 11.
43 P. H. Philip, 'The vicissitudes of the early British settlers at the Cape', *Quarterly Bulletin of the South African Library*, 40: 4 (1986), pp. 159–70. Both of Pringle's clerks, Maxwell and Gibson were declared insolvent, as were Alexander Tennant and John Murray senior. Some of these occurred in the Batavian period and the reason seems to have been that they had overreached themselves and were damaged by the collapse in the price of property and other goods after the British departed.
44 See the bound typescript 'Captain John Findlay, 1777–1851: this record has been compiled from the papers in the possession of George Schreiner Findlay of Pretoria', 1941, South African Library, Cape Town, which recounts Findlay's story and reproduces extracts from many of the letters. See also Natasha Erlank, 'Letters Home: the Experiences and Perceptions of Middle-class British Women at the Cape, 1830–1850', M.A. thesis, University of Cape Town (1995), and Joan Findlay (ed.), *The Findlay Letters* (Pretoria 1954).
45 Edmund H. Burrows, *The Moodies of Melsetter* (Cape Town 1954), pp. 23–4, supplies much of the background. The estate was said to be worth £47,000, but was sold for only £26,000. The effect of the Moodies on southern Africa was such that the papers of various branches of the family were deposited in the Swellendam *drosdy* (the local courthouse), the archives in what is now Harare, Zimbabwe, and the National Archives at Kew.
46 Lieutenant J. W. D. Moodie, 21st Fusiliers, *Ten Years in South Africa, including a particular Description of the wild Sports of that Country* (two volumes, London 1835), I, p. 1. 'Of all the situations above absolute want, I believe none can be more irksome and cheerless than that of a half-pay officer.' This and the other quotations come from pp. 2–5. Moodie clearly wished to emphasise his military status as a veteran of the Napoleonic wars (he had been commissioned in the Scots Fusiliers at the age of seventeen). He also sought to tap into the popularity of works on hunting, a common characteristic of travel and settlement

47 Burrows, *Moodies*, p. 24.
48 Collins's idea was subsequently published by Donald Moodie in his *The Record, or, A Series of Papers relative to the Condition and Treatment of Native Tribes of South Africa* (Cape Town 1838); Alan Lester, *Imperial Networks: Creating Identities in Nineteenth Century South Africa and Britain* (London 2001), p. 201.
49 Burrows, *Moodies*, p. 29 and ff.
50 Ibid., pp. 32–3.
51 Moodie to Lord Charles Henry Somerset, 30 March 1835, WCA: CO 3929/486.
52 Henry Goulbourn [senior official in the Department of War and Colonies] to Benjamin Moodie, 12 October 1816, copy in Moodie papers, National Library of South Africa (NLSA): MSB 690.1 (1).
53 WCA: GH vol. 1/20, ref. 151 (1816–17).
54 Burrows, *Moodies*, p. 35.
55 All this information comes from the original handwritten list of settlers, WCA: KAB, ref. VC 576.
56 Moodie, *Ten Years*, I, p. 49.
57 In 1835 Moodie was still memorialising the Governor on his losses, the inadequacies in the Cape laws for binding his 'apprentices' to him, the losses incurred as a result of frontier disturbances, not to mention the 'serious loss' from the sale of his estates in Scotland. WCA: CO 3929/486.
58 Burrows, *Moodies*, pp. 37–9.
59 These subsequent histories of Moodie settlers have been compiled from an appendix in Burrows, *Moodies*, pp. 172–93; Moodie, *Ten Years, passim*; and biographical reference works.
60 Moodie to Somerset, 30 March 1835, AWC: CO 3929/486.
61 'Of the two hundred Scotch servants and mechanics brought out to the Cape a few years ago by Mr Moodie, there is scarcely one (with the exception of a very few profligate characters) who is not now in prosperous and improving circumstances; and many of them whom I have met with, in various parts of the colony, had already cleared little fortunes of from £500 to £2000 sterling.' Thomas Pringle, *Some Account of the Present State of the English Settlers in Albany, South Africa* (London and Edinburgh 1824), pp. 47–8.
62 Moodie, *Ten Years*, I, pp. 155, 163, 221, 224, 328–36.
63 Robert Ross, *Status and Respectability in the Cape Colony, 1750–1870: a Tragedy of Manners* (Cambridge 1999), p. 137.
64 Burrows, *Moodies*, p. 53.
65 Moodie, *Ten Years*, I, pp. 52–3.
66 For the Bell litigation see AWC: CSC 2/1/1/72, ref. 5, illiquid cases, 1852. For other legal actions and letters of grievance see AWC: CO 4065, ref. 193, letters to Colonial Secretary Southey, 14 August 1852 and 14 December 1851; CO 4065/194, memorial to Lieutenant-governor Darling; CO 4060, ref. M. 51, letter to John Montagu, 3 February 1851; CO 39, ref. 9, letter to Colonel Bell, 10 April 1836. For Charles Bell see Phillida Brooke Simons, *The Life and Work of Charles Bell* (Vlaeberg 1998). An account of the litigiousness of Moodie can be found in his entry in the *Dictionary of South African Biography*.
67 Bell (1822–69) was born in Drumburgh, on the Cumberland side of the Solway, but was almost certainly of Scots parentage.
68 Donald had joined the navy in Leith in 1808 at the age of fourteen, following in the footsteps of an eighteenth-century ancestor, James Moodie, who had been a Royal Navy commodore. In the course of his administrative career in the Eastern Cape and Natal Donald compiled 'records of African tribes'. His son Duncan became an author. Another brother of Benjamin Moodie, Thomas, served in the Bengal infantry but also decided to stay and settle at the Cape. John, the writer

of *Ten Years,* did not, however, remain at the Cape, despite his favourable descriptions. He left for Canada and wrote a book about that colony. The Moodie family history tells us a good deal about distressed gentry, family influences and onward migration within the 'British world'.

69 Timothy Keegan, *Colonial South Africa and the Origins of the Racial Order* (London 1996), p. 64 and *passim;* Ross, *Status and Respectability,* p. 49.
70 His *The Record* was compiled to counter Philip's accusations in his *Researches in South Africa* (see below).
71 Among an extensive and useful, albeit generally antiquarian, literature see A. E. Makin, *The 1820 Settlers of Salem: Hezekiah Sephton's Party* (Wynberg 1971); M. D. Nash, *The Settler Handbook: a new History of the 1820 Settlers* (Plumstead 1987); Nash, *Bailie's Party of 1820 Settlers* (Cape Town 1982); Guy Butler, *The 1820 Settlers: an Illustrated Commentary* (Cape Town 1974); E. Morse Jones, *Roll of the British Settlers in South Africa* (Cape Town 1969, second edition 1971, published under the auspices of the 1820 Settlers' Monument Committee); Lynne Bryer and Keith S. Hunt, *The 1820 Settlers* (Cape Town 1984); and the lavishly illustrated Butler, *1820 Settlers.* Among older detailed accounts see Colin Turing Campbell, *British South Africa: History of the Colony of the Cape of Good Hope from its Conquest 1795 to the Settlement of Albany by the British Emigration of 1819, with Notices of some of the British Settlers of 1820* (Cape Town 1897); I. E. Edwards, *The 1820 Settlers in South Africa* (London 1924), and H. E. Hockly, *The Story of the British Settlers of 1820 in South Africa* (Cape Town 1948). Family history, as elsewhere, is a boom industry, generally among whites, in South Africa. Other works include C. Pama, *British Families in South Africa: their Surnames and Origins* (Cape Town and Johannesburg 1992), and Cecilie Swaisland, *Servants and Gentlewomen to the Golden Land: the Emigration of Single Women from Britain to Southern Africa, 1820–1931* (Durban 1993).
72 Lester, *Imperial Networks,* chapters 3 and 4.
73 Nevertheless, some settlers did break their indentures and went to live in Grahamstown. T. R. H. Davenport, 'The consolidation of a new society' in Monica Wilson and Leonard Thompson (eds), *The Oxford History of South Africa,* I (Oxford 1969), p. 279.
74 Nash, *Settler Handbook,* p. 15.
75 Ibid., p. 16; letter of J.H.R. to *Morning Chronicle,* 12 July 1823, on the state of settlers in South Africa in May 1823, Pringle, *Some Account of the Present State of the English Settlers,* p. 108. Ironically, the 'clerks, confectioners and piano tuners' may have been entered in the list of occupations in order to increase the chances of selection, since it was thought that the settlement required members of the 'ornamental' trades.
76 There were some independent settlers, some with considerable means, who must have had different motives from those of the majority of the migrants.
77 Hockly, *British Settlers,* p. 32, gives the surprisingly precise figure of 3,940 for the first wave.
78 Nash, *Settler Handbook,* p. 112.
79 Ibid., p. 108.
80 Campbell died after a fall from his horse. His grave can be seen at the botanic gardens at Rhodes University. His estate, Barville Park, still bears the name some miles out of Port Alfred. His son John spent sixty years in government service at the Cape, finally as resident magistrate in Cape Town, retiring in 1884 at the age of eighty. Another son, Frederick, had a career as an officer in the Cape Mounted Riflemen, serving in many of the wars against indigenous peoples. Campbell, *British South Africa,* pp. 191–2.
81 Jones, *Roll of the British Settlers,* pp. 7–15.
82 J. V. L. Rennie, *The Scottish Settler Party of 1820* (four volumes, Grahamstown 1991), I, p. 11. This monumental work, containing every conceivable detail on the party and its descendants down to the twentieth century well represents the scale of the fascination with this migration. The author's ancestors, the

Rennie family of East Lothian, joined the Pringle family later, as did Charles Jervis Buchan Syderserff (from Whittinghame, in East Lothian), whose naval career had been beached by the ending of the Napoleonic wars. Thomas Pringle described him as 'the younger brother of a Scottish laird, rich in blood but poor in fortune'. Syderserff was the nephew of Lord Hepburn and was related to Lord Dalhousie. He was therefore a classic younger son of the elite having to make his own way. Rennie also published a number of articles on aspects of the Scottish party. See *The Annals: Journal of the Grahamstown Historical Society*, 1: 2 (1972), pp. 10–16; 1: 4 (1974), pp. 3–6; 2: 2 (1976), pp. 2–8; 4: 2 (1984), pp. 75–80; 18 (1988), pp. 67–81.

83 Some descendants still live in the area, which bears a number of Scottish names. Given that the Scots' land was to the north and the west, it is almost as though there was some effort to replicate the demographic arrangement of the United Kingdom itself. For the route taken by the Scottish party see J. A. Pringle, 'Marking the route of the Scottish party of 1820 settlers', *Looking Back*, 20: 1 (1980), pp. 44–7. Pringle, a descendant of a member of the party, was the director of the Natal Museum in Pietermaritzburg. As so often happened, the Glen Lynden area came to be inhabited more by Afrikaners than by Scots, though all went to the same church. There is an anonymous typescript account of this church and its incumbents, 'Glen Lynden: the Scottish Settlers' Memorial Chapel', in the Cory Library, Grahamstown (CLG) MS 14, 755.

84 Eric A. Walker, *A History of Southern Africa* (1928, reprinted London 1962), p. 156; Davenport, 'Consolidation of a new society', pp. 278–9.

85 The original grant of 1,100 acres to Pringle's party was later increased to some 20,000 acres. Hockly, *British Settlers*, p. 78.

86 Makin, *The 1820 Settlers of Salem*. The minister of this party, the Rev. William Shaw, was born in Glasgow, though he was of Yorkshire extraction. The Salem community remains pleasantly English in appearance, with two Methodist churches (the original one of the 1820s and another dating from the 1850s) overlooking a cricket ground. But a grimmer racial reality lies beneath the outward sylvan character of the place. After the later church was built it became the 'white' church and the older one was the 'black'. This segregation was practised in many communities, well ahead of the imposition of apartheid.

87 This idea was developed by H. H. Dugmore, 'Reminiscences of an Albany Settler', a lecture delivered at the jubilee celebrations of 1870 and published in Grahamstown in 1871, quoted in Hockly, *British Settlers*, p. 64.

88 Thomas Pringle, *African Sketches* (London 1834), p. 124.

89 Pringle's first shelter was round, in the African manner.

90 Charlotte Erickson, *Emigration from Europe, 1815–1914: Select Documents* (London 1976), pp. 116–19.

91 Pringle, *Some Account of the Present State of the English Settlers*.

92 Angus Calder, 'Thomas Pringle (1789–1834): a Scottish poet in South Africa', *English in Africa*, 9: 1 (1982), pp. 1–28.

93 A. E. Voss, 'Thomas Pringle and the image of the "Bushmen"', *English in Africa*, 9: 1 (1982), p. 17. This article, pp. 15–28, contains much of interest on Pringle's attitude to indigenous peoples.

94 A. Keppel Jones and E. K. Heathcote (eds), *Phillips, 1820 Settler: his Letters* (Pietermaritzburg 1960), p. 254, quoted in Calder, 'Thomas Pringle', p. 3.

95 Thomas Pringle, *Narrative of a Residence in South Africa* (London 1835). This, Pringle's best-known work, formerly constituted Part II of his *African Sketches*.

96 Pringle, *Some Account*, pp. 17–18 and *passim*.

97 Beinart, *The Rise of Conservation*, p. 89.

98 Quoted in Pringle, *Some Account*, pp. 97–109.

99 Other Scottish names bestowed upon the region include Lyndoch, Eildon, Glen Gregor, Craig Rennie, Glen Thorn and Cheviot Falls. H. L. Huisman, 'Historical notes about places visited on the excursion to the Scottish settler valleys in the

100 See chapter 6.
101 In addition to various members of the Pringle family, the Ainslies (William was married to Thomas Pringle's sister Jessie) arrived later in 1833. They lived at 'Glen Thorn' for a period before moving on to other farms. Like many other settlers, they were swept up in the frontier wars. Ivan Mitford-Barberton and Violet White, *Some Frontier Families: Biographical Sketches of 100 Eastern Province Families before 1840* (Cape Town and Pretoria 1968), pp. 14–15.
102 The farm 'Lyndoch', bought by William Dods Pringle, a younger half-brother of Thomas, continued in Pringle ownership until the later twentieth century. Thomas Pringle's own farm, 'Eildon', likewise remained in Pringle ownership for more than 150 years. Another Pringle farm, settled in 1824 by John, brother of Thomas, was 'Glen Thorn' and it was similarly retained by Pringles to modern times. Huisman, 'Historical notes', pp. 36–9.
103 Pringle, *Narrative*, p. 160.
104 Mitford-Barberton and White, *Frontier Families*, seek to provide coats of arms and family histories for frontier settlers connecting them with noble British lines. Thus the settlers seem to become heroic conquerors, latter-day Normans, upon the eastern frontier. Participation in frontier wars becomes a set of noble actions between 'civilisation' and 'barbarism'. We might be more inclined today to see them as white 'robber barons', albeit inevitably swept up in the norms and mores of the time.
105 Murray Pittock, *Celtic Identity and the British Image* (Manchester 1999), pp. 64–70; Colin Kidd, 'Race, empire, and the limits of nineteenth-century Scottish nationhood', *Historical Journal*, 46: 4 (2003), pp. 873–92.

Winterberg Range', *Looking Back*, 14: 2 (1974), pp. 35–9, where there is a map of 'Scottish Settler Country', p. 37.

CHAPTER THREE

Radicals, evangelicals, the Scottish Enlightenment and Cape Colonial autocracy

Pringle was a figure of both the frontier and the Cape capital. He moved between the two, viewing himself as a patriarch and observant protagonist of settlers in the one and as a liberal writer and evangelical controversialist in the other. He travelled overland between the frontier and Cape Town in 1822, a journey which inspired some of his poems. In these he applied a romantic sensibility, heavily derived from Scott, to the African landscape, incorporating it into European aesthetic and literary norms.[1] Once in the capital, he joined a group of Scots who were busily creating the intellectual and religious institutions of the colony, who were involved in the formation of various companies and economic ventures, and who were usually locked in combat with the Governor, Lord Charles Somerset. Indeed, it may be argued that, although Somerset ruled with the royal mandate, in the longer term it was the Scots who had greater influence on the character and policies of the Cape. Ultimately the autocratic style of officialdom which emerged from the Napoleonic Wars, often perpetrated by the military governors of the period – half-pay officers who found employment in the colonies[2] – could not withstand the ferment of ideas that emerged from the Scottish Enlightenment as well as from an energetic evangelicalism. Both Somerset and his successor but one, Sir Lowry Cole, explicitly saw much of this activity as essentially 'anti-English'.

The Scots, of course, did not conduct these battles alone. At different times, and for differing purposes, they were involved in shifting alliances with the elite Cape Dutch as well as other English-speaking groups. This chapter will analyse some of these alliances and in doing so will demonstrate that 'Anglicisation', which has too often been seen in a curiously undifferentiated way in southern African history, was actually a highly complex and ethnically diverse process. Invariably the flag of language has been seen to stand as a central signifier for the whole of legal, intellectual, economic and political culture. In fact there were a number of symbolic flags in play and the significance of multi-ethnic white settlement, so carefully separated on the frontier by Bathurst, has never been adequately appreciated. The Scots were a relatively small group at the Cape, but the evidence suggests that because of the religious, economic and intellectual significance of that group, taken together with the forcefulness of some of its personalities, it punched much above its weight.

How many Scots?

The numbers of Scots and the trajectory of the statistics over the nineteenth century reveal some interesting phenomena. At the start of British rule there were not many more than 1,500 officials, 14,000 burghers, and 17,000 slaves at the Cape. By 1840 the population of the Colony had reached about 150,000, with Cape Town having over 20,000. As the British numbers built up (not least the military) in the succeeding thirty years, it is difficult to get a handle on precisely how many Scots there were, although their significance seems to be out of proportion to their numbers. If we take the founding of St Andrew's Presbyterian Church in the late 1820s as some kind of guide, we find that the organising committee was made up of some sixteen fairly prominent Scots.[3] There were twenty-eight subscribers to the raising of funds for the building, though it should be noted that those twenty-eight subscribed no less than £3,810 to the cost.[4] This gives some indication of their wealth. Even later in the century, in 1873, the white congregation was said to number no more than 100, although other congregations had been founded by then. Of course, not all Scots were Presbyterians, and some Presbyterians (notably some Northern Irish) were not Scots, although they probably had Scottish affiliations. Moreover, some who had been Presbyterians had become so accustomed to attending St George's Anglican Church that they stayed with it. When a call went out for the founding of a Presbyterian church in Port Elizabeth in 1860 it was said that there were some 300 Scots in that town.[5] In 1897 there were twenty-two European congregations of the Presbyterian Church throughout South Africa, with some 4,653 members.[6]

When we turn to the censuses, we find that the first major census in 1865 did not contain any breakdown of the place of origin of white settlers.[7] That of 1875, however, did.[8] Of 203,463 whites in Cape Colony, only 7.8 per cent claimed birth in England or Wales, 1.8 per cent in Ireland, and a mere 1.1 per cent in Scotland. That contrasts with the 2.3 per cent who gave Germany as their place of origin. We have to remember, however, that these figures are only about birth, that they are dependent on careful and honest completion of the census forms, and that many people born in the colony might still have seen themselves as, in some way, ethnically Scots, whether through parentage, education, religious or simply cultural preference. Many colonial born 'Scots' may well have had their sense of ethnicity re-fuelled by a return to Scotland for university training. In any case, the figures change dramatically later. In the 1891 census the English and Welsh figure remained at 7.3 per cent; the Scots had risen slightly to 1.8 per cent, while the Irish had fallen to 1.1 per cent.[9] In 1904, after a considerable growth in migration, the English and Welsh figure had become 10.94 per cent, the Scottish 2.71 and the Irish 1.48.[10] But in the first census of the Union (incorporating all four territories for the first time) in 1911 the percentage of whites born outside the country was now 20.4, of which the English constituted 48.6, the Welsh 1.4, the Scots 14.3 and the Irish 5.6.[11] (Hence roughly 70 per cent of the foreign-born came from what then constituted the United Kingdom.) This represents a fairly dramatic shift and reflects, of course, the very considerable migration of Scots to the Rand since the foundation of the gold mines. The Irish figure, proportionate to the whole, has dropped dramatically, presumably because of the massive Irish migration to North America in the period. The Scottish numbers have risen considerably, constituting about one Scot to 3.5 English at a time when the home population would have been about 1:8. This does, however, mean that the Scots proportion was lower in South Africa than it was in Australia, Canada or New Zealand. Astonishingly, in the latter Scots to English were often in the proportion of 1:2.

Somerset and the 'Scotch Independents'

Quantitative and qualitative assessments do not necessarily coincide. Prominence is not always a function of preponderance. It may even be the case, although this is debatable, that Scots influence declined even as their numbers increased in the later nineteenth and earlier twentieth centuries. It is certainly the case that the Scots never seemed so prominent as they did in the first few decades of British rule in Cape Town.

They constituted a significant mercantile group. They dominated some of the professions. They were instrumental in the founding of the major cultural and intellectual institutions of the time. They were central in the development of printing and publishing, most notably in the establishment of a free press. It will be the argument of this chapter that in all these activities they brought distinctive Scottish training and attitudes to bear on the administrative and developmental problems of the Cape. They established an ethnic network, social, political and professional, in which they supported and influenced each other. Their alliances with elite members of the Dutch community as well as some elements of the English were shifting and pragmatic. There is some evidence that their womenfolk also moved within Scottish circles. But, in maintaining links with the metropole, their attentions were divided. If their intellectual and religious connections partly lay in Edinburgh, their evangelical and political links were unquestionably with the centre of power in London.

When a coterie of Scots set about creating at the Cape a set of intellectual and scientific institutions that would replicate those with which they had been familiar in Edinburgh and other British cities they did so with very specific objectives in mind. Schools, the South African College, literary and scientific societies, a South African Museum, later a botanic garden, and a free press were not ends in themselves. They were designed to introduce some of the intellectual, humanitarian and evangelical ferment of the day. And no distinction was seen between these developments and research in the natural sciences, as well as financial, commercial and other economic activities. There was no sense that cultural and capitalist enterprises were in conflict. The essence of their philosophy was that the two were mutually and appropriately supporting. The bourgeois public sphere that they set about creating and dominating was intellectual, religious, political *and* mercantile all at once. It is thus entirely incorrect to see, as Keegan has done,[12] an 'uneasy coexistence' between the humanitarian and the commercial. On the contrary, Scots from Hume and Smith down to nineteenth-century liberals and utilitarians like Mill and Macaulay saw such 'coexistence' as essential to their designs. It was a constellation of ideas that also fed into the Manchester school of free-traders.

This is well illustrated by the activities of the leading Scots at the Cape between the 1820s and the 1850s. When Pringle arrived in Cape Town from the frontier he was appointed sub-librarian of the city's public library. He was soon joined by John Fairbairn (1794–1864), a friend from Edinburgh student days, who was to be highly influential in many issues and developments at the Cape over the next three decades. Fairbairn shared Borders origins with Pringle.[13] He was born at Carolside Mill, between Earlston and Lauder in Berwickshire, and was brought up in the Church of Scotland. The son of the miller, he developed a considerable interest in literature and went to Edinburgh University in 1810 and by 1812 had formed a firm friendship with Pringle. Fairbairn started in the humanities but in 1812 moved to medicine, attending classes in chemistry, pharmacy, anatomy, surgery and physics. Although he subsequently abandoned his medical studies, he must have developed broad interests which were to stand him in good stead in his subsequent activities at the Cape. He was active, with Pringle, at the Edinburgh Literary Society. In 1817 he was recruited by John Bruce, another Scot, to teach at the Bruces' academy (founded by two brothers) in Newcastle upon Tyne. Thomas Pringle's cousin, the Rev. James Pringle, was ministering at Clavering Place Chapel, so Fairbairn joined a Scots educational and religious colony in the city. Fairbairn soon joined the celebrated Literary and Philosophical Society there. Founded in 1794, this society still exists as one of the great examples of its kind. Fairbairn was a member from 1818 to 1823 and read many papers before its members, most of whom would have been sympathetic to liberal, humanitarian and Romantic interests.

But Fairbairn's links with Edinburgh were far from broken. Pringle had become the joint editor of *Blackwood's Edinburgh Monthly Magazine* (more commonly known as *Blackwood's*), which was intended to be a Tory response to the Whig *Edinburgh Review*. After a few issues (it is possible that he was out of sympathy with its politics) Pringle moved on to edit Constable's *Edinburgh Magazine*, and Fairbairn contributed to the latter from 1817. He continued to do so from Newcastle, often providing translations of German (and occasionally French) poetry, notably by Goethe and Herder, as well as original work of his own. Thus Pringle and Fairbairn helped to maintain Edinburgh's links with the European Romantic movement. In 1819 Pringle announced to his friend that he had decided to join the 1820 settlement scheme and tried to persuade Fairbairn to join him. The latter declined. But Pringle kept up the pressure from the Cape, and in 1823 Fairbairn relented and set out for the colony. In a letter to Pringle he wrote, 'Your hint about Magazines and Newspapers pleases me exceedingly,' and suggested that nothing should hinder them from becoming 'Franklins of the Kaap',[14] a reference to Benjamin Franklin (1706–90), who set up a printing press in Philadelphia, bought the *Pennsylvania Gazette* in 1729 and built up a reputation as a journalist. Pringle and Fairbairn might emulate this achievement in the Cape almost a century on and in doing so find their niche in history. Fairbairn used the word 'Kaap' perhaps in anticipation of the possibility of forging a sympathetic alliance with Dutch colonists. On arrival, his application for the vacant rectorship of the grammar school was turned down, and he and Pringle then founded a rival establishment, the Classical and Commercial Academy, opened in Harington House on the Keizergracht in December 1823. (Pringle had been tutoring private pupils since 1822.) Soon many of the Cape notables were sending their sons to this school, its name presumably indicative of the notion that it was to be something more than a grammar school, combining classical and practical studies.

The third major Scottish figure at the Cape was Dr John Philip, the highly influential superintendent of the London Missionary Society.[15] Philip was the son of a hand-loom weaver from Fife, born therefore into a social group that was to be most disadvantaged by the developing industrialism of the period. Well schooled, he moved north in the 1890s to work in a mill in Dundee, first as a clerk and then as a manager, an experience which may well have contributed to his sense of the social injustice inflicted upon workers, and not least child workers, in the period.[16] He had a dispute with his employer, probably over the issue of child labour, and left the mill. By this time he had fallen under the influence of the Rev. Thomas Durant, minister of the Congregationalist Church in Dundee, and in 1799 he went to the Congregationalist college at Hoxton to train as a minister. He was duly ordained in the Congregationalist Church, then increasingly powerful in Scotland, and in 1804 became minister of a church in Aberdeen. The congregation of this church proceeded to split, over an obscure issue of the theology of baptism, and Philip took over the larger and more significant section, soon establishing his influence throughout Aberdeen and the north-east. He was thus not unfamiliar with the business of controversy and schism. In 1809 he married a woman who not only bore him a large family but also became a vital associate in his ministry, both in the north-east of Scotland and at Cape Town. Jane Philip, indeed, became effectively an LMS administrator at the Cape. In Aberdeen he began to display his radical tendencies, his belief in the relationship between religion and politics, and his search for a particular kind of practical and involved evangelicalism. He clearly had some belief in the equality of the sexes, for he encouraged girls as well as boys to attend his prayer and Bible meetings. He was also a powerful and popular preacher, frequently filling a large church to capacity.

In 1817 Philip was invited by the London Missionary Society to take over the position of Superintendent at the Cape, an office previously held by Johannes van der Kemp and James Read (see the next chapter). After lengthy negotiations with his congregation, reluctant to see him go, he took up the offer and landed at Cape Town in February 1819. He soon became a highly controversial figure. His house in Cape Town was visited by all the most notable divines and missionaries of the period, as well as by most influential secular figures. As we shall see in a later chapter, he had many critics within the ecclesiastical as well as the lay worlds of the Cape. He was seen as assuming episcopal powers, as entering too enthusiastically into the secular realm, both in Cape Town itself and upon the frontier.[17] He was critical of fellow missionaries and earned the enmity of other celebrated Scots, such as Robert Moffat, the LMS missionary (from Ormiston in East Lothian) at Kuruman.[18] In this chapter, however, we are concerned primarily with his secular activities in Cape Town itself.

The educational activities of Pringle and Fairbairn, of which Philip would have approved, seemed to represent a relatively uncontroversial start to their 'improving' aspirations. Soon, however, their ambitions were to lead into a period of considerable turmoil in Cape Town. The Edinburgh student friends were quickly mixed up with other Scots, including Philip, George Greig (who arrived from Scotland in 1823), Alfred Robertson (who had landed in 1814), the merchant H. E. Rutherfoord and Archibald Robertson, later an influential Cape bookseller and publisher. This group, with others, were eager to turn Cape Town into a version of an intellectual, educational, scientific and publishing centre on the Edinburgh model.[19] Such literary and philosophical activity was to be closely bound up with the major religious and commercial exploits of the age. Thus their mental cosmos was not compartmentalised. While there were to be many and complex alliances of people and ideas, they were wholly eclectic in their interests. Moreover, frontier, missions, slavery, the status of the Khoi, commercial developments and the political influence of the settlers were all grist to their mill. And they considered that a central characteristic of such an outpost of enlightened activity was the existence of a free press as a printed forum for their ideas and an exchange of views.

But such a press would also become a hotbed of controversy, a turbulent centre for resistance to established power, a factional flag that would stimulate efforts at suppression by the Governor and inspire the hatred of settlers, as well as fierce tussles between the Cape metropole and frontier interests. Since the earliest days of British rule at the Cape the colonial government had set out to frustrate the operations of a free press. In May and July 1800 the Governor, Sir George Yonge, had issued regulations for the establishment of a printing press and the publication of a newspaper by the firm of Walker & Robertson (early Scots settlers who were also ship hirers and in the import/export business).[20] This official paper was the *Cape Town Gazette and African Advertiser* and the burden of the regulations was that no other organ of the press would be allowed.[21] These regulations were closely related to others respecting any association which was perceived to be Jacobin in its tendencies (which effectively covered all societies that might at any time criticise the colonial authorities). Thus the government was to exercise complete control and indeed eventually took the press into official ownership. The *Cape Town Gazette*, now a government sheet containing announcements of regulations, ordinances and appointments, remained the only publication.

Thomas Pringle first applied to establish a literary periodical, designed 'to enlighten South Africa', with the Rev. Abraham Faure (who had received part of his education in England) in January 1823. They proposed publishing a journal in English and Dutch in alternate months, avoiding 'the discussion of all controversial or agitating topics'.[22] This was approved by the Cape colonial secretary Colonel Bird, but Somerset soon overruled his subordinate's decision. He explained his action to the Colonial Secretary, Bathurst, with the accusation that Pringle was an 'arrant Dissenter', which was inaccurate, since Pringle had in fact been brought up in the established Church of Scotland.[23] Next George Greig tried in July 1823, promising to exclude 'personal controversy' and discussion of 'the policy of the administration of the Colonial Government', but he too was refused. (Greig in fact had the limited intention of supplying commercial information and offering space for advertisements, together with some literary material.) By December 1823 the Secretary of State in London had intervened and Pringle was permitted to publish. Fairbairn and Pringle co-operated in the issue of the *South African Journal*, a quarterly intended to be mainly literary in its content. Abraham Faure went ahead with issuing his Dutch rival, as it had now become, *Nederduitsch Zuid-Afrikaanische Tijdshrift* (the Dutch South African Journal), which lasted until 1843.[24] Greig, discovering that strictly speaking the ban covered journals but not newspapers, also set about publishing the *South African Commercial Advertiser* and then offered it to Pringle and Fairbairn for their editorship. Perhaps cheekily an application was made for the *Commercial Advertiser* to enjoy the same postage rights as the *Cape Town Gazette*.[25] Yet, to emphasise its difference, the new paper mixed a diet of poetry with law reports (including a case involving a critic of the Governor[26]) and politically sensitive material, such as the fortunes of the Eastern Cape settlers, as well as thinly veiled attacks upon despotic government (portrayed as a characteristic of continental Europe, though few readers would have failed to draw the inference that the Cape was another example).[27] An editorial proclaimed that 'No Government has yet been found capable of resisting, for any protracted period, the united voice of Public Opinion'.[28] This stimulated an attempt by the Governor to censor the *Advertiser* and Fairbairn and Pringle asserted their intention 'never to compromise our birthright as British subjects by editing any publication under censorship'.[29] The paper was closed.[30] Somerset ordered that Greig's press should be sealed, but the fiscal and his officers failed to seal the type. Greig duly brought out a remarkable pamphlet, produced on wetted paper with mallet and planer, without the help of the press. Greig and his employees worked all night on this, and then distributed hundreds of copies from the windows of Greig's premises, creating the sensation which Somerset no doubt wished to avoid.[31]

Somerset's general state of paranoia was not helped when a poster libel circulated in Cape Town. The posters were first spotted by the Scottish Captain John Findlay, the master of the *Alacrity*, whose family became (as we have seen) significant members of the Scots community at the Cape. The posters published accusations of a sexual relationship between the Governor and Dr James Barry, military doctor at the Cape, who treated Somerset and was known to enjoy a close friendship with him. It was alleged that someone passing Government House had observed Somerset and Barry *in flagrante* within. Barry was the son of an Irish artist, but his formative years had been spent in Edinburgh, where he had studied medicine. Clearly the accusation of what was thought to be a homosexual relationship was a very serious one for the time, although the story is greatly complicated by the fact that after his death, Barry was discovered to be a woman.[32] The publication of this libel offers an insight into the highly fevered atmosphere of Cape Town of the time, and obviously contributed to Somerset's sense of being under serious personal attack.

Somerset broadened his assault on those he perceived to be his enemies by attacking the Fairbairn–Pringle school. He considered it to be a 'seminary of sedition', a hotbed of Jacobinism, that the teachers were instilling 'the disgusting principles of Republicanism' in their pupils.[33] The number of pupils had been growing in 1824, reaching a peak of forty-seven, but under this onslaught some of them were withdrawn. Some claimed that this was because of a decline in standards, and it is possible that Fairbairn was neglecting his duties, while Pringle, under pressure, was beginning to lose interest. Meanwhile Somerset now ordered that Greig's press should be confiscated, enraging Philip, who considered it to be the property of the London Missionary Society,[34] and Greig himself was banished from the colony. This must have been galling for the cautious Greig, but he returned and became influential in disseminating publishing ideas. Greig's press was sold or licensed by the government to William Bridekirk, the owner of yet another newspaper, the *South African Chronicle and Mercantile Advertiser*, which had been published for a year. Bridekirk was pro-government but his *SA Chronicle*, roundly condemned by Fairbairn, lost money and closed in 1826. Toadyism did not pay.

Somerset also refused to contemplate Pringle and Fairbairn's efforts to found a South African Literary Society, no doubt on the model of equivalents in Edinburgh and Newcastle. Its first meetings took place in the home of Cape Town merchants, one of them the Scottish merchant Charles Pillans, who was also involved in the preparations for founding a Presbyterian church in the same year. An attempt was made to reconcile Somerset to the Literary Society by inviting him to be patron. Somerset asserted that he would 'oppose and thwart everything without exception which emanated from them [Pringle and Fairbairn], or in which they were concerned'.[35] The meetings of the society were declared to be illegal (under the 1800 anti-Jacobin regulations) and it was refounded successfully only in 1829. It may well have been because of this that the committee established to found a Presbyterian church had to assure Somerset that Pringle was in no way involved in the project, even although Pringle had been active in establishing a Presbyterian church for the settlers on the frontier.[36] Pringle himself feared that his presence might so stimulate the opposition of the Governor that the whole project would be jeopardised.[37] Pringle, prudently perhaps, chose to resign his post as sub-librarian of the public library and returned, for a period, to Glen Lynden on the Eastern Cape. Thoroughly frustrated by the atmosphere at the Cape, he was preparing to return to Britain (which he did in 1826), where he would become the secretary of the Anti-slavery Society.[38] From this influential position he maintained his interest in conditions at the Cape. Pringle was now anathema to the Governor, and he characterised the whole group as 'Scotch Independents',[39] dabbling in politics and dangerous to the running of the colony.[40]

However, Somerset was grappling with complex forces. A scion of the highest ranks of the British nobility, he found himself facing individuals of much lower social standing who were exerting influence beyond anything his upbringing could have envisaged. These people seemed, therefore, to be undermining a natural social order: he would have noted their adherence to ideas of legal equality, their religious dissent (in its broadest sense), and their notions of influence, if not power, open to talent – which he would have found disturbing – much more than their belief in a stable social hierarchy or their fundamental concern for the primacy of property – with which he could have found common cause.[41] Moreover, not only was he facing an apparently radical, enlightened group of Scots, he was also far from getting his own way in London. There he faced a Colonial Secretary, Bathurst, and a permanent under-secretary, James Stephen, who were at least partially drawn into the evangelical network and felt increasingly uncomfortable with Somerset's autocratic style. The Colonial Office considered, for example, that his treatment of Greig had been illegal. Bathurst contemplated dismissing Somerset, but drew back from doing so, no doubt fearing the alienation of important patronage networks. Somerset had indeed been Governor for an extraordinarily long period (from 1814), but getting rid of him was still not easy. He returned to Britain for another of his extended leaves in 1826 and was replaced only in 1827 after a change of government in London.[42] To a considerable extent it was the Scots, with their loud and polemical activities and in alliance with many in the merchant class, who engineered his downfall.

The press, educational and intellectual conflict of the years 1823–25 were part of a wider struggle which ran through the 1820s and early 1830s, including the governorships of Somerset's two successors, Sir Richard Bourke (a Whig who acted during Somerset's last leave) and Sir Lowry Cole. The establishment of a more organised administrative civil service and the removal of patronage and corruption had been recommended by a Commission of Inquiry appointed in 1822, which reported in 1826. This was paralleled by the introduction of a whole range of liberalising and humanitarian measures which appeared to transform the character of colonial governance, legal arrangements in respect of race and slavery, and the relationship between English and Dutch-speakers at the Cape. Scots were at the centre of all these controversies. First of all, press freedom had in fact been further delayed. Although the *Commercial Advertiser* had resumed publication in 1825, it was again closed between 1827 and 1829.[43] Fairbairn, who had published a condensed version of the first eighteen issues of the *Advertiser* in 1826 to offer evidence for the history of the conflict and the value of the paper, continued to campaign with great vehemence. He pledged himself to denounce maladministration and injustice and proposed that the *Commercial Advertiser* would be the 'advocate of our real and essential rights and privileges'. His provocative epigraph for the *Advertiser* was that 'the mass of every people must be barbarous where there is no Printing'.[44] In 1827 he departed for London, funded by a public subscription, to lobby the Colonial Office. There he received a sympathetic hearing from the new Secretary of State (only briefly in the office), William Huskisson. The result was ordinance No. 60 of 1829, which, though stopping short of full freedom of the press, nonetheless offered guarantees unknown before.[45]

Greig and the dissemination of the press

From 1830 newspapers began to flourish in centres outside Cape Town – like Grahamstown, Port Elizabeth, and Graaff Reinet. With the founding of the new British colony of Natal, a press was set up there too. Indeed, the struggle of Greig, Fairbairn and Pringle resonated through the nineteenth century and became a frequent touchstone for press and political freedoms, though increasingly framed in terms of white rights. In Grahamstown the publication of a newspaper was undertaken by a printer, L. H. Meurant (1812–93), who had been apprenticed to Greig and who had helped to produce the 'Facts'. There too a Governor, Donkin, had attempted to confiscate a press, but Meurant brought out the *Grahamstown Journal* in December 1831.[46] Though it saw its own freedoms as being closely connected with the struggle in Cape Town, it became so identified with settler interests that it was soon totally out of favour with Fairbairn and others who were seen to represent the opposing humanitarian faction. The *Journal* became the mouthpiece of the influential Robert Godlonton and others seeking to extend imperial power and dominate the African peoples of the frontier.

Yet another of Greig's protégés was David Dale Buchanan (1819–74). Buchanan, as his names imply, was born at New Lanark in Scotland. He reached the Cape in 1829 and studied under John Philip. He became an infant teacher and later worked for Greig for a number of years. In 1840 he founded his own newspaper, *The Cape Town Mail*, aided by a gift from Greig of an old press and type. In 1846 he moved to the new colony of Natal and founded the first newspaper there, the *Natal Witness*, which survives to this day. Buchanan had thoroughly imbibed the radicalism of his mentors and used the *Witness* (masthead motto: 'The Truth, the Whole Truth, and Nothing but the Truth') to pursue anti-authoritarian and humanitarian issues.[47] He conducted a vitriolic campaign against the Lieutenant-governor, Benjamin Pine, whom he considered to be an autocrat. One editorial bore the dramatic, if unsubtle, headline 'Pine and rapine' in which the offending official was described as 'our mountebank governor'.[48] After Buchanan's death the *Witness* continued to be consistently anti-government.

The influence of Greig and Fairbairn was also felt in Port Elizabeth, where John Philip's son, John Ross Philip (who knew Greig through his father), and the schoolteacher John Paterson founded the *Eastern Province Herald* in 1845 (from 1848 the *Port Elizabeth Telegraph*). Paterson ran the *Herald/Telegraph* until 1852 and owned it until 1857.[49] He always proclaimed himself as influenced by Fairbairn's editorials in the *Commercial Advertiser*, and was certainly heavily involved in the anti-convicts agitation. (When in 1849 thirty-six emigrant boys were landed at Port Elizabeth he suspected that they might be convicts.) He announced in the legislative assembly that he was a follower of Fairbairn and he believed that a man's rights should not depend on the colour of his skin.[50]

Reform and Emancipation

While the influence of Greig and Fairbairn – but not always their politics – spread to the Eastern Cape and Natal, additional newspapers were appearing at the Cape. One of them was the Dutch *De Zuid Afrikaan* in 1830, established by the advocate (educated in the Netherlands) Christoffel Brand.[51] Such a plurality of journals helped to open the fissures wider between different groups of colonists and between the English-speakers and the Dutch. Moreover, polemical pamphleteering was now common and led to much recourse to the law, litigiousness in which the Scots were as active as any other group. All this was exacerbated by the sequence of measures enacted in the later 1820s and subsequent years.

The founding of the Cape Land Board in 1828 constituted an effort to regularise landholding arrangements at the Cape. It was to lead to a considerable expansion of surveying activity, in which the Scots were closely involved. It would also overturn the somewhat haphazard arrangements of the Dutch East India Company, which had benefited the Dutch settlers. New legal dispositions were made to regularise judicial appointments, the Governor's judicial function as final court of appeal was removed, and some aspects of the English common law were introduced to operate alongside Roman Dutch law (the existence of which had given Scots an advantage at the Cape, since it was closer to their Scottish model).[52]

In this key year Philip chose to publish his *Researches in South Africa*, a highly polemical work in which he exhibited his striking blend of radical evangelicalism, belief in the need for political involvement on the part of clerics and missionaries (which would separate him from many who were not so persuaded), as well as his blend of Smithian *laissez-faire* economics and a profound conviction both in the sanctity of property and in the dignity of labour.[53] He also quoted Adam Smith on the notion that towns were the begetters of freedom, order, good government and industry, while Malthus had insisted that 'civil liberty' tended most to 'generate prudential habits among the lower classes of society'.[54] And it was in 1828 that he seemed to secure his triumph. Two ordinances set out to liberalise the labour arrangements of the colony. Ordinance 49 overturned the notion that the Bantu-speaking Africans across the eastern frontier should be kept entirely separate. They were now permitted to cross the border and seek work, regulated by the requirement that they must take out passes. This ordinance has been seen as the necessary corollary to the more famous ordinance 50, for which John Philip had campaigned ceaselessly. This gave the Khoi and other free persons of colour equality before the law. It decriminalised 'vagrancy' and abolished pass laws, compulsory labour service and child indenture while permitting Khoi to buy and own land, as well as giving them the opportunity to enter into free contracts of labour. Philip and Fairbairn would have preferred it to draw no distinction as to colour (to be 'colour-blind', as it is often expressed), but nonetheless it has long been seen as the triumph of early nineteenth-century liberalism.

Ordinance 50 had a number of key effects upon southern African society and upon the writing of its history. The promulgation of the ordinance finally broke the alliance between English-speakers and the Dutch, who viewed it as a direct attack upon their powers and upon the racial and labour arrangements, which they had previously dominated. It also helped to form the battle lines between the Cape liberals and humanitarians and the frontier settlers, who regarded themselves as facing the practical problems of labour, migration over the frontier, 'vagrancy' and the tensions between the rule of law and the unwritten laws of force which they felt were needed to regulate frontier relations. Moreover, while the fiftieth ordinance was formerly seen as a great triumph and the foundation of liberal and eventually colour-blind policies at the Cape, it has more recently been viewed as offering more in theory than in practice. While its objectives have to be assessed in conjunction with the combination of free transit and tight pass controls of black labour in ordinance 49, it did very little actually to change the standards of living and conditions of Khoi and other free persons of colour. Many cases were brought against 'masters' under its provisions but the economic and social situation of the Khoi changed little.

With the departure of Pringle, Fairbairn remained the most notable journalist and editor, fiercely throwing himself into every issue of the day. By now the *Commercial Advertiser* was owned as well as edited by him. He continued to be the sole editor until 1859, but after his death the paper expired in 1869. Throughout this period the *Advertiser* constantly took on a self-reflective mode. Fairbairn repeatedly alluded to the role of the paper in the establishment of a more civilised polity, as he would have seen it. Fairbairn firmly viewed himself as an editor centrally concerned with social reform. The *South African Commercial Advertiser* had been out of commission during the heady days of 1828, but it was fully involved in the debates leading up to the abolition of slavery. A central part of this was Emancipation. Fairbairn was a passionate abolitionist, as were some of the other Scots. In taking up this position Fairbairn helped to cement his alliance with the mercantile group, who sought an end of all monopolistic, autocratic and coercive practices, although some of them were slave owners themselves.[55] If the ordinance respecting the Khoi affected the Afrikaans stockholders and frontiersmen, the abolition of slavery was to damage the economic position of the substantial Dutch wine growers and arable farmers of the Cape, some of whom also operated as elite figures in Cape Town itself. In the later 1820s their fortunes were in any case at a low ebb, partly because their wine no longer received any protection in British markets, partly because its export had been damaged by its allegedly poor quality. The conditions of slavery had been ameliorated to a certain extent by new regulations in 1826 (and all slave laws were consolidated in 1830), but by the end of the decade the humanitarian/evangelical faction, headed by Thomas Fowell Buxton, Bishop Wilberforce and Zachary Macaulay, was gaining the ascendancy in London. In the Anti-slavery Society Thomas Pringle was able to bring knowledge of the situation at the Cape. Pringle died in London in 1834, shortly after the Emancipation law was passed. Since it was followed by a period of several years' forced 'apprenticeship', he never saw the slaves securing their full freedom.

It has been suggested that John Philip brought much less passion to the issue of slavery than he did to that of the social and political position of the Khoi.[56] But there remains good evidence that Philip used his connections with the powerful evangelical network in London to maintain pressure upon the moves to Emancipation.[57] He was also a frequent contributor to the *Commercial Advertiser*, under the pseudonym 'Colonist'. Some of the earliest issues of the paper had included material and editorials on the question of slavery, but anonymity cloaks whether these were written by Fairbairn or Philip. In any case, there was a significant difference between the campaign over the rights of the Khoi and the existence of slavery. The amelioration of Khoi conditions could be achieved only by agitation and legislation at the Cape. Slavery was a much wider issue involving colonies, like those in the West Indies, with a much more considerable slave population. Action could be taken only in London. If Philip did seem more muted in his concern about slaves (which is itself debatable) it was only because he recognised that the real centre of power was the metropole and that pressure had to be exerted through the humanitarian network. At the Cape itself, the Philanthropic Society was founded in 1828 to help deserving slaves and slave children to purchase their freedom. Once again it represented an alliance of evangelical and mercantile interests. A prominent member was the Rev. James Adamson of the Presbyterian Church; Pringle and Philip both made donations to it, and Fairbairn became a prominent committee member. Meanwhile, at the height of these campaigns, the relationship between

Philip and Fairbairn was further enhanced by marriage: Fairbairn married Philip's teenage daughter, Eliza, in 1831. (He had become an adherent of Philip's church, abandoning the Presbyterianism in which he had been brought up.) Philip and Fairbairn had paid a joint visit to the frontier in 1830, and in a speech at a dinner at the mission station at Bethelsdorp Fairbairn had announced that he despised no one because of poverty, honoured no one because of wealth and feared no one because of his power.[58] After the abolition of slavery in 1833–34 Philip and Fairbairn had one more triumph. In 1834 a vagrancy Act was proposed which they believed would have overturned the provisions of ordinance 50. They set up a fierce opposition to the measure, including in the pages of the *Commercial Advertiser*, which led to its disallowance by the government in London.

Fairbairn: commerce, finance and education

It is apparent that the evangelical/mercantile alliance had an economic interest in the maintenance of free labour provisions and, above all, in the recognition in London that slave owners had to be compensated. Philip and Fairbairn were firm believers in the primacy of property. They strongly argued the compensation case and were astute enough to recognise that the payment of such compensation (worth almost £1.25 million in the case of the Cape) would add greatly to the colony's liquidity. The payment of what was, in effect, a notable subsidy from London would greatly stimulate an ailing economy. From the point of view of the merchants, with their connections with London mercantile houses, the fact that such compensation could be paid only in the imperial capital would ensure that they would benefit from the percentage secured by agencies, a function that they could conveniently offer to the Cape slave owners, who, unlike their Caribbean counterparts, did not visit London.

This was indeed a form of 'philanthropy plus five per cent'. (Commission was a minimum of 5 per cent and could be quite a lot higher.) The economy of the colony duly moved ahead during the 1830s[59] and the balance in power began to shift from Cape agriculture to the rearing of merino sheep (a development which accelerated in the 1840s and from which Benjamin Moodie benefited, as we have seen[60]). The interior soon became more important than the Cape arable region, promoting the growth of both interior towns and of ports, like Port Elizabeth, on the Eastern Cape coast. Overall, this led to an expansion in the size of the bourgeoisie and growth in the press and educational institutions pioneered by Pringle and Fairbairn, among others.

But Cape Town itself would also be favoured by such wider economic advance, not least in the provision of financial services. It was to this field that the ever energetic Fairbairn was to turn his attention. Fairbairn had already been involved, in 1826, in an attempt to establish a Cape of Good Hope Bank, based on Scottish joint-stock principles and strongly supported in the *Advertiser*.[61] This failed, since the colonial government would not contemplate such a private venture. But the idea was revived with greater success in 1835. Fairbairn once again pointed out that a private joint-stock bank was a Scottish invention, that it should be one that was organised with branches, that in Scotland there was a bank for every 7,500 inhabitants, which went some way to explaining the prosperity of that country. This time the idea found favour and the bank opened its doors in 1837. Fairbairn next turned his attention to another Scottish notion, the principle of mutuality. By this system a company would be owned by its customers or members, with profits ploughed back into the business for the benefit of all. In 1847 he was instrumental in founding the Mutual Life Assurance Society, which still exists and is commonly known as the Old Mutual. In 1984 it helped to fund the publication of the biography of Fairbairn. As well as propounding the virtues of these financial arrangements in the *Commercial Advertiser* Fairbairn tracked the economic cycle at the Cape by publishing annual reviews of trade and economic development. In these he often predicted and pushed new developments, for example predicting in 1846 the spectacular growth of the merino sheep industry.[62]

But Fairbairn's commercial interests never interfered with his cultural and educational ambitions. He was influential in the founding of the South African College, in league with a coalition of Scots and Afrikaners, who formed the majority of the college's first council. Confronted with this alliance, Governor Cole considered that the college was essentially an 'anti-British' operation, by which he surely meant anti-English or anti-Establishment.[63] Fairbairn maintained an interest in the college for the rest of his life, serving again on its council in 1852 and becoming the chair of its governing body in 1855. He was also closely involved with the establishment of elementary and secondary schools, not least in the appointment in 1838 of another Scot, James Rose Innes, as the first Superintendent General of Education. In 1835 he encouraged the founding of a popular library in Cape Town, and served on the library committee of the main public library until the 1860s. A former medical student at Edinburgh, he argued unsuccessfully for the necessity of a medical school.

The range of Fairbairn's other concerns encompassed the creation of an Agricultural Society, opposition to stamp duty, involvement in the establishment of a coastal steamship company in 1836 (the Cape of Good Hope Steam Navigation Company, serving Cape Town and Algoa Bay or Port Elizabeth), the formation of municipal government for Cape Town in 1840, a temperance association, and above all the agitation against the landing of convicts at the Cape in 1848–49.[64] He took an interest in the development of harbours and roads (another very Scottish set of concerns, as is evidenced by the number of Scots involved in their construction), as well as in the provision of labour and the encouragement of immigration from Britain. Fairbairn and Philip also had strong views on the frontier war of 1835–36 and other aspects of the handling of Eastern Cape issues, which will be examined in a later chapter. Not surprisingly, perhaps, Fairbairn was loathed and admired in equal measure. Most Afrikaners came to abominate him, as they had done Philip. Fellow Scots, like Benjamin Moodie, fell out with him and Moodie sued him in a notorious libel action. Among those who admired him was the distinguished astronomer Sir John Herschel, resident at the Cape from 1834 to 1838, who was impressed by the quality of the *Advertiser* and by Fairbairn's editorials. F. S. Watermeyer, who married Fairbairn's daughter, founded the *Cape of Good Hope Observer* in 1849, at least partially influenced by the Fairbairn model. It has been said that Fairbairn became less radical in the course of the 1830s, that he became, in effect, a 'proto-colonial nationalist', much more interested in the rights of white colonists than of the region's indigenous peoples, that the humanitarian, philanthropic and egalitarian passions ebbed as he became more of an Establishment figure. Evidence for this has been seen in his support for the master and servant legislation of 1856. It would certainly be true that, as Kirsten McKenzie has put it, 'The *Advertiser*'s notion of "the people" was set against both an idea of aristocratic patronage and, at the other extreme, a disorderly underclass'[65] and it may be that that dichotomy became more pronounced as Fairbairn grew older. Yet he remained a polemicist to the end, and was intimately concerned with every controversy of his age, certainly bringing the liberal and nonconformist tone of the literary and philosophical societies, as well as some aspects of scientific endeavour, to the Cape.

Representative government

The last great agitation in which Fairbairn was involved, with some support from Philip, was the pressure for the granting of representative government to the colonists at the Cape. At first, councils for securing the advice of colonists were designed largely to draw off the steam of participatory agitation, to provide a representative fig leaf for gubernatorial autocracy. The first British administration had established a burgher senate in 1796, comprising six burghers appointed by the Governor and charged with advising on matters relating to roads, prices and taxation. In 1825, towards the end of Somerset's governorship, a Council of Advice was formed to provide a more formal setting for officials to discuss the issues of the moment and create a sense of corporate involvement in decision making and responsibility for outcomes. However, the Colonial Office was highly ambivalent about the devolution of some political influence to settlers. While settler representation could lead to considerable turbulence, as it had done in the West Indies, it was also seen as a means of avoiding dissent and 'separatism'. New South Wales had acquired some settler representation in the legislature in 1825. These ideas developed further after Lord Durham's report on Canada in 1839. The first stage of this process would involve the election of 'unofficials', representatives of the settler community, to a law-making council. The officials would still hold power, but their legislative ideas would be subject to more open debate. It was thus a further step on the path of free expression vigorously demanded by the Scots group in the 1820s. This 'representative government' would eventually develop into 'responsible government' (in the Cape in 1872), in which the 'unofficials' would come to form the majority and settler politicians would take over most of the administrative departments as Westminster-type Ministers.

The agitation at the Cape began as early as 1826. When two burghers resigned from the senate over the slave regulations of 1826 the Cape Town elite demanded to be able to elect their successors. This was refused, though in 1828, when the burgher senate was abolished, two burghers were invited to sit on the Council of Advice. Fairbairn duly threw himself into another cause, allied in this instance with the leading advocate Christoffel Brand. They jointly took up the cry of 'no taxation without representation' and, as we have seen, Brand founded the *Zuid Afrikaan* in 1830. It was to be a rare moment of unity, because Brand soon began to write of the possibility of a Dutch burgher revolt, at which Fairbairn immediately became loyal to the Governor (Cole), even approving of repressive measures to contain Dutch opposition to slave emancipation and other developments.

The Cape was never immune to world events and outside forces. The War of American Independence and the French revolution both had their echoes at the Cape. As we have seen, post-war British economic and social problems, the Scottish Enlightenment and the full force of evangelicalism all had considerable effects at the Cape. Now, in the wake of the Reform Bill and the arrival of a Whig government in London, further constitutional developments occurred there.

CAPE COLONIAL AUTOCRACY

Sir Lowry Cole was succeeded by the Whig Sir Benjamin D'Urban and he inaugurated nascent representative institutions, including Executive and Legislative Councils, with nominated settler representatives. Fairbairn's interest in representative institutions waned in the 1830s, partly because of the pressure of other issues, partly because he was anxious about the fitness of the colonists, and perhaps particularly the Afrikaners, to handle such a constitutional development. Moreover, in 1834 he was rejected as a potential member of a committee to press for representative government. This is an indicator of the extent to which his activities with respect to ordinance 50, anti-slavery and the disallowance of the vagrancy ordinance had made him thoroughly unpopular in the colony.

But in the 1840s, at a time when the Cape economy began to move ahead on a whole range of fronts, he again became closely involved. His reputation was enhanced by his fierce opposition to the landing of convicts at the Cape in 1848–49, an issue which created rare unanimity among colonists and settlers of all ethnic origins and political opinion. It has often been suggested that it was this anti-convict agitation which helped to lead directly to the devolution of some influence to the colonists. When the Governor, Sir Harry Smith, held an unofficial election for council seats Fairbairn was one of those elected. John Philip, on the other hand, had shown very little interest in representative institutions. He was anxious about what such a colonial assembly would do to the various reforms of the 1820s and early 1830s. He believed in the benign oversight of the imperial power, attempting, as he would have seen it, to balance interests and protect the weak. Between 1850 and 1853, when a new constitution with an elected legislature was introduced, considerable controversy raged. This was less to do with the granting of a legislature, which by then seemed assured, than with the nature of the franchise under which its elections would be held.

Yet again, alliances were reformed. The richer merchant class and the colonial officials favoured a franchise with a high financial threshold for admission, such that only whites could conceivably qualify. The other group, including Fairbairn and other radicals like Buchanan, supported by the Coloured population and some Dutch-speaking farmers, led by the leading Afrikaner and former Lieutenant-governor of the Eastern Cape, Sir Andries Stockenstroom, argued for a lower, colour-blind property qualification which would permit some Coloured voters to be enrolled.[66] Until his death in 1851 Philip supported this position. Fairbairn, Buchanan and others threw the weight of the liberal press behind the latter group and, perhaps surprisingly, it found favour in London. The colour-blind, lower-threshold franchise (with a property qualification of £25) was incorporated into the new constitution. Fairbairn was elected to the new assembly, though he failed to become its speaker, as he had hoped, perhaps because of the liberal position he had adopted. Nevertheless, he unwittingly helped to ensure that the shift from humanitarian to settler discourse was indeed propelled by this greater degree of settler political representation.[67]

This was regarded as the high point of Cape liberalism, although in practice the number of non-whites with access to the vote was always tiny. In any case, had the constitution been introduced several years earlier, at a time when more Coloured people held land on the Eastern Cape, there would have been more such voters, but the violence of the frontier had helped to wipe out their settlements there. The so-called 'colour-blind' franchise (though revalued considerably in 1892) survived well into the twentieth century.[68] But, as a modern revisionist historiography has asserted, it turned out, like ordinance 50, to be more important in theory than in practice, a matter of liberal pride, even for some a source of seemingly radical sentiment. Perhaps the prime importance of these measures lay in reflecting the manner in which some of the grand debates of Europe were transferred to, and modified by, the Cape. This era of liberalism and reform also became important as a central signifier for a liberal historiography, now much discredited as representing a crudely binary, positive-and-negative, approach to the past. In reality the era is fraught with ambiguities and ambivalences, with alliances and antagonisms that were never clear-cut, always shaping themselves and reforming according to the demands of any given moment. In any case, from the 1850s onwards Cape liberalism began to give way to the separatist views of the settlers of the Eastern Cape and elsewhere. The frontier wars were significant in this development, and it has been pointed out that the pseudo-scientific racist and anatomist, the Scot Robert Knox, derived some of his notions of the inevitability of 'the war of the races' while serving as a military surgeon in wars with the Xhosa.[69] In his book *The Races of Man* (1850) Knox revived ideas of polygenesis (that human races had different origins): he and his followers may well have influenced popular views, but as an anti-Darwinist he was often at odds with the scientific establishment. And as a confirmed atheist he cannot have been received with much enthusiasm by the missionaries and the surviving leading lights of this chapter.[70]

Intellectual and scientific institutions

The position of the library in Cape society was vital to the sense of pride of the elite, a group which saw themselves as placing the Cape within the intellectual, literary and philosophical traditions of Europe. They were effectively preparing for the incorporation of the hinterland of Africa while forming a crossroads between the American and Atlantic worlds on the one hand and the Indian Ocean and South Pacific territories on the other. Originally established in 1818, based on a private collection bequeathed in the eighteenth century, it was opened in 1822. It was moved to better accommodation in the Commercial Exchange (whose members had built a fine building in 1822) in 1828 and remained there until the new library and museum building was opened in 1860. As a subscription library it was principally a resort of the elite, although there were a number of attempts to create a more popular circulating library open to a wider (and almost exclusively white) public. As we have seen, both Pringle and Fairbairn were closely involved with the library, with Fairbairn taking on a significant role on its committee.[71] Pringle's successor, when he returned to the Eastern Cape, was Alexander Johnstone Jardine, another Scot from the Borders, who was librarian until 1845. In his period the holdings grew tremendously and its central position was acknowledged by George Greig, who described it in yet another of his publishing ventures, the *Cape Town Almanac* of 1832, as 'the pride and boast of the Colony'.[72] Jardine, like Pringle, was essentially a literary figure, who also combined librarianship with editing a journal, in his case the *Cape of Good Hope Literary Gazette* (1830–35).[73] Jardine was committed both to the idea of the circulating library and to the encouragement of the creation of libraries in country towns. There may have been an early one on the Eastern Cape. In 1848, probably related to Chartist and other revolutionary activity in Britain and Europe, there was a further move to create a more popular library, one which was strongly supported by the Presbyterian minister the Rev. James Adamson, but the lack of any major population of white skilled labourers ensured that the idea of mechanics' institutes, so successful in Canada, Australia and New Zealand, never really caught on at the Cape. The constituency for a popular library (with a lower subscription than that secured from the elite) was similarly small, though it may have helped to open opportunities for women.

When the Governor, Sir George Grey, encouraged the building of a new, classical library building at the foot of the government gardens in Cape Town, it was agreed that the building should also accommodate the museum. This elegant building (which still houses the South African Library today) was duly opened to great acclaim by Prince Alfred, Queen Victoria's son, in 1860. The museum also owed its origins to that decade of ferment the 1820s, primarily to the Scots doctor Andrew (later Sir) Smith (1797–1872), as its Web site acknowledges to this day. Smith was the son of a shepherd turned market gardener from Roxburghshire. The father had experienced some upward social mobility and Andrew continued the trajectory by pursuing medical studies in Edinburgh. He secured his degree in 1819 and joined the Army Medical Service.[74] He arrived at the Cape in 1821 as assistant surgeon to the 98th Foot, and subsequently rose rapidly through the ranks. He served on the Eastern Cape frontier from 1821 to 1825, arriving soon after the subsequently notorious military doctor Robert Knox had departed. Smith soon began to perform official functions with regard to the frontier and beyond. He was commissioned by the Governor and Commander-in-Chief to report on the Bushmen or San in 1828, on the Zulu and Port Natal in 1831, and set out on a major expedition between 1834 and 1836 to secure treaties with African chiefs beyond the frontier, an expedition which was fitted out by the Cape of Good Hope Literary and Scientific Association and supported by prominent Cape citizens. He was accompanied by the Scot Charles Bell, son of a tenant farmer near Crail, in Fife, who arrived at the Cape in 1830. He was well connected, being the nephew of the colonial secretary, inevitably another Scot, Colonel John Bell. Charles later became the government surveyor.[75] Their remarkable journey took them from Graaff Reinet north to Philippolis and on to Thaba Bosiu, in what is now Lesotho. They pushed on to Sekonyela's, close to the Wittenbergen range, then to Thaba Nchu, before crossing the high veld north of the Orange River to Moffat's mission at Kuruman. The truly epic part of the expedition then began. They travelled up to the Limpopo River, just crossing the Tropic of Capricorn, with a side trip into what was later the northern Transvaal. They returned to the colony via some of the Tswana chieftaincies and called again at Kuruman. Throughout, Charles Bell produced illustrations of the regions they visited, mainly water-colours of the people they met, their hunting exploits, their encounters with lions, the landscape, and mission congregations, including Moffat preaching to the Tswana.

In all this work Smith probably devoted more of his attention to ethnographic and natural historical studies. He was a notable hunter, and his justification of hunting on the grounds of zoological research probably had a considerable influence on other hunters who penetrated the interior of southern Africa in the nineteenth century.[76] He wrote a number of papers on the Bushman and, after his return to Britain, published his five-volume *Illustrations of the Zoology of South Africa* between 1838 and 1847. He brought back to Britain numerous specimens for museums. (His example of a giraffe was still on display at the Natural History Museum in South Kensington at the end of the century.) He was later appointed director-general of the army and ordinance medical department, became an enemy of Florence

Nightingale and was severely censured for dereliction of duty in the Crimean War.

The South African Museum was proclaimed by Somerset in 1825 and was inevitably depicted as having a taxonomic purpose, a means of classifying the examples of the animal, vegetable and mineral kingdoms that would be assembled by it. This would of course also have a practical purpose in helping to survey the natural resources of the colony and their economic potential. Smith was appointed the honorary superintendent.[77] Under Smith the museum's collections grew rapidly and he swiftly produced a descriptive catalogue. It is evidence of the growth of hunting interests in the interior (many officers and officials from India went to the Cape to spend their leave in the pursuit of hunting and its related activities of exploration and natural history study[78]) that a firm of taxidermists established itself at Cape Town in 1818 and became closely associated with the museum. These were, however, only tentative starts. Because of structural problems in the building housing them, the collections were moved in 1827. In 1829 Smith was instrumental in founding the South African Institution and the museum collections came to be associated with it. When Smith left the Cape in 1837 he took his own collection, loaned to the museum, with him, but the museum's holdings continued to grow until they were displayed in the new building in 1860 (and moved in 1895 to a classical building of its own at the other end of the government gardens).

Fairbairn had been prominent in reforming the Literary and Philosophical Society in 1829, the same year that Smith founded the Institution. The latter body was designed to be scientific and supposedly uncontroversial, exhibiting few of the liberal tendencies associated with Fairbairn's activities. In 1832 the Literary Society and the Institution, whose membership largely coincided, amalgamated, with many prominent Scots serving on the new body's committee (though Fairbairn seems to have lost interest at this point). Interestingly, Philip was a member of the council of the combined body, and Pringle, far away in London, became an honorary member. The Institution published the *South African Quarterly Journal* between 1829 and 1831 and again from 1833 to 1836, edited by Smith and James Adamson,[79] the formidable and austere Presbyterian divine who was also Professor of Mathematics at the South African College. Smith published many of his papers on a whole range of scientific and ethnographic subjects in this journal. He has been depicted as being particularly interested in his ambitions for his own career, but nevertheless his sixteen-year sojourn at the Cape left a considerable museological and scientific legacy.

The Rev. James Adamson was closely involved in yet another scientific and recreational development at the Cape. In 1848 a commission was established to create a botanical garden of a standard to be linked into the imperial chain of gardens.[80] This was a project supported by Sir William Hooker, the director of Kew. Of the five members of this commission, three were Scots (Fairbairn, Adamson and Rutherfoord) and one was a German, Ludwig Pappe, a medical doctor and apothecary who had trained in Hamburg and was subsequently appointed colonial botanist and Professor of Botany at the South African College. Once the garden was founded and developed it became a classic place of elite resort, complete with concerts by military bands. The concept of the garden was deeply embedded in the history of the Dutch colony (witness its central position in the layout of Cape Town), and ambitions were soon developed to make it an economic garden, closely concerned with horticultural and agricultural research, tying it more closely into patterns of international research.[81] Another Scottish connection was an architectural one. The firm of J. Boyd & Son of Paisley supplied the Cape botanic garden with one of its structures in 1875; in 1882 the same firm sent out the Pearson Conservatory to Port Elizabeth, and later furnished Durban with a Jubilee Conservatory. In 1895 the Cape Town garden was still being castigated for its lack of a fully scientific programme of sufficient rigour – and perhaps its glory days were to come only in the twentieth century with the creation of the great garden at Kirstenbosch – but still the garden was a notable addition to the bourgeois and intellectual amenities of Cape Town, particularly as they were so closely associated with other institutions. Thus, through the creation of all these literary, scientific and educational institutions, the objective was clearly to ensure that the bourgeois public sphere was also an enlightened and rational one, identified by its body of shared knowledge and its capacity repeatedly to add to it.

For the upwardly mobile Scots and other members of the Cape elite, status and respectability, denied them by autocratic governors, also lay in all forms of literary and scientific institutions.

Conclusion

By the middle of the nineteenth century the Cape had acquired the full range of literary, philosophical, educational, and scientific institutions, all supported by a flourishing periodical and press sector. With the exception, perhaps, of the Royal Observatory, directed in this period by a Cumbrian and an Irishman,[82] Scots had been central to all these developments. Moreover the college, library, museum, garden and observatory were more or less connected with wider international networks of learning, in which Scots can be found working in many other territories of the British Empire. Despite the continuation of forms of autocratic colonial government in the early part of the period, the 1820s were an extraordinary decade in the development of the intellectual, press, educational and scientific institutions of the colony, laying the foundations, sometimes firm, sometimes tentative, for the more significant developments of subsequent decades. The question arises whether all this would have happened without the Scots. They were not, of course, alone. There were many Dutch figures, some English, and key figures from Germany and Ireland involved in many of these developments. Sir Thomas Maclear, the influential Astronomer Royal, was from Northern Ireland. So was William Porter, the highly influential Attorney General at the middle of the century, much involved in the representative government and franchise issues. Both were Presbyterians.

Yet it is apparent that figures like Pringle, Philip, Fairbairn, Smith, Jardine and other Scots were not only central to many of the developments of the period but also brought a distinctively Scots intellectual, cultural and religious experience to bear. They consciously bridged the literary, press, scientific and commercial worlds, which they did not see as being antithetical in any way. They helped to create the alliance between the professional and mercantile elites. They also threw themselves into the racial, abolition, labour and frontier policies of the Cape, exhibiting here a coalition of concerns not only of their age, ethnicity and class but which had roots (in different ways) in Scots involvement in the British Empire from the eighteenth century.[83] It might be argued that the institutions of the bourgeois civic sphere would have inevitably appeared at the Cape at some point, but without the Scots these foundations might well have been delayed, and, above all, they might have taken different forms.

Notes

1 Angus Calder, 'Thomas Pringle, 1789–1834: a Scottish poet in South Africa', *English in Africa*, 9: 1 (1982), pp. 1–28.
2 C. A. Bayly, *Imperial Meridian: the British Empire and the World, 1780–1830* (London 1989); for greater detail, Zöe Laidlaw, *Colonial Connections* (Manchester 2005), and Alan Lester, *Imperial Networks: Creating Identities in Nineteenth Century South Africa and Britain* (London 2001).
3 Frank Quinn and Greg Cuthbertson, *Presbyterianism in Cape Town: the History of St Andrew's Church, 1829–1979* (Cape Town 1979). The first committee mooted contained twenty names. See also *St Andrew's, Cape Town: a Centenary Record, 1829–1929* (Cape Town 1929)
4 Quinn and Cuthbertson, *Presbyterianism*, p. 13.
5 Poster 'To Scotchmen resident in Port Elizabeth, 1860', Archives of the Western Cape (AWC).

6   'After 40 Years: a Sketch of the Growth of the Presbyterian Church of South Africa, 1898–1938', pamphlet reprinted from the *Presbyterian Churchman*, December 1939.
7   *Census of the Colony of the Cape of Good Hope, 1865* (Cape Town 1866).
8   *Census of the Colony of the Cape of Good Hope, taken 7 March 1875* (Cape Town 1877).
9   *Census of the Colony of the Cape of Good Hope, 5 April 1891* (Cape Town 1892).
10 *Census of the Colony of the Cape of Good Hope, 17 April 1904* (Cape Town 1905).
11 *Census of the Union of South Africa, 1911* (Pretoria 1912).
12 Timothy Keegan, *Colonial South Africa and the Origins of the Racial Order* (London 1996), p. 99. Keegan's account is one of the most valuable treatments of the period, with a penetrating analysis of the historiography, but he is often not so secure on the Scottish background.
13 H. C. Botha, *John Fairbairn in South Africa* (Cape Town 1984).
14 John Fairbairn to Thomas Pringle, 2 March 1823, quoted in J. Meiring, *Thomas Pringle: his Life and Times* (Cape Town 1968); see also John Robert Wahl, *Thomas Pringle in South Africa, 1820–1826* (Cape Town 1970).
15 Andrew Ross, *John Philip: Missions, Race and Politics in South Africa* (Aberdeen 1986).
16 For these two reasons the suggestion of Jean and John Comaroff that Philip and others concerned with abolition were involved in the 'thoroughgoing reconstruction of culture and consciousness entailed in the industrial revolution' seems inherently unlikely. Jean Comaroff and John Comaroff, *Of Revelation and Revolution: Christianity, Colonialism and Consciousness in South Africa* (Chicago and London 1991), I, p. 120.
17 Famously, Sir Lowry Cole described him as a 'more a *politician* than a missionary'.
18 Moffat believed in the mission to save individual souls. He felt that Philip was much too involved in politics and in wider social concerns.
19 Fairbairn explicitly held Edinburgh up as the ideal. Kirsten McKenzie, 'The *South African Commercial Advertiser* and the Making of Middle-class Identity in early Nineteenth-century Cape Town', M.A., University of Cape Town (1993), p. 43. See also McKenzie, '"Franklins of the Cape": the *South African Commercial Advertiser* and the creation of a colonial public sphere, 1824–1854', *Kronos*, 25 (1998–99), pp. 88–102.
20 Botha, *Fairbairn*, p. 16. For Walker and Robertson see J. L. Meltzer, 'The growth of Cape Town commerce and the role of John Fairbairn's *Advertiser*, 1835–1859', *Archives Year Book of South African History* (1994), pp. 110 ff.
21 Monica Wilson and Leonard Thompson (eds), *Oxford History of South Africa*, I, *South Africa to 1870* (Oxford 1969), p. 314.
22 Eric A. Walker, *A History of Southern Africa* (1928, reprinted London 1962), p. 160.
23 Ibid., p. 315.
24 J. Don Vann and Rosemary T. VanArsdel (eds), *Periodicals of Queen Victoria's Empire: an Exploration* (London 1996), pp. 252, 261.
25 AWC, GHv.1/38, ref. 570.
26 An account of this can be found in Wilson and Thompson, *Oxford History* I, p. 315.
27 It should be remembered that these struggles at the Cape were taking place relatively soon after similar events in England. The activities of William Cobbett and William Hone in pursuit of a free press had occurred a matter of years earlier. Ben Wilson, *The Laughter of Triumph: William Hone and the Fight for the Free Press* (London 2005).
28 *South African Commercial Advertiser*, 7 April 1824.
29 Botha, *Fairbairn*, p. 22; Thomas Pringle, *Narrative of a Residence in South Africa* (London 1835), p. 186.
30 The reasons for discontinuing the *Commercial Advertiser* are given in AWC, GH v.1/39, ref. 592.
31 George Greig, 'Facts connected with the stopping of the *South African Commercial*

CAPE COLONIAL AUTOCRACY

Advertiser', facsimile reproduction produced by the Africana Connoisseurs Press (Cape Town 1963).
32 Rachel Holmes, *Scanty Particulars: the Strange Life and Astonishing Secret of Victorian Adventurer and Pioneering Surgeon, James Barry* (London 2002). James Barry was certainly a close friend of Lord Charles Somerset and acted as medical adviser to him and his family. Holmes speculates that Barry may have been hermaphrodite.
33 Botha, *Fairbairn*, p. 25; Keegan, *Colonial South Africa*, p. 97.
34 Somerset described Philip's claim as 'contemptible prevarication'. He considered that, despite the shadowy presence of Philip, the LMS superintendent was the 'Head Huntsman' on the press controversy, with Fairbairn and Pringle as 'whippers-in'. Anthony Kendal Millar, *Plantagenet in South Africa* (Oxford 1965), p. 195.
35 Botha, *Fairbairn*, p. 28.
36 Quinn and Cuthbertson, *Presbyterianism*, p. 7
37 *St Andrew's: Centenary Record*, p. 6. It is suggested here that Pringle had told Earl Bathurst that he was so 'notoriously obnoxious' to the Governor, the Presbyterian project would be prejudiced. He also said that the Governor had negatived him from being on the Committee.
38 Pringle's remains were exhumed from the Bunhill Fields cemetery in London and taken to the Cape for interment in a crypt at the Scottish 1820 settlers' memorial church at Eildon in the Baviaans valley. This neatly reflects the strong historicism of settler groups anxious to cling to forms of legitimising history. Graham Wiltshire, 'The homecoming of Thomas Pringle from Bunhill Fields to Eildon', *The Coelacanth: Journal of the Border Historical Society*, 9: 1 (1971), pp. 7–9.
39 Technically only Philip was an 'Independent' in religious terms. Fairbairn had become one in Cape Town, partly through his association with Philip and his later marriage to Philip's daughter. Pringle was never an Independent in this sense. Somerset was not always down on Scots: as we shall see, he encouraged Scottish ministers to migrate to the Cape to revive the Dutch Reformed Church, and he also promoted the development of a school system strongly staffed by Scottish teachers.
40 Keegan, *Colonial South Africa*, p. 98.
41 For a study of respectability, and the manner in which it was defined by scandal and by the law, see Kirsten McKenzie, *Scandal in the Colonies* (Melbourne 2004), as well as Robert Ross, *Status and Respectability in the Cape Colony, 1750–1870: a Tragedy of Manners* (Cambridge 1999).
42 For a somewhat hagiographical biography of Somerset see Millar, *Plantagenet in South Africa*. Somerset certainly presided over an extraordinary period of transformation in Cape history.
43 The *Commercial Advertiser* had already been under attack in 1826 for 'false statements' and was to continue to be so for much of its history. See AWC GH 1/58, ref. 840. The second suppression is dealt with in GH 1/58, ref. 19.
44 Though Fairbairn did not attribute it, this is in fact a saying of Samuel Johnson's.
45 For a more sceptical account see A. D. Hall, 'Pringle, Somerset and press freedom', *English Studies in Africa*, 3: 2 (1960), pp. 160–78.
46 Meurant was half Swiss, half English and was born at the Cape. His father apprenticed him to Greig. In old age he wrote a celebrated book which set out to describe the heroic efforts to achieve a free press at the Cape and the manner in which he took this tradition to the frontier at Grahamstown. L. H. Meurant, *Sixty Years Ago, or, Reminiscences of the Struggle for the Freedom of the Press in South Africa and the Establishment of the first Newspaper in the Eastern Province* (Cape Town 1885), reprinted in a facsimile edition by Africana Connoisseurs Press (1963). The Johnson quotation (see note 44) appeared as the epigraph of this book too.
47 Balasundram Naidoo, 'David Dale Buchanan as editor of the *Natal Witness*, 1846–1856', *Archives Year Book for South African History*, 40 (1977), Pretoria 1982, pp. 121–248.
48 Basil Leverton, 'The *Natal Witness* and "open testimony"' in John Laband and

Robert Haswell (eds), *Pietermaritzburg, 1838-1988: a New Portrait of an African City* (Pietermaritzburg 1988), pp. 202-3.
49 His supposedly liberal views did not stop him selling the paper to the fiery settler protagonist Godlonton.
50 Pamela Ffolliott and E. L. H. Croft, *One Titan at a Time: the Story of John Paterson of Port Elizabeth, South Africa, and his Times* (Cape Town 1960), pp. 77-83, 115-16, 121.
51 Keegan, *Colonial South Africa*, p. 105-6. For the expansion of the press at the Cape and elsewhere in South Africa see Vann and VanArsdel, *Periodicals*, pp. 254-86.
52 Judge Menzies had been appointed for this reason. The Colonial Office had decided that Scottish lawyers should be sent as judges to the colonies. Menzies was originally offered New South Wales, then the Cape, even although, as Menzies himself pointed out, his political views were opposed to those of the Cabinet of the day. A good account of Menzies' career and his Cape appointment can be found in C. Graham Botha, 'The Hon. William Menzies, 1795-1850', *South African Law Journal*, 33 (November 1916), pp. 385-404, reprinted by the *Cape Times* in South African Pamphlets, 7: 5 (1916).
53 John Philip, *Researches in South Africa* (two volumes, London 1828).
54 Philip, *Researches*, I, pp. 369, 373.
55 Among Scots and Northern Irish, Hamilton Ross and Charles Pillans received slave emancipation compensation (£476 5s 8d and £143 13s 2d respectively). Meltzer, 'The Growth of Cape Town Commerce', p. 140.
56 Keegan, *Colonial South Africa*, pp. 113-15. Keegan takes Andrew Ross to task (accusing him of misrepresentation) in seeing Philip as an abolitionist, but evidence points the other way.
57 Pringle also had significant international connections, notably in the United States, and encouraged American missionaries to work on the eastern Cape. See Andrew Porter, 'North American experience and British missionary encounters in Africa and the Pacific, c. 1800-1850' in Martin Daunton and Rick Halpern (eds), *Empire and Others: British Encounters with Indigenous Peoples, 1600-1850* (London 1999), pp. 354-5.
58 Botha, *Fairbairn*, p. 66.
59 The trade through Cape Town grew from £630,000 average in the years 1831-35 to an average of £1,596,000 in 1836-40. This was followed by a recession in the early 1840s. Meltzer, 'The Growth of Cape Town Commerce', pp. 132-3.
60 Until they fell out over a libel action Moodie also wrote for the *Advertiser*, under the pseudonym 'Indicator'. In the Fairbairn correspondence he appears as B. M. of Swellendam.
61 For example, in an editorial in the *Commercial Advertiser*, 15 February 1826.
62 Merino sheep wool exports grew from 117,634 lb in 1835 to 3,194,602 lb in 1845. Between 1846 and 1855 the average value of the trade was £984,000.
63 Botha, *Fairbairn*, p. 137. See also W. Ritchie, *The History of the South African College, 1829-1918* (two volumes, Cape Town 1918).
64 Alan F. Hattersley, *The Convict Crisis and the Growth of Unity: Resistance to Transportation in South Africa and Australia, 1848-1853* (Pietermaritzburg 1965).
65 McKenzie, '"Franklins of the Cape"', p. 98.
66 For an account and interpretation of this period see Stanley Trapido, 'The origins of the Cape franchise qualification of 1853', *Journal of African History*, 5 (1964), pp. 37-54, and, for the later fate of liberalism, Trapido, '"The friends of the natives": merchants, peasants and the political and ideological trajectory of liberalism in the Cape, 1854-1910' in Shula Marks and Anthony Atmore (eds), *Economy and Society in Pre-industrial South Africa* (London 1980), pp. 247-74.
67 For an elaboration of this crucial shift in 'discourses' see Alan Lester, *Imperial Networks* (London 2001). In common with many others, Lester sees the malign influence of that Scot from Ecclefechan, Thomas Carlyle, as contributing to it in Britain and throughout the empire.
68 Ross, *Status and Respectability in the Cape Colony*, pp. 173-4, and Julie Evans,

Patricia Grimshaw, David Philips and Shirlee Swain, *Equal Subjects, Unequal Rights: Indigenous Peoples in British Settler Colonies, 1830s–1910* (Manchester 2003), chapters 4 and 7.
69 Andrew Bank, 'Losing faith in the civilizing mission: the premature decline of humanitarian liberalism at the Cape, 1840–1860' in Daunton and Halpern, *Empire and Others*, pp. 364–83.
70 For discussion of Knox see Saul Dubow, *Scientific Racism in Modern South Africa* (Cambridge 1995), pp. 15, 27–8, Nancy Stepan, *The Idea of Race in Science: Great Britain, 1800–1960* (London 1982), pp. 41–3, as well as Douglas A. Lorimer, *Colour, Class and the Victorians* (Leicester 1978), pp. 137–8, 150–1, and Christine Bolt, *Victorian Attitudes to Race* (London 1971), pp. 18, 22, 39.
71 One of the earliest circulating libraries in South Africa was in Scottish 1820 settler territory at Glen Lynden. A. G. van der Riet, 'An 1820 settler circulating library at Glen Lynden, Eastern Province', *South African Libraries*, 19: 4 (1952), pp. 99–102.
72 For the account of the library and of other intellectual institutions I am indebted to Saul Dubow, 'Literary and Scientific Institutions in the Nineteenth Century Cape Colony', unpublished paper, designed to be a chapter in Dubow's forthcoming book *A Commonwealth of Knowledge*. I am grateful to Professor Dubow for sending me a copy of this paper and for his permission to make use of it. See also Saul Dubow (ed.), *Science and Society in Southern Africa* (Manchester 2000).
73 Vann and VanArsdel, *Periodicals*, pp. 243, 262.
74 *Dictionary of South African Biography* and *Dictionary of National Biography*.
75 For Charles Bell's involvement in the Smith expedition see Phillida Brooke Simons, *The Life and Work of Charles Bell* (Vlaeberg 1998), which contains a map and many illustrations of the journey on pp. 30 ff.
76 John M. MacKenzie, *The Empire of Nature: Hunting, Conservation and British Imperialism* (Manchester 1988), pp. 93–4.
77 This is still acknowledged by the museum's website.
78 MacKenzie, *Empire of Nature*, notes the visits of some of these figures.
79 Vann and VanArsdel, *Periodicals*, p. 262.
80 Donal P. McCracken, *Gardens of Empire: Botanical Institutions of the Victorian British Empire* (London 1997), pp. 40–2 and *passim*. Eastern Cape gardens were subsequently founded in King William's Town (1865) and Port Elizabeth.
81 For this international context see Richard Drayton, *Nature's Government: Science, Imperial Britain, and the 'Improvement' of the World* (New Haven CT and London 2000).
82 The Royal Observatory was, however, later dominated by Scots, notably Sir David Gill.
83 See, for example, A. Mackillop and Steve Murdoch (eds), *Military Governors and Imperial Frontiers c. 1600–1800* (Leiden 2003), and Douglas J. Hamilton, *Scotland, the Caribbean and the Atlantic World, 1750–1820* (Manchester 2005).

CHAPTER FOUR

Scots missions and the frontier

The histories of the Cape frontier, of Scots military figures and of missionaries are inseparably intertwined. Yet, in a significant corpus of historical writing on the frontier, they have rarely been satisfactorily combined. Moreover, until recent times the Scots missionaries have seldom been examined as a separate ethnic group with different objectives and methods, even although their activities upon the frontier were important in both white and, more particularly, black history. The missionaries constituted a separate pressure group with connections with the imperial metropole and to Scottish society and its various Churches. They were frontier 'pioneers' who arrived when that frontier was still 'open' – that is, an incipient zone of contact between white and black, not yet fully under colonial rule. They often attempted to establish their mission stations during the period when the frontier was 'closing', that is, the time of turbulence and violence when imperial power was being established, sometimes aggressively, at times reluctantly. They usually withdrew when war broke out, but they also weathered the vagaries of imperial policy: successively efforts to set up buffer zones and treaty systems, the prosecution of forward policies and periods of apparent retreat, and finally the pushing of the colonial border through the frontier zone. Once this had happened the frontier had been 'closed'. Blacks were forced to adjust to the new conditions. And the missionaries began to make more headway with both their spiritual and their educational objectives. But, as Lamar and Thompson have pointed out, the white take-over of the American frontier was a great deal more complete than the southern African one.[1] Despite continual and endemic violence, African societies were more resistant and, in some senses, more ready to adjust and assimilate (in the sense of a two-way assimilation) than the indigenous peoples of North America.

The Eastern Cape frontier was distinctive in a number of ways.

African peoples were relatively densely settled, but the southern Nguni had no central political authority as the northern Nguni did. They constituted a set of separate chieftaincies, which both co-operated and conflicted with each other. The important chieftaincies in the mission zone were the Gaika and (beyond them) the Gcaleka.[2] The region to the west and south of the Winterberg range, incorporating the Zuurveld, was, as we have seen, more or less suitable for white settlement. It spawned a number of towns, Caledon, Cradock, Fort Beaufort within the colony; Grahamstown at its outer edge, later King William's Town beneath the Amatole range, and others deeper into what became known as Kaffraria and the Transkei. And it also had a coastal dimension which facilitated the approach of Anglophone white settlers as well as military forces. Initially the coastal bridgehead was Algoa Bay (Port Elizabeth) and later (from the late 1840s) East London. Scottish missionaries, in various societies, positioned themselves on this frontier and became embroiled in the processes of frontier closure. They acquired relatively large tracts of land; they established complex relationships, not always benign, with African peoples; with the colonial authorities; and also, often hostile, with settlers. The environment of the region constituted a significant underpinning of all of this activity. It seemed to offer attractive, extensively timbered and seemingly well watered land, beyond the relatively arid Karoo, suitable for some cultivation as well as the running of sheep and cattle. Yet its fertility was often exaggerated: it lurched from severe drought to excessive rainfall, and it sometimes experienced extremes of heat and cold. But its hills and river valleys also rendered it an appealing, even romantic, landscape for whites, offering some analogy with Scotland itself.

There were at least seven parties to these frontier conflicts. The British inherited the frontier problem from the Dutch, since Boer trekkers had reached what was to become the Eastern Cape frontier in the VOC period. There they became semi-detached, and sometimes wholly detached, from company authority, disputing land and cattle with the Xhosa, matching raid with counter-raid, as well as conflicting with Bushman and Khoi. Once British administration had been established the situation became a good deal more complicated. The Cape and the frontier became inseparably interlinked, both by administrative and military ties and by the processes of settlement, trade, labour extraction and the migration of some black people into the colony and its fringes. The arrival of British settlers and missionaries added both to the complexity and to the realisation that frontier policy was central to the overall administrative dispensations of the Cape. Thus the first party in these relationships was colonial officialdom, seeking the peace that would permit frugality in expenditure, the first requirement of administration, yet constantly creating fresh and costly crises through their efforts to consolidate the frontier. The second were the southern Nguni peoples, notably the Xhosa, who sought to retain land that they considered to be theirs as well as secure fresh territory for settlement, the running of their cattle, hunting and some cultivation. The third were the white settlers, Boer and English-speaking, pressing farther into disputed territory. The fourth were the Khoisan peoples within the colony, already under severe pressure, in the Bushman case to the point of being hunted to extinction, yet also partly assimilated as workers, as settler clients in the buffer zone, as converts and as military auxiliaries. The fifth were the missionaries themselves, seeking to establish their stations and recognising that their fortunes could be protected only by multilateral relations with the African peoples among whom they settled, the white colonists and the colonial administration. The sixth party was a diverse group of 'humanitarians', journalists, educators and incipient politicians in Cape Town observing and commenting on frontier affairs, while the seventh was the imperial government and the multiple forces and interests which operated upon it.

These parties were in a constant state of shifting alliances. The Xhosa, observing the value of missionaries as diplomats and protectors among the Griqua of the Orange River frontier, the Khoi, and later the Sotho,[3] at times sought similar missionary aid. The administration also attempted an alliance with missionaries in order to gain 'intelligence' on frontier conditions. The humanitarians (examined in the previous chapter) and settlers were initially united in their loathing of the administration, but this was an unnatural alliance which soon broke up into mutual antagonism. The Khoi allied with both missionaries and administration, but were ultimately betrayed. While Scottish missionaries also arrived in Tswana territory to the north-west of the colonial boundary, this chapter will concentrate on the Eastern Cape, which became a prime focus of evangelistic ambitions both in the southern African region and in Scotland itself. Other areas of Scottish activity included the Transkei and northern Natal.

The military frontier

The frontier wars continued intermittently over a period of a hundred years between the 1770s, when the Dutch had reached the zone during the VOC period, and the 1870s. They raged over a tract of land almost 100 miles wide, from the eastern edge of the colony to the Kei River. The British were caught up in these struggles, 600 miles and more from Cape Town, from the start of their rule. In 1798 they set the frontier of the colony at the Great Fish River. They later tried to clear the Xhosa from its fringes and form a buffer zone which became known as the ceded territory.[4] But the imperial advance was inexorable. Ultimately, the boundary reached not just the Keiskamma but the Kei beyond, and the new port of East London was founded by 1848.[5] Later annexations were to move northwards through the Transkei and into Pondoland, eventually reaching up to the border of Natal. Scots military men and missionaries were to be involved in this frontier region almost from the start of British entanglements there.

Robert Hart (1776–1867), from Strathaven, in Lanarkshire, arrived at the Cape with the 78th Highland Regiment in 1795.[6] He was involved (as an ordinary soldier) in the suppression of the Van Jaarsveld revolt in Graaff Reinet in 1798[7] and in the following year was active in the third frontier war, against Ndlambe. For the British this frontier constituted a Boer problem as well as an African one, and Hart was caught up in both. After 1802 he went to India before returning to Scotland to marry. By now an ensign, he was back at the Cape in the 1806 invasion. He again became a frontier warrior, as adjutant of the Cape Regiment (or 'Hottentot Corps') under Colonel John Graham (see below). In 1807 his regiment cleared the Xhosa from the Zuurveld region of the frontier, driving them over the Great Fish River. After the founding of Grahamstown in 1811–12 Hart and his wife were stationed there until 1817, at a time when the town was no more than a collection of huts and tents. He was appointed the superintendent of Somerset Farm, which supplied food and fodder to the troops at Fort Beaufort, introducing merino sheep, importing horses and building a water mill. He acted as guide to the 1820 settlers (notably his fellow countrymen, the Pringle family) and helped them with grain, seed and stock. He acquired an extensive frontier farm which he renamed Glen Avon and became *heemraad* for the area under the *landdrost* W. D. MacKay. Active in the building of the DRC church at Somerset East, he supported the Lovedale mission and later bequeathed £1,300 for the building of the Presbyterian church in the town. It was completed in 1870.

The career of William Don MacKay (1769–1831) also illustrates how quickly Scots were on the frontier. He was from Sutherland and arrived at the Cape in 1806. By 1808 he was ensign with the Cape Corps. He was involved in the suppression of the Slagtersnek rebellion[8] and then worked in the *landdrost*'s offices at Graaff Reinet and Cradock before being promoted *landdrost* at Somerset East. He married an Afrikaans woman and was proficient in the language, as his frontier career suggests. He was later Civil Commissioner at the Cape and Simonstown. Accused of ill treatment of Khoi, he sued John Philip for libel and won £200 damages and £400 costs, a crippling amount for Philip and his supporters to find.[9] As soldier and settler, frontier and colonial administrator, MacKay reflects the speed with which Scots were heavily embroiled in Cape affairs, as well as the degree of in-fighting that broke out among the Scots community.

If Hart has sometimes been called 'the father of the English-speaking settlers', then his superior officer, Colonel John Graham (1778–1821), was the principal frontier campaigner.[10] Graham represents the great difficulties of writing about this period. For long a hero to the whites, he has recently been described as a 'butcher' by President Thabo Mbeki, as part of the campaign to change the name of Grahamstown. But violent frontiers inevitably spawn butchers on both sides, and the military and settlement dispositions of the frontier were exceptionally complex.[11] Graham came from a family which took the name of its estate, 'of Fintry', in Stirlingshire. It indulged in the conceit of hanging on to this description even after they had fallen on hard times and sold the land. Graham was born in Dundee and in 1794 had enlisted in the regiment founded by his kinsman Thomas Graham of Balgowan, later Lord Lynedoch. His rise was rapid in an era of almost perpetual war, and by the time his regiment was involved in the second conquest of the Cape in 1806 he was a major. After the occupation he was charged with the reorganisation of the Cape ('Hottentot') Corps[12] and, as its colonel, led these Khoi troops, classic colonial auxiliaries whom he greatly admired, against the Xhosa of Ndlambe, clearing some 20,000 of the chief's followers from the Zuurveld.[13] He set up military posts along the frontier and was appointed civil and military commissioner in the region. In 1812 he wrote a letter to his father in which he described himself as administering an area larger than Scotland (a doubtful claim, but it reveals his attachment to a Scottish comparator). He is credited with founding Grahamstown (which the Governor, Sir John Cradock, decreed should be called after him), although Hart is also regarded as having chosen the site. He was keen to re-establish white settlement on land where many Boer farms had been abandoned. Graham had learned Dutch during a period campaigning in the Netherlands and was supposedly adept in his diplomacy with the Boers and their commandos.[14]

After a period in Europe (he seems to have been impatient to return to the action of the final period of the Napoleonic Wars) he returned to the Cape, only to find that Somerset had abolished his frontier post. The establishment of the Cape Corps was also severely cut and Graham was placed on half pay until he became commandant at Simonstown. Before his death he received news of the battle of Grahamstown, an action in the 1818–19 frontier war: the land of the town to which he had given his name remained hotly disputed. Within a year the 1820 settlers were arriving, supposedly to consolidate the frontier. Although, as we have seen, this settlement initially failed in its imperial objectives, the Scots settlers were to be caught up in the further frontier wars of 1834–35 (Hintsa's War), the 'War of the Axe' of 1845–46,[15] and the final conflicts of 1850 (Mlanjeni's War) and the Gcaleka War of 1877–79. Scots settlers fought with Boer commandos and as irregulars with imperial forces. They sometimes fought alongside other Africans or with their servants, some of whom they saw killed before them. The frontier wars were never simply black-versus-white struggles, although they were all prompted by disputes over land, cattle, labour, failed diplomacy and the nature of authority. They also produced a 'blow-back' effect within the colony when the supposedly loyal Khoi of the Kat River settlement (land which was also coveted by the settlers) rose in revolt in 1851.[16] But the principal pressure was on the Xhosa, whose land was dispossessed by settlers and the colonial administration. The Mfengu, refugees from the northern Nguni region,[17] were settled among them, a process furthered after 1857 when a Xhosa prophet, Mhlakaza, and his daughter, Nongquase, proposed that the whites would be thwarted and help would arrive if all cattle were killed. Such was the distress among the Xhosa that this suggestion was effected, producing a major demographic crisis and making more land available for the Mfengu.[18]

The missionary frontier

The Scots missionaries had a highly ambivalent relationship with both imperial and African authorities, and their fortunes ebbed and flowed with the vagaries of colonial policies. Hart and Graham had created some aspects of the frontier conditions which the Scottish missionaries would experience when commencing their spiritual campaigns, initially on the 'wrong' side of the effective border. And if their activities were conditioned by the nature of the frontier, there can also be little doubt that there was much that was distinctive about their Scottish experience and character. They themselves often wrote of historic Scottish frontiers and the cattle raiding that had taken place across them. Their own propaganda insisted that they understood the problems and were hardy and determined enough to overcome them. They became, in effect, landowners with 'tenants' (sometimes literally so, though by the early twentieth century they were repudiating this role)[19] who were drawn into a whole range of economic, environmental, spiritual and westernising relationships. The Scottish estate, of which some of them had had experience in Scotland, was a model in socio-economic as well as environmental terms. After the initial open frontier phase, ministers and teachers became increasingly well educated and were full of ambition, not just for conversions but also for the 'modernisation' process.[20] Education was at the centre of their mission. They were not unique in this, but they were particularly seized by the need for 'industrial' training.[21] Although they were seldom popular with settlers (who suspected their alleged affiliations with Africans and often wrote that they preferred 'raw Kaffir' labour to the missionary products), they saw themselves as having an obligation both to African and to colonial society to produce black artisans and an educated black proto-bourgeoisie while supposedly avoiding unnecessary competition with whites. Their educational policies were also designed to be self-sustaining, by producing 'Native Agents' – African teachers to spread the educational word, agricultural demonstrators to create a market-oriented farming mentality, and catechists for further conversion – the triple prerequisite of the religious objectives.

But we should see these activities as constituting a wholly reciprocal relationship. Early writings on missionaries took the white viewpoint.[22] A more recent and extensive historiography has adopted an African focus.[23] The intention here is to consider the effects upon the metropole as well as upon African peoples, for there can be no doubt that Scottish society was itself modified by the existence of the missions. As we shall see, a wave of local Scottish missionary societies, often focusing on Africa, emerged at the turn of the eighteenth and nineteenth centuries. It was not long before various Scots societies developed associated women's organisations in Scotland, helping to emphasise the ties with 'home'.[24] Sometimes these were framed along the lines of 'women's work for women', but often they raised funds for more general objectives, including the financing of 'native teachers'.[25] Such organisations were a setting for both middle- and working-class female activism, in which 'home missions' and 'foreign missions' were undoubtedly connected.[26] By the end of the nineteenth century women were beginning to play an increasing role in the governing structures of the Scottish Churches.[27] Their activities in the missionary field undoubtedly contributed to this. Another class pulled into the missionary endeavour were some of the industrialists of the central belt, perhaps particularly influenced by the example of David Livingstone. They became major contributors to missionary projects, and seem to have seen little conflict between the manner in which they severely held down workers' pay and conditions in Scotland while supposedly contributing to the 'raising' of the spiritual and economic situation of Africans.

If women's involvement led to a certain degree of social advancement and educational and economic liberation, however slowly these phenomena worked through, then that of industrialists may even have contributed to the radicalism of the Scots working class in the twentieth century. The existence of the missions also had a major effect upon the practical theology disseminated in Scots universities and theological colleges, and ultimately upon the convergence of the Free, United Presbyterian and Established Churches in the late nineteenth and early twentieth centuries. The South African Scottish missions, closely associated with their Indian counterparts,[28] and later joined by those in West, Central and East Africa, became significant sources of imperial propaganda, through meetings, lectures and publications (not least the major genre of missionary biography) as the century progressed. The Rev. James Stewart, the influential principal at Lovedale, entitled his first address to the General Assembly of the Free Church of Scotland 'The King of the World, or Christian Imperialism'.[29] By the end of the century they had enhanced and confirmed the Scots' sense of an imperial role and had consequently contributed to those aspects of a Scottish identity that were rooted in involvement in the British Empire.

If Scottish women were swept up into these imperial processes, missionary endeavour at the periphery was indeed strongly gendered. On the white side, women – initially as missionaries' wives, but also as unpaid workers – were very important in the organisation and running of missions. After a period when the earliest London Missionary Society missionaries formed unions with Khoi women,[30] Scots began to arrive with their white, often Scottish, wives. They too were 'pioneers' of the open frontier, embroiled in its turbulence and insecurities. From the middle of the century, as the frontier came increasingly under colonial control, wives became even more influential. Moreover, single women were beginning to arrive as missionaries and teachers, underpaid but still a vanguard of female professionalism, often more advanced in the missionary context than in home society, and consequently rebounding upon it. Nevertheless, marriage was still seen as the natural state of women, and independent female missionary workers who married were usually deemed to have resigned. The missions had a similarly paradoxical effect upon the gendered relationships of those Africans who were within the missions' orbit. The roles of women and men swiftly changed under mission influence. Men became agriculturalists[31] and eventually migrant labourers, while women were subjected to efforts to transform them into 'keepers of home and hearth' like their white counterparts, although some African women emerged as teachers and nurses in the later nineteenth and early twentieth centuries. If the influence of

African women in traditional society declined, it may have increased as male migrant workers left home and some women secured jobs.

Although the Scottish Churches were relatively slow to join the missionary enterprise, with the established Church initially resistant, Scots and those influenced by Scottish education were active from the early stage of frontier evangelicalism. Both the London Missionary Society (LMS), founded in 1795, and the Glasgow Missionary Society (GMS), established in 1796, were non-denominational and represented the new evangelical thrust which coincided precisely with the first British conquest of the Cape. The LMS attracted many Scots who had left the established Church and joined the Congregational movement. The Rev. John Love, the minister of the Scots Presbyterian church in Artillery Street, London, was one of the first secretaries of the society, and presided over the emergence of southern Africa as a major sphere for its operations. In 1799 he helped to select Dr Johannes T. van der Kemp (1747–1811) as a missionary for the Cape. Van der Kemp had had a colourful career as a Dutch soldier and a libertine (by his own confession) before he went to Edinburgh to study medicine in the 1780s.[32] After a family tragedy he joined the LMS and was ordained. At the Cape he headed for the eastern frontier region of the southern Nguni and set about establishing a mission on the land of the chief Ngqika (then called Gaika) of the Xhosa in the valley of the Tyumie River. But he withdrew almost immediately, partly because the Governor, Sir George Yonge, fearful of Jacobinism on the frontier, insisted on his recall. Van der Kemp instead founded a mission with mainly Khoi adherents at Bethelsdorp, near Algoa Bay. Another was founded farther east at Theopolis. These missions became a centre of considerable controversy with settlers and missionaries alike. Settlers claimed that the Khoi were drawn away from the labour market, that they were treated on a basis of equality[33] and that their inhabitants lived in a slovenly environment. Interestingly, when John Philip visited them on a tour of the frontier in 1821, he suggested that they would enhance their reputation by building in stone.[34] Stone- and brick-built architecture would indeed be a defining characteristic of the Scottish missions, physically symbolic of the shift from the open to the closed frontier.

After these hesitant starts, the LMS decided to send a director to report on the situation in southern Africa and make recommendations for future operations. The man chosen was John Campbell (1766–1840), the son of an Edinburgh greengrocer. Having been apprenticed as a goldsmith, he entered the ministry and soon revealed his evangelical credentials by founding the Religious Tract Society of Scotland in 1793. He produced religious books for youth and founded a Sunday school to which he hoped to bring young blacks from South Africa. He sailed for the Cape in 1812, after the death of van der Kemp and, encouraged by the Governor, Sir John Cradock, he spent almost two years in the interior. He became, in effect, an explorer, travelling through Namaqualand, Damaraland, Griqua and Bushman country and collecting natural historical and geological specimens. Partly as a result of his proposals, Robert Moffat, of Ormiston, in East Lothian, arrived at the Cape in 1817, within three years moving to Tswana country and founding the Kuruman mission.[35] The significance of the work of the Rev. William Anderson (1769–1852)[36] among the Griqua became better known, with Anderson performing political and diplomatic functions as well as spiritual. The LMS mission on the frontier was briefly re-established between 1816 and 1818 by Joseph Williams when a Xhosa prophet figure called Ntsikana, one of Ngqika's counsellors, decided to make a partial conversion.[37] The other influential convert was Nxele, who was a prophet attached to the chief Ndlambe.[38] Williams also built a furrow for irrigation purposes and this became a *sine qua non* of all missions, evidence of their advanced approach to agriculture. Campbell was back at the Cape between 1818 and 1821, arriving with John Philip, and once again visited mission stations, this time on the Eastern Cape frontier. He published his journals in 1815 and, in two volumes, in 1822.[39] His significance was twofold: he confirmed the LMS interest in the region, encouraging missionaries to travel there, and his books provided more information on this new British colony.

Back in Britain, Love had returned to Scotland in 1800[40] and became chairman and then secretary of the GMS. The GMS was, however, far from being a society on the lines of the LMS. Together with the Edinburgh equivalent[41] and similar societies founded throughout Scotland,[42] it was an 'auxiliary' movement, fund raising, holding meetings, issuing propaganda, in effect, and often sending money and recruits on to the LMS.[43] But the GMS developed greater ambitions: it did become directly involved in missionary endeavour and in the recruitment of missionaries. It attempted to set up a mission in Sierra Leone, but failed. It also considered India. At this point, Love, with his LMS experience, may well have been influential in persuading it to turn its attention to southern Africa.[44] As a result, the GMS, despite its somewhat enigmatic and apparently exiguous origins, became a celebrated force on the missionary frontier, until its energies ran out with the continuing secessionist tendencies of Presbyterianism in the 1830s and 1840s.[45]

Almost two decades after van der Kemp's first incursion into the frontier zone, Scots returned to the disputed region. They found a

Xhosa people who had already received some vestiges of Christian influence from Khoi who had moved in among them[46] and become their clients, as well as from Ntsikana and Nxele. Now the Rev. John Brownlee (1791–1871), formerly a gardener from Wishaw and an LMS recruit who arrived in the colony in 1818, was appointed 'government missionary' in 1820.[47] Somerset was initially unsympathetic to missionaries, who seemed to him to come from an inferior social class and to represent alarming political views, but he later changed his mind. He imagined that missionaries might serve as intelligence gatherers as well as agents of social change on the frontier, and developed a master plan in which each of the southern Nguni peoples would have a resident missionary providing information to the frontier authorities and encouraging the development of 'civilisation'. But although the idea survived in a limited form until 1830 the missionaries themselves were soon highly ambivalent about such a role, recognising the dangers of conflict with their spiritual purposes. The GMS, still under the influence of Love, sent two missionaries in 1821, and a further one in 1823, to the same area. These were the Rev. William Ritchie Thomson (1794–1891), from Tarbolton, in Ayrshire,[48] a catechist, John Bennie (1796–1869), who was ordained in 1831, and the Rev. John Ross (1799–1878) from Glasgow. Thomson held the office of government agent for much of the 1820s, but soon recognised that he was compromised by such a role and was often viewed with grave suspicion.[49] Bennie, despite a relatively slight education, turned himself into a Xhosa linguist (he also mastered Dutch),[50] while Ross, the son of the owner of a cotton-weaving business, was a graduate of Glasgow University.[51] All three worked at the mission founded by Brownlee, known variously as Gwali, Chumie (modern spelling Tyumie), near the place where van der Kemp had projected a mission. It was also frequently described as a particularly beautiful spot: once Thomson arrived he insisted that it should be laid out afresh with cottages erected parallel to the street, with gardens stretching out behind. (The Scottish parallel is clear.)[52] No wonder Thomson thought that, black faces apart, going to church was like dropping into 'a little Scotch village'.[53] Ross had arrived with a small printing press (he had worked in a printing office in Glasgow and regarded himself as a professional) and founded the considerable tradition of printing and publishing which became a mark of the missions of the area.[54] The first Xhosa words, using a primitive orthography (later superseded) invented by Bennie, were printed on this press in 1823. A larger press arrived in 1831, and was succeeded by others as printing technology improved.[55]

Ross and Bennie moved to the Ncera Valley in 1824, to a densely populated area, where they named the mission Lovedale (later Old

SCOTS MISSIONS AND THE FRONTIER

Lovedale) after John Love's death in 1825. In 1827 William Chalmers, a catechist, and his wife arrived on the frontier, together with James Weir and his mother, and Alexander McDiarmid and his wife. Weir and McDiarmid were highly qualified artisans and were entered as elders. Thus reinforced, Ross proceeded to found new missions. With McDiarmid he established Balfour (after Robert Balfour, first secretary of the GMS) in 1828. Burnshill (after the Rev. John Burns, one of the society's founders and chairman after 1822) was set up in 1830 at the former capital of Ngqika (d. 1829), fifteen miles east of Lovedale. Pirie (Rev. Alexander Pirie, first chairman of the GMS), was established in the same year deeper into the frontier regions. The Rev. James Laing and the Rev. William Chalmers[56] initially took charge of this mission, followed by the Rev. Donald McLeod and the Rev. William Stuart. This reflects the manner in which the GMS had unrealistically harboured major ambitions for a string of stations into the interior of Africa and it was perhaps partly this vision which motivated David Livingstone's journeys. Meanwhile, Brownlee and Thomson worked on at the Gwali mission until Brownlee (who had now returned to the LMS) opened a new Buffalo mission at what became King William's Town in 1826.[57] Each of these missions was founded with a number of outstations and schools, staffed by Africans, around which the Scots missionary was expected to make frequent itinerations. The triumph was always to build a stone church at each, often with contributions from Africans themselves.

These early missions and their missionaries come to life, if in a partisan manner, in the writings of John Moodie, the younger brother of Benjamin.[58] On a journey to the frontier he visited Uitenhage, where he found that both the clergyman and the schoolmaster were Scots (these were the Rev. Alexander Smith and James Rose Innes), before moving on to what he describes as the station at Lovedale, which dates his visit to 1826 or later. He found the Africans there graceful, modest and hospitable, and was generally complimentary about the missionaries. At that point they lived in 'low wattle huts' in a square with tolerable grounds round about. Two married missionaries had their wives with them (presumably Ross and Bennie), while 'young mechanics' helped in the instruction of their African charges. Although the missionaries served excellent Scotch whisky and toddy, Moodie thought them gloomy over dinner and he found the laborious translation at the church service rather tedious. He also thought the singing inferior to that of the Khoi (whom he considered easier to convert) and noticed that several members of the congregation fell asleep during the sermon and were nudged by more attentive neighbours. He moved on to the station at 'Tchumie', where he found the scenery 'beautiful and romantic', the mission's village lying in an amphitheatre, though suffering from poor soil and pasturage. Mr T. (presumably Thomson) lived in a neat cottage, furnished with much taste, and Moodie found him to be a person of 'liberal education, excellent abilities and unpretending manners . . . cordial, cheerful and lively'. He found the conversation 'less tinctured with the peculiarities of the sect'. But he found the LMS station at Tzatzoe on the Buffalo (presumably Brownlee's) rather different. It was thoroughly gloomy, lacking in singing and dancing and the 'cheerfulness' and 'innocent hilarity' which he considered to be the mark of true religion. Innocent amusements were rendered sinful, austerity and despondency reigned, and the whole place was 'melancholy and torpid'. He found it no surprise at all that 'so few kaffirs are interested', since they (in common with himself) were repelled by the missionaries' peculiar dogmas, their narrow prejudices and fanatical zeal. In the last analysis, he thought that the merchant's store was more important in the civilising process. From the whites' point of view he thought it not surprising that the missionaries were unpopular, since they were fostering a 'spirit of hatred to Dutch and British colonists' through their propensity to 'hatch stories of injustice'. Generally, the missionaries should give up their 'love of power and meddling'. Moodie's lively insights, typical of his work, provide an excellent portrait of contemporary attitudes to the attractions and failings of the missionaries and their position within colonial society.[59]

Scots missionaries: politics, land and war

We know something of John Ross's involvement in the politics of the frontier from surviving letters of his wife, Helen. In 1829 she wrote to her sister of the disturbances being caused to their area by the arrival of a commando and some colonial troops. The Xhosa chief, Maqoma, and his people were cleared from land which later became the Kat River settlement of the Khoi, ensuring that the Khoi were themselves targets in subsequent wars. At this time of tension the missionaries were visited by Captain Ross, from the north of Scotland, and Colonel Somerset[60] seeking vegetables and bread. She fired the oven to bake biscuits for them, but their visit was unwelcome, as it would give the mission a bad reputation among Africans. Her husband also remonstrated with them for making war on the Sabbath.[61] Indeed, Ross established close and fruitful relations with the chief Maqoma, elder son of Ngqika.[62] In a letter to her parents in 1830 John Ross's wife Helen wrote about the Maqoma case, revealing the extent of the political involvement of the missionaries. Dr Philip, Mr Brownlee, two French missionaries, Mr James Read and Mr Fairbairn had visited

Lovedale to discuss Maqoma's grievances. The chief came to dine with them and next day the party visited his place. Helen Ross describes the admiration the missionaries felt for him and the extent to which they were exercised by the grave injustice done to him. On another occasion her husband went over to Grahamstown to put Maqoma's case to the Governor, an action which aroused the great enmity of the settlers (although she went on to say, somewhat enigmatically, that it would have been much worse had he not been a Scottish minister).[63] As we have seen, Ross showed his allegiance by opening the Pirie mission, deeper into Xhosa country, and remained there until his death in 1878.[64] Some time before the 1850 war he attended a meeting in Grahamstown and was disturbed to hear the warlike sentiments of the settlers, echoed by some missionaries and clergy. Supported by James Laing (1803–72), who arrived at Tyumie in 1831,[65] he spoke passionately against an unnecessary war against the Xhosa, no doubt confirming the colonists' distaste for him.[66] Yet the repeated wars seemed to the settlers to prove that the missionaries had failed in their objectives, while the Kat River rebellion of 1851 was certainly blamed upon them.

In all the vagaries of the frontier, Brownlee's mission at King William's Town remained safe. The town became the capital of Kaffraria, was generally garrisoned by colonial troops, and became the place of refuge for Europeans when each war broke out. Elsewhere the missions were repeatedly swept up in war, their staffs forced to flee, leaving their charges and the buildings to their fate. While the frontier remained 'open' their position was highly ambiguous: they were caught between the Scylla of identification with colonial settlers and authorities and the Charybdis of supposed alliance with the Xhosa, placing them constantly at risk. The Tyumie mission was destroyed in the frontier war of 1835 when almost all the initial adherents (except three) went over to the Xhosa. It was attacked again in 1846, and finally destroyed in 1851, after which it was never rebuilt. Balfour was destroyed in 1835 and was not rebuilt, because the African population had been cleared from the area. Burnshill on the other hand was not damaged during the war of 1835 thanks to the influence of Ngqika's widow, Suthu. But it was burnt, along with Burnshill and Tyumie, in 1846. Notwithstanding John Ross's sympathy for the Xhosa, the Pirie mission was destroyed in 1835, 1846 and 1850 when the Rosses took refuge with the Brownlees in King William's Town. Whether or not a mission was attacked and burnt seems to have been connected with the perceived connection of the missionaries with the colonial and military authorities. Brownlee and Thomson were viewed with some suspicion, given their government connections, and were regarded as government spies. The Tyumie mission had been used by troops, as had a later station (Uniondale, founded 1849 by the Rev. Robert Niven)[67] which was destroyed in 1850, Niven and his family escaping at the last minute. It was never rebuilt. It is significant that after the 1835 war the new Lovedale (later the home of the Institution – see below) was founded some miles to the west of the old one, thereby placing it within the colonial boundary. This did not, however, save it from attack in the 1846 war, when it was compromised by its buildings being used as barracks. Later it was protected by the fact that a military outpost was built at Fort Hare, farther east.

But nothing could obscure the fact that the missions had so far largely failed in their objectives. The energetic founding of stations was not matched by rapid conversions: the Xhosa still had the upper hand and used the missions as they pleased. John Philip reported that many societies thought the missions in Kaffraria should be withdrawn,[68] and the Free Church seriously considered withdrawal in 1848 when a deficit of £2,400 was discovered in the annual expenditure. They were allegedly saved by the intervention of Dr Macfarlan, of Renfrew, who succeeded in raising money from some of the wealthier adherents of the Church.[69] One missionary, the Rev. John Cumming, who arrived in 1839 to found a mission at Glenthorn, was acute enough to recognise that once repeated hostilities were over the missions had a better chance of success.[70]

The missions were also saved by reinforcements, and the foundation of missions accelerated as the frontier closed. Among many, Alexander McDiarmid founded Macfarlan in 1853 and John Chalmers established Henderson in 1864 at Thomas River. Deeper into the Transkei, two missions were founded at Toleni and Mbulu in 1866: they were named Cunningham and Paterson respectively. John Ross's son, Richard, after eight years' education in Edinburgh, worked at Lovedale for eleven years and in 1868 moved to the Cunningham mission[71] in what was to become Fingoland. He then established outstations at Duff, Main, Somerville and Buchanan, which later secured enhanced status when they attracted missionaries from Scotland. It is an indication of the extent to which the frontier was well on the way to closure that these congregations remained largely loyal during the 1877–79 frontier war, although Ross himself was forced to barricade his house. His father's mission at Pirie also escaped damage at this time. Richard Ross worked at Cunningham for the rest of his career and he and his wife, Margaret Brownlee, are commemorated there by a granite monument on top of a nearby hill. His son, Brownlee John, continued at Cunningham.

A further five missions were founded in the Transkei, where there were nineteen stations in the early twentieth century. Many of these soon came under the control of African ministers. A mission was started among the Pondomise people in 1881, well ahead of the annexation of their territory in the later 1890s. In 1896 the Synod of Kaffraria was asked to send missionaries to the Pedi in the Zoutpansberg of the northern Transvaal. By 1905 three missions had been established, at Donhill, Stuartville and Gooldville by the Revs W. Mpamba, Yekelo Mbali and D. A. Macdonald respectively. 'Native Agency' had become a reality on a grander scale.

It has even been claimed that the Transkei land system was ultimately based upon the iniquities of the insecurities of the Scots tenantry.[72] The object of this system was to break communal land tenures and create an individualised peasantry. The Rev. Henry Calderwood, a Scottish missionary who had resigned from the LMS in 1846 and became native commissioner in the district of Victoria East, saw parallels between the 'injustice and hardship' of a bad land system in northern Scotland and the situation of Africans. He also found biblical justification in Joshua's settlement of the tribes in Palestine. Calderwood, supported by Richard Ross and Governor Sir Harry Smith, envisaged a small-scale peasantry in which each African male would have eight to ten acres of arable land, and grazing rights on commonage, in return for an annual rent and security of tenure.[73] The Mfengus had been settled with individual tenure and were the precedent. The idea was later transferred from Victoria East in the Ciskei to the Transkei and became more widely favoured by Cecil Rhodes.

Mission education: the Lovedale and Blythswood Institutions

As Calderwood's land proposals indicate, missionaries, particularly Scots missionaries, were concerned with much more than religious conversion.[74] They were, in effect, intent upon a complete social and cultural revolution. And the prime aid to such a revolution was Western education, the principal route to their civilising and Christianising mission. After the sixth frontier war the Lovedale mission was rebuilt several miles to the west of the original site at Ncera, and it became the setting for the development from 1841 of the most important educational establishment in the region, if not – in terms of black education – South Africa as a whole. But it was building on a well established educational tradition. In January 1842 the Presbytery examined the schools of the Kaffrarian missions. At Tyumie they found 124 scholars assembled (sixty-three male and sixty-one female – a striking near-equality of the sexes), seventy-five of them in European clothes. They proceeded to examine them in the geography of the Holy Land, arithmetic, reading and New Testament.[75]

At the newly founded Lovedale Seminary, later Institution, the missionaries sought to transform Africans into workers, at various levels, who would contribute their labour and skills to the settler economy.[76] But the original conception of Lovedale was infused with the early nineteenth-century race mentality of the frontier. It was designed to be a multi-racial establishment in which the children of missionaries and other settlers would be educated together with Africans. They would share all the activities of the school, although, perhaps symbolically, they would sit at separate tables in the dining room. (The justification for this was that whites paid more in fees and received different – presumably better in Western terms – food.) They also had separate dormitories. Although schools were founded at other missions, Lovedale was special in a number of respects. It grew to an extraordinary extent. Its buildings, funded locally and from Scotland, were of a high standard.[77] Its teaching staff was well educated. It set about the teaching of girls, and it began to attract black pupils from throughout southern Africa. It valued technical education from the beginning, but this was particularly stressed during the principalship of James Stewart, which began in 1870. It also represented the origins of tertiary education for Africans. It developed a Normal School to train teachers, and the future Fort Hare University College (which was eventually founded nearby) was partially planned within its walls.

Lovedale developed as a complete environment. Like eighteenth-century Scottish estate owners, the missionaries planted trees, 'stately oaks and pines'. There were gardens and a farm. All pupils were expected to work on outdoor projects for thirteen hours a week, on a campus that was three miles across. Pupils were taught that idleness and Christianity were incompatible, that intellectual development had to run parallel with technical, horticultural and agricultural activities. Photographs, mainly dating from the late nineteenth century, offer much evidence of this philosophy.[78] The gates to Lovedale open to an arboretum like that of a botanic garden. Pupils are marshalled for outdoor work parties. They sit at benches in workshops as at pews in church. Printing and bookbinding were significant from an early stage in the history of the mission and this opened out into major publishing and journalism ventures.[79] The surplus produce of farm and garden was available for sale, as were the products of the workshops and the printing establishment. Departments involved with brick making and building accepted construction contracts from local settlers and towns. For all these reasons the educational ambitions of Lovedale attracted the interest of the Governor, Sir George Grey. He so approved of its technical education that after a visit in 1855 he provided a government grant of £3,000 towards its development. This led to the opening of dedicated workshops in 1857

Lovedale's activities spanned the closing of the frontier in the area. The first principal was the Rev. William Govan (1804–75), born in Paisley.[80] He was an arts and divinity graduate of Glasgow University, recruited by the GMS, his salary to be paid by a wealthy merchant of Greenock. The school started out with nine white and eleven black pupils and Govan believed that they should be given the sort of education that they would have received in Scotland, including the learning of Latin and Greek.[81] But manual work and industrial training were also important almost from the start. The activities of Lovedale were interrupted by the seventh frontier war in 1845 and its building became a military fort. Govan and the missionaries withdrew to Fort Armstrong and did not return until 1850. In 1867 the Rev. James Stewart (1831–1905) arrived at Lovedale and almost immediately took issue with aspects of the education there. In effect he argued that there should be elementary education for larger numbers of pupils rather than a more advanced education for the few. Govan disagreed and both sent memoranda to the Free Church authorities. Stewart emerged victorious; Govan retired to Scotland in 1870 (he died in Dunoon) and Stewart took over the principalship, which he retained – apart from periods in Central Africa and travels overseas – until his death in 1905. Lovedale weathered the final frontier wars partly because there was a military establishment at nearby Fort Hare, and became a central institution of the closed frontier.

Stewart became one of the most celebrated missionary and educational figures of the period. He had been partly brought up in Edinburgh and partly on a farm, Pictstonhill, located between Perth and Scone. There he developed his oft-repeated agricultural philosophy of ploughing as an act of Christian service while working within the environment with a gun in one hand and a Bible in the other. He also developed a passion for botany and other natural sciences. At the farm, where his father was involved in establishing a Free Church after the Disruption, Stewart claimed that he had undergone a visionary experience in which he pledged himself to missionary activity in Africa. His education at Edinburgh was extensive: eight years in arts and divinity courses, followed by medical studies (interrupted by a visit to Central Africa to see Livingstone, then on his Zambezi expedition). Stewart's great social *coup* was to marry Mina, a daughter of the wealthy Glasgow shipbuilder Alexander Stephen. This gave him status as well as access to an opulent class of industrialists who supported and contributed to his many financial appeals. He raised considerable sums for buildings at Lovedale, for the founding of the Mfengu mission at Blythswood, for the Livingstonia Mission in northern Malawi and for the Gordon Memorial Mission on the fringes of Zululand. His wife became the rather grand chatelaine of Lovedale, the hostess of many visiting celebrities, from the colony and elsewhere, including members of her own family.[82] The Stewarts lived in a house which cost £800 (contributed by Mrs Stewart's friends) in addition to the sum granted by the committee for the purpose. Style had arrived on the frontier, an appropriate setting for the entertaining of notable imperial visitors.[83] One such was Alfred Milner, who, on one of his visits, opened the Muirhead Hall for the Girls' School.

Stewart became increasingly autocratic and irascible as his principalship moved towards mission elder statesmanship. This status was confirmed by his passionate adherence to British imperial expansion. He was a friend of General Gordon, Cecil Rhodes, Bartle Frere and Alfred Milner, the latter professing great admiration for him. The journalist W. T. Stead, editor of the *Pall Mall Gazette*, saw missionaries as the pioneers of empire and civilisation, and Stewart was viewed as a prime exemplar.[84] Not surprisingly, he was a strong supporter of the British cause during the Anglo-Boer War, which he saw as a righteous crusade.[85] He was kept informed by past students fighting in the war and he issued propaganda in the Lovedale newspaper, the *Christian Express*. He was also a proponent of the British imperial position while on a visit to the United States in 1899. He was optimistically convinced that the war was the means to greater justice for blacks, though he did not support a broader African franchise. There can be no doubt that under his influence Lovedale was a highly politicised place: it may be that this helped it to grow dramatically. He was active in journalism and in publishing, and towards the end of his life was passionate about the possibility of an 'inter-state college' which became the germ of Fort Hare, founded in 1916.

The creation of a girls' department at Lovedale in the 1860s was already based on a tradition of female education.[86] Women teachers, pioneers of white female professionalism, began to arrive from Britain at an early date. The Ladies' Kaffrarian Society sent out Miss McLaren in 1839 to establish a girls' school at Igqibigha, with Miss Ogilvie following her to marry Niven; Miss Thomson arrived in 1842, Isabella Smith in 1845, soon joined by the Misses Harding, Ross, McDiarmid and Weir.[87] When C. H. Malan, a committed evangelical and major in the 75th Regiment, visited the missions on the frontier in the early 1870s he found 'a lone Scotch woman, Miss Thompson' (this lady's name appears with and without the 'p')[88] near Heald Town.[89] A girls' school was established at Emgwali (or Mgwali) in 1861, under the auspices of the still active Ladies' Kaffrarian Society in Scotland, and Miss Blair later headed the Ross Industrial School for girls at Pirie. By 1868 the buildings for the Lovedale girls' school had been completed and a fresh infusion of women teachers had arrived, including Jane Waterston, the Misses MacRitchie (Marianne) and Macdonald, followed in 1881 by Mrs and Miss Muirhead.[90] Photographs of the girl pupils reveal the concentration on 'domestic science' and other female activities deemed appropriate within a Western concept of the 'separation of gendered spheres'. Missionary wives and teachers, certainly in the early period, also set about creating projections of themselves. Yet by the end of the century Lovedale had contributed to the development of black female professionalism: large numbers of African women teachers were trained and the medical mission began to train black nurses.

In 1886 Lovedale published a large book which set out to record the names and careers of its pupils, thereby demonstrating the success of its educational philosophy.[91] It was also a record of financial success, with attendant construction and other booms. At the time of publication Lovedale had twenty-two buildings, almost all stone-built. Its income included an average of £1,000 per annum in African fees (peaking at £2,000 in 1882). New educational buildings had cost £12,000 and a total of £30,000 had been raised in Scotland. Government grants had reached a total of almost £2,800 for the years 1880–87. The subtitle of the book read 'a record written in black and white but more in white than black'. This is clearly not to be taken literally, for there were always more African than European pupils in the school. Presumably it was intended metaphorically: that Western education had the capacity to turn black into white. One table listed the occupations of 2,058 'native' and 400 European 'alumni'. No fewer than thirty-eight occupations are recorded (plus eight other categories, including 'relapsed into open heathenism'). Of these, some are whites only (for example, fourteen magistrates, six doctors, six merchants, six civil servants, ninety-seven farmers), others are blacks only (202 agricultural workers, sixty-three carpenters, thirty-seven waggon makers, and obvious ones like 158 female native teachers and twenty-six native police), while a third are made up of both whites and blacks (eleven and sixteen ministers and missionaries respectively, four and six law agents, twenty-three and thirty-seven employed in stores). Such statistics of those prepared for life within the colonial economy were the badge of Lovedale's success.

But multi-racialism was almost at an end. By the 1890s racial separation was exerting itself. European numbers declined as more white schools opened, and white participation effectively ended when the

Scots Superintendent of Education of the Cape, Sir Thomas Muir, decreed that white teachers could not be trained there.[92]

The Mfengu mission at Blythswood was considered to be closely modelled on the Lovedale precedent.[93] The Mfengu were migrants who had been displaced from land farther north and settled on former Xhosa land: it has been estimated that some 16,000 Mfengu (then known to the whites as Fingoes) had crossed into the Peddie District in 1835. After the disastrous Xhosa 'cattle killing' of 1857 some 40,000 took advantage of the contraction of the Xhosa by settling on land between the Kei and Bashee Rivers. These people became noted for their responsiveness to marketing opportunities, their desire for Western education and their willingness to enter the colonial economy. Many also adhered to the imperial side in the frontier wars (though it was a great shock when some Mfengu took the anti-colonial side in the final war of 1877). Given these assimilative tendencies, they came to be greatly admired by figures like Cecil Rhodes. The minute books of the Presbytery of Kaffraria indicate that this mission was already under consideration as early as 1865, when a memorial was sent to the Governor, Sir Philip Wodehouse, requesting permission for its establishment. The Governor's reply approved of the intention but insisted that this implied no territorial rights: the missionaries would have to get concessions from friendly chiefs and headmen.[94] Presumably the presbytery did nothing until after 'Fingoland' was annexed to the Cape in 1871. In late 1873 Mfengu leaders, Luzipho, Veldtman Bikitsha, John Mazamisa and Bulube, summoned James Stewart of Lovedale and the Rev. Richard Ross (second son of John) of the Cunningham mission at Toleni twelve miles away and requested that they should be given a 'child of Lovedale', in other words a 'daughter' institution. Stewart told them they must raise money themselves.

The Mfengu proceeded to raise almost £1,500, placed the cash on a table, and allegedly announced to Stewart, 'There are your stones; now build.' Stewart raised £1,500 from the Free Church and another £1,000 from private sources. In the end, a total of £7,000 was raised, £4,500 from the Mfengu themselves. The mission was granted 2,000 acres of land free, and three master masons, under the leadership of David Munro (who later became a farmer near Lovedale) were sent out from Scotland to build it, supposedly in a Scottish baronial style. The Institution was opened in 1877, but was almost immediately closed for the final frontier war, when it was taken over as a fort, at which some 140 Europeans sought refuge during the war. It reopened in 1879 under the principalship of the Scot, the Rev. James Macdonald. Initially, it operated under the aegis of the Lovedale Educational Board, but later became independent. From 1882 a new principal, the Rev.

James McLaren, was particularly interested in the Xhosa language and published a new grammar with the Lovedale Press. He was also interested in tree planting, built a new manse, and in 1886 opened a girls' boarding department with Mrs Bennie (daughter-in-law of John Bennie) in charge. Later the role was taken on by Mary Campbell until she married one of the missionaries. In 1897 McLaren became inspector of schools in the Transkei, with some 200 schools under his authority. An in-service course for teachers was developed and soon there were two successful black teachers at the institution, Amos Quinta and J. B. Luti, although they aroused the animosity of the principal, William Moir, who apparently had the capacity to fall out with everyone. A girls' industrial school was headed by Mary McDougall for more than forty years. At the end of the Anglo-Boer War surplus stores were bought up and new buildings erected. There was a farm, which reached the size of 1,300 acres by 1903, and each hostel had its own vegetable garden. By the twentieth century it was said that the products of the school had entered almost all the professions.

Lovedale and medical mission

The Victoria Hospital was founded in 1898 and, after a faltering start, was taken over by Dr Neil Macvicar (b. 1871), the son of a minister near Peebles.[95] He had been apprenticed to a firm of lawyers in Peebles, but his main enthusiasm was reading about Africa, and he conceived the youthful ambition of fighting slave traders. He applied to, and was turned down by, the African Lakes Company, the Mackinnon East Africa Company and the Congo Free State. So he settled upon medical training at Edinburgh. Once he had graduated he went to the Blantyre Mission in Malawi, but he swiftly fell out with the missionaries there and left. In 1900 he met Stewart and was persuaded to go to Lovedale, where he remained for thirty-five years from 1902. He had a considerable interest in public health and also developed a research profile, publishing extensively on his studies of tuberculosis and scurvy among the inhabitants of the Lovedale area, significantly including returning labour migrants from gold and coal mines.[96] Two African nurses (Mina Colani and Cecilia Makiwane, former pupils in the girls' school) began their training in 1903, joining hospital assistants already under training. But this led to segregation. Until then Victoria Hospital had admitted white and black patients, but the matron decreed that African nurses could not possibly train with European patients, and in 1904 the European ward was closed. Macvicar saw himself as leading a scientific crusade against superstition (indigenous medical practices) and set about medically examining

Lovedale pupils, introducing health and hygiene as a school course, and founding the South African Health Society, which published health readers in Sotho and Xhosa. Macvicar was also involved in planning for the 'inter-state college' together with the journalist Tengo Jabavu, the Rev. J. Knox Bokwe (for twenty-five years Stewart's private secretary) and the Rev. S. P. Sihlali. Macvicar was subsequently medical officer of Fort Hare College for twenty-two years.

African ministers

The first African minister on the frontier was the celebrated Rev. Tiyo Soga (1829–71). He was born in a Xhosa community, the son of a senior councillor of Ngqika, at the time of Maqoma's dispossession and was educated at a United Presbyterian mission school ('Struthers' village school)[97] before moving on to Lovedale in 1844. His father, though not a convert, showed signs of westernisation by irrigating his land and using the plough, while Tiyo's brother Festiri also operated within this liminal space between European and African methods. Tiyo was sufficiently talented that the missionaries sent him to Glasgow at the time of the seventh frontier war in 1846. He travelled to Scotland with the Ross brothers and the son of William Ritchie Thomson, John Henderson of Park providing funds for his fare and his studies. He returned to the Cape as a catechist, but in 1851 he was back in Scotland to train for the ministry. He was attached to the UP Church, particularly the John Street congregation, which paid for his studies, including the acquisition of some medical knowledge at the Andersonian Institution.[98] (Subsequently the church's Juvenile Missionary Society paid his £25 p.a. salary on the frontier.) While at this church he met and married Janet Burnside. He had some striking effects during his time in Glasgow: he was, for example, involved in missionary work in the poor East End of the city and allegedly, with one or two exceptions, never experienced any colour prejudice. He met a fellow student, Robert Johnston, at the university and convinced him that he should go to the Cape frontier.[99] Tiyo's ordination seems to have been a dramatic affair, before a packed congregation with the Moderator and all the leading ministers of the UP Church present. The sermon was preached by the Rev. Henry Calderwood, of Greyfriars (later Professor of Moral Philosophy at Edinburgh and related to Henry Calderwood of Victoria East). The Moderator, Dr William Anderson, delivered an impassioned prayer in which he indulged in 'a tirade against the colonial policy of England', bestowing his wrath upon the Prime Minister, the government and the Colonial Secretary, whose 'blundering acts were confessed as if

SCOTS MISSIONS AND THE FRONTIER

by his own lips'. On the other hand, he presented supplications for 'the noble Kafir chieftain, Sandilli' (Sandile).[100]

Soon after their wedding in 1857 the Sogas returned to the frontier and founded the Emgwali or Mgwali mission, thirty miles from King William's Town, where a large number of Xhosa had been settled. There they were joined by the Rev. John Chalmers, the son of the Rev. William Chalmers, born on the frontier but inevitably sent to Scotland for his education. Tiyo's life story became a saint-like progression for his biographers.[101] He was said to have worked so indefatigably and lived in such poor, damp accommodation as to have contracted TB, dying an early death at another mission he founded at Tutura in 1867. Before he died he had provided himself with a literary profile by translating *Pilgrim's Progress* and the four New Testament gospels into Xhosa. His father also became a heroic figure in missionary annals, though some confusion was sown about his allegiance. He was killed by Mfengos in 1878, stoically awaiting his fate in his village after he had proclaimed his allegiance to Sandile.

Tiyo and Janet had four sons and three daughters,[102] all but two of whom studied in Scotland. Their sons were William Anderson Soga, who became a missionary and doctor,[103] John Henderson Soga, a missionary and Xhosa historian,[104] Allan Kirkland Soga, a government official and journalist[105] and J. F. Soga, a veterinary surgeon.[106] John Henderson Soga (1860–1941) was disabled from birth but had a remarkable career. He was educated in Glasgow 1870–77 and again in Edinburgh 1886–90, with his theological training following up to 1893. Like his father and two of his brothers, he married a Scots woman, Isabella Brown, of Glasgow, before working on missions in the Transkei. He retired, curiously, to Southampton in 1936 and one of his sons was killed there in a German air raid. Another son was named Richard Ross Soga, reflecting yet again the dynastic assumption of the names of admired missionaries. These naming practices also implied the cross-racial sympathies which the Sogas came to symbolise. It was said that Tiyo and Janet encountered no racial animosity in Glasgow, although there were problems after their return to South Africa. Yet their three sons (who would have later been classified as 'Coloured') also married Scots women at a time when the racial lines were hardening.

Tiyo Soga always insisted to his sons that they should think of themselves as 'Kaffirs' and they certainly maintained an interest in the history and culture of their black forebears. But they could not escape the fact that their inheritance was multiply hybrid – genetically as well as through their education, their religion and their work on the margins of two societies, interpreting modernisation to their fellow Africans. And the white part of their hybridity was unquestionably Scottish rather than British. It was said, for example, that Soga's dedication to the underdog was partly based upon his love of the Burns song 'A man's a man for a' that'. But Tiyo Soga has also been seen as representing an early form of negritude. As the first westernised South African who received a university education he has been credited with helping to develop both black consciousness and early concepts of African nationalism. Even if his thought was not so far advanced, he was certainly seen as a precursor by Africans, ministers, professionals and politicians who followed him.[107] More Africans were ordained soon after this death: the Revs Elijah Makiwane and M. J. Mzimba in 1875, followed by the Revs Candlish Koti, J. Knox Bokwe and Ndongo Matshikwe.

Scots women on the frontier

The number of Scottish women on the frontier in this period is remarkable.[108] As wives, teachers and, later, nurses they were lynchpins of the organisation and supposedly civilising objects of the missions. They were also key in maintaining contacts with Scotland, with their relatives and with the communities that supported them. They acted as hostesses to visiting dignitaries, as well as often bearing the brunt of child rearing and flight during the various frontier wars.[109] Several died of diseases contracted on the frontier or failed to survive childbirth. Despite the (often rudimentary) medical training of a number of the missionaries, treatment and care were minimal. One of their number, Mrs Niven, saw sights which reduced her to insanity. The marriages of others may have been slightly odd. Because the GMS recommended that missionaries should be married, it has been suggested that Laing's marriage to Margaret Drummond was virtually an arranged one, since the GMS preferred married missionaries. When his first wife died another lady, Isabella Mirrlees, was despatched from Scotland in 1842 to marry him.[110] The second wife of William Ritchie Thomson, Isabella Smith, of Kincardineshire, sister of Charles Abercrombie-Smith (later Auditor General of the Cape), arrived in Kaffraria to teach and train the daughters of missionaries. When she married Thomson in 1846 she was twenty-three and he was fifty-two. Yet she was independent enough to insist on continuing to teach as a condition of the marriage. As a result, Thomson's eldest daughter, by his first marriage, took over domestic duties, including the upbringing of the children of Isabella. Missionary chroniclers had no need to look far for stories of heroism: Mrs Chalmers, the widow of William Chalmers, declined to return home but went back to the

SCOTS MISSIONS AND THE FRONTIER

Tyumie Valley to continue her work with women and children. On his travels Major Malan noticed the significance of missionary wives, like the Mrs Laing, Bennie and Stewart, including their role in fund raising. The wives of Scots artisans were also active. Malan visited the sick wife of a master carpenter, 'a bright Christian Scotchman who came out from Scotland for the work of the gospel here'.[111]

The experiences of two women reveal the lifestyles and professional aspirations on the frontier in vivid ways. The first was Helen, the wife of the Rev. John Ross (d. 1862). She was the daughter of Bryce Blair, an engineer, of Kilmarnock, and married Ross shortly before he left for South Africa in 1823. Thereafter she remained on the frontier, acting, in the words of one of her obituaries, as 'mother', 'teacher', 'comforter' and 'guide' to the mission Africans, until her death in 1862, never once returning to Scotland.[112] She had to flee from her mission homes on five occasions, three of them from Pirie, and on four occasions house and contents were burned down. Three of her children died in infancy. Yet despite her hardships she was, it was said, noted for the warmth of her Scottish hospitality. Her grandson wrote she broke down only once, when a visiting Scot sang 'Ye banks and braes', and she insisted that it should never be sung in her presence again.[113] Even if apocryphal, the story reflects the family's continuing adherence to a Scots identity. Nor was she forgotten in Scotland. Another obituary was published in her home town, expressing pride that Kilmarnock should produce women of such sterling courage.[114] Although Helen Ross never saw her family again after her departure from Scotland, she maintained a correspondence with her parents and sister, as well as various friends, for many years. Copies survive in the Cory Library, in two volumes.[115] (Many other such caches of letters, connecting the Cape frontier with Scotland, must have been lost.) These letters record her orders home for clothing, shoes, tartan material, household goods, whisky and the like. She records the deaths of her children, the competence of her black servants (carefully clothed in European garb and moulded to her image),[116] the arrival of distinguished visitors, and, as we saw earlier, notable political events. She also seems to have mixed with some of the royal women of the Xhosa.[117] While she was mainly absorbed in domestic matters, she also led a prayer group for women and girls. At the missions, perhaps more than in the middle-class world of white women at the Cape, the domestic sphere overflowed into the public one and overlapped with the development of female professionalism. Her funeral was conducted by John Brownlee and Tiyo Soga, neatly representing the old and the new in the development of missionary personnel.

Jane Waterston (1843–1931) was a very different figure, representing not only a new sort of woman but also a different type of frontier.[118] Born in Inverness to a middle-class family which adhered to the established Church, she trained as a teacher and may also have received training as a nurse and midwife. In 1867 she travelled to Lovedale as head of the girls' school. Over a period of eight years she energetically built up this department of the Institution. She got on well with James Stewart, but she was highly critical of some of the missionaries, of the home authorities and even of the ladies in Scotland who supported missions. She also became a protagonist of better pay and conditions for women in the mission field. In 1874 she returned to Scotland to study medicine (she was eventually licensed in Dublin) and in 1879 she prepared to go to Livingstonia in Malawi. Perhaps mindful of her family responsibilities (she supported them after her father's bank crashed in 1878), she insisted on a salary of £200. She stayed only a few months, falling out with Dr Laws,[119] as she had done earlier when encountering Dr Dalzell (see below). These dominant men objected to her strong views on women's abilities and their concomitant rights.[120] Thoroughly disillusioned with what she described as 'religious humbug', she also fell out with the Foreign Mission Committee of the Free Church, which demanded repayment of the cost of her passage and outfit. She returned to Lovedale, but at this stage the FMC would not sanction the founding of a medical mission there. She left for Cape Town in 1883 and established a very successful medical practice. Her letters reveal the manner in which she maintained an extensive network of Scots contacts. A notable Cape Town figure, she received an honorary degree at the university in 1929.

Natal and the Gordon Memorial Mission

As we have seen, Scottish missionaries saw the southern Nguni and their Mfengu neighbours as a prime focus for their activity, but they developed some interest in Natal. A mission was established in Pietermaritzburg in 1867 and five others soon followed, including Mpolweni, where a Union College was founded in league with American Presbyterians. This was designed to educate African evangelists and ministers. Girls' and boys' institutions were also founded (the girls', interestingly, came first, in 1888). Impolweni eventually had 5,650 acres with Africans renting land. The Renier, Gordon and Kalabasi missions constituted outposts leading to the coal-mining districts of Dundee. Of these, the Gordon Memorial Mission became the most celebrated. The background to all these missions lay in the fact that James Allison left the Methodist Missionary Society and affiliated himself to the Free Church, encouraged by Dr Duff of Calcutta. Allison provided land at Mpolweni, and may also have done so for the Gordon Mission, and that may have directed the attention of its founders away from the original intention of working in the Free Church's zone in Kaffraria.[121] Meanwhile, James Henry Gordon, grandson of the Prime Minister and second son of the fifth Earl of Aberdeen, planned to devote his life to missionary work in Africa. But he was killed in a shooting accident at Cambridge University in 1868 and the Aberdeen family gathered together £6,000 for the founding of a mission in his memory.[122] Other donors added more funds. The mission was duly established in the Jobskop location, Msinga Natal, on land close to the Tukhela River, about 100 miles from Pietermaritzburg. The ubiquitous James Stewart selected the site and made some of the preliminary arrangements, undertaking a 1,000 mile round trip on horseback in order to do so.[123] In January 1871 the *Natal Witness* announced that Dr James Dalzell, an ordained medical missionary, had arrived in the colony to take charge. He remained for thirty years and became a powerful figure in the region. He was aided by his wife and her two sisters, the Misses Lorimer, daughters of the Rev. Dr Lorimer of Glasgow, who in the manner of Lovedale developed departments for women and girls.[124] The mission survived the disruption of the Anglo-Zulu War, and it was hoped that it would be a major centre of evangelisation after its conclusion. By the time of Dalzell's death the mission had twenty-one outstations, 300 communicants and 540 catechumens. Dalzell was an enthusiast for education, including agricultural and industrial training and suggested that his medical skills were key to winning over converts and also securing the support of local whites.[125] The income of the mission was derived from the rents of tenants (their numbers were probably restricted by the fact that plenty of land was available in the adjacent 'native reserve') and from the sale of produce. The mission survives to this day, with its land, buildings and gates on the hill beyond the Tukhela River crossing on the road to Dundee. In 2005 its sign still bore its affiliation to 'the Church of Scotland'.

Conclusion

The experience of Scots missionaries on the Eastern Cape frontier was an extraordinarily ambivalent one. They arrived with a number of convictions: that Christianity was the essential concomitant of civilisation; that their message was so overwhelmingly liberating that it would blow down 'barbarism' like the walls of Jericho; that in the process they would free women from drudgery and oppression, men from warfare and violence, as well as create enlightened agriculture, introduce the elevating forces of the market, and use science and medicine to free Africans of 'superstition'. The landscape would be domesticated through the use of Scottish names, the planting of trees and gardens. The reality was very different. They encountered hostility from those they had come to 'save' as well as from the colonists who were supposedly their co-religionists. They were frequently overcome by war, frustrated by official policy and intimidated by an intractable environment. Many experienced geographical, meteorological and ethnic dislocation, which helped to compound their isolation, melancholia and depression.[126] William Chalmers was said to be so distressed by the burning of the church at Tyumie in 1846, 'a severe trial . . . too much for me to bear', that he sickened and died early in 1847.[127] When they seemed to start to make inroads upon African society, through education and seemingly progressive agricultural practices, southern Nguni culture would prove resistant enough to produce 'nativist' reactions, returns to the old ways particularly marked between the 1840s and 1860s. While they worked for what they saw as 'God's Kingdom', they were irretrievably sucked into the conflicts of human kingdoms. Their own missions became petty principalities in which they themselves exercised significant degrees of temporal power, interacting with local chieftaincies and the colonial authorities.

Yet an era of considerable vacillation ultimately gave way to a period of greater certainty. Governors vacillated about the value of missions; missionaries vacillated about their relations with the administration and with settlers. Africans vacillated between the desire to utilise missions to their own ends, diplomatic, medical, commercial, and a sense that the missionaries were ultimately dangerous to their autonomy and to their occupation of their land. It was difficult for them to work out whether missionaries were genuine helpers and protectors or dangerous harbingers and protagonists of imperial rule. So often, particularly in the early years, they had the impression that all missions did was to bring down commandos or colonial troops around their ears. Mission adherents were sufficiently buffeted by conflicts that they could sometimes be loyal to the station and at others throw in their lot with resurgent Xhosa resistance. Yet, as Tiyo Soga's relatives demonstrated, certain aspects of the agricultural, commercial and educational messages of the missionaries could seem attractive if they could be adopted while stopping short of full conversion. Missionaries were also hesitant about the effectiveness of 'Native Agency' and whether Africans had the capacity or could be trusted to be their messengers. And, as Tiyo revealed, even their 'model Kaffir' could remain very much a man of his own culture. Yet the frontier missions also had a considerable impact upon Scotland. It was a commonly held view that 'there is much in common between the eighteenth-century Highlander and the African'.[128] Africa somehow demonstrated the speed with which Scotland itself had entered a modern industrial world. The education and attainments of the missionaries, as played out in so many life stories, seemed to illustrate the manner in which Scots from almost any social class could aspire to religious and educational, architectural and agricultural, engineering and industrial developments on a distant frontier. Those from quite straitened social circumstances could pay their way through university by working as tutors. It is not surprising that they brought their sense of self-help and their characteristic conviction in the multifarious benefits of education to the frontier. It was from this conviction that they represented a distinct ethnic identity and a different cultural and religious tradition that led them to believe that they were in the business of creating 'black Scotsmen'.[129] The phrase resonated down the century and was still being used by the Rev. E. Ntuli, Moderator of the Presbyterian Church of South Africa, in 1941.[130] By extension, female mission workers were in the business of creating black Scotswomen.[131] Indeed, several Lovedale students, including Sana Mzimba and Martha Kwatsha, went to schools in Scotland. While in Britain, Kwatsha became a Sunday school teacher, reversing the missionary role, and later married the Rev. M. J. Mzimba. Moreover, as Lesley Orr Macdonald has written, Scotswomen in the missions, and their supporters at home, were 'engaged in a wide range of tasks and responsibilities which offered able and innovative individuals levels of independence, professional development and authority which they could never have aspired to back in Scotland'.[132] Scots women may also have had a greater sense of personal agency and responsibility than those of other nationalities.[133]

Certainly in the era of certainty, the Free Church statistics seemed impressive. In Kaffraria there were thirteen missions and eighty-one Scots missionaries, twenty-eight 'native staff' and seventy-three day schools with over 4,000 pupils (a Christian community of 9,500). In the Transkei, fourteen missions, forty-five Scots missionaries, seventy-one African staff, 202 schools with 10,650 pupils (community of 17,712). And in Natal, five missions, eighteen Scots missionaries, eighteen African staff, 202 schools and 1,845 pupils (and a community of 10,985). But greater certainty had its dangers: the missionaries became more arrogant and high-handed. The Mfengu discovered that, despite the self-help character of Blythswood, whites were taking decisions without consulting them.[134] In an era when African Christianity was beginning to express itself in separatism and 'Ethiopianism' the

Scottish missions, coming from a tradition of such endemic schism, should not have been surprised when they also encountered secession. This was led by the Rev. Mpambani J. Mzimba (1850–1911), who completed the printing course in 1871 and was ordained in 1875. In 1893 he paid a visit to Scotland for the jubilee of the Free Church and succeeded in raising 'considerable sums of money' for the mission. The Presbytery refused to allow him the power to allocate this money as he pleased and he decided to secede, taking buildings and adherents with him. He built a church on a hill overlooking Lovedale. There can be little doubt that he was influenced by a combination of the development of separatist Churches in the period, the establishment of the (white) Presbyterian Church of South Africa in 1897, as well as discontent with the authoritarian tendencies of the white missionaries. James Stewart, for example, had insisted that 'Whites must rule' in an article in the *Christian Express* in November 1897. He was deeply hurt and embittered by Mzimba's secession.

By the end of the century the former radicalism of the Scottish Churches seemed to have drained away. A tradition of obedience to the civil authority was established and racially separatist tendencies emerged. Congregations became racially distinct and when the Presbyterian Church of South Africa was established it did not include the black missions, which would be overseen by a Missions Council, thereby maintaining control of policy in white hands. The Bantu Presbyterian Church emerged only in 1924.[135] Justifications about the avoidance of white dominance were bandied about, but the separation was all too convenient in the era of apartheid. When the Nationalist government, following its Bantu Education Act of 1955, took over mission schools, including Lovedale, there was scarcely a whimper of protest. It may even be the case that R. H. W. Shepherd, the last principal of Lovedale, approved of separate education, despite the original tradition of the Institution.[136] In the end, the Scots missions were locked in a paradox: they trained many future nationalists, but they themselves became segregationist and were careful to avoid confrontation with white governments.

Notes

1 Howard Lamar and Leonard Thompson, *The Frontier in History: North America and Southern Africa Compared* (New Haven CT and London 1981), introduction, p. 35. This work contains many important insights and set some of the agenda for southern African frontier studies. It was not however, the first approach to these comparative issues. M. Boucher, 'The Frontier and Religion: a Comparative Study of the USA and South Africa in the First Half of the Nineteenth Century', M.A. dissertation, University of South Africa (Pretoria 1966) is a valuable attempt at examining the religious aspects. Even earlier attempts to apply William Jackson

SCOTS MISSIONS AND THE FRONTIER

Turner's frontier thesis to southern Africa had been Eric A. Walker's lecture *The Frontier Tradition in South Africa* (Oxford 1950), Walker's study of the Great Trek of the Afrikaners, which reached its fifth edition in 1965, as well as some aspects of the works of W. M. Macmillan and C. W. de Kiewiet. See also Martin Legassick, 'The frontier tradition in South African historiography' in Shula Marks and Anthony Atmore (eds), *Economy and Society in Pre-industrial South Africa* (London 1980), pp. 44–79, and various chapters in Richard Elphick and Hermann Giliomee, *The Shaping of South African Society, 1852–1820* (London 1979).

2 The most striking and innovative study of the Xhosa is to be found in J. B. Peires, *The House of Phalo: a History of the Xhosa People in the Days of their Independence* (Johannesburg 1981).

3 The Paris Evangelical Mission arrived in the territory of the Sotho King Moshesh from 1833 and its missionaries became very significant diplomats and propagandists.

4 This was Somerset's 1819 policy.

5 In 1835 the Governor, Sir Benjamin D'Urban, annexed the territory between the Keiskamma and the Kei and named it Queen Adelaide's Province. London reversed this, but the area was acquired in 1846.

6 Ivan Mitford-Barberton and Violet White, *Some Frontier Families: Biographical Sketches of 100 Eastern Province Families before 1840* (Cape Town and Pretoria 1968), pp. 157–9, and entry in *DSAB*.

7 Adriaan Van Jaarsveld was a typical frontier freebooter who had been the 'hammer of the Bushmen', had been involved in driving the Xhosa beyond the Fish river, and had rebelled against VOC authority at the end of the company's rule as well as against the new rule of the British. Van Jaarsveld was representative of a Boer faction on the frontier that essentially sought freedom to pursue their own dispensations there.

8 This rebellion of Afrikaners on the frontier had partly resulted from the 'Black Circuit' of 1812, when the Khoi appeared to have been given legal rights. Interestingly, the Boers sought the support of the Xhosa chief Ngqika (Gaika), but he refused to enter into an alliance with them. This contributed to his later sense of betrayal by the British.

9 Andrew Ross, *John Philip, 1775–1851: Missions, Race and Politics in South Africa* (Aberdeen 1986), p. 116.

10 Winifred Maxwell, 'Colonel John Graham, founder of Grahamstown', *The Annals*, 3: 1 (1979), pp. 55–63, and entries in *DSAB* and *SESA*. For some of Graham's letters home see C. T. Atkinson, *Supplementary Report on the MSS of Robert Graham of Fintry*, Part II, 'Letters of Colonel John Graham from South Africa, 1805–1829', Historical Manuscripts Commission, not. 81 (London 1942).

11 Ben Maclennan, *A Proper Degree of Terror: John Graham and the Cape's Eastern Frontier* (Johannesburg 1986), offers the most detailed account of Graham's campaigns.

12 For an account of his efforts to create an appropriate uniform for this corps see Maclennan, *Proper Degree of Terror*, pp. 29–30, and Robert Ross, *Status and Respectability at the Cape, 1750–1870: a Tragedy of Manners* (Cambridge 1999), pp. 13–14.

13 Graham wrote that 'I must now in justice to my poor fellows, the Hottentots, say a word about them. They have not only fulfilled but far surpassed my most sanguine expectations ... When led by Europeans they seem regardless of danger ... They will march the whole of the hottest day, and if they get leave will dance all the succeeding night.'

14 Introduction by Atkinson to *MSS of Robert Graham*, p. xi. A comparison of the fighting capacities of Afrikaners and the Khoi can be found at p. 144.

15 The best account of this war is to be found in B. Le Cordeur and C. Saunders, *The War of the Axe* (Johannesburg 1981).

16 The reasons for the Kat River revolt (conducted by a minority of the Khoi) were many and various: they knew that they were disparaged by white settlers who

wanted their land; their land and possessions had been devastated in the War of the Axe; they may have been influenced by a Christian notion of liberation; some had significant connections with the Xhosa.

17 There has been considerable debate about the nature and origins of the Mfengu. This is summarised in Alan Lester, *Imperial Networks* (London 2001), pp. 89–90. They were sufficiently favoured by the colonial authorities that some others sought to assume the mantle of their identity.

18 For the best account of these events see Clifton C. Crais, *White Supremacy and Black Resistance in Pre-industrial South Africa: the Making of the Colonial Order in the Eastern Cape, 1770–1865* (Cambridge 1992).

19 John Lennox, *United Free Church of Scotland: the Story of our Missions* (Edinburgh 1911), p. 54.

20 The Wesleyans, for example, did not display the educational attainment of the Scots. Norman Etherington, *Preachers, Peasants and Politics in Southeast Africa, 1835–1880* (London 1978), p. 32.

21 According to the memoir of his grandson, John Ross visited the Moravian mission at Genadendal on his journey to the eastern frontier from the Cape. He was particularly impressed with the industrial training there. See note 64 below.

22 For example, Lennox, *The Story of our Missions*; J. Du Plessis, *A History of Christian Missions in South Africa* (London 1911), the works of Cape missionaries, and the articles in local (white) historical society journals cited below.

23 See Donovan Williams, 'The missionaries on the eastern frontier of the Cape Colony, 1799–1853', Ph.D., University of the Witwatersrand (Johannesburg, 1959), and Etherington, *Preachers*, represented early examples of the more sympathetic approach. More recent examples of the African focus include Jean and John Comaroff, *Of Revelation and Revolution* (two volumes, Chicago 1991, 1997), and L. de Kock, *Civilising Barbarians* (Johannesburg 1996). For a nuanced survey see Andrew Porter, *Religion versus Empire? British Protestant Missionaries and Overseas Expansion, 1700–1914* (Manchester 2004).

24 As early as 1800 the Northern Missionary Society in Inverness formed a Women's Society, raising funds, and organising meetings and sermons. By the time the Glasgow Ladies' Association for promoting female education in Kaffraria was formed in 1839 there was a considerable tradition of such activity. Lesley Orr Macdonald, *A Unique and Glorious Mission: Women and Presbyterianism in Scotland, 1830–1930* (Edinburgh 2000), pp. 112–13.

25 In 1825 the Dunfermline Ladies' Society offered to fund an African teacher, called Robert Balfour, at Chumie. The amount required was said to be slight, no more than £8 per annum (at a time when white missionaries generally earned in the region of £100 p.a.). Two other black teachers were called Charles Henry and John Burns, a naming policy clearly designed to illustrate the abandonment by these 'native agents' of African ways in favour of missionary ones. It did not work: Robert Balfour went over to the Xhosa in the 1835 war. It was also said that these early agents were of indifferent quality. Clearly, a much stronger educational infrastructure was required, as subsequently provided by the Lovedale Institution. Donovan Williams, *Where Races Meet: the Life and Times of William Ritchie Thomson* (Johannesburg 1967), pp. 65–6, 69. Another example (among many) of a native teacher funded by a women's association occurred in 1832. Thomas Brown was to be 'specially under the patronage of the ladies of Cumnock Union'. This was agreed at a meeting of the Presbytery of Kaffraria at Pirie, 4 October 1832, Presbytery Minute Books, CLG MS 9037. There are five of these minute books, covering the years 1824 (when the presbytery was established) to 1875. They are a mine of information and appear to have been very little used.

26 These connections between home and foreign missions are well described in Macdonald, *Unique and Glorious Mission*, particularly chapter 3. For a more general account of these connections, in the context of India and London, see John Marriott, *The other Empire: Metropolis, India and Progress in the Colonial Imagination* (Manchester 2003).

SCOTS MISSIONS AND THE FRONTIER

27 Macdonald, *Unique and Glorious Mission*, chapter 4.
28 Alexander Duff, missionary and educator in Calcutta, was always a major exemplar, and he visited the Eastern Cape missions in 1864. A. A. Millar, *Alexander Duff of India* (Edinburgh 1992), pp. 189–90.
29 The biographer of the dominant missionary, James Stewart, the Rev. James Wells, described his subject as subscribing and contributing, together with the Rev. John Mackenzie, to the expansion of the British Empire. James Wells, *Stewart of Lovedale* (London 1909), pp. 304 and 330. See also James Stewart, *The Assembly Addresses of the Rev. James Stewart* (Edinburgh 1899).
30 As a result of these liaisons, the social norm on the 'open' frontier, several missionaries were accused of 'fornication'. Yet his Khoi marriage inevitably made James Read acceptable and welcome when he became minister to the Kat River settlement, which had been founded in 1829 but moved into a disastrous (from the Khoi point of view) revolt in 1851. For other missionaries the temptations of a relationship with a local woman were seen as a major sin. Robert Moffat threatened his fiancée with this possibility as a means of inducing her to join him in southern Africa. Wendy Woodward, 'The petticoat and the kaross: missionary bodies and the feminine in the London Missionary Society, 1816–1828', *Kronos*, 23 (November 1996), pp. 91–107, particularly pp. 91–2. Woodward points out that missionaries tended to sexualise indigenous women but not European ones.
31 The introduction of the plough, to be drawn by oxen, shifted agricultural labour from women to men. It may be that influential Xhosa women lost power at this time, as authority, including prophetic and religious authority, became male-dominated. It was said that missions became refuges for women persecuted or displaced in their own society, but women were also displaced by missionary agency when their husbands became monogamous. Nomathamsanqa Tisani, 'The shaping of gender relations in mission stations, with particular reference to stations in the East Cape frontier during the first half of the nineteenth century', *Kronos*, 19 (November 1992), pp. 64–79. Tisani's article reminds us that the Xhosa had names for the geographical and other phenomena which missionaries incorporated through their naming policies.
32 An account of van der Kemp's time in Edinburgh and his studies there can be found in Ido H. Enklaar, *Life and Work of Dr J. Th. Van der Kemp, 1747–1811, Missionary Pioneer and the Protagonist of Racial Equality in South Africa* (Cape Town and Rotterdam 1988), pp. 15–18.
33 Van der Kemp and Read insisted that the Khoi should be free, live on a basis of equality with whites, and be released from all forms of compulsion. Elphick and Giliomee, *Shaping of South African Society*, p. 380.
34 Ross, *Philip*, pp. 98–9.
35 Robert Moffat, *Missionary Labours and Scenes in Southern Africa* (London 1842, reprinted 1846). By this edition this book had already sold 18,000 copies, demonstrating the immense popularity of missionary works in this period.
36 Anderson was born in London, the son of an Aberdeen merchant who had moved south. He arrived in Cape Town in 1800, a member of the second party of the LMS. Within a few years he had moved to Griqua country on the Orange River.
37 Ntsikana even wrote a hymn which was said to be a great favourite with African congregations.
38 Nxele's Christianity was much more apocalyptic than Ntsikana's. In 1818 he led the forces of Ndlambe against Ngqika at the battle of Amalinde. He was captured and exiled to Robben Island. Natasha Erlank, 'Re-examining Initial Encounters between Christian Missionaries and the Xhosa, 1820–1850: the Scottish Case', unpublished paper. This is based on a chapter of Erlank's Ph.D. thesis, 'Gender and Christianity among Africans attached to Scottish Mission Stations in Xhosaland in the Nineteenth Century' (Cambridge 1998). I am grateful to Dr Erlank for supplying me with a copy of the paper.
39 Rev. John Campbell, *Travels in South Africa, undertaken at the Request of the London Missionary Society, being a Narrative of a second Journey in the Interior*

of that Country (London 1822). The work was dedicated to the Governor, Rufane Donkin.
40 He became minister of Anderston Church in Glasgow.
41 The Edinburgh Missionary Society was founded in the same year as the GMS and changed its name to the Scottish Missionary Society in 1819. It never had its own missionaries or stations in the field.
42 Similar societies to the GMS and the EMS were founded in Stirling, Greenock, Paisley, Kelso, Perth, Dundee, Aberdeen, Inverness, Elgin and Nairn. These were all 'praying societies' interested in missionary activity, although sometimes the concern was primarily with 'home missions' in the growing industrial cities. There is a paradox here: on the one hand, difficulties in travel ensured that such bodies were founded on a local basis, yet there was clearly a national fashion being replicated around the country.
43 Peter Hinchliff, 'Whatever happened to the Glasgow Missionary Society?' *St. Hist. Eccl.* 18: 2 (1992), pp. 104–20. Hinchliff discovered that, because of the nature of its organisation, the manner in which its activities were handed over to the Free Church of Scotland and the United Presbyterian Church of Scotland, and the subsequent lack of interest in its archive – apart from legal documents – its papers had largely disappeared. Some of the missionary records of the Free Church are to be found in the National Library of Scotland.
44 'Notes on the early History of the Glasgow Missionary Society' compiled by R. H. W. Shepherd, handwritten, CLG, MS 8722. This seems to be partly based on the 'Report of a Special Meeting of the Members of the Glasgow Missionary Society held in the Trades Hall, Glassford Street, Glasgow, Monday 4th March 1837'. The GMS was originally constituted by twenty-two ministers and thirteen laymen. The fissiparous nature of the Scottish Churches was well reflected in the fact that they were representatives of the 'Relief', 'Auld Licht Burgher', 'New Licht Burgher', 'Antiburgher', 'Reformed Presbyterian' and 'Establishment' connections of the Presbyterian Church.
45 In 1837 the GMS split (over the issue of affiliation to the Establishment or adherence to independence). One part gave itself the unwieldy name of the Glasgow Missionary Society according to the Principles of the Church of Scotland, the other the snappier Glasgow African Missionary Society. Bennie, Ross, Laing, McDiarmid, Weir and the missions at Lovedale, Burnshill and Pirie adhered to the former, while Chalmers and Niven, the missions at Tyumie and Igqibigha went with the latter. In 1844 the GMSPCS, slightly paradoxically, handed over its assets and operations to the Foreign Missions Committee of the Free Church, while the two stations of the GAMS went to the United Presbyterian Church three years later.
46 Elizabeth Elbourne, '"To Colonise the Mind": Evangelical Missionaries in Britain and the Eastern Cape, 1790–1837', D.Phil. (Oxford 1991) and 'Early Khoisan uses of mission Christianity', *Kronos*, 19 (1992), pp. 3–27.
47 Brownlee was accompanied by a Xhosa convert, John or Jan Tshatshu, who acted as interpreter and guide, revealing the manner in which the mission was, initially, a joint enterprise. Tisani, 'The shaping of gender relations', p. 71.
48 It was said that his mother was related to Robert Burns.
49 Williams, *Where Races Meet, passim.*
50 The Presbytery Minute Book, 1824–36, helpfully contains the signatures of ministers and elders, the dates when they came into office, and also the dates of their ordination. Bennie signed it as an elder in 1821 and again as a minister in 1831. John Ross signed in March 1823 and his two sons, Bryce and Richard, in 1850 and 1856. CLG MS 9037.
51 Ross left a fragment of autobiography, undated, in the CLG MS 3664. His father was from Sutherland, where family estates had been lost, so he became a spirit and wine merchant in Glasgow. He later owned a weaving mill. John studied geology as well as arts and divinity at university, adding some medical studies. The Cory Library also contains a copy of a letter by Ross, dated 11 August 1866,

addressed to a Mr McKenzie in Glasgow, in which he describes his 'heart and all its desires' as being drawn 'to Scotland, the land of the brave and the leal'. It is clear that Ross never lost his ethnic identity upon the Cape frontier, even although he never visited Scotland from his arrival at the Cape in 1823 until his death in 1878. He was probably a Gaelic-speaker, since he attended the Gaelic chapel in Glasgow with his father.
52 Williams, *Where Races Meet*, p. 44.
53 Natasha Erlank, 'Kilts for loincloths: Scottishness in the Eastern Cape in the Nineteenth Century', unpublished paper, p. 3.
54 'I was not an amateur printer,' Ross, fragment of autobiography. See also M. Berning and S. Fold, 'Scots missionaries on the frontier', *The Annals*, 17 (1987), pp. 4–8.
55 Some of these presses later found their way into the South African missionary museum in King William's Town. A. Murray McGregor, 'Notes on missionary establishments and sites visited by members of the historical society, May 15–16, 1976', *Looking Back*, 16: 3 (1976), pp. 67–74.
56 Chalmers signed the Presbytery Minute Book in May 1832.
57 Brownlee was credited as the founder of King William's Town, and was commemorated in a large brass tablet on the town clock. His son, Charles Brownlee, became proficient in Xhosa, was swept up in the frontier wars and was appointed 'Gaika Commissioner' by Governor Sir Harry Smith. Brownlee helped to negotiate the peace in the 1852 war; he was magistrate at King William's Town, and Secretary for Native Affairs in the first colonial ministry. He held various other posts and was also a farmer. He visited Scotland on three occasions. He compiled anthropological and historical material on the Xhosa. Hon. Charles Brownlee, *Reminiscences of Kaffir Life and History and other Papers, with a brief Memoir by Mrs Brownlee* (Lovedale 1896).
58 Lieutenant J. W. D. Moodie, *Ten Years in South Africa, including a Particular Description of the Wild Sports of that Country* (two volumes, London 1835), II, pp. 233, 255–97.
59 In volume I Moodie had been far more severe on missionaries. There he referred to the 'republican habits of our sectarians', who were half religious and half political, setting themselves up as 'judges between masters and apprentices'. He thought they fostered discontent and insubordination among Africans, partly because they themselves sprang 'from the lower classes, ignorant of human nature' and were 'warped and perverted' by 'religious dogmas'. Moodie, *Ten Years*, I, p. 204. Moodie was presumably thinking of Philip here, among others, and reveals the social snobbery, as well as fear of 'uppity' employees, that infused attitudes to missionary values and activities. He was clearly partially converted to a softer view by his visits to the mission stations on the Eastern Cape frontier.
60 Colonel Henry Somerset, Lord Charles's son.
61 Helen Ross to her sister, 13 October 1829, CLG MS 2638 (1827–49). Other letters are in MS 2637 (1823–27).
62 Maqoma and his people had been cleared eastwards from frontier land: in April 1830 Dr John Philip saw Boer farmers heading for Fort Beaufort to claim farms on his former land. W. M. Macmillan, *Bantu, Boer and Briton* (Oxford 1929, reprinted 1963), p. 41.
63 Helen Ross to her parents, 17 April 1830, CLG MS 2638.
64 Like so many other missionaries, Ross and his wife Helen established a dynasty. Bryce Ross (1825–99) was born at Lovedale and went to Scotland for his higher education in 1846, attending both Edinburgh University and the Andersonian Institution in Glasgow for medical studies. He returned in 1851 (arriving at the recently established East London), worked with the 'refugees' from the war in King William's Town and then became a teacher and boarding master at Lovedale for ten years. He wrote a geography, a reader and a hymnbook for the Xhosa and served on the 'Board of Revision of the Kaffir Bible'. His younger brother Richard Ross (1828–1902) likewise returned to Scotland for his education and married a

daughter of John Brownlee. His son, the Rev. Brownlee John Ross (1865–1944), educated like his father at Edinburgh University and New College, worked at Lovedale and Cunningham. He was said to have a deep attachment to the land of his fathers and the clan history of the Highlands which he used to impress Africans with the social similarities of the Scottish condition! He was frequently to be seen in a kilt. There is a biographical record of the Ross family in the CLG MS 9167. A death notice of Bryce Ross in an unidentified newspaper is also there, PR 1182. Bryce Ross recounted his journey to East London and King William's Town in a letter to Dr Macfarlain (sic) of Renfrew which was reprinted in the *Scottish Guardian*. CLG MS 7945. Brownlee Ross wrote memoirs of his grandfather, father and uncle which were published in the *Daily Despatch* and were republished in *Brownlee J. Ross: his Ancestry and some Writings, with an Introduction by R. H. W. Shepherd* (Lovedale 1948). Shepherd added a sketch of B. J. Ross himself. Bryce Ross's son, Dr John Ross, became a notable doctor. Educated in Glasgow, he developed an interest in public health and served in the final frontier war. Obituary, *Cape Mercury*, 5 September 1891.

65 Laing was the son of a shepherd who attended the parish school in Sanquhar, Dumfriesshire. He studied under and worked with Dr Thomas Chalmers at Edinburgh University and with the Society for the Relief of the Destitute Sick in that city. He took some medical courses at the Andersonian Institution and with Robert Knox at Edinburgh (but it is hard to establish whether he imbibed Knox's racism). He was taught Xhosa by Bennie, though was never very proficient. He moved to Burnshill in 1831 and stayed there for most of his career. In 1860 he attended the General Assembly of the Free Church, collecting £2,800 for the Kaffrarian missions on this visit. He brought out his nephew, John Laing, who became the member of the legislative Assembly for Fort Beaufort, and Robert Stocks to be a master printer at Lovedale. His son was Dr John Drummond Laing. For forty-one years Laing kept a daily journal, now deposited in the Cory Library. S. Fold, 'The missionaries and their society: the Glasgow Missionary Society', *The Annals*, 17 (1987), pp. 8–12. There is also an article on Laing in *The Coelacanth*, 11: 2 (1973), pp. 43–6.

66 Fold, 'Missionaries and their society', p. 9.

67 Uniondale was so named to celebrate the coming together of the Secession and Relief Presbyterian Churches into the United Presbyterian Church of Scotland in 1847. Niven had arrived early in 1835 and had originally founded the Igqibigha – a rare use of an African name – in 1836.

68 This was in a letter to the Foreign Secretary of the LMS in April 1846, clearly influenced by the outbreak of the War of the Axe. Williams, *Where Races Meet*, p. 145.

69 Lennox, *Story of our Missions*, p. 32.

70 Ibid. Cumming wrote that only when the power of the chiefs was broken would there be a 'brighter prospect of the benign influence of the gospel' being more 'generally diffused' in the region.

71 This may have been named after the wealthy Cunningham family of Fairlie, of whom Sir James and Sir William Cunningham were known to the missionaries.

72 Erlank, 'Kilts for loincloths', p. 6. See also *Brownlee J. Ross, his Ancestry and some Writings*, pp. 28–9

73 Calderwood fell out with the LMS over its humanitarian stance and he has been seen as a significant figure in the shift towards a more settler-orientated policy.

74 It is perhaps dangerous to stress the notion of Scottish 'exceptionalism' too much. Many missionary societies operated in similar ways. However, while other industrial schools were founded, only Lovedale survived and prospered. Moreover the Wesleyans (for example) were much more associated with the settler cause and official standpoints during the wars. They were sometimes favoured by governors as a result. Lester, *Imperial Networks*, pp. 100, 135–6.

75 Presbytery of Kaffraria Minute Book, CLG MS 9038. The school at the Burnshill mission had forty-four school pupils and an average church attendance of 115.

76 This account of Lovedale is based upon R. H. W. Shepherd, *Lovedale, South Africa, 1824–1955* (Lovedale 1956); Wells, *Stewart*, and various pamphlets, including Shepherd, 'Lovedale South Africa' (Lovedale n.d., probably 1931); Shepherd, 'Short Biographies of Galla Rescued Slaves now at Lovedale' (Lovedale 1891); Shepherd, 'The Jubilee of Lovedale Missionary Institution, July 1891' (Lovedale 1891). See also James Stewart, *Lovedale Missionary Institution* (Edinburgh and Glasgow 1894) and Glasgow Missionary Society, 'Quarterly Intelligence: the Opening of the Lovedale Seminary', South African Library.

77 Later in the century the buildings were said to be so extensive that it was impossible to take a comfortable walk round them.

78 These photographs are to be found in Wells, *Stewart, passim*. Others are to be found in the pamphlets, note 76.

79 For accounts of Lovedale printing see J. Atkinson, 'The Lovedale Press: a Review of Recent Activities' (Lovedale 1931), S. G. V. Crawford, 'Lovedale Press, 1823–1875', *The Coelacanth*, 14: 1 (1976), pp. 28–37, and the various histories of Lovedale by Shepherd. Robert Moffat's mission at Kuruman also developed a notable press. See F. R. Bradlow, 'Printing for Africa: the Story of Robert Moffat and the Kuruman Press' (Kuruman 1987). This press, also active from the 1820s, published religious works in several languages, periodicals, school texts, advice on alcohol and the ubiquitous *Pilgrim's Progress*.

80 Much later, Govan was commemorated in the naming of Govan Mbeki, a leading African National Congress politician and father of Thabo Mbeki.

81 Stewart later abolished the Latin and Greek and it was said that some students objected to what was perceived as a discriminatory policy!

82 Her brother and his wife, together with two children, paid a visit to the Eastern Cape and to Lovedale in 1886. They moved in elite imperial circles in London, on board ship and in the colony. They were received like visiting royalty wherever they went, not just at the missions but also in Cape Town, Port Elizabeth, Kimberley (where John Stephen bought diamonds from Alfred Beit), Bloemfontein and Grahamstown, with flags flying, arches of welcome, bands playing and schoolchildren lined up in serried ranks. As major benefactors of Lovedale and of the Free Church they clearly saw it as their due. An account of this journey can be found in a transcript of the original diary kept by Mrs Stephen, to be found in the South African Library in Cape Town.

83 Wells, *Stewart*, pp. 342–9.

84 We need a closer consideration of the role of missionaries in imperial expansion in the Eastern Cape and Natal in the nineteenth century. J. H. Procter's article 'The Church of Scotland and British colonialism in Africa', *Journal of Church and State*, 29 (1987), pp. 475–93, briefly alludes to the late nineteenth century in Malawi.

85 G. C. Cuthbertson, 'James Stewart and the Anglo-Boer War, 1899–1902: a Nonconformist missionary perspective', *South African Historical Journal*, 14 (1982), pp. 68–84.

86 Girls were said to be more amenable to education in the early days of missions, partly because they were more settled and therefore 'available' than the men.

87 Lennox, *Story of our Missions*, pp. 28, 70.

88 Miss Thompson or Thomson turns up in the United Presbyterian Missionary Record in 1852, when she is described as labouring among the Fingoes, four miles from the nearest European. Macdonald, *Unique and Glorious Mission*, p. 124.

89 C. H. Malan, *Rides in the Mission Fields of South Africa* (London 1872).

90 The 1868 and 1881 names are derived from *Lovedale Past and Present*. Significantly, the first names of the women are usually not mentioned and generally we know less about them than about the men.

91 *Lovedale Past and Present: a Register of Two Thousand Names, a Record written in Black and White, but more in White than Black. With a European Roll* (Lovedale 1886).

92 Shepherd, *Lovedale* (1956), p. 15.

93 This account of the history of the mission (called after Captain Blyth, the magistrate of the district, who was an Anglican) is based upon Andrew Murray McGregor, *Blythswood Missionary Institution, 1877–1977: 'Ora et Labora', the Story of the Great Scottish–Fingo Institution in the Transkei* (King William's Town, 1977) and Wells, *Stewart*, pp. 112–22. Wells reported that in 1907 the institution had eleven Europeans and seven Africans on its staff. There were 370 pupils, including 170 in the training school. The departments including a training school and a practising school for teachers; boys' and girls' industrial departments, boys' and girls' boarding departments, and a book and stationery store.

94 Wodehouse's letter is dated 5 September 1865. Minute Books, Free Church Presbytery of Kaffraria, June 1845 to October 1865, CLG MS 9039.

95 R. H. W. Shepherd, *A South African Medical Pioneer: the Life of Neil Macvicar* (Lovedale 1952).

96 Tuberculosis was one of the several terrible prices Africans had to pay when encouraged by taxation, overcrowding on the land, and the progressive denial of marketing opportunities for their produce, to head for the mines as labour migrants.

97 So named because of a £10 annual donation from Dr Struthers' Glasgow congregation.

98 The Church apparently paid out £202 for his university education and then raised over £132 to kit him out as a missionary. John A. Chalmers, *Tiyo Soga: a Page of South African Mission Work* (second edition, Edinburgh, London, Glasgow and Grahamstown 1878), p. 99. This work was immensely popular and went through several editions. Chalmers had access to a number of sources on Soga that were subsequently lost, as well as collecting a large quantity of oral memoirs of him.

99 Johnston was in Kaffraria only briefly before he was called to minister in Grahamstown. He later became minister of the Presbyterian church in Port Elizabeth.

100 Chalmers, *Tiyo Soga*, p. 89. Sandile was the Xhosa chief in this period.

101 A good example is H. T. Cousins, *From Kafir Kraal to Pulpit: the Story of Tiyo Soga* (London 1899), in which Soga becomes a South African prophet and disciple, 'a model Kafir', but also (p. 160) an example of the fact that 'no difference of kindred, or tongue, or people, or nation, shall ever obstruct' the fellowship of Christianity.

102 One daughter entered missionary work in the Transkei. Another went to Glasgow and never returned: she became a singing teacher there.

103 W. A. Soga took medical and divinity degrees at Glasgow, was ordained, and founded the Miller Mission, Elliotdale, Transkei. From 1900 he concentrated on his medical work.

104 J. H. Soga was educated at Glasgow High School, Dollar Academy and Edinburgh University. After his ordination he became missionary in Bacaland, Mount Frere District, Griqualand East. He founded the Mbonda mission, and later replaced his brother at Elliotdale. His children with Isabella Brown went to Scotland for their education, one of them taking an engineering degree at Glasgow. One of his daughters taught at Blythswood. He published a good deal, including *The South Eastern Bantu* (Johannesburg 1930) – which contained a sketch of the family in its introduction – and completed some of his father's translations. See also T. D. Mweli Skota (ed.), *The African Yearly Register, Illustrated National Biographical Dictionary (Who's Who) of Black Folks in Africa* (Johannesburg n.d. but 1920s), p. 259. Skota was the general secretary of the African National Congress in Johannesburg.

105 A. K. Soga attended the same schools as J.H. and studied law at Glasgow University. At the Cape he became an officer in the Public Works Department in the Transkei.

106 J. F. Soga also attended the schools in Glasgow and Dollar and took his degree at the Dick Veterinary College. He became a government veterinary surgeon at the Cape and was active in suppressing the rinderpest epidemic of 1897.

107 Donovan Williams, *Umfundisi: A Biography of Tiyo Soga, 1829–1871* (Lovedale 1978), pp. xix, 118–27.

SCOTS MISSIONS AND THE FRONTIER

108 In an extensive literature on women missionaries and gender see in particular Norman Etherington, 'Gender issues in South East African missions, 1835–1885' in H. Bredekamp and R. Ross (eds), *Missions and Christianity in South African History* (Johannesburg 1995); Deborah Gaitskell, 'Rethinking gender roles: the field experience of women missionaries in South Africa' in Andrew Porter (ed.), *The Imperial Horizons of British Protestant Missions, 1880–1914* (Grand Rapids MI, 2003); and the articles in D. Ackerman, J. A. Draper and E. Mashinini (eds), *Women Hold up Half the Sky: Women in the Church in Southern Africa* (Pietermaritzburg 1991).
109 They were often attended by Khoi midwives.
110 *The Coelacanth*, 11: 2 (1973), pp. 43, 45.
111 Malan, *Rides*, p. 138.
112 Obituary by Rev. J. A. C. Chalmers, CLG MS 3425. Another obituary, written by William Govan, appeared in *Indaba*, the Lovedale journal, in December 1862.
113 *Ross: Ancestry and some Writings*, p. 6.
114 *Kilmarnock Weekly Post*, 3 January 1863.
115 CLG MS 2637 (1823–27) and 2638 (1827–49). The copies were made by John Ross, but whether this occurred before they were sent or from the originals after her death is not recorded. Ross himself never returned to Scotland, so the former is a possibility.
116 Natasha Erlank, 'Missionary Wives and Perceptions of Race in the early Nineteenth-century Cape Colony', paper presented on the workshop on women's history, South African Historical Society conference, 1995, deals with the symbolic significance of clothing and the presentation of the body at mission stations.
117 Tisani, 'The shaping of gender relations', p. 77.
118 This brief account of Waterston's career is based on Lucy Bean and Elizabeth van Heyningen (eds), *The Letters of Jane Elizabeth Waterston, 1866–1905* (Cape Town 1883); Macdonald, *Unique and Glorious Mission*, pp. 133–6; *South African Scot*, April 1906, p. 121.
119 Waterston wrote in despair, 'I was judged fit to teach Anatomy in London. I am thought fit for the Alphabet here.' Waterston to Stewart, 14 February 1880, in Bean and van Heyningen, *Letters*, p. 170.
120 She also fell out with dominant women. Elizabeth Garrett Anderson disapproved and Waterston found her 'hard and godless'. Bean and van Heyningen, *Letters*, pp. 104–5.
121 I am indebted to Norman Etherington for providing this convincing, if slightly speculative, information about the connection with Allison. It should be noted that the mission was under discussion before the death of James Gordon. The constitution of the mission, formally established in 1874, cited the Earl and Countess of Gordon, Lord and Lady Polwarth, the Hon. John Campbell Gordon and Lady Elizabeth Gordon as its founders. The Scottish management was made up of three members of the Gordon family, two members of the Free Church Foreign Missions Committee and its convenor, who acted as chairman.
122 Alexander Duff wrote a memoir of the Gordons, *True Nobility: Sketches of the Life and Character of Lord Haddo, and of his Son, the Honourable J. H. H. Gordon*.
123 Wells, *Stewart*, pp. 110–11.
124 There was, for example, a sewing school for girls run by Mrs. Dalzell.
125 Dalzell, despite his mission affiliations, was keen to separate himself from non-white people. When the town of Pomeroy was laid out on the road to Dundee, beyond the Gordon Memorial Mission, a number of Africans claimed that they had been dispossessed of land and asked for compensation. Dalzell bought a plot in this new township and built a 'substantial freestone house value £300–£400' on it. He asked to be able to purchase the adjacent land to enclose it with trees and a substantial fence 'to protect it from coolies and Arabs'. His request went as high as the Governor but was rejected. Dalzell to Magistrate Umsinga, 20 January 1890, KZNA SG 216/1890.

126 Williams, *Where Races Meet*, pp. 42–3.
127 Lennox, *Story of our Missions*, p. 31.
128 Ross: *Ancestry and some Writings*, p. 6.
129 Robert Niven first used this phrase in 1845. Williams, *Where Races Meet*, p. 156. In 1848 Niven also suggested that Africans should be clothed in kilts. Erlank, 'Kilts for loincloths', p. 3.
130 'Lovedale's Centenary: A record of Celebrations July 19–21, 1941' (Lovedale 1941), p. 15. These celebrations made much of the distinctive Scots contribution to education, while the Bishop of Grahamstown insisted that even the Anglican Church in South African had been mainly influenced by Scotland. Tshekedi Khama, paramount chief of the Tswana and a former student of Lovedale, was present at this centennial celebration and also made a speech.
131 On the missionary education of girls see Deborah Gaitskell, 'At home with hegemony? Coercion and consent in the education of African girls for domesticity in South Africa before 1910' in Dagmar Engels and Shula Marks (eds), *Contesting Colonial Hegemony: State and Society in Africa and India* (London 1994), pp. 110–28.
132 Macdonald, *Unique and Glorious Mission*, p. 128.
133 Ibid., p. 132.
134 McGregor, *Blythswood*, p. 8.
135 This later became the Reformed Presbyterian Church of South Africa. The two branches came together again only in 1999. Graham Alexander Duncan, 'Presbyterian expressions in Southern Africa, in the context of 350 years of the Reformed tradition', *Nedgeref Teleogiese Tydskrip*, 42: 2 (2002), pp. 423–31. See also Duncan, 'Scottish Presbyterian Church Mission Policy in South Africa, 1898–1923', M.Th., University of South Africa (Pretoria 1997).
136 Shepherd (born 1880) was brought up in poor circumstances in Dundee and was said to have been influenced by meeting a Xhosa student, Mdana Xaba, at Edinburgh University. He was sent to Tembuland in 1920 and arrived at Lovedale in 1927. A prolific writer and proponent of the Lovedale Press, he established a friendship with Alexander Kerr of Fort Hare University College. He was Director of Publications of the Lovedale Press for a period and published *Literature for the South African Bantu: a Comparative Study of Negro Achievement. Report of a Visit to the USA under the Auspices of the Visitors' Grants Committee of the Carnegie Corporation* (Pretoria 1936). He became Principal of Lovedale in 1942. He was Moderator of the General Assembly of the Church of Scotland in 1959, ironically a period of radicalism in the Church with regard to the break-up of the Central African Federation. His biographer suggested that he had 'tried too hard to be impartial' and had been subjected to some criticism for his failure to attack the Nationalist government. G. C. Oostuizen, *Shepherd of Lovedale* (Johannesburg 1970), p. 79. The record of the General Assembly of the South African Church in attacking apartheid was better, and the Rev. Rob Robertson established the first racially integrated church (since 1948) in East London in 1962.

CHAPTER FIVE

Continuing migration to Natal, the Cape and the Transvaal

Migration to Natal

From the 1850s there were fresh attempts to encourage migrants to move to South Africa, particularly to Natal. The colony of Natal had been annexed by the British in 1843 in order to frustrate the Boer Voortrekkers in their desire to establish a republic there, a settlement which had led to conflict with the Zulu which would become a major element of the Afrikaners' historical mythology. English-speakers had been operating in Natal, mainly as hunters and traders, from the 1820s, but once the protection of the imperial power appeared to have been offered them, their numbers began to grow rapidly. The identity of the Natal settlers has aroused interest from at least the inter-war years, first through the work of Alan F. Hattersley and more recently through the extraordinary research of Shelagh O'Byrne Spencer. Hattersley published his *The British Settlement of Natal: a Study in Imperial Migration* in 1950 and it contained a separate chapter on Scots.[1] This was, perhaps, the most notable of a whole series of works on the history of Natal by Hattersley, including volumes of documents, from each of which some information can be gleaned on Scots settlement.[2] The problem with Hattersley's work, however, is that it is not always as well referenced as it might be, and his general assertions (for example, that eastern Scotland 'showed less interest in migration') are not always accurate. By contrast, the research of Spencer demonstrates remarkable detective work in tracking down countless individual white settlers who arrived in Natal. Her multi-volume register, characterised by extraordinary detail and a great range of sources, is the work of a lifetime and in 2005 she had only reached G in the alphabet, volume 7.[3] But accounts of individual settlers certainly offer valuable insights into the interactive character of migration, conditions in Natal and questions of identity.

Scots inevitably arrived in Natal before the new emigration schemes of 1849–50, some arriving from the Cape as hunters and traders.[4] Of these perhaps the most remarkable was William Cowie (1809–56), the Scottish Voortrekker. Cowie was born in Scotland in 1809. Having arrived in the Cape as a young man, in 1837 he married Magdalena Laas, the daughter of Andries Laas. He trekked with her family into Natal in that year, and in 1838 he was one of a commission of six sent to Port Natal to discover the reaction of the British to the advent of the Boers. The former were sufficiently vulnerable to welcome protection, so the trekkers annexed the region and Cowie was appointed *veldcornet* to the Bay area (later Durban). He secured a large farm, but he soon became *persona non grata* among the Afrikaners. He disapproved of the commando led by Pretorius which invaded Zululand, replaced Dingane with Mpande as king and returned with some 36,000 cattle. Cowie fed news of this 'cattle commando' to the Cape newspapers and therefore to the Cape administration. When Captain T. C. Smith arrived with troops in 1842 to commence the process of imperial take-over, Cowie decided his future lay with the British. Inevitably the Afrikaners regarded him as a renegade and set out to capture him. But he was never taken.

Under the British administration Cowie performed a number of functions. He hunted elephants in Zulu country, he was agent for the registration of farms and also agent for the *Cape of Good Hope and Natal Shipping and Mercantile Gazette*. He bought and sold farms and attempted to secure a government appointment, whether as postmaster at Durban, agent to the Zulu or superintendent of one of the African locations, notably Umvoti. He was unsuccessful in all these, but he did remain *veldcornet* at Durban until 1849. Ultimately, Cowie's British imperial identity was more important than either his Scots or his assumed Afrikaans affiliation.

The Proudfoot family are interesting because they had had a trading relationship with the Cape since the Napoleonic Wars, importing Cape wool. Thomas Proudfoot was sufficiently successful to purchase an estate, Craigieburn, near Moffat in Dumfriesshire. His two younger sons James and William left for the Cape in the early 1840s. William began to farm in the Baviaans valley in 1842, while James headed for Natal to indulge in big game hunting.[5] Both recognised the trading potential of Natal, and James opened a store at Port Natal, later Durban. William started a stock farm which he duly called Craigieburn and became captain of the Karkloof troop of the Natal Carbineers. He became a classically violent frontier figure, leading contingents against Bushmen and Africans. He took upon himself the defence of settlers in the region north and west of the Umgeni River in territory which was described as 'the very picture of some parts of Forfarshire and Aberdeenshire', although the latter counties were presumably less violent. The Proudfoots were large shareholders in the Durban to the Point railway.[6] Another early migrant was John Anderson, a shoemaker from Auchterarder who was already prosperous by the time the later settlers arrived.

It so happened that the start of publicity for Natal as a new migrant destination coincided with problems in the Scottish economy. In the 1840s there was a downturn in the fortunes of the cotton industry. The railway panic, when the initial overheated boom in railway construction and share issues faltered dramatically, brought problems for construction as well as iron and steel production. Commercial houses also suffered, and in 1847 one of the East India Company firms, Gemmel Brothers, failed. Population continued to be decanted from agricultural areas in the fertile Lowlands and people were still being cleared from Highland estates. Wages were depressed, unemployment was high and some heavily indebted farmers were encountering losses.[7] At the same time, famine in Ireland brought a wave of Irish migration into Scotland, inevitably exacerbating competition for jobs. By 1851 over 18 per cent of the total population of Glasgow had been born in Ireland.[8] The years from 1847 to 1851 were, in any case, a period of high emigration from Britain as a whole, for the stumble in the Scottish economy was of course part of a larger picture. Moreover, by this time the British government was promoting emigration, utilising the system of Edward Gibbon Wakefield: passages were financed through the sale of Crown land, a policy supervised by the Land and Emigration Commissioners, operating particularly in Australia and New Zealand.

It was in this atmosphere that the new colony was beginning to be noticed. Newspapers carried information about the fresh destination and prospectuses were published. Natal was promoted as a region of great physical beauty (with some areas that allegedly looked like Scotland), with a good climate, fertile soil and a colonial administration that was offering generous land grants to immigrants. Some salient facts were not mentioned. Much of the land available had been cleared of Africans through a mixture of European and African agency in relatively recent times. It was sandwiched between areas of dense black settlement, with populations that were far from reconciled to the white presence. Despite the relatively large black population within the colony, there were likely to be labour difficulties if Europeans took the option of being owners and supervisors unwilling to perform manual labour themselves. Moreover, no convenient ports had been created, and the interior of the continent was in the hands of Afrikaners. Nevertheless, fifty-eight ships sailed with emigrants for Natal between 1848 and 1852. Of these, five left Glasgow[9] and one sailed from Leith,[10] although many Scots migrants travelled on ships clearing Liverpool and southern ports.

Byrne and other settlements

These prospects attracted the attention of an extraordinary traveller and financier called Joseph Charles Byrne (1800–63). Byrne was born in Dublin and, having made money as a stockbroker in Liverpool, travelled widely in North America, Australia, New Zealand and Cape Colony. Throughout these travels he studied migration opportunities and publicised them in his book of *Wanderings*.[11] He had clearly been particularly taken with southern Africa (although some doubt has been cast on whether he travelled as extensively as he claimed), for he followed this with two emigrants' guides, one to the Cape of Good Hope and one to Natal.[12] He was assiduous in publicising his schemes, in lecturing, in placing advertisements, and he even founded an emigration newspaper.[13] In the years 1849–50 he was responsible for sending a considerable number of migrants to Natal through his Natal Emigration & Colonisation Company. Byrne's scheme seemed on the face of it ingenious, though it was criticised by Donald Moodie, the younger brother of the instigator of the Moodie settlement, who was by then a member of the administration in Natal.[14] Byrne was to deposit £10 with the commissioners for each migrant he took to Natal, and would receive in return fifty acres of land. But each of his migrants would receive only twenty acres, leaving him thirty in hand. Once he was able to certify that the migrant was settled, he would have his £10 deposit returned. He had to cover the shipping costs and other expenses. Other migration entrepreneurs set out to establish similar schemes, and the publicity ensured that yet more people travelled independently.[15] Between 1849 and 1851 almost 5,000 people arrived in Natal (so this migration was roughly equivalent to the 1820 settlement on the Cape frontier). A considerable number of them, probably disproportionate to the relative populations, came from Scotland. Two Byrne ships, the *Ina* and the *Conquering Hero*, left from Glasgow.[16]

But, like so many migration entrepreneurs, Byrne failed to make his activities a commercial success; he was declared bankrupt and left for Australia (after a visit to Natal to attempt to sort out his affairs).[17] The reasons for this tell us much about the colony and about the nature of the migration. A great deal of land had already been unproductively alienated, so what was left was relatively poor in quality, had inadequate access to water or was remote in location. So much land was available for the market that Byrne had no hope of selling his surplus acres. Moreover, many of the migrants failed to take up land, but headed for the towns (at this stage mainly Durban and Pietermaritzburg) to seek employment or open businesses there, and a glance at the extraordinary range of occupations represented among them indicates why this should have been so. As with the 1820 settlement, a migration which was supposed to be about land settlement actually attracted people who had little interest in farming. And, as in 1820, the land grants were too small for the environmental conditions, and farms were consequently uneconomic. This was so obviously the case that Lieutenant-governor Pine was constrained to add twenty-five acres per person to the twenty-acre grant made by Byrne.

The unscrupulous Byrne probably organised the emigration of some 2,200 people, almost half the entire movement, many of them Scots. Insights into the motivations for emigration, into Byrne's dishonesty, into the conditions the emigrants encountered on arrival, and into the opportunities available to them, can be found in reminiscences written by Jane Arbuthnot, the wife of the settler James, towards the end of the nineteenth century.[18] The Arbuthnots, who came from Peterhead, found 'the prospect of procuring native servants for menial work' particularly appealing, as they had heard of 'the hardships undergone by educated ladies and gentlemen for want of domestic servants' in the United States. In 1848–49, looking for better opportunities and a superior climate, they began to notice references in newspapers and pamphlets to Natal. They hoped to put together a party, but in the end they managed to recruit only a ditch digger called Peter McKay, who had been to Natal already as 'cook and bottle washer to a hunting party travelling far into the interior with several wagons in search of big game'. His Irish wife would also join the party, together with a nursemaid, Jane Smith, to look after the Arbuthnots' five children.

Having made their decision and formed their party, they travelled to London to purchase the equipment they thought would be necessary in their new home. There they saw Byrne in his grandly appointed office with the walls adorned with pictures of Zulus (clearly designed to attract emigrants rather than put them off). In the absence of banks in Natal, they trustingly handed over their capital of several hundred pounds to him (he seemed 'plausible and kind') on the understanding that his agent in Natal, John Swales Moreland, would return the money to them on arrival.[19] They never saw it again. (Moreland had been authorised to pay it out, but Byrne had become insolvent in the interim.) Eventually they sailed on the *Unicorn* from Liverpool in June 1850. The *Unicorn* also carried Charles Scott, a Church of Scotland minister and schoolmaster from Peterhead, William Campbell, the Free Church minister at Alexandria, in Dunbartonshire (who travelled to improve his health), and about seventy Highlanders who had been on the land. As a final injustice, Byrne boarded the ship as it departed and insisted on taking another sum of money from each passenger before he would permit it to sail.

This largely Scottish party reached Durban in September 1850 after an adventurous journey of ninety-six days. As Durban had no harbour and a very dangerous bar on what was often a very stormy coast, landing was difficult. The *Minerva* had been wrecked on the shore the previous month, and simply getting to the beach in the inner harbour could be a dangerous business, with rowing boats frequently swamped. Durban itself was almost two miles inland and at this stage consisted mainly of tents and huts, all likely to be inundated with sand. One of the more notable buildings was the Highlander Hugh MacDonald's hotel facing the scarcely developed Market Square.[20] James Arbuthnot set out on foot to find his land, which was between Pietermaritzburg and Richmond, near the Illovo River, eventually returning to collect his family, who were struggling as best they could in the absence of the capital stolen by Byrne.[21] By this time their nursemaid, Jane Smith, had left them and set herself up with a laundry business. She employed some Africans and was soon successful, an interesting example of female colonial entrepreneurship. The McKays stayed with the Arbuthnots when they trekked inland, a journey taking two weeks. They found abandoned Dutch gardens and were able to salvage some seeds from them. They soon had a successful vegetable garden on their land, but after three years they moved from Illovo to Umzinto, near the hot, damp coast, south of Durban, where they were pioneers in sugar planting. Arbuthnot was elected to the legislative council of Natal under representative government and was prominent in forming volunteer corps at Richmond and Umzinto. He also dabbled in clay deposits and, at the invitation of the Lieutenant-governor, wrote an emigrants' guidebook which was published in Edinburgh and Aberdeen in 1862. Scots migrants were clearly valued in the colony.

A fellow passenger on the *Unicorn* was George Lamond, who also wrote his reminiscences.[22] He was robbed of his cash on the *Unicorn* and had to be helped by James Arbuthnot, who had of course lost money to Byrne. After their arrival they both helped with the rescue of passengers from another wreck, the *British Tar*, and Lamond later joined the Arbuthnots when they trekked inland. Lamond was fairly well connected, for he was welcomed at Government House by Benjamin Pine, the Lieutenant-governor, and was given a job in the colonial Treasury. But in 1851 he moved on to work at a coastal estate called Compensation, where he 'helped to make and eat the first sugar manufactured in Natal'. In 1854, at the invitation of the Lieutenant-governor, he returned to government service in the audit office. Some migrants moved in the other direction, into farming. John Smith, a baker from Montrose, also a passenger on the *Unicorn*, started out as a confectioner for a few years, but in 1856 he bought a farm called Fox Hill, a favourite resort of hunters. Smith was elected to the legislative council in 1886 and used his position to promote the granting of Responsible Government (which came to Natal in 1893). Other Scots migrants included W. M. Collins, who became postmaster-general of the colony in 1853; Alexander Gordon, who used the proceeds of the sale of his army captain's commission to bring a family party to 'New Glasgow', subsequently settling on a farm called Aberdour. Some surveyors and engineers displaced by the railway crash emigrated to Natal (and later Scots were to be prominent in the development of Natal railways). Other professions represented were construction foremen, masons, carpenters, tailors,[23] weavers,[24] millwrights,[25] a cotton mill manager,[26] a cleric who became a farmer,[27] a boatbuilder,[28] shoemakers, ferrymen, innkeepers, storekeepers, land surveyors, a tidewaiter and customs officer, and many others. Some probably entered their occupation as 'agriculturalist' even when they were not. An example is Robert Carruthers (1826–88), who was a printer from Inverness, a member of the family who owned the *Inverness Courier*.[29]

The *Ina*, which arrived from Glasgow in March 1850, carried a remarkable passenger called Thomas Duff (1825–1905), who travelled with his father, John (1784–1864). Duff senior probably lied about his age in order to be accepted, since he appears in the lists as aged forty-five when he was in reality in his mid-sixties. The Duffs came from Logiealmond in Perthshire and it is clear that Thomas had had a good education. After his arrival he wrote a series of letters home which were subsequently collected and published as a pamphlet (in 1850 in both Aberdeen and Perth, price 4*d*) with the title *First Impressions of Natal by a Perthshire Ploughman*.[30] The original introduction to the pamphlet dilated on the spread of 'civilised life' and 'practical religion' and pointed out that though Thomas was 'more familiar with the plough than the pen, he yet possesses an education superior to most of his class even in Scotland'. Moreover, his views on Natal offered comparisons with 'the Scotchman's own colony in Upper Canada'. The Duffs lived in the 'Emigrants' Shed' in Durban for several weeks, and Thomas's letters offer a vivid impression of life in the town, of the journey up-country, and of efforts to settle on their land on the Umhloti River.

Duff was particularly impressed with the Africans of the colony, whom he described as 'Zulu refugees': he admired them 'for their tractable and friendly dispositions', their honesty, and their willingness to work if treated well. He worked beside them landing cargo on the beach and also on attempts to break down the bar and scour out the entrance to the bay so that more vessels could come into the inner harbour. In the early days of settlement black and white were much more inclined to work together on manual labour. Perhaps as a result of this experience, he decided to do everything to learn the local African language and was perturbed that no decent grammar yet existed to help him to do so. The harbour works and breakwater operations were under the supervision of 'a Scotchman', Mr Milne.[31] Inevitably, many of Duff's comparisons as to landscape, vegetation and soil quality were with Scotland. He visited other Scots who lived near by and quoted their hopes for the economic future of the colony. He also compared the prices of foodstuffs and was particularly impressed that meat in Natal was so cheap (while much else was dear). 'We have a steak at least once a day to our coffee,' with rice and pumpkin, also cheap, and 'a good soup to dinner'. He lamented the absence of a bookseller in the colony, and consoled himself with his *Book of Scottish Song* and *Chambers's Information for the People*, both of which he had brought out with him. There can be no doubt that the Scottish identity of the Perthshire Ploughman was important to him. Respectability for him meant abstemiousness, and he berated other settlers who spent too much in the alehouse.

Some of the Scots went to visit the German colony at 'New Germany', not far to the west of Durban (189 emigrants had arrived in 1848 to grow cotton), in order to discuss prospects. Eventually the Duffs moved to their ninety acres on the Umhloti, Thomas proclaiming that he was 'absolutely angry at such a country lying waste'. He soon recognised that the scarcity of wood and water would create problems, as would the absence of transport and marketing opportunities. For most of the 1850s, after he had completed his sequence of letters home, Duff attempted to supplement his income with trading in Zululand; he lost his herd of cattle to lungsickness in 1856; in 1861 his home was destroyed by a fire which spread from adjacent cane fields. Such misfortunes were the common experience of settlers, as was Duff's later career. He turned to storekeeping and sugar growing. In 1881 he moved (by this time he had a family) to a farm on the Mooi River.

There is no way of knowing whether Duff's published letters encouraged any other migrants to leave Scotland, but there were other ways in which the white population of Natal was boosted during this period. One group of settlers were former soldiers, particularly of the 45th and 91st Regiments, who took their discharge and remained in the colony, some of them ahead of the 1849–51 schemes. John Anderson (1816–89), of Auchterarder, had joined the 45th Regiment in 1836, was sent to

Natal in 1843 and took his discharge in 1847. He became a boot and shoe maker in Pietermaritzburg and ended up with a very considerable business. William Anderson (1818–98) was from Glasgow. He arrived at the Cape in the 27th Regiment and was discharged in 1845. He went to Natal in 1849 and received land near Pietermaritzburg. He was later a stationmaster with Natal Government Railways, starting at Berea Road station. James Cruickshank (1827–1907), from Stirlingshire, was a soldier in the 45th and then the 91st, serving in the seventh frontier war of 1846–47. After a return to Britain he settled in Natal and became a farmer, fruit grower and landowner. He died in Scotland. William Cunningham, born in Falkirk in 1819, also arrived with the 45th to serve in the seventh frontier war. He was discharged in 1859 with a disability pension and became a farmer in the Byrne Valley with a store for African trade. He called his farm Dunbar and brought out a niece and a number of other relatives.

Indeed, many of the Byrne and other settlers subsequently sponsored family members and friends, particularly after the new colonial land grant proclamation of April 1857. James Brown (1796–1873), possibly from Banchory, arrived on the *Unicorn* and served for a while on Lieutenant-governor Pine's staff. He subsequently became a resident magistrate, a ferryman, and combined being the gaoler in Ladysmith with the office of messenger to the court and provisions contractor for the prisoners. Between 1857 and 1859 he brought out his wife, a daughter and a son, as well as three married daughters and their husbands. John Gavin (1821–75), from Kincardineshire, who was described as a blacksmith, engineer, iron and brass founder, also exhibited the versatility of the early settlers. He arrived in 1850, failed to take up his land grant[32] but was involved in sugar production until a devastating flood in 1856 destroyed all the cane he had planted (a disaster for many other settlers). His brother David joined him and over subsequent years he sponsored at least thirty family members as settlers. By 1860 he had established the Caledonian Foundry in Durban, where he advertised his brass and iron castings, ship repairs and bell founding. He was described 'as a sterling, hard-working Scotchman'. He served on the Durban town council and conducted comparative tests on British and Natal coal. Surprisingly, he went back into sugar and died a horrible death when he fell into a pan of boiling juice. John Gray (1827–1900), probably from Glasgow, was a tidewaiter and weigher in the Customs department, and later a storekeeper and sugar planter. He brought out up to ten relatives in the later 1850s. He was president of the Durban Building Society and treasurer of the Regatta, but despite these signs of prosperity he subsequently became insolvent and left Natal.

As well as these family networks, it is noticeable that many emigrants established beneficial settler networks on board ship. For example, the farmer A. Macnab seems to have employed labourers on his farm who had all been emigrants on the *Conquering Hero*. Another group of Scottish friends, who had met on the *Aliwal* from London in December 1849, settled on a farm near Durban and produced oats, potatoes, beans and other crops for the town's market. There James Bell, born in Cramond Bridge in 1828, the son of a hand-loom weaver who had become a quarryman, was joined by his friend John Smith (these two had originally intended to go to Australia but had stopped off in Natal) and fellow passengers George Haigh, Robert Morrison, James Patullo and (later) Frank Patullo. Bell also traded with Zululand and later went to work at the Umzinto Lodge sugar estate of James Arbuthnot.

It is tempting to imagine that Scots had a high reputation as hardworking, go-getting settlers but, as we shall see, the success stories can readily be countered by the record of 'ne'er-do-wells'. Moreover, some of the successes met their nemesis in the trade downturn of the 1860s, when there were a number of insolvencies. Archibald Ferguson (b. Stornoway, 1826) was a wheelwright and waggon builder who was an active freemason and a member of the Durban town council, becoming acting mayor. He was insolvent in 1863 and seems to have moved out of Natal into the South African Republic. John Brown (1824–83) from Saltcoats, arrived in 1850 and opened a general store in Durban. He bought up various town blocs, became a commission agent, and then director and chairman of the Commercial & Agricultural Bank of Natal. Other directorships followed, and he was also agent for the Union Steamship Company. He opened stores in Pietermaritzburg and Ladysmith. He was a JP and captain of the Durban Rifle Guard. By the 1860s he was worth a lot of money and had valuable properties. But his finances were complex and overstretched. The economic problems of the 1860s duly hit him hard.

Success stories

An instance of extraordinary upward social mobility which reveals the opportunities afforded settlers is the career of James Ellis. Ellis (1806–87), from Blackford, in Perthshire, was a worker on the Lynedoch estate of Baron Lynedoch of Balgowan. He considered his emigrant's land grant of 105 acres to be 'equal if not superior to any Lynedoch'. Within a year of his arrival in 1849 he bought a 3,000 acre farm thirty miles from Pietermaritzburg for £150. He may have been enabled to do this through pooling resources with three sisters who had arrived in Natal.³³ This farm was known by the Afrikaans name Wilde Als Spruit, but he divided his section into two blocks and named them Lynedoch and Balgowan.³⁴ His smirk of satisfaction may well be imagined. Thomas Duff was certainly impressed by his 'farm, or rather an estate' when he encountered him. But Ellis had other jobs too. He was overseer of roads, later 'Street keeper and Overseer of Public Works', and also became a notable bridge builder. In 1865 he was postmaster of Fort Nottingham in the Natal Midlands. He was active in the Congregational Church and on his death left a number of legacies to Scottish charities as well as to relatives who had stayed at home. It is clear from this that he wished to reassert his identity and broadcast the manner in which he had, through colonial settlement, moved from humble estate worker to an estate owner himself. But his multifarious activities, as with other settlers, make it apparent how difficult it was to make money from the land alone.

Walter Brunton (1825–76) was from Peeblesshire, arrived as a steerage passenger in 1852 and became a lime burner, boatbuilder, merchant and shipowner. Although he did not take up his settler's land grant, he subsequently acquired 1,000 acres and also began to plant sugar on another block of land near the coast. He owned vessels which made voyages to Mauritius and Melbourne; he set out to establish a business in the eastern Transvaal goldfields (it was not a success) and he opened the Prince of Wales Hotel in Durban. He sat on the Durban town council and was a director of the Natal Printing Company. The *Natal Witness* described him as one of the foremost among the 'Scotch clique' which should more correctly be called 'the working men of Durban'. This was clearly intended as a compliment, but the article could have been written by a Scot! Brunton also stood surety for a number of the members of his family as settlers. Peter Cormac Sutherland (1822–1900), from Caithness, had an extraordinarily adventurous career before becoming influential in Natal. His parents had emigrated to Nova Scotia but returned to Scotland after they had been disappointed by prospects there. Sutherland became a medical student at Aberdeen and also went to sea as a medical officer on Aberdeen whalers. He made two voyages to the Arctic on Franklin expeditions, which helped to give him a reputation as a scientist and geologist. George Barrow, of the Colonial Office, advised him to go to Natal, where he became government geologist in 1854. He set up a geological survey, pursued interests in botany and natural history, and was surveyor-general from 1855 until 1887. As a doctor he also chaired the committee which granted permission to practise in Natal. He designed the layout of various Natal towns and opposed the granting of Responsible Government.³⁵

Other notable success stories included the brothers Buchanan. Their activities in primary education will be examined in the next chapter, and David Dale Buchanan's role in the Natal press has already been noticed in Chapter 3. As well as being a newspaper proprietor and editor David (1819–74) owned a printing, bookbinding and stationery shop; he was also an advocate who was, at one stage, acting attorney-general and a member of the Executive Council. As a sort of Natal version of John Fairbairn, he was a founder of the Natal Fire Assurance & Trust Company, was attorney to the Natal Bank and founded the Natal Political Association. He reported on master–servant relations and on emigration. He also helped form the Immigration Aid Society to help needy immigrants. Always a controversialist, he regarded Lieutenant-governor Pine as a tyrant and was opposed to many of the policies of Theophilus Shepstone. Like Fairbairn, he fought libel actions. He became a member of the legislative council, and acted as an adviser to the Sotho king Moshesh, fiercely taking the Sotho side when the treaty of Aliwal North handed over a large tract of their territory to the Orange Free State. His older brother Ebenezer (1812–97) also became a lawyer (after time as clerk in David's office) and served on the Pietermaritzburg town council, as town clerk, treasurer, market master and later Registrar of Births, Marriages and Deaths. He held the government contract for the control and sale of gunpowder. He owned a property which was named Haddington after his birthplace. The Buchanans were active Congregationalists.

It is noticeable that some of the early settlers maintained social and economic connections with 'home'. James Blackwood (1824–99) arrived in Natal in 1850, and formed a partnership with a fellow passenger to open a store. Successful, he started a new partnership as importers, exporters and general merchants in association with William Couper, a merchant, of Glasgow. Blackwood moved back and forth, remarrying in Glasgow in 1859, and the company erected a fine two-storey establishment in Durban. He became one of the first town councillors and was active in the Presbyterian Church. Robert Carruthers, who has already been mentioned as falsifying his occupation, moved back and forth between the family printing business in Inverness and his work in Pietermaritzburg. He also visited Australia, and died in Inverness. Alexander (1825–66) and David (1828–1905) Forbes were employed in the family timber business in Pitlochry, but their business was ruined when a ship they owned, bringing timber from the Baltic, sank, uninsured, in the North Sea. The two brothers sailed for Natal on the *Unicorn*. They were good shots and became hunters and traders, later farmers. They never lost contact with Scotland: one called his farm Killiecrankie; the other called his Athole or Atholl. As a result of his travels it was David who advised Alexander McCorkindale (the uncle of his wife) to establish New Scotland to the west of Swaziland (see below). Forbes also dabbled in diamonds, gold and coal. Connections with Scotland were facilitated by journeys 'home': more prosperous settlers took advantage of steam and reduced journey times over migrant sail.

Some of the migrants arrived in a fairly prosperous condition. Archibald Murray, the son of a Paisley stationer, was able to buy no fewer than 3,000 acres and was effectively the founder of the village of Pinetown, not far inland from Durban. When the Rev. Charles Scott arrived, Murray invited him to Pinetown to minister to the Scots settlers there. John and Walter Macfarlane were from Highland gentry stock, who briefly farmed before entering the administration and politics. John became a magistrate and a highly unpopular (among Africans) native administrator. Walter entered the legislative council when it was established in 1856, and became its second speaker after Donald Moodie. By 1858 he was in opposition (for his influence on 'native policy' see below).[36] Another Macfarlane relative, G. J., became mayor of Pietermaritzburg, where a number of Scots served on the town council.[37] Hugh Maclean, laird of Coll, who had fallen seriously into debt after buying estates on Mull, sent many of his tenantry to the United States and contemplated sending more to Natal in 1849. He despatched his two sons, Alexander and William, to buy land. A sugar estate was purchased and a few tenants emigrated, but the number seems to have been small.

Some passed through and failed to settle. Among the wealthy who pitched up in Natal was John Shedden Dobie (1819–1903), from Beith, in Ayrshire. He was from a comfortably-off background (his father was a lawyer-landowner) and was intended for the law, but he threw over his studies for a life of adventure. He even studied veterinary science with Professor Thomas Dick at Edinburgh, and, as a lover of all things equine, attended the Eglinton tournament in 1839. He kicked around the world, to Australia, Gottland, California, Samoa and back to Victoria, where he became a land holder. But in 1862, after land legislation that disadvantaged him, he headed for Natal, spent time in Durban and Pietermaritzburg, and went into sheep. But a number of diseases, including foot rot, blue tongue and heart water, defeated his efforts, and in 1866 he left for South America. He returned to his small Ayrshire estate, which he had now inherited, in 1870. His historical significance lies in the fact that he kept a journal while in Natal, and it offers a snapshot of the state of the colony in these years, together with information on many of its leading white settler citizens.[38]

Ne'er-do-wells

But Scots migrants were far from being uniformly hard-working and successful. Peter Davidson (b. 1814), joined the Royal Navy and was discharged in Cape Town. He may have been involved in laying out the grounds of Admiralty House in Simonstown, and moved on to Natal in 1847. There he supervised the settlement of Germans brought out by the Jung & Bergtheil company to 'New Germany' and was the company's farm manager. He was regarded as a skilful agriculturalist, particularly interested in developing cotton. He tried to develop a Scottish settlement, but drink was his undoing and he became known as 'Drunken Davidson'. John Duff Doig, born 1817 in Perthshire, was a labourer, bricklayer and builder who was regarded as a good tradesman but was imprisoned for outrageous and violent conduct. The career of James Cleghorn, who arrived in Natal in 1844 and was a pioneer cotton grower, is instructive as illustrating the rough-and-ready arrangements and often unsuitable appointments on a colonial frontier. Having been a seller of firewood in Pietermaritzburg, he became a clerk in Shepstone's office. As a result he was appointed assistant magistrate in the Umvoti location, partly because he had good language skills. He was, however, utterly inadequate for the post and was soon exposed as conducting his own extra-legal retribution. He was frequently in a 'pitiable state of intoxication'. He was dismissed and embarked on a number of financial disagreements with the administration.

Andrew Ferrier (1830–68) sailed on the *Ina* as servant to Captain Alexander Gordon. He settled on a farm at New Glasgow on the Umhloti River and took over a farm, Glenside, running to 2,715 acres. But he was an inveterate drinker, ended up in prison and sold his farm in 1865. He moved to New Scotland in the Transvaal and died there soon afterwards. Alexander Forbes (1816–89) was from Aberdeen and was another heavy drinker. He was a baker who was in Cape Town by 1845, when he was married to Margaret Stewart Lyell (1827–99). Convicted of drunkenness, he and his wife left for Natal in 1847. He established the Port Natal Baking Establishment, but his drinking turned ugly when he began to beat Margaret. What happened next reveals the vulnerability of a wife facing this kind of abuse. By 1850 she could take no more, left Forbes and took her children to live with William Slack. Later she left Slack and lived with a soldier of the 45th Regiment, G. A. Rafter. She had no fewer than twelve children with Rafter. Facing financial problems, she became a laundress and a seamstress. She also, disastrously, became wet nurse for the baby of one Alexander Anderson for a payment of £2 10s a month. The payments soon stopped and the baby was abandoned with her. She sought redress, but without much success. Meanwhile Forbes went from bad to worse. He was described as an 'ill-conditioned little Scot', a 'drunken and dissipated character', usually covered with bruises and wounds from drunken brawls, and a disgrace to the Durban Volunteer Guard, of which he was a member. Interestingly, one of his submissions in the divorce case, which he instituted, was his resentment that Margaret was bringing up his children as Catholics. Rafter was presumably an Irish Catholic and Margaret's adherence to her partner's (later, husband's) Church caused domestic sectarianism to surface in Natal.

Women and entrepreneurship

Margaret Forbes tried to sustain herself by taking in laundry and sewing. We have already seen how Jane Smith became an entrepreneur with her own laundry. Other women took over their husband's job or set up their own business. Jane Arbuthnot, after her husband's death and financial difficulties, established herself as a carter, conveying sugar to Durban. The details of the wife of Thomas Clouston (born on Bute in 1809) are not known, but in the 1890s she became postmistress of Fort Nottingham, a post previously held by her husband and her father. John Fleming (1822–1902), from Strathaven in Lanarkshire, was a carpenter and builder who became mayor of Pietermaritzburg. He married Anne Shackelton, who was already established as a milliner. Her two sisters joined her and also set up in the millinery business. By the later nineteenth century many Scots women must have been employed in such clothing trades, often as proprietors, throughout southern Africa. Scots women must also have been involved in prostitution, a relatively hidden phenomenon, since prosecution was apparently rare. We do know of a Scottish woman called Catherine Wood who, in the earlier decade of 1840–50, had many convictions for prostitution at the Cape.[39] More must have been driven into the same trade later in the century. But whether sex working represents enterprise or oppression remains a matter of some controversy. Still, a great deal remains to be done in these areas of the writing of the history of women.

White population and later settlements

Population figures for this period are elusive, but by the late 1850s it would seem that there were about 8,000 whites in Natal and as many as 200,000 Africans (that is, not including the considerable population to the north in Zululand).[40] Other figures suggest that there 14,000 whites in 1863 and some 150,000 blacks.[41] Thus the proportion of whites varied from 4 per cent to 9 per cent during this period, a tiny proportion compared with that of the Cape. By the time of the first systematic census of Natal, in 1904, the African population, now including Zululand, was almost a million.[42] The Indian population (Indian migrants had arrived to work on the sugar plantations and build the railway lines) was eventually in excess of the number of whites. Thus, until well into the twentieth century, the number of Natal whites was small, and this fostered their sense of threat. For them the irony was that, despite the large preponderance of blacks, they were unable to secure all the labour they wanted. From the earliest days of the colony the 'native policy' (closely identified with the 'agent' and later Secretary of Native Affairs, Sir Theophilus Shepstone) was the confinement of Africans upon reasonably extensive reserves, controlled by a form of indirect rule through supposedly traditional (but sometimes invented) chiefs and headmen. Inevitably, settlers were not happy with this policy. They wanted to see the reserves reduced, with Africans forced out into what they saw as the modernising (and presumed liberalising) labour market. Thus administrative policy towards Africans should be almost entirely geared to the requirements of the white-led economy. This view was strongly expressed by a commission to offer advice on 'native policy' set up by the Lieutenant-governor in 1852 and reporting in 1854. It was of course made up entirely of whites, a mixture of Afrikaners and British. Among them was Walter Macfarlane, who later became a strong critic and leader of the anti-Shepstone faction on the legislative council. No doubt Scots represented many opinions on the nature of colonial administration, but some not only identified themselves with settler policies but also led the assault upon officialdom. Nevertheless, Shepstone's policy by and large survived. Colonial policy was devoted to raising the number of whites.

As we have seen, between 1858 and 1866 efforts were made to bring out friends and relatives of existing settlers, with a proportion of the cost of the passage provided and grants of land reintroduced. (They were discontinued in 1869.) Under this scheme some 1,580 settlers were introduced to the colony. In the early 1870s there were fresh efforts to promote emigration. The (English) astronomer and meteorologist Dr Robert James Mann, formerly the Superintendent of Education, was appointed Special Emigration Commissioner for the Natal government, and he published an *Emigrants' Guide* in 1873.[43] This stressed the availability of land and castigated Boer profligacy. Mann claimed that the Byrne settlement had disproved the Afrikaner notion that a farm was uneconomic if it were smaller than 6,000 acres.

Natal was only half-way to Australia, and its alleged blessings were forcibly laid out. He also stressed the great growth in the sugar industry and the ease of reaching the colony. In the twenty years since the Byrne scheme, transport had been revolutionised. Many sailing ships (for example, those of John T. Rennie, originally of Aberdeen, and Bullard & King) still made the voyage in sailing times of fifty-two to ninety days. But by then there was also a twice-monthly Union Line steamship service from Southampton, carrying the mails. The cost of steamship second class was virtually the same as sailing ship cabin, although sailing steerage by sail was a good deal cheaper.[44] The size of steamships and marine engine technology had advanced rapidly. The first mail contract to the Cape in the 1850s had specified forty-two days, not a massive saving on good sailing ship times. The small ships of the Union Line did not progress beyond Cape Town at that time, and passenger numbers were virtually insignificant. The mail service was extended to Durban in 1863, and by 1876 the mails ships were required to reach the Cape in twenty-six days. By the time that diamond discoveries were beginning to feed their galvanising effects into the southern African economy, getting there had become a great deal easier and more comfortable.

Nevertheless, James and Helen McIntosh, who arrived in Natal in 1869, travelled by sailing vessel and took three months on the voyage.[45] McIntosh had started a business in Ayr in 1866, but soon decided to emigrate. They took up a farm, but found that it did not pay. McIntosh then moved into transport riding, with a 'fleet' of eighteen waggons and 400 oxen, initially travelling to the Free State and the goldfields at Barberton, later to the Transvaal and even Delagoa Bay. He built up a number of businesses, including a wattle farm, his stock farm (and transport headquarters) 'Breadalbane', near Ladysmith, and a wholesale business in Durban. He soon possessed a number of Durban properties, including a public house. He had a business in Lourenço Marques, and was associated with another in Johannesburg. He placed his sons and a son-in-law in the management of each of these enterprises and was extremely rich when he died at an advanced age in 1925.

Of those who arrived from the early 1870s one of the most interesting was Charles John Smythe (1852–1918).[46] He was the grandson of Lord Methven and grew up in Methven Castle, near Perth. Through his mother he was related, by marriage, to the Earls of Elgin. He was attracted by the prospects of sugar farming and emigrated to Natal in 1872, but he moved on to prospect for gold in the eastern Transvaal. Eventually he settled as a stock farmer at Nottingham Road, north-west of Pietermaritzburg. He married the daughter of another

Perthshire man, Margaret King. She had developed a considerable knowledge of stock on her father's farm and contributed a fair amount to Smythe's success. In a classic Scottish echo, they named their farm Strathearn, and Smythe soon became a major figure in the community. In 1893 he entered the Natal legislative assembly on the granting of Responsible Government. By 1897 he was speaker and two years later he became colonial secretary (second to the Governor). Between 1905 and 1906 he was the Premier of Natal, but not even his kinship with the Colonial Secretary, Elgin, could save him after the Zulu Bambatha revolt. His government's poll tax had been its immediate cause, and he resigned in protest against courts martial and executions conducted by the imperial troops. This was a jurisdictional dispute rather than a humanitarian one. He was a representative at the National Convention discussing Union (the Natal representatives' effort to promote the alternative of federation failed) and became the first Administrator of Natal after Union (1910–17).[47]

Of the many places in Natal that were given Scottish names, few were more important than Dundee. Such naming policies were, as we have seen, fairly common. A Scots surveyor named one farm in the Biggarsberg (just north of Dundee) 'Cundy Cleugh'. Another district farther south became Camperdown, presumably after the estate and district of Dundee which commemorated Admiral Duncan's victory off the Dutch coast. These allusions to an alien geography represented the inscription of white affiliations upon the landscape, the efforts of settlers to create a space which seemed familiar and friendly, and equally a symbol of possession by whites and of dispossession for blacks. Renaming has become a hot topic in modern South Africa, but the founders of Dundee had no idea that their actions would ultimately be so controversial. The region lay in a sort of empty triangle north of the Tukhela River, a no-man's-land with a light black population, in neither Afrikaner- nor British-settled territory, even if it technically belonged to the latter. It was subject to raiding by both the Swazi and the Sotho, while Zululand was very close. There were some Boer farmers there; a few British settlers arrived in the 1850s, and two Edinburgh-trained doctors (Prideaux Selby, of Alnwick, and John Robson, from Hawick) took up residence. From 1860 a family from Scotland's Dundee began to arrive.[48]

Thomas Paterson Smith reached Natal in 1855 after five years on the Victoria goldfields in Australia. He took over a 3,000 acre farm and named it Dundee. He was soon joined by a younger brother, Peter (1828–1911), with his wife, Ann (1824–1908), and family.[49] The Smiths became involved in brick making, building, tree felling in the Cundy Cleugh, as well as building up a herd of South Devon cattle and a flock of merino sheep. Their fortunes improved when they began to exploit a seam of coal discovered on the slope of Talana Hill.[50] When the scale of the seam became more obvious Peter sent for Cornish miners. Other seams were worked by Peter's son and his son-in-law, Dugald Macphail (from Inveraray, Argyll, landed in Natal in 1864), and soon a town began to grow up.[51] Nearby mining centres were Coalfield and Glencoe. The Dundee Coal Company was founded in 1885 and agitated for an extension of the Natal Government Railways (NGR). Dundee became a significant place, with notable public buildings, a Caledonian Society, a Presbyterian church, and boasting many Scots concerts and dances. William Craighead Smith, Peter's son, lived in a substantial house called 'Balgray', while Dugald Macphail built 'Craigside'.[52] When a weekly newspaper was founded it was called the *Dundee and District Courier* (the Scottish equivalent is also the *Dundee Courier*).

The Anglo-Zulu War sent the inhabitants into laager and resulted in the deaths of some of its male inhabitants, but it also produced boom conditions for the town. Then in 1882 Peter Smith invited a Dundonian mining engineer, William Maconochie,[53] to emigrate to Natal and the coal mines of the area were soon producing four-fifths of the total coal output of the colony. The Anglo-Boer War was much more serious for the town. An early British defeat took place at Talana Hill on Smith lands (Peter and Ann's home became a dressing station) and the Transvaal Afrikaners occupied the town for eight months. The celebrated siege of Ladysmith took place a short distance away. But after the lifting of the siege Dundee began to boom. There continued to be problems: local Africans were often discontented with the white presence, and the Zulu Bambatha tax revolt of 1906 was sufficiently close to cause alarm. Cattle stocks (it is good cattle country) were devastated by East Coast Fever.[54] Nevertheless, the Dundee Coal Company (which had several Scots directors) continued to flourish. It has been said that 'hard and canny Scots' virtually monopolised the managerial positions: examples included Jock Ferguson, Robert Campbell and Jimmy Watson (who appropriately came from the Scottish Dundee).[55] Welsh, Cornish and English miners worked at the lower levels, often supervising black labour. Today the Talana Museum preserves the history of the Natal 'Coalopolis' and commemorates the Boer War battle. A cemetery contains the gravestones of its Scots founders[56] and the houses of Peter and William Smith have been restored.

The gold boom from the 1880s produced notable spin-off economic growth for Natal. Durban and Pietermaritzburg flourished. The railway line into the South African Republic became important, and the Durban harbour works were developed considerably. Scots masons and carpenters seem to have been greatly valued in the colony.[57] In 1889 a recruiter called Walter Peace, the Natal government agent, was active in Scotland engaging masons for the NGR, under the supervision of the resident engineer. Peace held a meeting at a granite yard in Aberdeen, attended by 100 masons. Within a month the *Aberdeen Journal* reported that fifty of them had left for Natal, and they were followed by another fourteen.[58] Peace's requests for advertising, travel and agency expenses connected with the 'engagement of the Scotch masons' are in the KwaZulu Natal archives. One of his bills was for £588 to the Union Steamship Company for the passages of these 'Scotch stone masons'.[59] Peace was also actively recruiting joiners and sent out forty to Natal for public works, including the railway to Johannesburg. The Durban Harbour Board was employing many Scottish carpenters. A wonderful letter of complaint survives from an Englishman who chose to sign himself 'John Bull'.[60] He had been taken on as a carpenter in March 1890 but claimed that he was one of fifteen or twenty who were discharged to make way for twenty tradesmen shipped out from Scotland. Why, he demanded to know, is it that only 'Scotchmen' get work with the Harbour Board and also with the Carriages Department, while Englishmen are outsiders here? Is this 'a Scotch Colony or an English one'? Moreover the Scots received higher wages, and the writer lamented the fact that he had not a 'Mc' on his name. He also complained of the iniquities of a Scots foreman who spent his time fishing off the North Pier.

The boom also helped Scottish exports. It was said that it was cheaper to import iron balconies than to make them locally, and that most such balconies in Pietermaritzburg came from Glasgow.[61] In 1891 Durban harbour received a successful tender for a sand pump hopper steamer to be built at William Simons of Renfrew.[62] The engineer-in-chief of the Harbour Board at the time (he held the office from 1888 to 1895) was Cathcart W. Methven (1849–1925), born in Portobello.[63] This raises the question whether Scots in prominent positions took their orders to familiar suppliers in Scotland, or whether they were simply considered to be the cheapest and the best (cheapest perhaps because of the relatively low wages offered to Scots workers at the time). It is certainly the case that many of the locomotives for the NGR came from Dübs & Co. of Glasgow and the first locomotive superintendent had been a Scot called Milne. Later the celebrated general manager of the railways, Sir David Hunter, was convinced of the superiority of Scots in all railway matters.[64] He imported a brother to fill a senior managerial position. Dübs was so powerful that it had its own agent in the colony, a Mr Lorimer. When enormous pressure was put on capacity during the Anglo-Boer War a local Scots engineer called Reid built engines locally to a modified Dübs design. These were subject to a large number of derailments, and members of the Natal legislative council began to complain of a Scots conspiracy which ran the railways, and not very effectively. At the same time Hunter embarked on propaganda by founding the NGR Lecture and Debating Society: he gave the inaugural lecture himself and extolled the virtues of Scots engineering. The controversy was stoked up when in 1902 the railway workers went on strike over pay and conditions.[65] If the railway employers, hostile to unions, were often Scots, it is also the case that the unofficial Labour member of the Natal legislature who strongly supported the strike was William McLarty (1858–1940), born in Arran and a successful businessman.[66] Scots continued to dominate many railway engineering and managerial posts. Reid's successor was David Hendrie (1861–1940), who was born in Inverness and had experience on the Highland Railway and with Dübs. He was locomotive superintendent of the NGR between 1903 and 1910; he designed both engines and carriages to be constructed locally, inspiring the admiration of Smuts. If he encouraged local industrialisation, he imported many components from Scotland.

Many notable Scots in the sugar industry took their orders for sugar-processing machinery to Scottish firms. One of the most noted sugar pioneers, Sir Marshall Campbell (1848–1917, from Glasgow) arrived in Natal with his parents in 1850. Campbell managed the Muckle Neuk sugar mill and moved on to the Aberfoyle, Umhloti and other estates. His brother Samuel Campbell (1861–1927) was born at Muckle Neuk and was the founder of the Natal Technical College. Marshall floated his Natal Sugar Estates in 1895,[67] made a large fortune and inevitably moved into directorships, including the press. He became a member of the Natal Assembly and, after the Anglo-Boer War, served on the Imperial Boundary Commission and the South African Native Commission. He consulted Gandhi and Gokhale about the difficulties of Indians in Natal, and was opposed to further Indian immigration. He claimed that he had all the African labour he needed and had no requirement for indentured Indians.[68] Labour needs could be satisfied by whites and blacks.

Scots were clearly influential in key sectors of the Natal economy, but the question arises how far this was reflected in white population figures. The Natal census of 1904[69] offers a breakdown of the birthplaces of non-colonial-born whites, who constituted almost half the total at that time. Of these, 25,891 had been born in England and Wales, 8,704 in Scotland and 2,229 in Ireland. There were considerable numbers born in Germany (1,917) and in Norway and Sweden

(1,342), with no fewer than 2,861 born in Australia. The latter figure reflected the demographic relationship between the colony and Australia. Many migrants dropped off in Natal, while others travelled from Australia when the mining and sugar sectors grew considerably. Many of these 'Australians' may well have had some aspects of a Scottish identity in their make-up. But, leaving these to one side, Natal, a colony often thought to be distinctly 'English' in tone, actually had one in four of its (non-Irish) British-born population from Scotland, that is, at least double what it should have been in terms of relative home populations. Even the figure of those born in the Cape Colony, 6,384, was smaller than that for Scotland. There were almost 4,000 whites of Scots birth in Durban; over 1,300 in Pietermaritzburg, while the figures for such settlements as Dundee, Newcastle (another coal-mining centre) and Ladysmith in the north of the colony revealed an even higher proportion of Scots. These figures do not of course take account of second-generation colonial-born 'Scots', who may well have still identified themselves with aspects of Scots ethnicity, culture and religion. If we turn to the religious breakdown, almost 13 per cent of the white population (roughly one in seven) were adherents of the Presbyterian Church, together with the Free Church, the United Free and the Church of Scotland. The Dutch Reformed Church produced a figure of 11.5 per cent and the Church of England (and presumably Episcopalians) 39 per cent. Since the Presbyterians would have been largely Scots or Scots descendants in ethnicity, we again find a Scots component which is out of proportion to that of the relative populations within the United Kingdom. And there would have been a fair number of Scots in other denominations. Thus the colony of Natal experienced disproportionate migrations of Scots.

Immigration to the Cape

In the same period there continued to be a steady stream of settlers at the Cape. The archives of the Secretary to the Immigration Boards at Cape Town and Port Elizabeth in the late 1850s and early 1860s offer a great deal of information on immigration on specific ships. These records often contain names, places of origin, occupations, prospective employers and even potential pay of the immigrants. These are just a few representative examples. In May 1858 397 Scots arrived on the *Gipsy Bride*, no fewer than 234 from Lanarkshire and eighty-six from Dumfriesshire. The occupations profile of these reveals thirty-three trades, with no fewer than seventy stonemasons, twenty-five joiners and carpenters, thirteen general labourers and ten farm labourers, with handfuls of quarrymen and millwrights. Many of the single women were arriving as domestic servants.[70] In this period there is little indication that white immigrants were competing with black labour, at least at the Cape itself. The *Lord Raglan*, arriving in September 1859, carried 172 Scots, 151 of them from Forfarshire. The *Matilda Atheling*, arriving the previous month, similarly had a high proportion (thirty-seven out of fifty-nine) from the Forfar area. The Scots on another ship, the *Wellington*, arriving in February 1860, came mainly from Aberdeen and Edinburgh. Fewer Scots seemed to arrive in Port Elizabeth.[71] In 1860 the *Aberdeen Journal* announced the appointment of Alexander Bruce as local agent for assisted emigration to the Cape. He organised the emigration of some thirty migrants and in 1831 left himself with a further fifteen. Matrons' diaries also survive from vessels sent out by the British Ladies' Female Emigration Society between 1860 and 1880, but these seem to have contained relatively few Scots.[72]

There were, moreover, recruitment schemes for particular occupations. Many Cape police were recruited in Scotland, though they were bitterly disliked because they did not speak Afrikaans. They were also displeased with the work, staying only briefly, complaining of the arduous duties and poor pay. In 1872 half the force decamped for the diamond fields, indicating yet again migrant mobility within the colony.[73] Meanwhile, further attempts to encourage agricultural migration to the Cape in the late 1870s and early 1880s were surrounded by controversy. In 1873 an emigration agent was appointed to work in London and British immigration was financed by the sale of Crown land. In 1877 Scottish migrants arrived on several ships to take up land in the Eastern Cape, on the Kei River. Some 361 Scots arrived from eastern, central and southern Scotland to settle the frontier, as in 1820, though now extended farther east. As usual, the migrants' hopes were largely dashed. The promised quality of the land was hopelessly optimistic; access was difficult; the East London inhabitants and press were not happy, on the grounds that the new migrants were not of the appropriate type; and the settlers arrived in time for the final frontier war. Further attempts were made in 1880, when 105 Scots arrived, and 1881, when plans were laid for the recruitment of a further 300. But the Kei River settlement was a failure, reflecting again the problems of planned agricultural settlement at the Cape.[74]

New Scotland

By the 1850s, when the geopolitical pattern of South Africa had been largely established, with two colonies and two republics, many white immigrants used the Cape and Natal as staging posts before heading into the interior. These settlers exhibited little desire to cling to the imperial nurse and were happy to head for the Boer republics if opportunities for land or, more likely, commercial and career advancement could be found there. As we shall see, many Scots turned up in the Transvaal and, to a lesser extent, the Orange Free State, well before they were sucked in by the mineral revolution and the great gold boom. But as well as hard-headed, go-getting individuals there were also some wildly unscrupulous people and madly ambitious schemes about. The sense of limitless opportunity for whites in southern Africa in the period seemed to stimulate these hopelessly illusory plans. Such a one was the grandly named New Scotland. This project turned out to be as fiercely unpractical as it was ludicrously speculative. It was hatched by Alexander McCorkindale, who was born in Glasgow in 1816.[75] He was probably a commercial traveller for Glasgow and Paisley firms making machinery for cotton mills, and this gave him a clear idea about downturns in the cotton industry.[76] Early in 1856 McCorkindale set out for Natal with his English wife and a party of relatives and twenty-two boys from a reformatory who were apprenticed to him.[77] He used his capital to settle at a place on the Senquasi or Sinkwazi River, close to Zululand, with the intention of growing cotton. But he was soon restless. He dreamt of establishing a new settlement and approached, in turn, the Orange Free State and the Transvaal to secure blocks of farms upon which he could settle fellow Scots. As we have seen, he was related by marriage to another Scot, David Forbes, a hunter and trader in Natal since 1850. He claimed that the area to the west of the Swazi border (the boundary of Swaziland had only recently been 'established' through a land grab, dressed up as a concession from a Swazi chief) had affinities with Scotland, and in 1864 he proposed to McCorkindale that it might be an ideal place to settle Scots. McCorkindale was soon fired by the idea and formed a company, the London & South African Commercial Agricultural & Mining Company, which later became the Glasgow & South African Company. Although they never progressed beyond a merely shadowy existence, he applied to the Transvaal government for 200 farms at £40 each (at this stage to be located throughout the Transvaal) on which to settle immigrants. McCorkindale suggested that he would bring in farmers, mechanics, traders and miners. To convince the republic's authorities of his commitment, he became a Transvaal burgher the same year. By then he was concentrating on the New Scotland territory.

Fortunately for McCorkindale, he had already become known to President Pretorius, who supported the scheme. From the point of view of the Transvaal this was a proposed settlement which had some parallels with that of 1820 at the Cape. The Swazi border was disputed and turbulent. By settling it with farmers capable of bearing arms the republic would consolidate its hold on the region and have a ready-made commando available to repulse Swazi inroads. But McCorkindale went further. He proposed that he could make the River Usutu navigable and would be able to provide an outlet for the Transvaal through Delagoa Bay. This was a dearly cherished ambition of the landlocked republic, at a time when Portugal's claim to that area of southern Mozambique had not been fully confirmed. Pretorius himself paid a visit to Pietermaritzburg in 1866 to facilitate the settlement and to induce the colony to relax duties on goods associated with the scheme. The administration refused and Pretorius was even more convinced that his republic required an independent outlet to the sea. As well as producing an ambitious harbour scheme, McCorkindale claimed that he was founding a commercial bank able to lend the Transvaal as much as £250,000. This was too good to be true for the struggling republic. McCorkindale returned to Britain in 1865 to set about raising capital and recruiting migrants, taking with him Pretorius's daughter, Christina, who wished to see Europe. McCorkindale was barely successful in raising money or men, though he did bring out some of his own relatives and persuaded some Scots in Natal to move to New Scotland. In September 1866 the *Times of Natal* reported that fifty families associated with McCorkindale were about to leave the Noodsberg area of the colony for their new homes in the Transvaal.[78]

Not the least of the shady aspects of the scheme was McCorkindale's claim that he had secured extra land from the Swazi. This was fictional. It is not surprising that Africans on the putative border described McCorkindale as 'Gwenya', the Crocodile, a perfect image of a predator swimming in shallow waters. Nevertheless, the company acquired forty farms at £40 each and some fifty people settled near a lake which was called Chrissie to flatter Pretorius's daughter. The three districts of New Scotland were named Industria, Roburnia[79] and Londina South. McCorkindale set up his headquarters at a place he called Loch Banagher, but he became a victim of his own ambition in 1871 when he died of malaria at Delagoa Bay while conducting a survey for his harbour. His will was as unpractical as his schemes had been and he left behind financial complications that occupied his widow for the rest of her life.[80] The Transvaal soon repudiated his schemes, and some of the Boers who participated in the notorious filibustering commando into Zululand in 1884 claimed that their farms had been expropriated by the Transvaal government and the estate of McCorkindale. This commando, which sought to put Dinizulu on the Zulu throne, defeat a rival faction and acquire major land for itself, seems to have been made up of a mixture of these disaffected Transvaal farmers, richer elements seeking to extend their land holdings, some Germans, and settlers from Natal, a few of whom may have had Scottish connections. They established the 'New Republic', based on Vryheid, incorporated into the Transvaal in 1888 and handed over to Natal after the Anglo-Boer War.[81]

One of the earliest maps of the Transvaal, produced by Friedrich Jeppe and A. Merensky, clearly demarcates New Scotland, with the township or farm of Hamilton prominently shown.[82] The names of Scots continue to flit in and out of the history of the region for some time.[83] Jeppe[84] published a very useful almanac in 1877, in which some of the New Scotland officials are listed.[85] McCorkindale himself had been appointed *veldcornet* of New Scotland. Later there was a magistrate and native commissioner called Robert Bell, who commanded the Border Corps (its secretary was R. Stewart) and was involved in a commando against the Swazi in 1876. Bell was later murdered. A settler called E. J. Buchanan applied to take over his role. A schools commission was established for the area, initially under the chairmanship of Bell, and later of S. T. Erskine, the government land surveyor.[86] After McCorkindale's death J. S. Aitken came out from Glasgow to administer New Scotland on behalf of the company. A New Scotland Farmers' Association was formed which set up an agricultural co-operative society. But the turbulence of the area was well illustrated when disputes over cattle ownership broke out.[87] Moreover, it was alleged that Boers were crossing the Swazi border in order to cut timber, for this was a well wooded region and sawmills had been established. (Mrs McCorkindale attempted to capitalise on this.) But many of the Scots left. A few Scottish names survive to this day, but it is significant that Roburnia was renamed Amsterdam and Hamilton seems to have disappeared from the map. New Scotland, some of it positioned in what should have been Old Swaziland, became a new slice of Afrikanerdom, just as the Baviaans River settlement of 1820 was also largely taken over by Boers. Today what was New Scotland has been subsumed into the Ermelo District of Mpumalanga province.

If the land which Scots supposedly settled was invariably taken over by Afrikaans people, many of the Scots (as in the early 1820s) headed for town, where they were soon performing significant roles in commercial and official life. The Jeppe almanac reveals the extent of Scots penetration of the Transvaal even in the period ahead of the mineral revolution and the gold boom. In the 1870s Pretoria had hotels with the names Edinburgh and Waverley, Lydenberg had a Caledonia

Hotel and Rustenburg had Brown's Temperance Hotel. All these appear to have been run by Scots. Government land surveyors in Pretoria included Peter MacDonald (who listed himself as a chartered engineer), A. H. Walker, W. A. B. Anderson, G. P. Moodie (one of the by now extended Moodie clan), F. McDonald and H. M. Anderson. Leading contractors of the time included Traill (who was an Orcadian) and George MacKenzie (who described himself as stonemason and builder), while merchants, importers, agents and auctioneers have Scottish or Irish names like McLaren, Reid, McCormack, Cruickshank and Macaulay. Although it is dangerous arguing only from name evidence, it is apparent that Afrikaners played a comparatively small role in the non-agricultural sectors of the economy and in government service, where most of the names are those of English-speakers, many of whom may well have been Scots. One of the early prospecting sites of the Transvaal was known as the New Caledonia goldfield. Thus, although specific Scots settlements like that of New Scotland invariably have a whiff of failure about them, there can be little doubt that Scots were highly influential in key areas of the booming Transvaal economy in the later nineteenth century. Scots were also active in the Orange Free State. One migrant from Aberdeenshire, William McKechnie, son of a minister, died in Bloemfontein in 1877 at the age of thirty-eight. Surprisingly, he was already a member of the Volksraad.[88] In subsequent chapters we shall see that this was also true of the professions.

South Africa and the migration boom

The mineral revolution and the ensuing boom, occurring just when Canada and Australasia were economically depressed, stimulated a remarkable migration from Scotland. A sudden rise took place in 1889, and in the 1890s South Africa was the most popular destination for Scots apart from the United States. The first census of the Union of South Africa in 1911 revealed that there were 1,276,242 whites in South Africa. Of these 181,891 were born in the United Kingdom, over 20 per cent of them from Scotland. (The figures for England, Ireland and Wales were 69 per cent, 8 per cent and 2 per cent respectively.)[89] The gender imbalance was pronounced. Of the Scottish-born figure of 37,138, males numbered 24,397 and females 12,741. The distribution in the four provinces was striking. Twenty-six per cent of Scots-born were in the Cape, 19 per cent in Natal, 7 per cent in the Orange Free State and 48 per cent in the Transvaal. There was thus little doubt where the main pull had come from, while the overall Scottish percentage was double what it should have been proportionate to the population of the British Isles. Scots were clearly more likely to migrate to South Africa than the Irish or Welsh. This partly reflects the propensity of Scots to migrate; it also reveals the extent to which colonial authorities in South Africa had set out to recruit Scots for specific professions. It is perhaps no wonder that this period became one in which the various badges of Scots identity, in societies, sports and Presbyterian churches, proliferated (see Chapter 8).

Scots had had another major effect upon the mining boom in the Transvaal. Though the gold deposits there were strikingly extensive, the quality of the ore was very poor. It was soon apparent that older methods of extracting gold, by passing the crushed ore over a mercury bed, would be hopelessly uneconomic. The solution to this difficulty was discovered in a Glasgow laboratory. In 1887 two brother chemists, Robert and William Forrest, working with John S. MacArthur, confirmed the solubility of gold in potassium cyanide. Although the process was also used in Australia, New Zealand and elsewhere, it was particularly applicable on the Rand mines. The process was patented in 1890, but by then it was already in use in the Transvaal. It could be said that this process, together with the great costs of mining at deep levels, ensured that the mines would adopt the cheap labour option, holding the pay of African mine workers down to a virtually irreducible minimum, ensuring that that labour would be migratory and that white labour would be used only for supervisory roles.

There was a fresh burst of migration after the Anglo-Boer War, to such an extent that a north-eastern presbytery was reported in the *Aberdeen Journal* in 1904 as complaining about the number of young men emigrating to South Africa.[90] At the same time there was considerable emigration of women to South Africa, largely under the auspices of the South African Expansion Committee, later known as the South African Colonisation Society. Many of the women were intended for domestic service and were expected, through marriage, to maintain the momentum of the post-war reconstruction and Anglicisation policies. For example, forty Scotswomen were sent to the Transvaal by the *Raglan Castle* in June 1903. Among these were twenty 'cook-generals', five 'good cooks', as well as parlour maids, nurse housemaids, waitresses, a nurse, a nursery governess and a secretary.[91] 'Scotch families' proceeded as assisted emigrants on the same vessel and arrangements were made for wives to follow earlier male migrants. But the boom was relatively short-lived. In late 1903 and early 1904 reports began to appear in the *Edinburgh Evening News* and *The Times* that the migration of women as domestic servants to the Transvaal was proving disastrous. It was alleged that they were being paid lower salaries (£4 per annum) than their black counterparts, and that they were not being taken care of. A substantial correspondence ensued in which the South African Colonisation Society and the Transvaal Immigration Office attempted to refute the charges.[92]

But more significant checks were at work. The South African economy was highly cyclical; the region was already developing major social problems. (As well as the importation of Chinese labour and the drive for greater numbers of black migratory workers, there was a growing corps of rural 'poor whites' and white urban unemployed.) Moreover, as in the past, agricultural settlement failed. One of Milner's schemes was post-war soldier settlement. This was supported by the right-wing Imperial South Africa Association in Britain, various politicians and Rand mining interests. The Scottish dimension was provided by Simon Fraser, Lord Lovat (1871–1933), who had raised the Lovat Scouts from estate workers and others near Beauly. He hoped that some of his men would settle. The young John Buchan, novelist, Tory and future Governor General of Canada, was made secretary of the Land Board. But the scheme was doomed: land had to be bought up at premium rates; the agricultural sector took a serious downturn almost immediately; and the settlers were reluctant to present themselves. Indeed, the numbers of migrants was now tailing off and after the First World War the Afrikaner-dominated government of the Union started to curtail migration from Britain. Migratory patterns incorporated southern Africa from time to time, particularly in periods when social distress in the metropole coincided with depression in other colonies. Scots had been swept up in these periodic spurts to a disproportionate degree, but the problems of the environment, land availability, dramatic swings in the economic pendulum, racial separation and attendant labour competition had always acted as powerful brakes upon migrant enthusiasm.

Notes

1 Alan F. Hattersley, *The British Settlement of Natal: a Study in Imperial Migration* (Cambridge 1950), chapter VII, pp. 178–93.
2 Alan F. Hattersley, *More Annals of Natal, with Historical Introductions and Notes* (London 1936); Hattersley, *Later Annals of Natal* (London 1938); Hattersley, *Portrait of a Colony: the Story of Natal* (Cambridge 1940); Hattersley, *Pietermaritzburg Panorama: a Survey of 100 Years of an African City* (Pietermaritzburg 1938); Hattersley, *Portrait of a City* (Pietermaritzburg 1951).
3 Shelagh O'Byrne Spencer, *British Settlers: a Biographical Register in Natal* (seven volumes, Pietermaritzburg 1981 and following years).
4 Most of the examples that follow are taken from the works of Hattersley or, more notably, Spencer.
5 Tabler lists a number of Scots hunters and traders, including William Henry Drummond (1845–79), younger son of Viscount Strathallan, who hunted with his associate Dalziel in 1876–77, Robert Newton Dunn (1794–1847), the father of the celebrated John Robert Dunn (1833–95), St Vincent William Erskine, Townsend

Erskine, McCorkindale's surveyor in New Scotland, David Leslie (1839–74), MacLachlan, MacLean (first names not known), Norman Magnus MacLeod (1839–1929), Monies, George Pigott Moodie, John Ross, John Robert Thomson (1788–1878) and others. Edward C. Tabler, *Pioneers of Natal and South Eastern Africa, 1552–1878* (Cape Town and Rotterdam 1977), *passim*.
6   Tabler, *Pioneers*, p. 22.
7   Two examples were Robert Aitken, who abandoned a loss-making farm near Falkirk, and George Trotter, from West Lothian. Both farmed in Natal.
8   Charles Withers, 'The demographic history of the city, 1831–1911' in W. Hamish Fraser and Irene Maver (eds), *Glasgow II, 1830–1912* (Manchester 1996), p. 149.
9   These were the *Ina*, which left Glasgow in March 1850; *Conquering Hero*, June the same year; *Albinia*, April 1851; *Lady Sale*, May 1851; *Isle of Wight*, September 1851.
10 *Urania*, August 1851.
11 J. C. Byrne, *Twelve Years' Wanderings in the British Colonies, 1835–1847* (London 1848).
12 J. C. Byrne, *Emigrant's Guide to the Cape of Good Hope* (London 1848) and *Emigrant's Guide to Port Natal* (London 1848).
13 *Byrne's Emigrants' Journal*, which inevitably carried accounts of successful settlement, letters from happy settlers, reports of profits on land sales, etc.
14 D. Moodie to Secretary to Government, Cape Town, 14 March 1850, printed in Hattersley, *More Annals of Natal*, pp. 28–9. Moodie correctly predicted that the allotments would be unfit for cultivation, that there would be 'much privation and distress' and that the wrong sort of professions would be attracted, like 'clerks and persons formerly employed in manufactories', who would give 'untrue accounts of their previous occupations . . .'
15 There were seven companies or organisations involved, including one from Germany (Bergtheil & Jung).
16 Other schemes, apart from Byrne's, which attracted some Scots included the Christian Emigration and Colonization Society. This was essentially a Methodist-run enterprise, associated with the Earl of Verulam, and 400 settlers emigrated under its aegis. Emigrants were settled on the Cotton Lands, land originally allocated to the failed Natal Cotton Company, with its centre at 'Verulam'. 'New Glasgow' was in the same area. Settlers connected with a Scots aristocrat came from the Duke of Buccleuch's Hampshire estates and migrated under the care of the Byrne company. They were mainly English.
17 Despite now having a justifiable reputation as an unscrupulous operator, Byrne continued to dream of emigration schemes, including one from Ireland to Brazil, and even cooked up a plan to send people to French New Caledonia.
18 'From Scotland to Natal', from the Reminiscences of Mrs James Arbuthnot, a MS in the possession of Mr Crofton Arbuthnot in Hattersley, *More Annals*, pp. 29–38.
19 The justification for this was that money was often stolen on the voyages. 'Several hundred' is the vague figure given by Jane Arbuthnot. Spencer's account suggests £200.
20 Hugh MacDonald had been a master mariner. He had made many coastal voyages between the Cape and Natal before settling to open his hotel. His hotel was also famous for its billiard rooms (opened 1850). Ian Morrison, *Durban: a Pictorial History* (Cape Town 1987), p. 10. It may have been the same MacDonald (often also spelt McDonald in the sources) who opened the first coffee shop in Pietermaritzburg in 1847. Bill Guest, 'Economic development of the capital city, 1838–1910' in John Laband and Robert Haswell (eds), *Pietermaritzburg, 1838–1988: a New Portrait of an African City* (Pietermaritzburg 1988), pp. 120–9, especially, p. 121.
21 Despite all these problems, Arbuthnot wrote home to the *Aberdeen Journal* in 1852 to suggest how much more successful it was possible to be in Natal than in Buchan. Marjory Harper, *Adventurers and Exiles: the Great Scottish Exodus* (London 2003), pp. 28–9. Arbuthnot had been asked by farmers in north-east Scotland to

report to them. Marjory Harper, *Emigration from North East Scotland* (Aberdeen 1988), I, p. 320, has a longer account of this incident.
22 'Mr George Lamond helps to grow sugar at Compensation', Hattersley, *More Annals*, pp. 92–4.
23 James Millan opened a successful tailoring establishment in Pietermaritzburg. Another tailor was Peter Lennox, from Galloway.
24 David Gray, from Paisley, opened a roadside inn and later farmed at 'Cathkin', named after Cathkin Braes in Glasgow.
25 John and William Craig, from Ayrshire, became waggon builders in Pietermaritzburg.
26 Georg Macleroy emigrated for his health, promoted cotton growing, became government immigration agent, then registrar of deeds and manager of the Natal Bank.
27 William Mackenzie, the son of a lawyer, abandoned the ministry and took up farming at 'Cramond'.
28 Walter Brunton, from Peebles, who sailed from the Clyde on *Ina*, became a boat-builder at Cato's Creek, on Durban Bay.
29 This family is commemorated in a memorial in Inverness town hall.
30 As a piece of ephemera this has become an extremely rare item. It was published in full as 'A rare piece of Africana', *Natalia*, 7 (1979), pp. 7–23, introduced by S. P. M. Spencer.
31 In 1850 Milne also set about anchoring the sand on the Point by planting 'Hottentot's fig'. Beverley Ellis, 'White settler impact on the environment of Durban, 1845–1870' in Stephen Dovers, Ruth Edgecombe and Bill Guest (eds), *South Africa's Environmental History: Cases and Comparisons* (Athens OH and Cape Town 2002), p. 39.
32 By a proclamation of 1872 any settlers' grants not taken up, with appropriate title, by 1873 would be forfeited. Many were, reflecting the lack of interest in land of a fair number of settlers. Many simply realised that it was largely worthless, hardly worth their while in negotiating the bureaucracy to establish their title.
33 One sister, Elizabeth, was housekeeper to Colonel Boys, who acted as governor before the arrival of Benjamin Pine. Boys was the officer commanding the 91st Regiment in Natal. At the time of Duff's arrival, there were some 100 troops in Durban and 600 in Pietermaritzburg.
34 Balgowan later became a station on the Durban-Johannesburg railway line. It replaced 'Curry's Post' founded by sergeant-major George Curry who had retired from the local garrison. Maryna Fraser, 'A Brief History of the Farm "Bosch Hoek"', *Natalia*, 15 (1985), pp. 95–99, particularly p. 95.
35 Presumably, as an official, he had no desire to come under settler ministerial supervision. After a strikingly adventurous life Sutherland was killed in a carriage accident in Pietermaritzburg.
36 Hattersley, *Portrait of a Colony*, p. 121.
37 Ibid., and J. Forsyth Ingram, *The Story of an African City* (Maritzburg 1898).
38 A. F. Hattersley (ed.), *John Shedden Dobie: South African Journal, 1862–1866* (Cape Town 1945).
39 Katherine Elks, 'Crime, Community and the Police in Cape Town, 1825–1850', M.A. thesis, University of Cape Town (1986), pp. 55, 155.
40 Theophilus Shepstone suggested that there were 210,000 Africans in Natal in 1862, with roughly 600 immigrating from Zululand each year. Monica Wilson and Leonard Thompson (eds), *The Oxford History of South Africa* I, *To 1870* (Oxford 1969), p. 385.
41 Neil Parsons, *A New History of Southern Africa* (London 1993), p. 119.
42 *Census of the Colony of Natal, April 1904*, presented to HE the Governor of Natal, June 1905.
43 Robert James Mann, *The Emigrant's Guide to the Colony of Natal* (London 1873). Mann also edited for publication Henry Brooks, *Natal: a History and Description of the Colony* (London 1876), which inevitably laid stress upon immigration and the advantages of the colony.
44 The figures were: steam, first, £38 17s; second, £26 5s; sail, cabin, twenty-five guineas; steerage, sixteen guineas.

45 Kathleen Power McIntosh, *Some old Natal Families* (Pietermaritzburg 1974), pp. 4–6.
46 Daphne Child, 'Scottish aristocrat became top Natal figure', *The Settler: Journal of the 1820 Settlers' Association of South Africa*, 62: 3 (1989), pp. 12–13.
47 Another later settler was Edward Mathers (1850–1924), the son of a printer and publisher in Edinburgh. He arrived in South Africa in 1878 and became the founder-editor of the *Natal Mercury*. He worked for various other newspapers and became a major publicist and propagandist for the mineral and mining prospects of southern Africa. He also wrote handbooks for migrants and remained a dedicated imperialist.
48 Sheila Henderson, 'Colonial Coalopolis: the establishment and growth of Dundee', *Natalia*, 12 (1982), pp. 14–26.
49 Peter was born on the family farm in the parish of Guthrie, while Ann was born at Craighead, both near or in Dundee. Their gravestones are at the Talana Museum.
50 Coal had been known in the area since as early as 1838. Ruth Edgecombe and Bill Guest, 'An introduction to the pre-Union Natal coal industry' in Bill Guest and John M. Sellers (eds), *Enterprise and Exploitation in a Victorian Colony* (Pietermaritzburg 1985), pp. 309–41.
51 Eventually there were three adjacent townships: Dundee, Dundee Proper and Dundee Extension. They were amalgamated in 1896.
52 Talana Museum pamphlet, 'The Founders of Dundee'.
53 The Talana cemetery has a gravestone commemorating James McConnachie, possibly a son of William, who was born in Dundee, Scotland, in 1867, worked for the Natal Government Railways and died in Dundee, Natal, in 1898.
54 There were rival companies, including the Elandslaagte Colliery Company, in which the farmer S. Mitchell-Innes had an interest.
55 Bill Guest, 'Commercial coal mining in Natal: a centennial reappraisal', *Natalia*, 18 (1988), pp. 41–58, especially p. 49.
56 Talana Museum pamphlet 'Talana Museum Cemetery'.
57 Scots construction workers had been heading for the United States in large numbers in the 1880s, but when the American boom came to an end South Africa and Australia became significant destinations. Charlotte Erickson, *Leaving England: Essays on British Emigration in the Nineteenth Century* (Ithaca NY and London 1994), p. 209.
58 Harper, *Emigration from North East Scotland* II, pp. 7–8.
59 Correspondence on this recruitment can be found in the KwaZulu Natal Archives E1/18 LIB 336.1889, dating from March/April/May 1889.
60 KwaZulu Natal Archives, NHB 117 (A) 1891, vol. 1/2/8.
61 Melanie Hillebrand, '"A bad row of teeth": Pietermaritzburg's architecture' in Laband and Haswell, *Pietermaritzburg 1838–1988*, p. 48.
62 KwaZulu Natal Archives, NHB 117 (A) 1891, vol. 1/2/8.
63 Methven had been assistant harbour engineer and engineer-in-chief of the Greenock Harbour Trust for eighteen years. He reported on various harbours throughout southern Africa and also became an architect of note, designing many buildings in Durban. He was president of the Natal Institute of Architects and was also associated with the Royal Institute of British Architects and the Institution of Civil Engineers. He was active in the South African Association for the Advancement of Science and was involved in the organising committee of the Natal Technical College, in the founding of the Durban Art Gallery and in the design of the organs of the city halls in Durban and Pietermaritzburg.
64 Hunter, who had been general manager of the railways since the 1880s, always attracted controversy. He was exceptionally well paid (a salary of £1,200 in 1885) and had presided both over the expansion of the railways and over their lack of financial success. Hein Heydenrych, 'Railway development in Natal to 1895' in Guest and Sellers (eds), *Enterprise*, pp. 58–9.

CONTINUING MIGRATION

65 W. H. Bizley, 'The political career of Mr Reid's "ten wheeler"', *Natalia*, 19 (1989), pp. 43–9.
66 See chapter 7, p. 223, for an account of McLarty's career.
67 One of Campbell's partners was David Don (1841–1906), who was born in Brechin. He was successful as a financier and helped Campbell to buy the Natal Central Sugar Company, a subsidiary of the Oriental Banking Corporation, of which Don was the manager. Campbell was a bibliophile who built up an extensive library, now in the hands of the Durban municipality. His nephew emigrated from Scotland to South Africa in 1876 and became editor of *The Times of Natal*.
68 Joy Brain, 'Indentured and free Indians in the economy of colonial Natal' in Guest and Sellers, *Enterprise*, pp. 209 and 226–7. See also Peter Richardson, 'The Natal sugar industry, 1849–1905: an interpretative essay' in Guest and Sellers, *Enterprise*, pp. 181–97.
69 The commissioner for this census was Sir Thomas Keir Murray, son of the founders of Pinetown.
70 AWC: IBC 6, 7, 8, 9. The F. J. Boonzaier collection also contains records of emigrant ships arriving at Port Elizabeth in the same period. These reveal the names of numbers of Scots and their occupations.
71 AWC: PIB 8, 9.
72 AWC: PIB 13.
73 Nigel Worden, Elizabeth van Heyningen and Vivian Bickford Smith, *Cape Town: the Making of a City* (Cape Town 1999), p. 231. A good account of class formation and racial segregation can be found in Vivian Bickford-Smith, *Ethnic Pride and Racial Prejudice in Victorian Cape Town: Group Identity and Social Practice, 1875–1902* (Cambridge 1995).
74 Harper, *Adventurers and Exiles*, pp. 139–41.
75 Useful accounts of McCorkindale's schemes can be found in A. N. Pelzer, 'Alexander McCorkindale en sy skemas 1864–1866', *Historia*, 15: 1 (1970), pp. 6–23, and Pelzer, 'Die invloed van McCorkindale se haweskemas op Britse belangstelling in Delagoabaai', *Historia*, 15: 2 (1970), pp. 74–80.
76 Hattersley, *British Settlement of Natal*, p. 183.
77 Spencer, *British Settlers* II (Pietermaritzburg 1983), p. xx.
78 Ibid. II, pp. 164–5.
79 Presumably this was intended as homage to Robert Burns, but I can find no confirmation.
80 She died in 1879.
81 Graham Dominy, 'The New Republicans: a centennial reappraisal of the "Nieuwe Republiek" (1884–1888)', *Natalia*, 14 (1984), pp. 87–97.
82 Friedrich Jeppe, *Die Transvaalische oder Suid-Afrikanische Republik* (Potchefstroom 1868). This book is in German, though the legend of the map is in English.
83 Papers relating to McCorkindale and New Scotland can be found in the Transvaal archives in Pretoria. Entering New Scotland into the data base of this archive produced no fewer than 444 hits. Some of this history of New Scotland is based upon a selection of these documents.
84 Jeppe was a German who had emigrated to South Africa in 1861 and described himself as a cartographer. He became the postmaster at Potchefstroom in 1866 and then demonstrated the extraordinary opportunities available in the Transvaal in the period. He was postmaster-general from 1868 to 1875 and in 1877 was appointed government translator and controller of statistics.
85 Fred (sic) Jeppe, *Transvaal Book Almanac and Directory for 1877* (Pietermaritzburg 1877).
86 Other members of the school commission were D. Forbes (presumably McCorkindale's informant), J. Arthur and D. Napier.
87 Papers on this incident, in which, it was alleged, the Swazi had removed cattle belonging to Africans on the Transvaal side of the border, can be found in the

Pretoria archives: SS 241/2747 (1877); SS 242/2957 (1877) on an alleged and potential alliance between the Swazi and the Zulu; and SS265/364, 1878, where E. J. Buchanan desires that Bell's wishes should be borne out by going to Swaziland to investigate the alleged cattle theft.

88   An interesting insight is provided into the maintenance of Scots identity in the British Empire by the fact that the *Aberdeen Journal* – and presumably other local papers – carried many death notices of emigrants who had left north-east Scotland. Many of these relate to South Africa. Marjory Harper, 'Emigration from North East Scotland', Ph.D., University of Aberdeen (1984), II, table VII.

89   Here I analyse the census figures rather differently from the method used in Chapter 2.

90   Harper, 'Emigration from North East Scotland', II, p. 12. For women's migration see pp. 232–4, 246, 274, 276n.6 and the table on p. 286, which indicates that 2,000 women emigrated from Britain under the auspices of the South African Colonisation Society and more than 4,000 more up to 1915. The proportion of these who were Scots is not known.

91   Transvaal Archives, Gov. 475 PS117 C1/4. This file contains correspondence between Chamberlain and Milner relating to the South African Expansion Committee and contains names and employments of all the women emigrants.

92   Transvaal Archives, Gov. 718, PS 36.

CHAPTER SIX

Professionals: the Church and education

Scots went further than simply exporting aspects of their civil society and cultural forms to South Africa. As Jonathan Hyslop has convincingly argued, they also despatched their social tensions and divisions, as well as their propensity for radical politics and trade union activity.[1] On the one hand, the most visible and prominent Scots were unquestionably either bourgeois or of rising social aspirations: educated professionals and business people, usually Presbyterian and eager for respectability, embracing a mix of ambition and continued adherence to Scottish cultural norms. But, at the lower end of the social order, Scotland contributed people who had often emerged from despair. As we have seen in Chapter 5, those who emigrated in the schemes of the later 1850s and early 1860s were driven from Scotland in search of better opportunities. Many of them embarked on something of a roller-coaster of economic highs and lows, while some became notorious as drinkers and often saw the interior of courtrooms. A few found new forms of despair in unfamiliar surroundings. Others later came to be part of an exploited white labour force on the Rand. Concentrated in relatively large numbers, and aware of their comparatively lowly place in the vast wealth formation of the time, they were ripe for unionisation. Key members of the leadership, like many of the workers themselves, came from Scotland. Black labour, of course, occupied an even more lowly place, but in this period there was no question of white and black making common cause. This chapter and the next deal primarily with the successful Scots: professionals, businessmen and union leaders. Moreover, it will chart the ways in which key professions were often dominated by those who were educated in Scotland. In migrating to southern Africa they invariably aspired to positions of power and influence which might have been beyond their reach in Scotland itself. The Church and education will be examined first, followed by other professionals, businessmen and radicals.

The arrival of Scots to dominate many of the familiar and emergent professions occurred from the start of British rule. As we have seen, Lord Charles Somerset, despite regarding some Scots as anti-Establishment and dangerous to the good order of the Cape Colony, favoured the appointment of Scottish ministers and teachers to develop and maintain the Dutch Reformed Church and rudimentary educational institutions as what he would have regarded as means of social cohesion and the maintenance of civilised standards. This established a tradition which was, in many respects, to be continued throughout our period.[2]

The Church

Dutch Reformed

There is but one statue outside the Dutch Reformed Groote Kerk in Cape Town and it is of the Rev. Dr Andrew Murray junior. He is also commemorated in a seated statue in front of the DRC church in Wellington, while his brother John stands in stone in front of the DRC seminary in Stellenbosch. They represent the take-over of the Dutch Church by Scots in the nineteenth century. This happened because the decline in the number of Dutch clerics and a crisis in their recruitment in the Netherlands[3] ensured that ministers had to be found from the country which was apparently overproducing them, Scotland. So successful was this strategy that by 1824 eighteen out of twenty-five of the ministers of the first independent synod of the DRC were Scots. Perhaps significantly, this synod formalised the severing of ties with the parent Church in Holland. It also established three presbyteries on the Presbyterian model.[4] Several of these ministers had been introduced to the colony by the Rev. George Thom, who had been sent to Britain to recruit ministers (and teachers) in 1820. Assisted by Professor McGill of Glasgow University,[5] he contrived to recruit six additional ministers to those already at the Cape. Among the latter was John Taylor (1778–1860), from Scone, who had arrived at the Cape, under the auspices of the LMS, in 1816. He left the LMS on arrival and was appointed by Somerset to be minister at Beaufort, thus becoming the first to serve the DRC. He baptised the future President Kruger at Cradock in 1826. There was a further injection of Scots in 1860, when the Rev. William Robertson travelled to Britain and recruited a further nine ministers, as well as four missionaries and two teachers.

George Thom (1789–1842) was born and educated in Aberdeen. He arrived at the Cape in 1812, having been recruited by the LMS.[6] A minister of the Church of Scotland, he later joined the DRC and became *predikant* of the church in Caledon. He was noted for speaking extremely good Dutch. Among his recruits, Andrew Murray (1794–1866) was born in Clatt, Aberdeenshire, and came from the 'Auld Licht' tradition of Scots Presbyterianism.[7] Educated at King's College, Aberdeen, he was soon marked out for overseas service. In 1821 he declined to go to Newfoundland but accepted Thom's call to the Cape. He went to Utrecht to learn Dutch and sailed to the Cape in 1822, keeping a diary of the voyage.[8] He was inducted at Graaff Reinet, the successor to the Rev. Abraham Faure,[9] and served there for forty-five years. His sons, John (1826–82)[10] and Andrew (1828–1917), were sent back to Scotland to be educated in Aberdeen and from 1845 in Utrecht. They were duly ordained, and returned to the Cape in 1848. Andrew was inducted at Bloemfontein in 1849 and moved on to Worcester in 1860, Cape Town in 1864 and Wellington in 1871, developing schools in each place.[11] He was a prolific writer, led major evangelisation tours and is regarded as one of the great leaders of the DRC in the nineteenth century. Another brother, Charles Murray (1833–1904), succeeded his father as minister of Graaff Reinet. Another of Thom's recruits was Colin Fraser (1796–1870), born in Ross-shire and educated in Aberdeen. He arrived at the Cape in 1824 and served the church in Beaufort West until 1862. His son, the Rev. Colin McKenzie Fraser (1837–1911), was sent to school in Inverness in 1852 and moved on to Marischal College, Aberdeen, before Utrecht. He married a Scots woman, Isabella Paterson, in Aberdeen, and returned to South Africa in 1862. He was minister at Philippolis from 1863 to 1907 and his daughter married the future President Steyn of the Orange Free State.[12] She was a striking and influential woman, as her biographer has demonstrated. The other recruits were the Revs Alex Smith, William Thomson, Henry Sutherland and George Morgan.

William Robertson (1805–79) was the son of a farmer, of Inverurie, in Aberdeenshire. A graduate of King's College, Aberdeen, he arrived at the Cape in 1822, recruited by Thom as a teacher. He went to Graaff Reinet and taught many Afrikaans pupils who were later to be influential in the Cape and the republics. In 1827 he returned to Scotland to study at Aberdeen and Edinburgh before making the usual language and theology pilgrimage to Utrecht. He was successively minister in Clanwilliam, Swellendam and Cape Town. He was influential in founding schools and the theological seminary in Stellenbosch before returning to Britain to recruit more ministers and teachers. One of his recruits was the Rev. Andrew McGregor (1829–1918), of Golspie, who was educated in Edinburgh and Utrecht, and was ordained in 1858. He was minister at Robertson until 1902 and married Robertson's daughter. Another was David Ross, of Auchenblae, the son of a weaver, who reached Cape Town, after the customary period in Utrecht, in 1862. He was originally trained in law and maintained an interest in legal studies. He served several congregations and established a number of schools. The Natal DRC was also not immune to Scots influence. The Rev. James Turnbull (1825–94) was a Presbyterian minister at the Cape from 1859 to 1867 but moved to the DRC on becoming the minister of that church in Greytown, Natal. He was actively sympathetic to the Boer cause in the war of 1880–81.

This ministerial migration exhibits a number of interesting phenomena. The first is the manner in which these clergymen had a tendency to create ecclesiastical dynasties. Andrew Murray had no fewer than five sons (John, Andrew junior, William, Charles and George) who became DRC ministers. Four daughters married ministers and four grandsons, the sons of Charles, became missionaries in Nyasaland, Malawi. John Murray was the first professor of theology at Stellenbosch. Colin Fraser also had a son who became a DRC minister. Moreover, these families tended to intermarry. Most of the ministers came from the north-east of Scotland and almost all of them were educated at Aberdeen, although many went on to Edinburgh for theology. As a result of this extensive recruitment, many of the key churches of the Cape DRC were in the hands of Scots ministers for much of the nineteenth century. They included Graaff Reinet, Beaufort West, Philippolis, Swellendam, Wellington, Worcester, even Stellenbosch and Cape Town itself. After the Great Trek, Bloemfontein was also a Scots ecclesiastical stronghold, helping to bind the republic to the Cape at least in ecclesiastical ways. Many of these were enormous parishes, from which additional congregations were carved out, often bearing the name of the minister or a place associated with him. Examples include Robertson, Murrayburg, Aberdeen and Fraserburg. Although the Scots *predikants* invariably identified with Afrikaner rather than imperial interests, they were not uniformly popular. In the 1820s some congregations were already becoming resentful of the preference being given to Scots. Some ministers were regarded as too autocratic, their attitudes to church organisation and their own authority engendering friction with their congregations. There were disputes over the refusal of baptism, the form of church services, and hymn singing. Conservative Afrikaans congregations objected to theological and other influences that were emerging from German pietism and Methodism in the period.[13] But congregations were generally more positive about Scots ministers' concern with education, the founding of Sunday and day schools[14] and their involvement in the nascent institutions of higher education, such as the Stellenbosch Gymnasium, which transmogrified into Victoria College and then the University of Stellenbosch. As further evidence of the crossover effect, they often had other outside interests such as geology, botany, the collection of fossils, and the law, which mitigated any tendency to fundamentalism.

But the open question must be whether they Scotticised the DRC or whether they were, in turn, Afrikanerised. Fry has suggested that the DRC effectively became a Scots kirk in the course of the 1820s.[15] But in this Fry allowed his chauvinism to get the better of him. Some ministers brought Scots wives with them, but many were married at the Cape, generally to women with Dutch or German names. Almost all of them received some acculturation at Utrecht. They often became devoted to the Boer cause, though the Great Trek caused them real dilemmas.[16] Most of the Scots ministers were opposed to the trek, holding that it was spiritually more important to remain within the colony than to head off into the lawless and godless region beyond the frontier. David Livingstone was concerned that Scots ministers aided and abetted the Voortrekkers, but such was not really the case. The Scots rolled up to minister in Dutch churches only after the republics had been established. The Rev. David Ross was accused of high treason for his Boer sympathies during the Anglo-Boer War and spent twenty-four days in prison. The Rev. George Murray (another of Andrew's sons) went to Ceylon with Boer prisoners-of-war to minister to them. Some of them spoke and wrote excellent Dutch; others were better with the spoken than with the written language. But all became closely associated with their Boer congregations. By the third generation they were unquestionably assimilated Boers, and it can be said that this part of Somerset's Anglicisation project had foundered on the rock of Scots' capacity for linguistic and cultural assimilation. Yet it is certainly the case that they modified the theology of the Dutch Church and introduced an evangelical thrust to it. Colin McKenzie Fraser caused considerable discontent in his congregation by showing interest in missionary activity among blacks. And the first DRC foreign missionary was the Rev. Alex McKidd (1821–65), a millwright from Thurso, recruited by Robertson in 1860, who became a missionary in the Zoutpansberg in what became the northern Transvaal (now Limpopo province). He married an Afrikaner woman who was the first Afrikaans person to enter the mission field.

Although it is a mixed picture, they may also have added to the joylessness of the Dutch Reformed Church. Some Afrikaners still say that the Scots introduced a heightened sense of Calvinism, of puritanism and of sin.[17] C. M. Fraser secured legislation in 1898 to restrict Sunday trains and gambling. He too was arrested during the Boer War, perhaps for the wrong reasons, and was sent to be chaplain of the concentration camp at Norval's Pont. But in some cases the Scottish ministers liberalised some of the more extreme aspects of fundamentalism in the DRC and many brought wider cultural and intellectual interests than would have been displayed by their Dutch predecessors. If they became socially and linguistically assimilated with their congregations, they brought fresh educational and theological outlooks to bear. In the end the DRC became something of a Dutch/Scots hybrid. Religious ideas and practices are modified in their transference across the globe like any others. Aberdeen, Edinburgh, Utrecht, Cape Town, Graaff Reinet (or wherever) were all nodes of intellectual, theological and social power and influence that fed into the make-up of these ministers, even if the perspectives derived from Scottish origins could remain of considerable significance. Different 'chemical' compounds went into the making of the second and third generations, but such South African-born individuals were still often educated in Scotland and brought that experience, together with the perceptions of a different age, to bear in very different geographical and ethnic settings.

Presbyterian

There were of course Scottish Catholics,[18] Episcopalians,[19] Methodists, Baptists and, above all, Congregationalists[20] in South Africa but, except in the case of a few celebrated individuals, they do not show up well in the record. Inevitably, they tended to merge with fellow Catholics or with other members of the Anglican communion and the 'Free Churches'. On the other hand, Scottish Presbyterians of various types initially worshipped in the Dutch Reformed Church until their numbers warranted the formation of a separate English-speaking Presbyterian Church. Sometimes the Presbyterians were initially invited to use the Dutch Church for their services. Throughout there was close co-operation between the two Churches, particularly given the presence of Scots ministers in the DRC. Nevertheless, the development of a separate Presbyterian establishment ensured a further clerical migration from Scotland. These ministers came from either the Church of Scotland or the Free Church but, given the relatively small numbers, the tradition of schism in the Scottish Churches had little opportunity for expression in South Africa, although, as we have seen, it did manifest itself in the activities of the different missionary societies. In order to understand the continuing growth of the clerical profession, it is necessary to chart the development of Presbyterianism itself. Moreover, it is apparent that any attempt to maintain multi-racial congregations in the first half of the nineteenth century became increasingly impossible as the racial order of the colony became progressively more rigid. It should also be remembered that the Presbyterian Church would have been a locus of 'respectability'. Many Scots, perhaps particularly from lower down the social scale and among military personnel, probably had nothing to do with it or indeed any other Church.

The first formal practice of Presbyterian worship was for whites, and soldiers, only. It probably occurred in relation to the lengthy service of the 93rd Highland Regiment (the Sutherland Fencibles) at the Cape.[21] There were no military chaplains at that period, but around 1808 the troops founded a Calvinist Society 'for worship and mutual edification'.[22] In 1812 the Rev. George Thom, still in the Church of Scotland, was invited by this society to form a congregation from among the soldiers. He duly did so, utilising a missionary chapel for its services. The first communion was celebrated by Thom in 1813, but the following year the regiment was posted back to Britain and the congregation lost a considerable proportion of its members. Indeed, it was said that Presbyterianism had a remarkable effect upon the discipline and morals of the regiment. In 1818 Thom was appointed Dutch Reformed minister at Caledon and the Rev. John Philip took over his duties in respect of Scots troops and other Presbyterians. To the distress of some members, who had thought that the Congregationalists were joining them, Philip effectively transferred the congregation into his own denomination and the worship ceased to be strictly Presbyterian.

In 1823–24 fresh attempts were made to resuscitate Presbyterianism at the Cape. The celebrated Rev. J. Dunmore Lang of Sydney, New South Wales, had preached that settlers in the colonies should be permitted to practise their own denominations. (Lang was always wary of the influence of established Anglicanism and of Roman Catholicism.) This published sermon, circulated at the Cape, is an interesting example of inter-colonial influences. In 1824 Earl Bathurst, the Secretary of State, proposed to the Moderator of the Glasgow Presbytery that financial aid should be granted to Presbyterians to establish their own churches. A public meeting, under the chairmanship of the prominent Cape Town merchant Alexander Macdonald was held later that year and a committee was formed, with no fewer than six, mainly Scots, DRC ministers as members, together with notable Scottish colonists, such as the surgeon James Abercrombie and the lawyer-merchant Charles Stuart Pillans, the librarian and editor Alexander Johnstone Jardine, the saddler Mackenzie, Findlay, Nisbet and Paton.

The resolutions of the meeting were published as a handbill.[23] Private donations and government support raised rather more than the cost of the building, £3,600; the burgher senate granted a piece of land known as Cooper's Yard and offered the use of the town quarry.

The laying of the foundation stone was performed with much Masonic ceremony, reminding us of the close connections at the time between the Scottish Church and Freemasonry. The committee sought the help of the presbytery of Edinburgh to find a potential incumbent.[24] The Rev. James Adamson was duly appointed by that presbytery and arrived at the Cape in November 1827. He was the son of the minister of Cupar in Fife, had established his intellectual credentials by contributing articles to the *Edinburgh Philosophical Journal* and was to receive the handsome salary of £400 per annum. As we have seen in Chapter 3, he was to become highly influential in many educational and intellectual developments of the city. A kirk session was constituted, including several members of the committee and Judge Menzies. St Andrew's Church, in a simple and rather severe Doric classical style in the Presbyterian tradition,[25] was duly opened in May 1829, meriting an enthusiastic report in the *Commercial Advertiser* which included a listing of the amounts raised in the early collections.[26] The Dutch Reformed Church, represented by Mr Von Manger, contributed 1,000 rix dollars (about £75) to the new church, while the officers and men of the 72nd Regiment pledged to contribute one day's pay. The throng attending the opening was so great that two companies of the 72nd and some civilians were unable to find room.

St Andrew's Church (initially known as the 'Scottish Presbyterian Church') was soon significant in the abolitionist activities at the Cape. Even though some of its members were slave owners (who would therefore benefit from compensation), the church resolved to institute mission work among the 'apprentices' preparing for full emancipation. Although this was discussed from 1836, it was not until 1838 that the mission was established. It was hoped that a Mr Nisbet, a missionary in Bombay who was residing at the Cape for the recovery of his health, would be associated with the mission, but he returned to Bombay. Subsequently St Andrew's was the first church to offer membership to blacks and in consequence the membership received a considerable infusion of converts from the former slave population. Although the mission was Presbyterian, it was placed under the control of a Lutheran, the Rev. G. W. Stegmann, and its services were generally separate from those of the predominantly white congregation, though organisationally they were theoretically together. The mission services were conducted in Dutch.[27] Between 1838 and 1841 1,000 adult former slaves joined the mission, which permitted Adamson in 1862 to declare that the church had been highly influential in ensuring that Islam had not spread among the ex-slaves to the extent that it might have done. There was also a very successful mission school which soon met in a dedicated hall completed in 1842.[28] In 1841 this mission school had 500 on its register with a daily attendance of 350. The mission additionally operated as a welfare society to attempt to keep its members out of the hands of pauper provision.[29] In 1841 the crusty Adamson resigned his charge in the midst of a dispute and promptly sued the congregation for the return of money he claimed he had expended on improvements out of his own pocket.[30] He was replaced by the Rev. George Morgan, who was 'called' by a large proportion of the congregation, including those Coloureds who were able to sign their names. But Morgan and Stegmann soon clashed and Stegmann withdrew most of the members of his mission into a separate congregation. It may be that these disputes serve to confirm the view that the emancipation of the slaves ultimately led to a hardening of racial attitudes at the Cape.

Despite his Welsh name, Morgan was a Scot who had been highly recommended for the Thom recruitment in 1823. He was a graduate of King's College in Aberdeen, had been a tutor in Ross-shire and the minister of Gairloch. He went to the Netherlands to learn the language (not very successfully, since it was said that he always read his Dutch sermons) and sailed for the Cape in 1825. He was appointed DRC minister in Somerset East, where he established a considerable reputation as a preacher and for the austerity of his tastes. He failed to endear himself to his Dutch congregation by condemning dancing, horse racing, card playing and the like, and he also argued fiercely against the Great Trek. That may partially explain why he was eager to accept the call to Cape Town in 1841, transferring from DRC to the Scottish Presbyterian. Another of his passions was to secure the independence of the Church from all government interference, perhaps an echo of controversies in Scotland itself.[31] For him, religious freedom and political liberty were two sides of the same coin. He conducted many marriages of freed slaves (the registers constitute an important source) and always signed himself as 'minister of the Scottish church'.

Presbyterianism tended to wax and wane according to the state of the Cape economy: for example, it went into a trough in the depression of the 1860s and 1870s, and the surviving part of the mission was closed in 1878, partly because, with the departure of Stegmann, it had been difficult to appoint a Dutch-speaking evangelist. Adamson had failed, on a visit to Scotland in 1840, to persuade the Church of Scotland to take it over. The mission congregation was predominantly black and Coloured, but it is difficult to establish exactly what happened to these members. Many would have joined the DRC for language reasons. Others accepted the invitation to join St Andrew's, but geographical separation of the races in Cape Town reduced the degree of integration of the past. Progressively the St Andrew's congregation would become largely white and exclusively English-speaking, although Morgan had always argued that the Church should minister to all without 'class distinctions' (by which he also meant distinctions of race).[32] He also suggested, as part of his rearguard action, that having a bilingual Church was akin to the situation in Scotland. Nevertheless, there continued to be attempts to keep missionary work going among blacks in the slums of the city, but now at arm's length and as a separate evangelistic organisation. Adamson, indeed, claimed that he had used his salary from the South African College to foster this mission work. A mission was also opened in the Ndabeni location, largely under the control of African evangelists.

Despite the co-operation, at least in personnel, between the Church of Scotland and the Free Church at the Cape, the Scottish Disruption of 1843 did have repercussions there. A Free Church was opened in Cape Town in 1846, under the aegis of the Revs E. Miller and E. Gorrie, who had been ordained in Edinburgh. This church, very well positioned near Greenmarket Square, was started but never completed. It incurred considerable debts and was closed in 1851.[33] The identification of St Andrew's as 'Scottish' led to discontent on the part of Irish Presbyterians, who founded their own church in 1889. It was perhaps for this reason that the 'Scottish' name was dropped in 1895. What Morgan would have thought of this is not recorded, since he had retired in 1871 and was succeeded by the Rev. John Munro Russell, son of the minister of Glendaruel Free Church, Argyll, who had been ordained in the Free Church in Edinburgh. He presided over a considerable expansion in the provision of Presbyterian churches and also became influential in the councils of the University of Cape Town. At a time of massive growth in the population of Cape Town (from 40,000 in 1880 to 250,000 in 1928) churches were founded in Woodstock (1893), Gardens (at the foot of Table Mountain, near the Mount Nelson Hotel)[34] and Mowbray (1904), with more to follow. Gardens represented a double shift in the centre of gravity: a geographical one into relatively salubrious suburbs farther into the lower slopes of Table Mountain, and a social one into an essentially white bourgeois congregation. It started out as a Sunday school in an iron building in the 1880s and by 1894 it had 180 scholars on its roll. The site for a church was acquired in 1899 and the building was completed in 1903 at a cost of £9,000, with an additional £1,000 being spent on the organ. (The church has remained notable for its music and other cultural activities.)[35] The first minister was the Rev. J. J. McClure who transferred from the Irish Presbyterian Church. By now, partly because of geographical location, partly because of the predilection of congregations, and finally because the mission

THE CHURCH AND EDUCATION

organisations were separate both organisationally and in terms of their 'clientele', the new suburban churches were almost universally white in character.

Meanwhile the Scots on the Eastern Cape frontier had been holding services since their arrival. They built a church at Glen Lynden by 1828 and the Rev. John Pears arrived as the first minister.[36] He did not stay long, moving on into educational work, and the church, which still stands, was eventually handed over to the DRC, the Scots being soon in the minority in the area. Longer-lasting Presbyterian churches were founded in Port Elizabeth (1870),[37] East London,[38] Somerset East,[39] Grahamstown (1827),[40] King William's Town,[41] Adelaide,[42] Pietermaritzburg (1880),[43] Durban, Ladysmith,[44] Kimberley (1878), Pinetown,[45] Pretoria,[46] and Bloemfontein (1898)[47] as well as in many other towns. As we have seen in Chapter 5, the first minister at Pinetown was the Rev. Charles Scott, who arrived in Natal on the *Unicorn* in 1850. The Rev. William Campbell, originally from Thurso, in Caithness, a Free Church minister on the same ship, set about establishing the Presbyterian Church in Natal. He had been commissioned by the Free Church Colonial Committee, after the Glasgow agent of Byrne's emigrant company, Robert Beveridge, had suggested that a minister should be appointed to accompany the Scots emigrants. A meeting of Presbyterians was held in Pietermaritzburg in October 1850 and Campbell attempted to minister to Scots in both Durban and Pietermaritzburg. He was called to the latter town in 1851, and between late 1853 and early 1854 he set out on an extended journey to the United States, Canada, Ireland, England and Scotland. He raised £1,225. He also tried to promote further emigration.[48] Meanwhile Presbyterian services had been taking place in the Congregational and Dutch Reformed Churches.

The new church was duly completed in 1864.[49] A number of prominent early settlers, such as William Arbuckle and James Brown, were instrumental in managing this and the construction was achieved through the help of the mason John McPherson.[50] McPherson literally had several strings to his bow. As well as mason and plasterer he was a fiddler, much in demand to provide musical entertainment. In 1851 he began to offer dancing classes in Pietermaritzburg, grandly describing himself as 'Professor of Dancing from Edinburgh'. He charged half a guinea for a monthly lesson and seems to have done well.[51] Whatever Campbell thought of this activity, the church still stands, on one of the prime sites of the city. It is now known as Pemba Kahle and houses the education department of the adjacent art gallery. Campbell, who seems to have had a high conception of the status of minister, also set about building an exceptionally large manse which stimulated some hostile comment, one critic suggesting that it was as grand as that of 'the rulers of the land'. The acquisitive Campbell seems to have taken the land due to his servant Euphemia McIntyre, who accompanied the family to Natal, Campbell having paid her passage. But he failed to secure the 100 acres promised to him under the Byrne scheme. When he attempted to seek compensation through the land awards under the proclamation of April 1857 he was turned down. Although he ensured that the distinctions of the Disruption were ignored, and Presbyterians in Natal initially avoided the schismatic tendencies of home, Campbell's imperious personality ensured another split. In 1865 a probationer, the Rev. John Smith, arrived from Scotland to support him in conducting services in Pietermaritzburg and the surrounding parishes. They soon fell out, and in 1870 Smith founded the Second Presbyterian Church in Pietermaritzburg. Campbell's other contribution to public life was that he served on an eight-man education commission in the colony in 1853. He was also instrumental in the formation of the presbytery of Natal in 1882, by which time there were at least four ministers in the colony.[52] His ambition to keep the Presbyterians together failed: in the 1860s a mission of the Free Church was opened in Pietermaritzburg with the Rev. John Bruce as its first minister.[53]

A document dating from 1860, appealing to the 300 Scots in Port Elizabeth to found their own church, is fascinating in its invocation of identity. This public notice proclaimed that Scots were attached to the land of their birth, that they loved 'to expatiate on the beauty of its scenery' and the 'records of its people', that 'fond memory loves to dwell' on its 'rugged mountains, verdant dales, romantic glens and classic streams', all invoking the 'tenderest associations'. Visitors to Port Elizabeth were surprised at the lack of a Scottish church, a standing reproach. Scots were indebted to their Church for their prosperity, since the Church had taught 'lessons of industry, frugality and self-denial'. They should therefore show their gratitude by stirring themselves to create a church that would be the 'pride and boast of the country'.[54] This appeal is instructive for its association of landscape and geographical features with the social traditions of the Scottish Church while also suggesting that Scots owed their colonial success to its principles and practices. It makes it clear that important elements of identity were bound up with the Church. Moreover, the considerable growth in the number of Presbyterian churches in the nineteenth and early twentieth centuries represents the manner in which Scots fanned out across the country and, in particular, arrived in the Boer republics in the 1880s and 1890s.

As the number of Scots on the Witwatersrand built up after the discovery of gold, one Scots minister became a peripatetic founder of churches. This was the Rev. James Gray (1852–1938), who had been minister in Harrismith.[55] He established a congregation in Johannesburg as early as 1887 which met in a building which later became a hotel, but St George's Presbyterian church in Joubert Park was built soon afterwards.[56] He moved on to establish a congregation in Pretoria, where he was also influential in helping to found the State Library.[57] Presbyterian churches were also established in Fordsburg, Jeppe, Germiston (named after a farm in Lanarkshire), Boksburg and Klerksdorp, all in the Witwatersrand area. Calls went out to Scots ministers to come to take charge of these. In the 1890s several Presbyterian congregations were established in the principal towns of what would become Southern Rhodesia, and Gray was again influential in this. But Gray became closely identified with the *uitlanders* and was *persona non grata* in the republic when war broke out. He became chaplain with the Scots Fusiliers. After the fall of Pretoria[58] he returned as pastor of St Andrew's, chaplain of eight military hospitals and state librarian until 1902. In 1903 he collected £1,500 in Britain for a war memorial window at St Andrew's, completed in 1907. His later career took him to Trinity, Grahamstown and to Clifton in Johannesburg. In 1921 he unveiled the David Livingstone statue at the Victoria Falls.

The association of these Churches with Scotland itself, including the use of the word 'Scottish', continued until the 1890s. But, although these connections were to continue into the twentieth century, it was in that decade that the first signs of an independent organisation began to appear. The presbytery of the Cape was formed in 1893. (Natal's seems to have preceded it.) Other presbyteries soon followed, and a General Assembly was first established in 1897. This, nevertheless, reveals the relatively slight scale of the Church. In 1898 there were thirty-seven congregations with a total of 4,653 members and thirty-seven ministers.[59] There were also ten 'native congregations', nine in Kaffraria and one in Pretoria, and eighteen mission stations with 702 members (what seems like a pitifully small number, but presumably it refers to fully communicant members).[60] A photograph of the members of the General Assembly which met in Cape Town in 1898 reveals thirty-eight unsmiling and severely Victorian figures. Among them was the Rev. W. A. Soga, MD, son of Tiyo, and two other unidentified black faces.[61] At this point the assembly was trying to display its multi-racial credentials, even if the blacks were in a tiny minority.

So far, the history of the Presbyterian Church and its Scottish affiliations seems predominantly male. But there were, obviously, women in the congregations (and two donated independently to the subscription for the St Andrew's church in Cape Town). Women also played a traditional role as Sunday school teachers. (The school which preceded the Gardens church listed six female teachers in 1894.) As early as 1846 a Ladies' Missionary Association had been founded at St Andrew's church to parallel a Gentlemen's equivalent (clearly it was thought inconceivable that men and women should serve together, though the existence of a women's society so early is significant) and women had generally associated themselves with the work of mission. Later, in keeping with the emergence of so many women's organisations around the time of the Anglo-Boer War, pressure developed in those years for the founding of a Presbyterian Women's Association. It was initially resisted, but the 1904 assembly was attended by the wives of ministers, and Mrs Andrew Brown and Mrs James Gray (identified as was the custom in that period with their husband's Christian names) set about establishing such a body.[62] Mrs Gray, when her husband was Moderator in 1902, had attended assemblies in London and Edinburgh, had been impressed by the work of women, and had brought the idea back to South Africa. Mrs Brown (presumably a recent migrant) had been active in Scotland in the Scottish Mothers' Union, in temperance and social work and in the Girls' Guild. The pamphlet history of the movement indicates that initially the women suffered from criticism and misunderstanding of their activities, but the movement soon spread throughout the Presbyterian networks of the country. They involved themselves in temperance and other social work, as well as in closer Sunday observance (which presumably helped to establish their credentials with the male body of ministers). They also tied up with Caledonian Societies to establish the 'Lonely Settler Campaign' which set about identifying and helping those in isolated districts (and therefore presumably most at risk from the consolation of drink or even inter-racial sex), including sending out postal packages to them. The annual reports became a record of membership and of money raised, and one interesting feature is the extent to which white and black numbers were included in these statistical accounts, including the money-raising activities of black members. What is not clear, however, is whether these worked together in the same branches or were established in separate ones. In 1913, for example, it was said that there were 2,138 whites and 1,787 blacks in the Orange Free State; in 1916–17 there were 2,344 white members and 1,327 black in Durban. In King William's Town the African numbers exceeded the white (3,500 to 2,400 in 1919), while in Cape Town there were relatively few black women involved. African women seem to have been particularly active in raising funds for the Orphanage Building Fund. At this point women seemed to be asserting their gender role across the colour line, but their opportunities to do so would become increasingly limited. They were also establishing the parameters of respectability and in doing so were attempting to raise others to their own bourgeois status.

Education

Schools

A South African encyclopaedia asserts that the primary and secondary curricula of the country's schools (here dealing primarily with whites) were particularly modelled on those of Scotland.[63] The reasons for this are not hard to find. It is not just that many of the earliest teachers were Scots, it is also the case that the most influential superintendents of education in at least three of the territories that eventually made up the Union were Scots. At the Cape, the first superintendent was James Rose Innes, himself recruited as a teacher in the 1820s. Later in the century his successor (but one), generally regarded as the most influential of all educational administrators, was Sir Thomas Muir. The first superintendent in the Orange Free State was John Brebner, while the influential counterpart in Natal was Robert Russell. All four of these figures placed an indelible stamp upon the educational system of the separate colonies and republic, ensuring that there would be a fairly high degree of uniformity at the time of the Union. If this was the case in the state school system (as well as in many mission schools, as we saw in Chapter 4) it was less true of the private school sector, which was modelled on the English 'public' schools.[64] But all these fed into a tertiary sector which (both in its white and black forms) was indelibly influenced by Scottish models.

This was even true at infant and primary level. The Haddington-born James Buchanan, partly influenced by Joseph Lancaster, creator of the Lancasterian school system, founded a school for the children of workers at Robert Owen's New Lanark. He later moved to London. All three of his sons, William, David Dale and Ebenezer, emigrated to the Cape, the latter two later moving on to Natal. William and David had been heading for New Zealand, but were persuaded to stay at the Cape when their connections with James and his school system were recognised. Ebenezer went to the South Seas with the missionary John Williams and spent some time there before returning to South Africa. William founded a school, mainly for the children of slaves, in 1830, and later added a department for whites. David, at a very tender age, assisted him before being sent into the interior to open a school for the Khoi. Their father, James, mother and sister Agnes arrived in Cape Town in 1839 and began to help William with his school. Curiously, James had also been intending to sail to New Zealand. Cape Town often scored in this way from being en route to other places.

To revert to the 1820s, it is a strange aspect of the 'Anglicisation' policy at the Cape that Somerset felt that the educational arrangements designed to concentrate on English-language instruction could best be carried out by Scots. As we have seen, George Thom was sent to Scotland to recruit a sort of job lot of ministers and teachers, clearly designed to demonstrate to the Afrikaners of the colony that the authorities had their spiritual needs in mind when setting about educating them in 'English' ways. Yet this early recruitment did not turn out to be an unqualified success. Only James Rose Innes, Archibald Brown and William Robertson had degrees, all from Aberdeen. Robert Blair, from Glasgow, William Dawson, from Aberdeen, and James Rattray, from Dundee, were not graduates but were trained primary teachers. Rattray had also taught in a school for the deaf in Dundee. All had learned some Dutch before departing and spent the voyage trying to improve their language skills. At the Cape, they fanned out to their various educational assignments: Dawson was sent to George, Innes to Uitenhage, Rattray to Tulbagh, Brown to Stellenbosch and Blair (eventually) to Caledon.

As we shall see below, only Rose Innes was to have a notable career in education, while Robertson switched to the ministry. Rattray took to drink after the death of his young son and was dismissed; Brown neglected his duties, left his job in 1831 and opened a private school; Blair gave up teaching to become Clerk of the Peace; while Dawson plodded on in George until he retired in 1840 (he was older than the others). Interestingly, he was then appointed 'instructor to the heathen', but it is difficult to establish precisely what that entailed.[65] There were twenty-seven of the 'English Free Schools', founded by Somerset, in the country districts but they were never popular, and the standard of teaching was often poor. In the 1830s attempts were made to reform the system, although these were postponed because of the usual financial constraints. It was only with the appointment of James Rose Innes as the first superintendent-general of education that education for whites at the Cape began to be developed properly.

Innes (1799–1873) was born in Banffshire and educated at King's College, Aberdeen, graduating in 1822. As we have seen, he was recruited by Thom and sailed for the Cape, where he became government instructor at Uitenhage. There he successfully used Dutch as a medium of instruction (what had happened to Anglicisation?) and was a popular teacher. He further asserted his solidarity with the Afrikaans population by becoming a deacon in the DRC. In 1830 he became professor of mathematics at the newly founded South African College, at a time when many schools were in decay. In 1837 the colonial secretary, the Scottish Colonel Bell, wrote a memorandum for the Governor, Sir George Napier, on the unsatisfactory state of education in the colony. Fairbairn at the *Commercial Advertiser* had already conducted a campaign against the school commission[66] and he and Sir John Herschel joined Bell (a close friend of both) in pressing for a fresh start. A new government education department, albeit grossly understaffed, was created and Innes duly became the superintendent-general in 1839. His first move was to return to Aberdeen in 1840 and recruit six more Scottish teachers, bringing them back to South Africa on the *Greyhound* from Portsmouth.[67] (One of these teachers, John Paterson, was to become one of the most influential figures in the Eastern Cape.[68]) The number of schools in the colony proceeded to grow quite rapidly. In 1827 there had been twenty-seven village schools, with an average roll of fifty pupils. By 1844 there were twenty-five mission and twenty government schools with almost 5,000 pupils. In 1859, when Innes resigned, there were 18,000 pupils. Innes continued to staff the schools with teachers recruited in Scotland (but not exclusively) and transferred many characteristics of the Scots system to the Cape. He arranged for subsidies to be paid to missions for their educational activities, which were directed primarily at Africans. He was instrumental in founding a Normal School in Cape Town in 1842, which trained students for the civil service and business as well as teaching. Innes was, however, subjected to some criticism for the state of the educational system, but nevertheless he was appointed a member of a new Board of Examiners and became its secretary.[69] Aberdeen University awarded him a DL in 1860. Innes's son, another James Rose (1824–1906), became undersecretary for native affairs in the Cape administration, while his grandson was the celebrated chief justice of the Transvaal (1902–10) and of the Union (1914–27), Sir James Rose Innes (1855–1942).[70]

Scots teachers continued to be prominent at all levels at the Cape. As we have seen in Chapter 3, John Paterson (1822–80), from Rubislaw in Aberdeenshire, opened the first senior government school in Port Elizabeth in 1841.[71] In 1845 he founded the *Eastern Province Herald*. In 1855 he became chairman of the town commissioners and was a member of the legislative council from 1854 to 1874. Another Paterson, Thomas (1815–98), also became a teacher in Port Elizabeth, but in 1847 he was ordained and became minister of the Congregational church in Uitenhage. Yet another, William, from Macduff, became rector of Paarl Gymnasium and died at Paarl in 1880. Joseph Reid (1819–85), born in Rothiemay, had been appointed head of the government school in Port Elizabeth in 1848 and in 1850 became proprietor of the *Eastern Province News and Port Elizabeth Chronicle*. Later, James McLeish (1832–62), born in Perth, contrived in his short life to be the teacher at the government school in Swellendam and then the first headmaster of the Grey Institute in Port Elizabeth. James McLean (1878–1955), from Stranraer, was another teacher at the Grey High School, who was prominent in a variety of sporting organisations, embracing bowling, swimming, cricket, and rugby. He was also active in the educational union, the Teachers' Association.[72]

The Cape education department remained as something of a shoestring administration through the period when Langham Dale was in charge. In 1892 it still had a staff of only five, but in that year the most influential educationalist of all arrived in the colony. Thomas Muir (later Sir Thomas) was born in Lanarkshire in 1844. He was educated at universities in Glasgow, Berlin and Göttingen and joined the mathematics department of Glasgow University in 1871. In 1874 he became head of maths and science at Glasgow High School. His distinction as a mathematician was confirmed when he became president of the Edinburgh Mathematical Society and won a medal (on two occasions) of the Royal Society of Edinburgh for mathematical research. The new Superintendent General of Education transformed the department in the years up to his retirement in 1915.[73] By 1910 it had thirty-nine officials, including a significant inspectorate whose personnel he trained. He founded a journal in 1901, *The Education Gazette*, to develop greater corporate awareness and keep teachers in touch with developments, as well as a central Education Office library. He surveyed the educational needs of the colony, founded many schools, improved buildings and set the department on course for the introduction of compulsory education (for whites). Given his background, it is perhaps not surprising that he promoted agricultural and industrial education. He also introduced woodwork, needlework, singing and nature study into primary schools. (The gender implications are probably obvious.) He established training colleges and set about ensuring that the entry requirements of universities and other tertiary institutions were met. It has been said that 'many of the best traditions of Scottish education were included in his contribution to Cape education'.[74] Meanwhile he continued his mathematics research, publishing many papers in learned journals and a number of books. This secured for him an international reputation which was confirmed when he became a Fellow of the Royal Society in 1900. He was also closely involved with the cultural life of the Cape.[75] In 1901, neatly demonstrating the Scots grip on education, he appointed Adam Gordon MacLeod (1862–1907) from Glasgow as Deputy Inspector of Schools.[76]

THE CHURCH AND EDUCATION

It was not just the Cape where the educational system was largely dominated by Scots. The Orange Free State educational service was effectively set up by another. John Brebner (1833–1902), the son of a small-scale farmer, was born in Auchenblae. Educated in Laurencekirk and at Aberdeen Grammar School, he went on to Marischal College in that city. After a period as a schoolteacher at the grammar school (he was also ordained as a minister in the Free Church), he failed to secure the rectorship when it became vacant in 1856. He was then recruited by William Robertson to take on the rectorship of Albert Academy at Burghersdorp in the Cape Colony. He was also invited to become minister of the Scots Kirk in Port Elizabeth, but declined. He arrived on the Eastern Cape in 1861 and was initially taken aback by the lack of cultivation, as he saw it, of the people on the Zuurveld and by the primitive character of the school. But he soon raised a considerable sum of money for the building of a new school and the pupils flocked in. He learned Dutch quickly and charmed pupils and their parents with his musical ability. In 1869 he moved on to Somerset East, where he helped in the establishment of Gill College and became its first Professor of Classics. The third James Rose Innes was one of his pupils. This experience brought him to the attention of the Volksraad of the Orange Free State which offered him the post of Inspector of Education, which he occupied from 1874 to 1891, when he was appointed the first Superintendent of Education.

In 1874 he toured the entire republic and was startled by the rudimentary nature of its educational system. There was no means of training teachers, but the Rev. Andrew Murray junior, minister of Bloemfontein, set about establishing a training college for girls to prepare them for primary work. Brebner had to cope with a territory where the white population was highly scattered and had to persuade a Volksraad, whose members were themselves relatively untutored, to supply the funds. Nevertheless, under his supervision the system grew from having only ten government schools with twelve teachers and 348 pupils in 1874 to one in which there were 199 schools, 293 teachers and 8,157 pupils in 1898. There were also forty-two private schools. He himself wrote a handbook for teachers. He became an elder of the DRC church in Bloemfontein and frequently preached there. In 1881 he toured Europe and the United States (and also visited Scotland, where he promoted some teacher recruitment) in order to study recent educational developments. He became extraordinarily influential in the Free State. It was said that President Brand frequently consulted him and, at the time of the Jameson Raid, he was actually acting state secretary because the state secretary had become acting president during President Reitz's illness. He was also a director of the national bank of the Orange Free State. In 1896 he founded a Normal School in Bloemfontein and in the same year he secured £6,000 from the Volksraad for the provision of schools for poor whites. By that year the number of Scots had grown to such an extent that a Presbyterian church was founded in the capital. Because, as the anonymous author of a memoir wrote, he never 'forgot that he was a Scotchman', he was active in the development of this church, became an elder and frequently took services. He was also a founder member of the Caledonian Society. It is said that he was greatly admired by the Volksraad, and it is clear that his combination of piety, holy orders and learning appealed to Afrikaners in the republic. The timing of his retirement in 1899 was fortunate, since it obviously saved him from any conflict of loyalties.[77]

Like Brebner, Robert Russell (1843–1910), the most influential superintendent of the Natal education system, was of humble origins. His educational attainments were also relatively slight. The son of a tailor, he was educated at the Church of Scotland training school in Edinburgh. He enrolled for an arts course at the University of Edinburgh but did not obtain a degree. Despite this, he was appointed headmaster of the newly opened Durban High School in 1866, a neat demonstration of the opportunities for rapid promotion in the colonial setting. He held the post until he became Inspector of Schools in 1874.[78] Four years later he was Superintendent and secretary of the Council of Education.[79] After Responsible Government was granted to the colony, he was reappointed Superintendent and also served on the Natal Civil Service Board. He presided over a considerable expansion of education in Natal, in many respects aligning the Natal system with that of the Cape. He was instrumental in founding the tertiary Maritzburg College in the mid-1880s and subsequently served on the council of the University of the Cape of Good Hope. He wrote one of the first geography and history textbooks to be used in Natal,[80] and toured Europe in 1897 to study educational methods in Britain, Sweden and elsewhere.[81] In 1901 the colonial minister of education proclaimed that Russell 'is possessed of high administrative and organising ability; he is an educational enthusiast, and the present satisfactory state of the primary schools of this Colony is due in very large measure to his efforts. I am of the opinion that his services are entitled to special recognition, pecuniary and otherwise.'[82] Russell retired in 1903.[83] His successor was Charles John Mudie, born in Dundee in 1857, who was recruited by Natal as a teacher in 1883 and was Superintendent from 1904 to 1917. He was an enthusiastic supporter of the Natal Technical College and advocated the establishment of a university college.

If Innes and Muir, Brebner and Russell left an indelible stamp on

THE CHURCH AND EDUCATION

the educational systems of the Cape, the Orange Free State and Natal,[84] ordinary Scottish teachers worked in the schools of many of the most significant settlements. One such was Robert Templeton. Born in Kilmarnock, he went to Glasgow University, where he encountered the Rev. John Chalmers, later minister of Trinity Church in Grahamstown, who was to deliver his funeral address in 1886. Templeton secured a distinguished degree and was successively a master at Kilmarnock Academy and Madras College in St Andrews.[85] He went to New College in Edinburgh to study for the ministry, intending to go to either India or China, but while there he met some students from the Cape. As a result he went to Lovedale as a teacher, but soon moved on to take charge of schools in Uitenhage, Bedford and then to a new non-denominational public school in Grahamstown.[86] He was regarded as the most influential teacher and Head on the Eastern Cape frontier, and many students who had distinguished careers studied under him.[87] At a later period, one of the most influential head teachers in the Transvaal was a Scot, C. D. Hope, who seems to have specialised in establishing new schools. In 1901, during the British occupation of the capital, he founded the Pretoria Boys' High School. In the following year he went on to found the Jeppe Boys' High School in a suburb of Johannesburg, where a number of Scots had settled and there was a Presbyterian church. In 1904 he moved on to Potchefstroom, another town with a considerable Scots community, and founded yet another high school. After this intensely peripatetic period he settled in Potchefstroom for the rest of his life, even refusing to take on the headmastership of the notable King Edward's School in Johannesburg when offered it in 1908.[88]

While Hope was opening and heading schools, anxiety to recruit Scottish teachers had re-emerged during the Anglo-Boer War and in the reconstruction period which followed. The concentration camps (which the British called 'refugee camps') inspired Campbell Bannerman's celebrated remark about 'methods of barbarism', but they also stimulated intense education efforts. Milner's education secretary, Edmund Beale Sargant, discovered that a self-help school had been created at one camp, and this caused him to found one at Norval's Pont in early 1901. Soon the idea was spreading throughout the camps and the British administration explicitly saw this as a means to Anglicisation. Emily Hobhouse, who created a political storm with her condemnation of conditions in the camps, saw the schools as 'the only bright spot in camp life'.[89] By the final months of the war there were 17,000 children attending camp schools in the Transvaal and 12,000 in the Orange River Colony, considerably more than in public schools in those territories. All these schools had to be staffed, and the expectation was that they would be staffed by women. The call went out for patriotic teachers from the United Kingdom, all of whom had to pass the test that they believed in the annexation of the two republics and would work to reconcile the inhabitants of the camps to their new status in the British Empire. Recruitment started in 1901 and interviews were conducted throughout Britain. Sir Henry Craik of the Scotch Education Department (SED) was soon involved and insisted that experienced elementary school teachers would be best rather than 'highly strung' women from Girton or Newnham. This was essentially a class as well as an ethnic point. He was effectively saying that lower middle-class Scots would prove more adaptable than upper-class English. In the end, thirty-three places in the recruitment went to Scots and sixty-seven to England and Wales. There were several thousand applicants and soon a new contingent was called for, in the same ethnic proportions as before. One-third of all recruits were also expected to come from the other 'white dominions',[90] clearly with the objective of spreading some kind of imperial patriotism.[91]

Craik made the ritual point about the sympathies between Scots and Afrikaners and it does seem that Milner's English project was duly diluted by Scottish and Presbyterian recruits. (Some of the teachers from Canada, Australia and New Zealand may also have been of Scots and Presbyterian background.) Indeed, when in 1902 a Scottish official in the Colonial Office, Graham, had suggested that all teacher recruits should be Scots Milner had been sceptical on the grounds that they integrated too readily with Afrikaners.[92] But, with the end of the war, there can be little doubt that the Scots recruitment was designed to allay the religious fears of Boers in the former republics. This is later reflected in the transmission to the Secretary of State of a translation of a letter in the Pretoria newspaper *De Volkstem* of 11 May 1904 in which six DRC clergymen expressed anxieties about policy relating to education and religion, in particular on the appointment of teachers from England and the consequent influence of the Church of England.[93] Recruitment, of both men and women, had continued in the aftermath of the war and Scots again featured prominently. The Colonial Office had made enquiries at the SED about the salaries required as an inducement to Scots to migrate, as well as the pension requirements and other conditions.[94] Teachers had already begun to travel to posts in the Transvaal and the Orange River Colony by February 1902.[95] By May of that year, the Colonial Office was informing the SED that more teachers were required from Scotland.[96] These teachers were offered £300 per annum if they found accommodation and food for themselves and £200 if they were provided with accommodation and rations. Sometimes the accommodation amounted to a tent at one of

THE CHURCH AND EDUCATION

the 'refugee camps'. Some were accompanied by their wives, who were often also teachers, so that the administration secured two at the same time. A good deal about these arrangements emerges from complaints made by a Scots teacher, W. A. Reid who was unhappy with his conditions. Reid's wife was also teaching and their combined pay was £510.[97]

In 1904 Milner was seeking thirty-five young male teachers. A number of Scots had already accepted appointments and the High Commissioner sought information on their qualifications.[98] A year later, the Colonial Office again informed the SED that it was seeking to recruit yet another large batch of teachers for the Transvaal. These included five assistants and ten headmasters, who were expected to be men; four infant assistants, ten primary assistants and six more for other schools (three of whom were to be Jewish), all of these women; and another four males, together with five headmasters, for Johannesburg. It was hoped that these recruits would sail in June in order to take up appointments in July. The SED responded that it was doing its best to find the teachers but that the salaries were too low for the men (no mention of the women!) of the standing and attainment required.[99] Another tack was an attempt to find scholars to receive bursaries to study at the Normal School at Pretoria in order to qualify as teachers for the Transvaal Education Department, but once more the SED was dubious, suggesting that the inducements were not good enough. Initially only one candidate presented himself, the son of a minister who had a leaving certificate recognised by the Scotch Code, secured at Hutcheson's Grammar School in Glasgow, and recognised for admission to Glasgow University.[100]

Although the actual numbers are hard to come by, obvious questions arise from this further attempt to boost the number of Scots teachers and students in South Africa. The first is why the SED was prepared to be as co-operative as it was. It might be assumed that its first responsibility was to ensure that sufficient teachers were forthcoming to staff schools in Scotland. It can only be surmised that there was at least a degree of overproduction such that they were prepared, perhaps in the interests of imperial patriotism, to comply with the requests of the Colonial Office in finding recruits for a variety of different categories of schools – temporarily in the camps, on farms (farm schools were common in the former Boer republics), as well as in towns and cities. The second must be why some teachers were prepared to offer themselves, particularly if the inducements were not much greater than could be secured in Scotland itself. Moreover, in some places at least, such teachers were going to bury themselves in fairly remote schools, lacking much in the way of intellectual or cultural sustenance. During the period of the war, patriotism may have operated as one motivation. But they were presumably also driven out by a relative lack of jobs at home, by the continuing poverty and social deprivation of so many Scottish communities, and by the expectation that opportunities for promotion and for higher salaries would be better in South Africa. South Africa was also, of course, competing with Canada, Australia, New Zealand and other territories of the empire. It is also important to remember that, whereas the nineteenth-century recruitment had been almost entirely male (though wives often took up teaching or auxiliary roles, for low or no pay), women teachers were now being employed in quite large numbers. We should also notice that it was a time of intensive recruitment of nurses and servants.

There can be little doubt that the appointment of so many Scots (and there were of course Afrikaner teachers as well) served to dilute the original vision of Milner and Sargant. Anglicisation was invariably an imperial ambition that foundered on practicalities. Still, it would be good to know how Scottish teachers adapted to the demands of the camp and town schools in the new imperial territories, how well they learned Afrikaans, how far they used the language in their teaching, what their relations were like with Afrikaner pupils and their parents, and how long they stayed in the profession rather than moving on into marriage or other posts.[101] Nevertheless, the effects of the Scottish influence upon the educational system in South Africa could emerge in strange ways. At the time of the Boer War, William Robertson (perhaps related to the original teacher migrant, William Robertson) was a DRC minister in the Free State responsible for appointing chaplains to the concentration camps, where, as we have seen, the schooling was often undertaken by Scottish teachers. When Robertson wrote a pamphlet about the camps, he reflected on this:[102]

> The fruits of these educational institutions will be reaped in after years. I fear I have to accuse some of the respected ladies from North of the Tweed of putting an indelible stamp of the Scottish national character on the characters of our children. When Mrs. Robertson was visiting a friend in the Bloemfontein camp, this worthy woman praised the schools, and among other things made special mention of the singing which was taught in them. A five year old girl was called to sing to my wife, and to her astonishment the little one struck up 'Far awa' frae bonnie Scotland' . . .

Higher education

Scots seem to have played as disproportionate a role in higher education as they did in school teaching. We have already seen in Chapter 3 how closely they were involved in the founding of the South African

THE CHURCH AND EDUCATION

College and in intellectual institutions at the Cape. This was also the case when the University of the Cape of Good Hope was founded in 1873, initially primarily as a qualifying and examining body. In 1916 the university sector was divided into two independent universities, Cape Town and Stellenbosch, together with the federal University of South Africa, which was the degree-awarding body for a number of colleges, including those in Grahamstown, Durban, Pietermaritzburg, Bloemfontein, Pretoria and the Witwatersrand. Indeed, because it was so difficult to export the collegiate systems of Oxford and Cambridge, it was generally the case that the Scottish universities offered the model for tertiary development around the British Empire. In the case of South Africa, M. Boucher has asserted that 'no student of our university system can fail to be struck by the high proportion of Scotsmen who have, over the years, aided its development'.[103] A correspondent in a Cape journal argued in 1880 that more Scottish professors should be recruited, 'for they are so much better than the products of Oxford and Cambridge'. There are perhaps several reasons for this. The first is that, as in Scotland, the dividing line between secondary and tertiary education was blurred. Second, Scotland invariably supplied professors in practical, scientific and medical disciplines. And third, it may well be that Scots were less interested in cultural or intellectual Anglicisation.

Scots, or descendants of Scots, also had a tendency to call other Scots. The Minister, Andrew Murray, decided in the 1870s that the new DRC Normal College for the training of teachers in Cape Town should have a Scots principal. He summoned James Reid Whitton (1849–1919) from Perthshire, who had trained at Moray House and was principal of Melrose Public School. He took up his post in Cape Town in 1878 and also directed a small school. It has been estimated that more than 800 pupils were influenced by him, and he has been credited with raising the standards and esteem of the teaching profession in South Africa.[104]

The roll call of academics is certainly impressive. The early professors of the South African College included the Rev. James Adamson, James Rose Innes, the Edinburgh graduate the Rev. John Pears (who was briefly minister at the Scots church at Glen Lynden),[105] and soon there were others with names like Roderick Noble, Gorrie and Pillans (the latter from Edinburgh University). John Fairbairn, John Philip and the surgeon James Abercrombie were all members of the early council, with Sir David Tennant as its secretary. Later professors and lecturers included John Croumbie Brown, Presbyterian minister, botanist and forester (see the next chapter), Guthrie, Ritchie, Corstorphine, Crawford,[106] Beattie, Buchanan, Brown, Clark, Edgar, Loveday, Jolly,

Reyburn, Gilchrist, Stuart-Thomson, Leslie. Most of these were graduates of Glasgow, Edinburgh or St Andrews. Courses were also based on Scottish models. A diploma in engineering was instituted as early as the 1860s, following closely the Glasgow example. There were few takers until the development of mining called for more engineers in the 1890s. Courses in civil engineering, land surveying and navigation were similarly based on Glasgow.[107] Half of all the members of the first administrative council of the University of the Cape of Good Hope in 1873 had Scottish backgrounds, while 40 per cent of the graduates selected for posts had Scottish degrees. Victoria College, Stellenbosch, also had many Scots on its professorial staff, including Thomas Walker, A. Macdonald, A. H. Mackenzie, J. T. Morrison and William Thomson. Gill College at Somerset East was originally founded as a tertiary institution through the bequest of Dr William Gill, the local district surgeon from 1828 to 1863. Gill was English-born, but had studied medicine at Glasgow.[108] As well as his medical activities, he took up farming near Cookhouse and built up a considerable flock of merino sheep. He bequeathed an estate of well over £20,000 and left the bulk of it to the founding of the college. The foundation stone was laid in 1867 and it opened in 1869, modelled on Glasgow University. It was inevitably largely staffed from Scotland, but later failed to maintain its tertiary status. It ceased to be a college in 1903 (when Rhodes University College was founded in Grahamstown) and became a high school.[109] Scots also turned up on the staff of the University College in Natal, notably Alexander Petrie, from Banffshire, an Aberdeen graduate, who held the chair of classics for many years,[110] and the botanist John William Bews.

Scots were prominent as vice-chancellors: Thomas Walker,[111] Sir John Buchanan, Sir Charles Abercrombie Smith, Sir Jock Carruthers Beattie and William Ritchie were all vice-chancellors at the Cape. Indeed, the University of Cape Town was so dominated by Scots that it was jokingly referred to as the 'Scottish mission to the Jews', since the student body was somewhat biased in the direction of members of that faith. Carruthers Beattie also pointed to the significance of Scottish networks. The South African College and UCT were always closely associated with St Andrew's church. Other institutions were similarly colonised. The geologist George Corstorphine from Edinburgh, who had worked in Cape Town, was instrumental in founding the School of Mines and Technology in Johannesburg (which later developed into the University of the Witwatersrand) and became its first principal. Among his staff was John Orr of Glasgow, who had held a chair of mechanical engineering at the mine school in Kimberley before moving to the Rand. Though it reflects an era of discrimina-

THE CHURCH AND EDUCATION

tion, Scottish universities were instrumental in extending qualifications to women. St Andrews had created the LLA (Lady Licentiate in Arts) in 1877 and made it available to students resident in the colonies. The Transvaal Technical Institute offered a course leading to this qualification in Edwardian times.

From about 1905 pressures emerged for the founding of a South African Native College which would offer tertiary training to Africans for the first time. (Members of the Coloured and Indian communities would also join its student body.) A coalition of forces was active in this, including Scots missionaries (it was a favoured scheme of James Stewart), African nationalists and journalists such as Tengo Jabavu, and what was described as a 'philanthropic section of Europeans'.[112] It took ten years before the college left the planning stage, and it was established at the time when all South African tertiary education was reorganised in 1915. It was opened in the following year by Louis Botha. The choice of site is instructive. It was resolved to use one of the forts of the frontier wars era, on land owned by the Scots mission, near Alice and across the river Tyumie from Lovedale itself. The college was consequently located in a liminal zone, the classic point of contact invested with missionary, military and also frontier settler history. Thus higher education for Africans, a central aspect of the limited (for blacks) modernisation project in the new Union, would occur at the edge rather than the centre, its marginality re-emphasised during the apartheid era. It was also, of course, a convenient place in terms of the fairly dense African populations of the Ciskei and the Transkei and, despite its relative remoteness, could also be accessed from the Free State, the Transvaal and Natal. The first principal, Alexander Kerr (1884–1970), was a Scot, educated at Edinburgh University and Moray House training college, and he remained in the principalship until 1948. When he arrived at East London in October 1915 he was met by the Rev. George Blair of the Presbyterian Church and by John Tengo Jabavu, the editor of the first vernacular-language weekly paper, *Imvo Zabantsundu*, and a member of the first governing council of the college. Here were representatives of the coalition that had fostered the new institution. Kerr, only just over thirty, once again illustrated the opportunities for responsible positions at a young age in South Africa.

The college started off by offering both upper secondary as well as tertiary education, since the opportunities for qualifying for university-level entry were so limited, itself an indictment of black education.[113] The first intake of students numbered no more than twenty, including two women. There were only two members of staff, and students were entered for degrees of the University of South Africa.

Although the further history of the college lies outside the scope of this book, its foundation was certainly deeply influenced by Kerr and his Scottish educational background. Kerr himself pointed out that in the days of primitive schooling more than a hundred years earlier, white and African schools had not been dissimilar. But European schools had been transformed over that period, drawing well ahead of those for blacks.[114] Similarly the universities had catered to white needs. Kerr, in one of his testaments, referred to Africans as 'the victims at once of political and economic expediency, of fallacious race theories, and of obsolete social customs'.[115] In a striking passage he described the college's function as being to teach 'the broad and universal facts of science, laying bare the skeleton of nature's garment as well as that fashion of it peculiar to South Africa. Man's use of nature is one of its main concerns.'[116] The medium of instruction was a combination of the languages of the students with English, and education at Fort Hare was provided with a Christian slant. Arts, science and teacher training soon established themselves as the major disciplines, with theology, agriculture and business studies lagging rather further behind. Even if African professional opportunities were to be severely circumscribed, Kerr set about a broadly based education. It reflects much of the Scottish influence of the period. Many future African nationalists were trained there, together with students from elsewhere who were to be prominent politicians in their own countries.[117]

Notes

1. Jonathan Hyslop, 'Cape Town Highlanders, Transvaal Scottish: military "Scottishness" and social power in nineteenth and twentieth-century South Africa', *South African Historical Journal*, 47 (2002), pp. 98 ff.; Hyslop, *The Notorious Syndicalist: J. T. Bain, a Scottish Rebel in Colonial South Africa* (Johannesburg 2004).
2. The card indexes of ministers and missionaries in the Boonzaier Collection in the Archives of the Western Cape contain biographical details of some 120 Scottish ministers and missionaries who arrived in South Africa in the course of the nineteenth century. AWC: Boonzaier, A 2039, box 23.
3. There were said to be 100 churches in the Netherlands without ministers in the period.
4. M. Boucher, 'The Frontier and Religion: a Comparative Study of the USA and South Africa in the First Half of the Nineteenth Century', M.A. dissertation, University of South Africa (Pretoria 1966), p. 27.
5. Professor of Divinity, 1814–40.
6. Thom was actually heading for India but decided that there were opportunities at the Cape and decided to stay there.
7. A number of secessions characterised the Protestant Church in Scotland in the eighteenth century. These were invariably based upon dissident views of patronage, establishment and subservience to the civil authority. Followers of the 'Auld Licht' tendency believed that the civil magistrate must regulate ecclesiastical affairs,

THE CHURCH AND EDUCATION

while the 'New Licht' wished to escape from such authority. Both of these came together in 1820 to form the United Secession Church. It is interesting that government subsidies for the employment of ministers at the Cape were ended only in 1875.

8   The passengers on the tiny 180 ton *Arethusa* comprised, in addition to Murray, Thom, his wife, two children and a maid; the clergymen Alexander Smith, W. R. Thomson, George Morgan, Colin Fraser and H. Sutherland, as well as the teachers James Rose Innes, Archibald Brown, William Robertson, James Rattray (and his wife) and William Dawson and his wife. Murray's diary reveals that it was an exceptionally eventful voyage, with gales, thunderstorms, contrary winds, becalming and a grounding on the Cape Verde Islands when the captain was discovered to be drunk. Esmé Bull, 'Rattray and Black – two Scottish schoolmasters', *Familia*, 28: 4 (1990), pp. 54–62, particularly p. 54.

9   Faure went to the Cape to be involved in, among other things, journalism. We encountered him in chapter 3 as an associate of Thomas Pringle.

10 In his capacity as professor at Stellenbosch John published no fewer than twenty-nine books, ranging from theology to lessons from the Bible and sermons.

11 J. Du Plessis, *The Life of Andrew Murray of South Africa* (London 1920).

12 Elbie Truter, *Tibbie: Rachel Isabella Steyn 1865–1955. Haar Lewe was haar boodskap* ('Her life was her message') (Cape Town 1997).

13 Boucher, 'The Frontier and Religion', pp. 20–7 and 47. Boucher even sees the Scots authoritarian tendencies, as well as the arrival of more Catholics and their priests at the Cape, as contributing to the motivations of the Great Trek.

14 The medium of these local elementary schools was often Dutch, emphasised by the so-called Lancasterian monitorial system in which older children taught the younger.

15 Michael Fry, *The Scottish Empire* (Phantassie 2001), p. 139.

16 J. W. Claasen, 'Skotse predikante en die geestelike bearbeiding van die Voortrekkers', *Hervomde Teologiese Studies*, 50: 1 (1994).

17 An archivist in Cape Town, Jacob van der Merwe, insisted that this was the case when I discussed my project with him.

18 One of the most prominent Catholics seems to have been Alexander Wilmot (1836–1923), born in Edinburgh. He was a civil servant in Port Elizabeth from 1853 and became Postmaster in that town in 1859. He was a member of the Legislative Council for twenty-one years and was active in the Temperance Alliance and the Volunteer Artillery. He was a prolific writer who was prominent in a number of charities. Pope Benedict XV made him a count of the Holy Roman Empire and he also held knighthoods of the Holy Sepulchre and of St Gregory. Margaret Harradine, *Port Elizabeth: a Social Chronicle to the End of 1945* (Port Elizabeth 1994), p. 285. One Natal settler, Alexander Forbes, complained that his wife was bringing his children up as Catholics. For their story see Chapter 5.

19 Among Natal settlers we can identify George Adams and James Arbuthnot as Episcopalians. See the relevant volumes of Shelagh O'Byrne Spencer, *British Settlers in Natal, 1824–1857: a Biographical Register* (Pietermaritzburg 1981 and following years).

20 As well as the celebrated LMS missionaries who were Congregationalists, the Buchanan family, educationalists, lawyers and newspaper editor, also adhered to that denomination, as did Natal settlers James Ellis and Alexander Forbes.

21 The account of the origins of Presbyterianism which follows is based on Frank Quinn and Greg Cuthbertson, *Presbyterianism in Cape Town: the History of St Andrew's Church, 1829–1979* (Cape Town 1979), *St Andrew's, Cape Town: a Centenary Record* (Cape Town 1929), as well as the entry on Presbyterianism in the *Standard Encyclopaedia of South Africa*.

22 *St Andrew's, Cape Town*, p. 7. There were initially only forty members, perhaps not surprising, since the society insisted that they should avoid entertainments like theatre and dancing.

23 'Resolutions passed at a Public Meeting of the Scottish and Presbyterian

Community on the 25th Day of November', printed by W. Bridekirk at the *Chronicle* office.

24 The list of subscribers illustrates the wealth of some members of the Scots community in the period. Charles Pillans contributed £400; Macdonald, Nisbet and J. Monteath £300 each, with £200 from Findlay, Mackenzie and others. Two women appeared on the list because the Loudon family seem to have resolved to contribute separately: Mrs Loudon £30, her husband £20 and their daughter £20. It would seem that Mrs Loudon had independent means and controlled the purse strings.

25 Neoclassicism was still standard in the 1820s, but even later, as suitable for churches in which preaching and the pulpit lay at the centre of worship; the Church of Scotland and other Presbyterian traditions continued to build in classical styles long after Gothic Revivalist buildings had become standard in England.

26 Dr Abercrombie protested about the name 'St Andrew's', insisting that it was a relic of Popery.

27 G. C. Cuthbertson, 'The impact of the emancipation of slaves on St Andrew's Scottish Church, Cape Town, 1838–1878', *Studies in the History of Cape Town*, 3 (1984), pp. 49–63.

28 The missionary impulse in St Andrew's was always strong and was represented in the founding of two societies in 1846.

29 G. C. Cuthbertson, 'The St Andrew's Scottish Church Mission in Cape Town, 1838–1878', *Contree: Journal for South African Urban and Regional History*, 9 (1981), pp. 12–18.

30 This did not stop him continuing to be an active member of the congregation.

31 Interestingly, in 1845 a Bengal civil servant, passing through the Cape and influential in the Calcutta Free Church, accused the Church of suffering from Erastianism and the operation of patronage. Morgan responded by insisting that the church was entirely free of patronage and was not under the jurisdiction of the Church of Scotland.

32 Cuthbertson, 'The impact of the emancipation of slaves', p. 60.

33 The site was eventually used for the Metropolitan Methodist Church, which survives.

34 For the history of the Gardens Church see E. C. Frost, 'History of Gardens Presbyterian Church, 1890–1940' (Cape Town 1940): Western Cape Archives Library, pamphlet, Vol. 18, JP 810. Gardens Church continued to 'call' its ministers from Scotland down to modern times. The present minister, the Rev. James Patrick, is Scots-born and trained. Gardens Church is now the most active in the central part of the city of Cape Town. St Andrew's still stands but is somewhat marooned in the road system near the dock area. Its congregation is now rather small.

35 All the works eventually cost £13,000, saddling the church with a debt which was discharged by 1921. It received some notable bequests. Frost, 'History of Gardens'.

36 The church is said to follow a Scottish 'T plan' style with heavy buttresses. When a new DRC church was built near by in 1874 Presbyterian services were again held at Glen Lynden. These continued until 1958, when a new 'settler memorial church' was dedicated, with Glen Lynden serving as a black missionary church. Apartheid had asserted itself. H. L. Huisman, 'Historical notes about places visited on the excursion to the Scottish settler valleys in the Winterburg range', *Looking Back* (Historical Society of Port Elizabeth), 14: 2 (1974), pp. 36–9. Another Presbyterian church was founded in the area by John Pringle on his farm, 'Glen Thorn', in 1840. Presbyterian services continued to be held there until the later twentieth century.

37 Some of the records of the presbytery of Port Elizabeth are in the Cory Library.

38 The first East London Presbyterian church was built on the west bank of the Buffalo River. The early services, from 1850, were held in a store before St Andrew's was built on a commanding site. The first minister was the Rev. John Russell.

THE CHURCH AND EDUCATION

Another Presbyterian church was built at Cove Rock in 1878. Services were also held in the Old Mutual Hall in Market Square, moving to St George's Hall in 1881. In 1901 the imposing St George's Church was opened, followed by more Presbyterian churches in the city in the twentieth century. *East London Centenary, 1848–1948: Official Souvenir Brochure* (East London 1948).

39 This church was badly damaged in a storm of 1877.
40 The records of this church 1827–62 can be found in the Cory Library.
41 A photograph of this church is in the Western Cape Archives: AG 12132.
42 This was known as the Agnes Mary Black Memorial Presbyterian Mission Church and is still in use.
43 A photograph of this church is in the AWC: AG 1474. Also KZNA: NAB C 317.
44 This church was converted into a hospital during the siege of Ladysmith in January 1900.
45 A fragment of a register of births and deaths from this church, dated 1851, is in KZNA: NAB A145
46 Ceremony of laying foundation stone of new Presbyterian Church Pretoria, AWC: AG 11556.
47 A pamphlet published on the seventy-fifth anniversary of the Bloemfontein St John's Presbyterian Church in 1973 (Bloemfontein 1973) can be found in the AWC: VAB St John's.
48 The details of Campbell's activities are to be found in the fourth volume of Spencer, *British Settlers*, pp. 24–6. This is partly based on A. Petrie, *The Presbyterian Church of Pietermartizburg, 1850–1950: A Centenary Review* (Pietermaritzburg 1950).
49 A number of sources, including the Pietermaritzburg town guide, give 1852, but it seems unlikely that the church would have been built before the fund-raising tour.
50 A. F. Hattersley, *The British Settlement of Natal* (Cambridge 1950), p. 191.
51 Alan F. Hattersley, *Portrait of a City* (Pietermaritzburg 1951), p. 31. For the early social and cultural life of Pietermaritzburg see also Hattersley, *Pietermaritzburg Panorama* (PMB 1938).
52 One of the oddest expressions of identification with the Presbyterian Church in Pietermaritzburg occurred in 1913 when a Mr and Mrs George Phimister applied for the remains of their two children to be exhumed from the English Church Cemetery to be reburied in that of the Scotch Church. Permission was granted and Mr Coney, undertaker and embalmer to the Chief Magistrate, got to work. It may be that it was simply easier for the Phimisters to visit the Scottish Cemetery, but it is also possible that they saw it as Presbyterian or Scottish ground rather than Anglican. KZNA: 1 PMB 3/1/1/1/1, MC 210–13.
53 Ian Darby and Patrick Maxwell, 'World Religions in Pietermaritzburg' in John Laband and Robert Haswell (eds), *Pietermaritzburg 1838–1988: a New Portrait of an African City* (Pietermaritzburg 1988).
54 'Printed circular addressed to Scotchmen resident in PE, being a plea for the formation of a Presbyterian Church in that city, October 1860', donated by the Rev. R. Orr, AWC: A 2449.
55 Gray was from Eddleston and was educated at Glasgow Academy and Edinburgh University. Tuberculosis forced him to seek a healthier climate and he was inducted at Harrismith in 1883, then to the goldfields in 1887. He was fourth Moderator of the General Assembly of the Presbyterian Church of South Africa and founded the Presbytery in Southern Rhodesia.
56 Moray Macdonald Franz, 'An introduction to the contribution made by the Scots to the development of Johannesburg', *Between the Chains: Journal of the Johannesburg Historical Foundation*, 15 (1994), pp. 18–22.
57 He and F. T. Nicholson collected £700 and presented this amount to the republican authorities to establish the state library.
58 An indication of the interest in Scotland in the Anglo-Boer War is that a pub in Crieff, Perthshire, was named the Pretoria. It retains the name to this day, has

an active soldier as its pub sign, and contains memorabilia and photographs relating to the fall of Pretoria. So far as local memory serves, it was named by a publican who returned from the war.

59 Rev. Dr D. Wark, 'After 40 Years: a Sketch of the Growth of the Presbyterian Church of South Africa, 1898–1938', reprinted from the *Presbyterian Churchman*, December 1939. By 1938 there were eighty-four congregations with 18,665 members.

60 This was said to have experienced a tenfold increase by 1938.

61 One may have been the Rev. E. Makubala from Kaffraria and the other the Rev. P. Matshikwe, who had been ministering in Simonstown before going to Somerset West.

62 Pamphlet, 'Presbyterian Church of South Africa Women's Association, 1904–1927' (Cape Town 1927).

63 *Standard Encyclopaedia of South Africa*, entry on 'Curricula'.

64 Peter Randall, *Little England on the Veld: the English Private School System in South Africa* (Johannesburg 1982).

65 The careers of these teachers are detailed in Bull, 'Rattray and Black', pp. 55–9.

66 V. D. Westhuizen, 'Die Skool Kommissie 1804–1839', *Archives Year Book for South African History* (1953, no. 2).

67 These teachers were John McNaughton (who was sent to Wynberg), Patrick Black (to Worcester), George Bremner (to Paarl), John Paterson (Port Elizabeth) and Joseph Reid (Somerset East). George Cromar followed later. These teachers supplemented some from England who had been recruited by Sir John Herschel. This group was rather more successful than the first lot. McNaughton taught competently in Wynberg until his retirement. Black, who came from a distinguished family in Musselburgh, worked with Rattray in Worcester and married Rattray's daughter Isabella, who was also a teacher. He suffered from severe health and financial problems and died in 1847. Bremner taught in Paarl, Graaff Reinet and Swellendam, then settled in Cape Town. One of his pupils was President Burgers of the Transvaal, who offered him a senior post in the Transvaal just before he died at the age of fifty-three. Cromar left teaching to have a very successful career as a legal clerk, Clerk to the Peace, and later Civil Commissioner and Resident Magistrate of Albert. He was the founder of the Standard Bank of South Africa.

68 Paterson (1822–80) gave up teaching for journalism and business, being replaced by Joseph Reid as head teacher of the government school in Port Elizabeth. (Reid also became town clerk of Port Elizabeth.) He founded the *Eastern Province Herald* in 1845, later the *Port Elizabeth Telegraph*. Initially he wrote anonymously so as not to jeopardise his government post, but in 1847 he resigned and became the paper's editor. He subsequently became involved in banking, in a general store, in insurance and in a building society. He bought up town land cheap and became exceptionally rich. (When forming the company of Paterson & Kemp, general merchants, he put in £30,000 capital.) He became an MLA, was described as an excellent speaker and always retained a strong Scots accent. He made frequent visits back to England and Scotland in the 1860s and 1870s. Pamela Ffolliott and E. L. H. Croft, *One Titan at a Time: the Story of John Paterson of Port Elizabeth, South Africa, and his Times* (Cape Town 1960). One contemporary memoir credited him with being the instigator of the Port Elizabeth town hall, the Grey Institute, the North End Park and other PE institutions and architecture. R. W. Murray, *South African Reminiscences* (Cape Town 1894), p. 91. Murray also noted the influence of other Scots of his time.

69 See entries on Innes in *DSAB* and *SESA*. See also John D. Hargreaves, *Academe and Empire: Some Overseas Connections of Aberdeen University, 1860–1970* (Aberdeen 1994), pp. 79–80.

70 Sir James Rose Innes, unusually, received all his education at the Cape but he went to schools in Uitenhage and Bedford, where he came under the influence of the Scots teachers, Mr Gibson and Robert Templeton. He spent a lot of time

THE CHURCH AND EDUCATION

in the Scots community at Lynedoch and other places where the 1820 settlers had carved out their farms. As well as being the grandson of the first James Rose Innes, he was the great-grandson of Robert Hart, the officer who founded Somerset East. Yet he professed himself eager to be called an Afrikaner, but declared that he could not share their view of the 'Native question'. James Rose Innes, *Autobiography* (Oxford and Cape Town 1949), pp. 3–8.

71 Paterson drowned in the wreck of the *Senegal* at Madeira when on a visit back to Britain.
72 These examples are from Harradine, *Social Chronicle*, pp. 269, 273, 275.
73 A great deal of detail about Muir can be found in Herman M. Dalebondt, 'Sir Thomas Muir en die Onderwys in Kaapland tydens sy bertmer as Superintendent-General van Onderwys 1892–1915', doctor of education dissertation, Stellenbosch University (1942).
74 *SESA*, vol. 7, p. 634.
75 See his obituary in *The Education Gazette*, 5 April 1934.
76 MacLeod was educated at Glasgow University and the Free Church Training College. Arriving in Cape Town in 1889, he briefly taught at the Normal School before becoming headmaster of Beaconsfield Public School and then the first Principal of Simonstown High School. He listed his interests as Celtic literature and customs and he became honorary chieftain of the Cape Highland Society.
77 Anon., *Memoir of the Life and Work of Rev. John Brebner, M.A., LL.D., late Superintendent of Education in the Orange Free State, South Africa* (Edinburgh 1903).
78 He took office in January 1875. For details of Russell's career see J. Forsyth Ingram, *The Story of an African City* (Pietermaritzburg 1898), pp. 120–3.
79 Russell's predecessor had been R. J. Mann (arrived in Natal in 1857), who had no qualifications for the post. He later became Emigration Agent in the United Kingdom.
80 Robert Russell, *Natal, the Land and its Story: a Geography and History for the Use of Schools* (Pietermaritzburg 1891). This text went through several editions.
81 He was impressed by technical education in Sweden and founded a technical school in Natal on the model of Uppsala. While in London he gave a lecture on education in South Africa at an 'educational gathering' sponsored by the Society of Arts and the Countess of Warwick. Ingram, *Story*, p. 123.
82 Minute by the Minister of Education to the Prime Minister, KZNA: AGO 1/8/81, 460A/1901.
83 He received obituaries in *The Times*, 5 July 1910, and *The Scotsman*, 6 July 1910.
84 If George Bremner had not died prematurely he might, at the invitation of President Burgers, have performed a similar function in the South African Republic.
85 This was a college to which many sons of civilians and military people in India and other colonies were sent for their education.
86 'In Memoriam: the Address delivered over the Bier on Thursday 21 January and the Sermon preached on Sunday evening 24 January 1886 on the Occasion of the Death of the Rev. Robert Templeton, Principal of the Public School, Grahamstown', by the Rev. John M. Chalmers, Minister of Trinity Church, South African Pamphlets, Vol. 18, CLG.
87 Rose Innes, *Autobiography*, pp. 6–7, provided a eulogistic sketch of the career and character of Templeton. Describing him as a man of rare quality, he wrote that a future Prime Minister of the Cape, two Chief Justices, a High Commissioner of the Union, judges of the Supreme Court and several leading barristers were all influenced by him.
88 Franz, 'Introduction to the contribution made by the Scots', p. 19.
89 Emily Hobhouse, *The Brunt of the War and where it Fell* (London 1902), p. 121.
90 Canada and Australia were asked to supply forty teachers each and New Zealand twenty.
91 Eliza Riedi, 'Teaching empire: British and dominions women teachers in the South African War concentration camps', *English Historical Review*, 120: 489 (2005), pp. 1316–47.

92 Donald Denoon, *A Grand Illusion: the Failure of Imperial Policy in the Transvaal Colony during the Period of Reconstruction, 1900–1905* (London 1973), p. 78
93 Enclosure in Milner to Chamberlain, 23 May 1904, NAP: Gov. 150, F1. Similar letters appeared in the *Potchefstroom Budget* and the *Western Chronicle*.
94 The reply to these enquiries was contained in Scotch Education Department (SED) to the Colonial Office (CO), 20 May 1902, NAP: Gov. 18 Gen 440/02.
95 Chamberlain to Milner, 7 February 1902, and Chamberlain to Milner, 21 June 1902, NAP: Gov. 11, Gen 95/02 and Gov. 18, Gen 440/02.
96 CO to SED, 16 May 1902, Gov. 18, 429/02.
97 Milner to Chamberlain, 28 March 1903, Gov. 131, Gen 187/03 and enclosures.
98 Their names were Messrs Bruce, Martin, Bain, Jude, White, Kay, Adam, Gillespie, Dallas, Jack, Campbell and Wood.
99 Lyttelton to Milner, 27 May 1905, with enclosures of correspondence dated 18 and 20 May. NAP: Gov. 320, 76/03.
100 Lyttelton to Selborne, 26 June 1905, NAP: Gov. 389, 76/05.
101 One piece of oral evidence relating to a later period emerged in the town of Winburg in the Free State. When introduced to Christoffel van der Linde, the town guide (b. 1920), he was intrigued by my name. This elicited the information that when he was a boy in the inter-war years the 'most popular young woman in the town' was a Miss Mackenzie from Scotland who taught in the school. She spoke Afrikaans and attended the DRC Church.
102 William Robertson, *Concentration Camps* (Cape Town 1903), p. 13.
103 M. Boucher, 'Some observations upon the influence of Scotland in South African university education', *Historia*, 14: 2 (1969), p. 98.
104 Entry by O. C. Erasmus in *DSAB*, III, pp. 841–2.
105 Pears had taught at Abbotshall, near Kirkcaldy, and was well connected. He had even been on a walking tour with Thomas Carlyle. William Ritchie, *The History of the South African College, 1829–1918* (two volumes, Cape Town 1918), I, pp. 58–9.
106 Lawrence Crawford (1867–1951) was born in Glasgow and educated at the university there. He became Professor of Maths at the South African College in 1898 and was in post until 1938. He was secretary and vice-chairman of the Senate of the University of South Africa for many years and was influential in a number of scientific bodies in Britain and South Africa.
107 M. Boucher, 'The University of the Cape of Good Hope and the University of South Africa, 1873–1946: a study in national and imperial perspective', *AYBSAH*, I (1972).
108 In a letter of the Rev. John Ross, 11 August 1866, to a Mr McKenzie of Glasgow, Gill is referred to as 'a countryman of ours' who, 'with all the canniness of his country, gave a great impulse to education on the frontier districts by leaving £20,000' for a college 'to have the University of Glasgow as a model, where he had his medical education'. He goes on to say that Gill arrived at the Cape at the same time as himself, that he made his money honestly and was a kind and considerate physician to the poor. 'He never took a fee from a missionary.' Gill's canniness was clearly extraordinary to have built up such a sum over a period of some forty years. CLG: MS 3243.
109 'H.L.H.', 'Some notes on the history of Somerset East', *Looking Back*, 15: 2 (1975), pp. 45–9; Boucher, 'University of Cape of Good Hope', p. 35.
110 S. J. H. Steven, 'Professor Alexander Petrie', *Acta Classica*, 2 (1959), pp. 7–10.
111 Walker (1847–1916) was born in Leith and educated in Edinburgh. He also attended courses in the Netherlands and Berlin. He was headmaster of the school in Paarl, 1876–78, before moving on to Stellenbosch. After a period as examiner and administrator in the University of the Cape of Good Hope he became Vice-chancellor in 1911.
112 CLG: Alexander Kerr Collection, PR 4105, folder 1/8, undated document but post-1948.
113 Secondary instruction ended only in 1937.

114 CLG: Alexander Kerr Collection, PR 4105, folder 1/8, document dated 7 November 1937.
115 Ibid. It is interesting that there is no entry on Kerr in the *DSAB*.
116 Ibid.
117 Two examples were Seretse Khama of Botswana and Charles Njonjo of Kenya.

CHAPTER SEVEN

The professionals: the environment, medicine, business and radicals

Scots and the environment

The relationship between Scots, their vision of Scotland and the landscape of the Cape has already been noted, particularly in respect of Thomas Pringle, in Chapter 2. But these environmental connections between Scotland and the Cape go much deeper. They can be identified as central to the development of the intertwining of environmentalism and evangelicalism in nineteenth-century southern Africa. Scots had a striking influence upon environmental ideas and the emergence of the sciences relating to forestry, agriculture, climate, hydrology and animal husbandry. Debates connected with drought, aridity, deforestation and dramatic climate swings had wider global significance, and these were in turn influenced by the Cape experience.

Moreover, Scots were highly influential in such practical fields as road building and surveying, which had scientific dimensions in the study of palaeontology and geology, the publicising of natural resources and discussion of the physical geography and geomorphology of the subcontinent. Medical men also had broad interests, and the Scottish medical schools were an important source of doctors for South Africa. Running through all these was a major interest in natural history, often acquired in Scotland, which fed into fascination with southern African fauna, first by hunting and then through conservation. No doubt many businessmen would have shared these interests, and it is certainly the case that a significant number of Scottish businessmen were deeply implicated in the economic transformation of the subcontinent, particularly in the era of the 'mineral revolution', with its distinctive and often damaging effects upon race relations, labour migration, and black dispossession and overpopulation on supposedly tribal land.

Migration and dispossession were also, of course, characteristic of Scottish social history. But some aspects of the landscape changes in Scotland preceded the Clearances and major emigration. The deforestation of Scotland had been noted by visitors, such as Boswell and

Johnson, in the eighteenth century, and improving landowners had been concerned to reforest their land. Two notable examples were the Dukes of Atholl in Perthshire and the Earls of Haddington in East Lothian. Interestingly, key figures who emigrated to the Cape came from both these areas. The planting of trees and the transformation of arable agriculture in the eastern counties and central belt of Scotland were seen as part of a redemptive process that fed into the mix of enlightened and evangelical ideas that were the intellectual inheritance of missionaries and others in the early nineteenth century. (It also helped to decant population into the towns and overseas.) The mission station would act both as a source of religious revival and dissemination of the Christian faith and as a setting for the renewal of the environment. Souls would be redeemed not only by the preacher but also by the planter of trees, the creator of gardens and the spreader of good agricultural practice. The missionary would be like the improving landlord and, as we have seen, the mission station would be the equivalent of the great estate, with its villages, its church (standing in for the great house), its working environment (sawmill, garden, workshops, irrigation system), hospital, school, the homes of the professionals, later the post office, telegraphic communication and other physical manifestations of the spread of the modern world.[1]

The frontier setting of mission stations re-emphasised such environmental objectives. For Robert Moffat, from Ormiston, in East Lothian, the degraded state of the environment around his mission station at Kuruman, and the evidence of increasing aridity and decline, were symptomatic of the essential sinfulness of the Tswana people of the area.[2] If they were saved, so would be their environment. Having moved beyond the Cape frontier in 1821, he published his *Missionary Labours and Scenes in Southern Africa* in 1842. The book is full of natural observations and, indeed, represents an intriguing tension between some of the science of the day, which Moffat actually footnotes, and his inclination to view the landscape in religious terms.[3] It was a landscape which could be made to work for Christians, but which served up drought and erosion for the 'heathen', tree-cutting Africans. Towards the end of the book there is an engraving of the mission, with ordered hedges, paths, plantings and buildings contrasting with the wildness beyond.[4]

Moffat's son-in-law David Livingstone echoed this by suggesting that one of the problems of the African was that he lacked a 'correct notion of the controul [sic] he exercises over the affairs of the world'.[5] If 'affairs of the world' can be deemed to embrace nature, then we can detect Livingstone's sense of a God-given capacity to exercise quasi-divine control. As a product of the central belt of Scotland, Livingstone had good reason to share an entire constellation of environmental ideas that were current at the time, though he was much less censorious and more inclined to an optimistic vision than Moffat. But he certainly carried on his travels images of enclosure, draining, improved farming practices and selective breeding that he would have seen in the agriculture of Lanarkshire, as well as new approaches to water supply through canalisation and irrigation, the application of fossil fuels, and his almost obsessive notion of the redemptive power of steam technology. Command over the environment had been greatly developed in the Scotland of his day, and there was no reason why that should not also happen in Africa. Indeed, it was a central notion of Romanticism that the wild could be physically and culturally tamed. It was also a major tenet of imperialism that, while Africans were allegedly at the mercy of their environment, whites could command and control it, in a perfect analogy of their political and military authority.[6]

Among Scots who brought these evangelical visions to the environment, few were as significant as John Croumbie Brown (1808–95).[7] Born in Haddington, he was the grandson of a distinguished theologian[8] and himself became a Congregationalist minister. He joined the LMS and was sent to Russia in 1833, subsequently joining the mission at the Cape between 1844 and 1848.[9] Some of his sermons were published as *Pastoral Discourses* in 1847 and often treated environmental as much as religious concerns. In 1847 he undertook a tour of the Cape which was to influence the subsequent direction of his career. He returned to Scotland in 1849 to study botany and in 1853 was appointed lecturer at King's College, Aberdeen. He returned to the Cape in 1862 as the Colonial Botanist and Professor of Botany at the South African College. In his official position he was indefatigable in his travels and in the causes he adopted, and is now regarded as having been far ahead of his time. He became almost obsessed with his 'maverick campaigning',[10] a controversialist who was sometimes dubbed a fanatic. He was dismissed in 1866 when the office was laid down at a time when the administration was retrenching during a recession. It had not helped that he had become unpopular with settlers, while scientists had criticised him for neglecting what might be described as pure botany. His concerns were primarily practical, particularly in the areas of agriculture and of forestry. Licking his wounds, he returned to Scotland and dedicated himself to writing and lobbying for environmental and forestry causes. His range of publications in this period was remarkable and confirmed his influence in forestry and environmental circles.[11] In all this he never had any doubt about the significance of Scotland and the Scots. When advocating the foundation of a national school of forestry, he wrote that 'Scotchmen can be most efficiently, and at the least expense, trained up so as manage our Colonial forests advantageously. That is a particular point to which I have given attention.'[12] Some Scots were appointed foresters later in the century, though not as many as Brown might have wished.[13]

For Brown, an increased knowledge of flora and the environment should be dedicated to the development of resources. He was interested in indigenous plants and wished to amass collections of them at the Cape Botanic Gardens; he also argued that the museum should act as a repository for specimens of Cape agricultural products. He reported on diseases in fruit trees, on the quality of grazing, and theorised about the problems of desiccation. He was convinced of the destructiveness of firing the veld (which both Africans and Afrikaners saw as regenerative), advocated the creation of dams and, above all, wrote abut the importance of forestry and the folly of not controlling forest fires. His annual reports as Colonial Botanist were major documents addressing all these issues and linking his observations and ideas with the science of the day. He also recognised the need for 'inter-colonial' action. In 1863 he sent circulars to a range of officials, at both senior and district levels, in many colonies, including St Helena, Victoria and India, asking for their reactions, and presumably the extent to which they were confirmed by their own observations, to his desiccation and climatic theories.[14] He had a considerable influence on Sir Joseph Hooker, director of Kew Gardens, who helped to disseminate Brown's ideas to other parts of the British Empire.

Brown considered that forestry had a much wider environmental – and consequently economic – significance than merely the timber resource. Thus he took up the long-standing scientific debate about the relationship between desiccation and deforestation and applied it to the Cape.[15] What has been described as his 'environmental gospel'[16] rested upon his conviction in the trinity of scientific knowledge, associated religious implications and aspects of social reform. This led him to sanctify belief in forest protection and tree planting, restrictions upon grass burning and the provision of irrigation, together with the beneficent effects of plant collecting, an understanding of pests and diseases, and experimental knowledge about soils and much else. He embraced Darwinian evolutionism, which helped to heighten his anxiety about human-induced species extinction. But his theology was gentler than that of Moffat. Whereas the latter saw original sin and the punishment of God in environmental degradation, Brown laid greater emphasis on a providential opportunity afforded by the application of scientific knowledge and the consequent extension of nature's potential bounty. Similarly, he countered a certain amount of the

Afrikaners' fatalism in their sense of God's punishment through disaster – that could be averted only by purer living and adherence to God's laws – with a passionate belief in human and environmental redemption through observation, experiment, science and sensible policy.[17] Whereas, in Moffat's 'blame game', indigenous people were the prime agents of the devastation of divine creation, Brown was more even-handed in his ascription of responsibility to both African land use and European practices. It was this that helped to induce his downfall.

In Brown's proto-ecological philosophy science and practical forestry, agriculture and environmentalism were inseparably intertwined. But above all he viewed himself as a professional scientist (if in clerical garb). Andrew Geddes Bain (1797–1864) was a wholly different figure, a practical man who developed his significant interests in science out of his powers of observation. He was a self-taught road surveyor and engineer, a profession which brought him into constant contact with the geology and palaeontology of the country. He also represented the upwardly mobile colonial Scot in classic form. Born in Thurso, he was educated in Edinburgh after the early death of his parents and became a saddler. He sailed to the Cape in 1816 (probably accompanying his kinsman, Lieutenant-colonel William Geddes of the 83rd Regiment) and within two years married Maria Elizabeth von Backstrom, with whom he had a large family.[18] In 1822 he opened a saddlery in Graaff Reinet and by 1825 he had set himself up as a trader and hunter, particularly serving the area around the mission at Kuruman, where his fellow Scot Robert Moffat was active. He travelled to the region that is now Botswana on several occasions (once encountering the Smith expedition) hunting for ivory, not always with great success. He was soon caught up in the violence and turbulence of the frontier: he was attacked by the Ndebele and lost his waggons. In 1829 he set off on a major expedition across the frontiers on both east and west and this time secured a major load of ivory. He supervised the construction of the Van Ryneveld Pass near Graaff Reinet (1832) and was involved in the Sixth Frontier War in 1835.[19] With his reputation as a surveyor established, he was attached to the Royal Engineers in 1836, working on frontier military roads such as that between Grahamstown and Fort Beaufort (1837–45).[20] The Governor ordered that it should be named the Queen's Road in honour of the recent accession of Victoria.[21] This secured him the job of inspector with the Cape Roads Board and he proceeded to engineer a series of spectacular passes: Michell's (1848), Bain's Kloof (1853) and Katberg (1854).[22] Bain himself discovered the route for the Bain's Kloof Pass and wrote to the government in great excitement, making a reference to the other great object of exploration of the day, that 'the grand problem is solved and the North West Passage is discovered!'[23]

Bain had long been a student of the geology of southern Africa, encouraged by a reading of Lyell's *Principles of Geology*, which he borrowed from Captain Graham, Civil Commissioner of Grahamstown, in 1837. While involved in road building he developed a major geological survey of southern Africa which he published in a series of articles in a local magazine.[24] He had already sent his results to the Geological Society of London and received the plaudits of the leading members of that society together with £200 from the government for his efforts. As a result of this, the noted imperial geologist and president of the Royal Geographical Society, Sir Roderick Murchison, suggested he should be appointed Cape Geological Surveyor, but there were no funds available. In 1854 he helped to discover the copper resources of Namaqualand, which produced a speculative rush that was not matched by the results. He also collected fossils and sent some of his specimens to the Geological Society of London, including unknown examples, one of which, *Diognodon bainii*, was called after him. He was a lively character, frequently writing satirical letters to the papers (which resulted in at least one libel action). He could also be crusty and made enemies, but he is commemorated in a number of memorials[25] and has been dubbed 'the father of South African geology'.[26] Early in the twentieth century another Scots geologist, Dr Corstorphine, considered that Bain's work had stood the test of time.[27] His son, Thomas Charles John Bain (1830–93), was apprenticed to his father and had an equally successful career as a surveyor and engineer. He was also a palaeontologist and ethnographic collector. Further descendants were involved in large-scale farming, one of them also acting as magistrate at Calvinia on the Eastern Cape.[28]

Bain senior was a friend of Charles Davidson Bell (1813–82), an interesting case of an able young Scot 'on the make'. He also provides a test case in the complexity of identities at the Cape. He was born on a farm near Crail in Fife and sailed to the Cape in 1829 as a teenager. His uncle, Colonel John Bell (1782–1876), had been appointed colonial secretary and his father sent him out to utilise these connections to make his career. The idea worked to an extraordinarily successful degree. Colonel Bell had given up a mercantile career (in his father's firm) during the Napoleonic Wars to join the army and had eventually served as a Peninsular campaign officer, which, as for so many others in that network, became a passport to imperial service. In 1822 he was deputy quartermaster-general at the Cape and within five years had arrived at the position of second in the administration to the Governor, a position he retained until 1841. He administered the government in the Governor's absence on several occasions. He was married to a daughter of the Earl of Malmesbury, who was also elder sister of the wife of the Governor, Sir Lowry Cole. Bell was an urbane and sociable figure, a lively raconteur who became the centre of social life in Cape Town. He was also an amateur artist and architect,[29] frequently amusing his guests by asserting his identity in 'talking scotch' (a neat example of internal and external expectations in identity).[30] He was later knighted and became a full general.

Colonel and Lady Catherine Bell had no children and the nephew was taken into their home as a surrogate son. There he met everyone who mattered at the Cape. He became a clerk in his uncle's office, moving on to the audit office, then into that of the master of the Supreme Court and later clerk to the Governor's council. He had already emerged as a talented artist and draughtsman, interests he had developed soon after his arrival, when he went on his own minor expedition to Cape Point, sketching and mapping as he went. As we have seen in Chapter 3, he was a member of Andrew Smith's expedition to the interior between 1834 and 1836. These interests prompted him to seek training as a land surveyor; in 1840 he duly joined the survey department, becoming surveyor-general in 1848, a post he held until his resignation in 1872.

He conducted surveys on the eastern frontier, living in Grahamstown for two years, as well as visiting Namaqualand on two occasions, the second to report on the copper discoveries there. He served on a commission investigating events on the leper and psychiatric colony on Robben Island, and even acted as surveying engineer on the building of the Cape Town to Wellington railway line. He was also involved in the Cape Town dock works. He was a director (from 1850) and later chairman (1865–73) of the Old Mutual insurance company, and other business interests included directorships of the Commercial Bank and the Umzinto Sugar Company as well as links with the Wynberg Railway and Green Point tram companies. He became the first chairman of the General Estate and Orphan Chamber and he served on the Fine Arts committees (later the South African Fine Arts Society) which were involved in presenting art exhibitions from 1851 onwards. Active in Freemasonry, he was master of Good Hope Lodge 1852–56. This bald account of his career places him at the centre of the life of the Cape in the period, but it constitutes only a part of his multifarious activities. He became an artist of note, if remaining strictly an amateur, although it may be that only a fraction of his output survives. He drew and painted landscapes, Cape street scenes, ethnographic subjects, animals, the hunt, and historical canvases relating to the history of the Cape. His surviving work has been resurrected in recent times and has been placed alongside that of the East Anglian Thomas Baines (a much superior artist), Thomas Bowler and George Ford, who was Smith's principal artist on an expedition to the Tropic of Capricorn.[31] He designed the first Cape stamps, a frontier service medal, banknotes for two banks, the insignia of the Old Mutual and the coats of arms of the South African College and the Orphan Chamber. He also designed significant silver items (including an epergne for his friend Andrew Geddes Bain,[32] celebrating the construction of Bain's Kloof Pass, and a trigger for Prince Alfred to activate the first load for the dock works in 1860), sculpted and carved, worked in wood block, engraving, etching, litho tint, lithography, and developed an interest in photography.

Bell's circle included John Fairbairn, Charles Piazzi Smyth (later Astronomer Royal of Scotland), Bain, John Steuart (master of the Supreme Court, who came from and returned to Perthshire), Sir John Herschel, the professors of the South African College, and other members of the elite. He married into two very influential families, first the daughter of the wealthy merchant J. B. Ebden (this led to divorce) and second the daughter of Anthony David Krynau, the patriarch of an old Cape family of German descent. His first marriage was contracted in the Anglican church and the second in the DRC Groote Kerk, although he was a Presbyterian. He acquired his uncle's fine country house, Canigou, at Rondebosch, and also maintained a house at Green Point. It might be thought that he had carved out such a significant position in Cape society that he would feel wholly integrated into it. Yet he always maintained his Scottish connections (helped by the fact that his parents lived to a great age). He returned to Scotland on leave on three occasions, and eventually retired to Edinburgh (with a wife and a new family who had no connection with the country at all). Piazzi Smyth wrote of Bell's 'pent-up passionate admiration for his native land' and 'the fervid love and even ecstatic devotion' he always bore for it.[33] Indeed, in letters home he wrote of his nostalgia for 'the land o' cakes'. He never broke his ties, and, despite the locations of his weddings, he clung to his Presbyterianism sufficiently fiercely that he was displeased when his eldest son married a Catholic and outraged when his grandchild was baptised into that Church.

Bell clearly developed multiple identities at the Cape. He identified himself with English-speaking settlers, invariably depicting Afrikaners as fat, uneducated and lazy. Yet his most celebrated artistic productions relating to historical events involved Bartolomeu Diaz ('The Isle of the Holy Cross') and Jan van Riebeeck ('The landing of Van Riebeeck, 1652' and 'The Strandlopers' visit to Van Riebeeck'),[34] clearly constructed as introducing a beneficent civilisation and Christianity to the region. He was also consciously setting out to introduce the grand history painting tradition to the Cape. In his contemporary art he demonstrated the prejudices of the era. Khoi people are usually depicted as drunken, grotesque and incapable of taking advantage of the opportunities open to them. (His portrayal of rural Khoi is more sympathetic.) The Cape Malays are given a much better 'artistic press': they emerge, equally stereotypically, as neat, tidy, pious and hardworking. Yet his humour emerges in the ways in which he often revealed whites in rather ludicrous situations. He offers some valuable documentary images of Cape Town street scenes of the period and he was clearly enthralled by the landscape, people, animals and hunting exploits he witnessed and recorded on his various journeys. Some of his illustrations of the Seventh Frontier War were published in the *Illustrated London News*. Much of his artistic work also aspired to a quasi-scientific representation, although he often playfully added lively human interest even to these. He was a colonial sojourner who readily moved between sophisticated Cape society and the environmentally and ethnically primitive (as he would have seen it) interior, expressing some sympathy for indigenous people and their right to land (for example in Namaqualand). He also described Africans as 'civil, hospitable and kind', comparing their treatment of travellers to that in his native Scotland.[35] His marriages connected him with families from other white ethnic communities who would have considered themselves committed settlers.[36] Yet he seems to have clung to his Scottishness and, surprisingly, given the comforts of his highly paid office and the fine houses which he occupied, he was determined to return to Scotland after an early retirement and immerse himself in Scottish cultural affairs. It has been suggested that he saw himself as an 'agent of British rule'[37] but the case is perhaps more complicated than that. Even after his return to Scotland he paid one more visit to the Cape, no doubt encouraged by the improvements in marine transport, by the affiliations of his second wife, as well as by his own interests. In Scotland he became a Fellow of the Royal Society of Edinburgh, of the Society of Antiquaries of Scotland and of the Scottish Meteorological Society. In all his professional and artistic interests he revealed a passion for pursuing new techniques and, given the manner in which Piazzi Smyth introduced him to lithography in 1848 and his distant relative the celebrated Scots photographer John Adamson to photography in 1857, he probably saw Scotland as nurturing innovations and therefore opening up new artistic and scientific worlds. These were connections which he did not wish to lose. For him, almost a lifetime spent in a colony was a means to an enriched and wholly interactive technical and cultural life, one which was above all constantly inventive.

In the later nineteenth century the environmental professions saw increasing professionalisation. More public posts became available and the private sector greatly expanded with the mineral revolution. George William Smith, a surveyor and architect, reflects the manner in which South Africa was part of a wider imperial system. Born in Glasgow, he arrived at the Cape, with experience on the Caledonian Railway, in 1858. Initially a railway engineer on the Cape to Wellington railway, he was soon town engineer and municipal surveyor in Port Elizabeth, and a land surveyor in Natal. He also worked in Australia, India, Canada and southern Europe in the 1870s and returned to Port Elizabeth in 1880 to take up a partnership in a prominent firm, securing contracts at Barberton and on the Rand, as well as on the Knysna goldfields in association with Sir Donald Currie.[38]

During Smith's lifetime the expansion of the public sector was rapid. As we have seen, despite the economic significance of geology, there was no money available for the creation of a government post in the 1850s. Even Brown's post as Colonial Botanist was vulnerable. But the increasing sophistication of some disciplines and growing belief that science did indeed offer answers to agricultural and environmental problems led to further government appointments and eventually to the growth of the relevant departments. From the later 1870s developments in veterinary science greatly enhanced research into the many animal diseases of southern Africa. A variety of explanations, related to environmental causation, the application of the new germ theory and later to greater understanding of entomological and epidemiological phenomena, came to be propounded in respect of various of these destructive ailments. William Branford was appointed Cape Colonial Veterinary Surgeon in 1876. Trained in London, he had been appointed professor at the Royal (Dick) Veterinary College in Edinburgh in 1869. His successor, Duncan Hutcheon (1842–?) was a Scot who qualified in Edinburgh in 1871 and worked in Scotland before taking up the Cape post in 1880. He faced Afrikaans farmers who considered that efforts to control diseases in cattle and sheep were no more than a 'futile wrestling against Providence',[39] but he also had powerful supporters in the Cape farming and political establishment. Moreover, brought up in the Calvinist tradition in Scotland, he had a sufficiently deep knowledge of the Bible to be able to match Boer farmers text for text. He presided over a considerable extension in the size and powers of his department and subsequently extended his influence by becoming Director of Agriculture.[40]

In 1889 Hutcheon was joined by two other vets, one of them Jotella

F. Soga, the son of Tiyo Soga and his Scottish wife, who had almost inevitably trained in Edinburgh. At that time he was probably the most senior black in Cape government service and he quickly distinguished himself in studying plants that transmitted diseases to animals. He began to publish his results in the *Agricultural Journal of the Cape of Good Hope*, a journal which was founded soon after the creation of the Department of Agriculture in 1889. Hutcheon also published numerous articles in this journal which, surprisingly, had a circulation of some 6,000 in the 1890s.

By the end of the century such issues were being addressed throughout southern Africa. Moreover, visiting 'experts' were bringing international ideas from the new sciences of agriculture, bacteriology and epidemiology to the region. One of the earliest was Robert Wallace, Professor of Agriculture and Rural Economy at Edinburgh, who was invited to report on the Cape in 1896. Another was Sir David Bruce (1855–1931). Bruce was born in Australia of Scottish parents, but they returned to Scotland when he was five years old. Brought up in Stirling, he became an enthusiastic naturalist. He studied medicine at Edinburgh and qualified in 1881. He joined the Army Medical Service, but soon developed an interest in bacteriological research and went to Berlin to study with the greatest practitioner of the age, Robert Koch. He joined the British garrison in Natal in 1894 and was involved in a military expedition the following year on which a large number of horses died of 'horse sickness', the disease transmitted by the tsetse fly in the subtropical regions. In the late 1890s he worked on trypanosomiasis in Natal, together with the colony's veterinary surgeon and a scientist in Pretoria. This work was interrupted by the Anglo-Boer War. (Bruce was in the siege of Ladysmith.) He continued to research human sleeping-sickness in Africa (notably in Uganda) and returned to South Africa in 1905 as the president of the Physiology section of the British Association for the Advancement of Science.[41] Regarded as a major researcher in insect-borne diseases, his work constituted considerable advances in the understanding of the tsetse fly and the trypanosome to which it is host. He gave evidence to important British government inquiries, and subsequently became Surgeon General of the Army Medical Service with the rank of major-general.

While Bruce was concerned with the bacteriology of the vectors of diseases which passed from wild to domestic animals, as well as having serious implications for humans, other Scots were becoming increasingly interested in the preservation of game after an era of devastating destruction. Early in the nineteenth century, southern Africa had swiftly become known as a hunter's paradise at a time when the cult of the hunter was transferred from Scotland to the empire.[42] Within the United Kingdom, Scotland was the prime location for shooting, primarily the stag, and architecture, concepts of manliness, and the relationship of the royal family and the elite to the environment became inseparably bound up with this form of the hunt. The resulting trophies and the associated art became one of the decorative elements of the age.[43] Roualeyn Gordon Cumming, born in 1820, from Altyre, in Morayshire, certainly developed his passion in Scotland before transferring it to southern Africa on an extended hunting trip between 1843 and 1848. He discovered the Cape, like so many others, on a journey to India, where he was a subaltern in the Madras Light Cavalry. However, he developed such a taste for shooting that he abandoned his military career and became a full-time hunter and showman. In South Africa, Cumming claimed to see parallels between the social and technical aspects of Scottish and African indigenous hunters. He combined an interest in exploration and the frontier, which he found to be a conveniently violent place, with a notion that hunting, natural history and the display of the trophies of the hunt were vital to the development of the imperial ethos.[44] He also contributed to the longer-standing realisation that profits from ivory could help to fund other activities in Africa.

Cumming helped to turn hunting in southern Africa into a publishing and theatrical event. He displayed his trophies, to some acclaim, in the Cape, for example at Colesberg,[45] and attempted to turn them to account (though with less success) in London (initially in 1851 at the Great Exhibition in the Crystal Palace) and Scotland. Nevertheless, he and the hunters who followed him, including several Scots, served to raise the public consciousness, particularly among the middle class, of southern Africa and its animal riches. Royalty, like many African chiefs, asserted its authority over the land through the destruction of game, though whites were infinitely more profligate. In 1860 Queen Victoria's son Prince Alfred was treated to a game drive at which it was estimated that some 6,000 head of game were killed.[46] More generally, the advancing frontier of hunters, Boers, missionaries, farming and settlement produced a tremendous retreat of the numbers and incidence of the distinctive southern African fauna in the course of the century, and as anxieties about extinctions (such as that of the quagga) and rapidly declining numbers grew there were calls for legislative and other action to help preserve species and stocks.

One of the principal figures involved in the establishment of the new game reserves was James Stevenson-Hamilton (1867–1957), a Scot whose family owned a small estate in Lanarkshire. Stevenson-Hamilton had a military career which took him to southern Africa in 1898, where he served in Basutoland (Lesotho) and then in the Anglo-Boer

War.[47] After the war he became the warden of the Sabi Game Reserve in the north-eastern Transvaal, and over the next forty years or so he turned this reserve into one of the most celebrated in Africa as the Kruger National Park.[48] He extended his own powers as a zoologist, as a park warden, as an administrator of the game regulations and of Africans who lived alongside the game, and above all became a major publicist for animal conservation.[49] He also cleverly hitched the park to the political and cultural aspirations of Afrikaners, not least in its naming.[50] He represented an extraordinary layering of identities: he always saw himself as a Scot – and retired to the family estate – but he was also British in his imperial affiliation, and powerfully committed to the African landscape, its animals and its peoples.[51] If Gordon Cumming represented a supreme version of the hunting paradigm, then Stevenson-Hamilton was wholly converted to the conservationist one, and each was influenced, in different ways, by his Scottish origins.

Grove has written that 'the emergence of a critique of the environmental impact of settlement in the British colonial empire was pre-eminently a Scottish phenomenon'.[52] In some respects this was also the case with hunting and conservation, given the significance of Scotland within the Victorian consciousness of landscape and game. Moreover, it was largely true of the developing fields of veterinary science, agriculture and bacteriology. All this was clearly based upon the fascination with the natural world that was certainly a feature of Scottish culture in the century,[53] as well as upon agricultural diversity and practices across Scotland, and above all on the manner in which new disciplines had established themselves in Scottish universities, notably Edinburgh. The range of medical, biological and forensic disciplines (which helped to inspire Arthur Conan Doyle) was joined by veterinary science, agriculture and, soon afterwards, forestry.

Medicine

The Archives of the Western Cape contain card indexes of professionals compiled as an aid to family history by F. J. Boonzaier, covering the years 1705–1982.[54] A survey of the doctor files reveals that roughly 600 medical men who were Scots or trained in Scottish universities arrived in South Africa from Scotland in the nineteenth and early twentieth centuries. This figure was scarcely matched by the total of those with qualifications from London, Dublin, (later) Queen's Belfast or an international group from Leiden, Berlin, Göttingen, Heidelberg and Paris. Boonzaier used a number of sources, notably the requests for permission to practise at the Cape and in the other territories, and it may well be that the figures cannot be completely accurate. Nevertheless it is clear that the Scots dominated the medical services of the region. It has been noted that between 1870 and 1897 (and presumably in the years beyond that date) almost every graduating medical class of the University of Glasgow sent one or more of its members to South Africa.[55] Edinburgh was probably most prominent in this respect, but the University of Aberdeen also figures strongly.[56] This coincides with the period when medicine at the Cape became increasingly professionalised in terms of licensing, controlling organisations and administration.[57] Moreover, Scots were dominant in the medical schools of South Africa once they came to be founded in the twentieth century.[58] For example, one of the first medical professors at the University of Cape Town was Arthur Wellesley Falconer (1880–1954), born in Stonehaven and trained in medicine at Aberdeen. He was assistant to the professor of internal medicine at that university before taking up the chair in Cape Town. He later became the second vice-chancellor of the university, 1938–47.

To return to the earlier period, it is noticeable the extent to which Scottish doctors were often active in other fields. There are a number of reasons for this. Scottish medical training continued to encourage versatility, interest in other disciplines and concern with issues of public health. Another is that doctors inevitably became prominent figures in their communities in a period when there was, perhaps, little competition. In doing so they generally acquired a good deal of public respect. Third, in some places they were usually able to make themselves financially secure relatively quickly and could then indulge their other interests. The obverse was also true. For example, no fewer than twenty-three qualified doctors arrived with the British settlers in Natal in the 1840s, many of them Scots or trained in Scotland, but only twelve remained in the colony because of the difficulty of making a living from general practice in the period.[59] Even among the twelve, several became farmers, and one joined the civil service. Another, Dr James Mack, who founded the cottage hospital in Pietermaritzburg, became insolvent in 1855.[60] But generally doctors had access to members of the elite (whether as patients or as social contacts) who were able to encourage and help them in their ambitions.[61] There were, of course, many Scots doctors who must have pursued their profession in both cities and rural towns without making much impression on wider public life.

Although we know that Scots doctors arrived during the Dutch period at the Cape, the first to land with the British invading force was Dr William Somerville, who was born in Edinburgh in 1771. He was with Sir James Craig's expeditionary force and was described by the general as 'an extremely clever and useful young man'. He was surgeon to the garrison during the first occupation and also held the post of Inspector of Government Lands and Public Buildings. He must have been an able linguist, for he became Dutch translator to the Governor, Sir George Yonge, and Secretary to the Court of Appeal. He was sent to Graaff Reinet as assistant resident commissioner in 1801 and was then appointed to the Commissary of Lands and Woods at Algoa Bay. He conducted a number of official expeditions to the interior, but left the colony in 1805. As we have already seen, James Barry, Robert Knox and Andrew Smith followed him as military doctors and also maintained wide interests. James Abercrombie (1798–1870, born in Edinburgh) arrived with the Moodie settlement and soon became very active in colonial affairs. He was instrumental in the development of the Cape harbour works and was active in the Presbyterian Church and in educational matters. He was elected to the first Cape legislative council in 1854 and again in 1865. Yet he kept up his medical interests, returning to Scotland in 1840 and 1846 to improve his qualifications. He was active in the suppression of the serious epidemic of 1867, but it impaired his health. He returned to Scotland for medical attention, illustrating the fact that he clearly saw the country as the fount of medical wisdom, but returned to die at the Cape. Both his sons became doctors.

Two other early doctors were Alexander Cowie (1797–1829) and Ambrose Campbell (1799–1884). Cowie arrived in 1823 and was given permission to practise by James Barry, but he soon found the lure of the interior too strong to resist. He set out as a trader to Dingane at the Zulu capital and led an expedition to Delagoa Bay. He contracted malaria and died. Campbell was the son of General Campbell of the 1820 settlement. He was born in Inverness, but may have received his medical training outside Scotland. He spent his career in Grahamstown, opening the first hospital on the Eastern Cape. He inevitably served in frontier wars and was drawn into frontier politics, purchasing newspapers and opposing the settler party led by Godlonton. He owned the *Colonial Times* for a period and founded the *Echo*, which was designed to be a literary, scientific and critical magazine, clearly intended to raise the intellectual tone of the remote districts. It lasted only six months. A fiercely anti-establishment figure (and some settler historians have given him a bad press as a result), he became increasingly eccentric in old age.[62] He also conducted a fierce professional dispute with the other doctor in Grahamstown, Atherstone. Perhaps this helps to explain why he moved on to be district surgeon in East London 1872–75.

Few doctors became more prominent in public life than Sir William

Bisset Berry (1839–1922). He was educated at Marischal College in Aberdeen and became a ship's surgeon with the Union Mail Steamship Company, settling at the Cape in 1864. He practised at Burgersdorp, in the Orange Free State and at Queenstown on the Eastern Cape. He was instrumental in founding the Frontier Medical Association in 1886, became active in municipal affairs, was the first mayor of Queenstown and sat on several government commissions on 'native affairs' and education. He was elected to the Cape legislature in 1894, joined the councils of the South African College and the University of Cape Town, became speaker of the House and was elected to the Union parliament in 1910. He abandoned his medical practice only in 1908. He was another figure who was interested in the 'intellectual civilisation' of the frontier, for he left his considerable library to Queenstown with money to open a public library. But the classic case of a Scots doctor who controversially involved himself in the affairs of southern Africa was Dr Leander Starr Jameson (1853–1917), born in Edinburgh though trained in London. Jameson arrived at the Cape in 1878 and went to the diamond diggings at Kimberley. Through his friendship with Cecil Rhodes he was involved in the conquest of Rhodesia (Zimbabwe), the disastrous raid (1896) and later became Premier of the Cape (1904–05). Throughout his adventurous career, perhaps best noted for his political and administrative incompetence, he always maintained his connections with Scotland and took Rhodes on a shooting holiday there in 1901.[63]

Donald Macaulay (1867–1920) was born in Wester Ross and was trained in Edinburgh. He arrived in the Transvaal in 1897 and became a prominent medical officer on a succession of mines.[64] He served on various medical commissions and became a notable researcher, particularly in miners' psithis, scurvy and pneumonia, serious conditions that afflicted large numbers of black miners. Obviously, the mines had a pecuniary interest in a healthy work force, although they took few steps to improve the horrendous conditions under which miners worked. The tradition of Scottish doctors active in public affairs continued into the twentieth century. Peter Allan (1886–1956), born and educated in Edinburgh, became a significant tuberculosis researcher, was active in public health in Cape Town and became secretary of public health and chief health officer of the Union at the time of the Second World War.[65] John Muir (1874–1947), born in Castle Douglas and educated at St Andrews and Edinburgh, arrived at the Cape in 1896 and combined his practice with research into haemophilia. He later became more interested in botany, particularly in the dissemination of seeds by ocean currents, and published extensively in this and other botanical fields. To these figures we can add the missionary medics who were noted in Chapter 4. All these doctors were generally Establishment figures who were interested in the spread of scientific values, research and education, as well as good medical practice, as they would have defined it, in a colonial setting.

In one field, that of psychiatric medicine, Scots had a considerable influence upon practice in South Africa. In 1888 Cape Colony set about a restructuring of its mental health services and appointed Dr William Dodds to take charge.[66] Dodds had been the deputy medical superintendent of the Royal Asylum of Montrose at Sunnyside, where he had helped to pioneer therapies unknown elsewhere. In an age when vast Victorian institutions had become effectively prisons for those adjudged to be mentally ill, the staff at Sunnyside sought restoratives in the natural world of the hospital's grounds and land leased from adjacent farms. Vegetables and other crops were grown, and the inmates were also provided with amateur dramatic and musical events. Sunnyside had become celebrated as one of the most humane psychiatric institutions of its type.[67] Its staff were trained in the notion that physical health was fundamental to treatment, together with 'minimal restraint, kindliness, fresh air and useful occupation'.[68] It also had a remarkable *esprit de corps* among its staff. This included the publication of a magazine, *The Sunnyside Chronicle* (founded by Dodds), which is an invaluable source for staff news and the relationship with both Natal and the Cape.[69] The profits from subscriptions to the magazine went to the 'patients' amusement fund'.

The first indication of a connection with South Africa was when the superintendent of the asylum in Petermaritzburg, inevitably a Scot, Dr Hyslop, requested that Sunnyside should send out some nurses to Natal. Mrs Hyslop, formerly Miss Brown, had been the Lady Superintendent at one of Sunnyside's hospitals and therefore knew the institution well. Four nurses volunteered – Margaret Findlay, Mary Findlay, Margaret Stewart and Mary Jane Collinson, together with a housemaid, Barbara Stewart. They duly sailed on the Union ship SS *Mexican* in June 1889.[70] Mary Collinson wrote long letters back to Sunnyside describing their voyage and their reception in Maritzburg, where all the local Scots gave them a big welcome.[71] Within two years the *Chronicle* was reporting that only two remained in the hospital, one having died and the other two having married.[72]

Within a month the *Chronicle* was reporting that Dr Dodds had been recruited to be the superintendent of the new asylum in Cape Town as well as visiting physician to the asylums on Robben Island and Albany. Dodds resigned, was given a grand departing dinner as well as a tea party by staff and patients, and sailed for the Cape in September 1889.[73] He too sent accounts of his voyage and arrival back to the Sunnyside magazine. He was soon followed by a junior physician from Sunnyside, Dr Frank L. Collie, who went to Durban to work in the hospital there.[74] (When his health broke down, he recuperated with Dodds at the Cape and later became a railway doctor on the line north of Kimberley.[75]) A migration network had now been firmly established. In June 1890 the *Chronicle* reported that 'the stream from Sunnyside to South Africa has not ceased', two male and two female nurses having left in May to join Dr Dodds at the new asylum in Mowbray at the Cape. The two males can be identified, as they had been, with Dodds, ardent members of the Sunnyside cricket team. They were J. Donaldson and G. Carey. In December the magazine averred that:

> So many of the rank and file of Sunnyside forces, besides superior officers, have been drafted off to South Africa that we cannot help feeling an almost paternal solicitude for the welfare of the Colony. In the great future which lies before it we doubt not it will reflect due credit upon the Institution whence some of its adopted children have been drawn.[76]

Later the *Chronicle* referred to 'the New Cape Sunnyside, or Valkenberg, as they call it out there'.[77] Yet another junior doctor from Sunnyside, W. A. Skinner, who worked at the Montrose hospital between 1896 and 1899, went to the Natal asylum in the latter year. However, his premature death was reported in July 1904.[78]

The contribution of Dodds was remarkable. The Cape lunacy law effectively criminalised mental illness. Patients were kept in prisons or were locked up in various unsuitable buildings. Soon after his arrival Dodds wrote a report seeking to transfer Sunnyside techniques to the Cape. He considered various possible sites for a new hospital, and the new Valkenberg hospital (which still exists) was duly built at Mowbray, near Cape Town.[79] It was regarded as a remarkable centre for psychiatric care. It should be stressed that it was for white patients, but Dodds also took an interest in blacks as he became more powerful within the Cape hospital service.[80] The several migrants to Natal also introduced Sunnyside methods there. Moreover, it was not only doctors and nurses who emigrated to the Cape and Natal. G. Grant, who had been one of the gardeners at Sunnyside, went to the Natal government experimental farm at Cedara, near Howick, in 1902 and reported back on its work and its methods to the *Chronicle*.[81]

Dr Dodds, in common with many other doctors, was inevitably swept up into the medical services during the Anglo-Boer War. Others arrived, including the celebrated creator of Sherlock Holmes, Arthur Conan Doyle, who was born and trained in Edinburgh, though of Irish parentage.[82] Medical services in Scotland also set about creating special hospital provision staffed by Scots personnel. One such was the Edinburgh and East of Scotland South African Hospital. Six doctors, six sisters and a matron of the Army Nursing Reserve Service, seven dressers and thirty-nine male attendants, together with a laundress and sisters' maid, under the command of Sir James Clark, appointed by the War Office as military executive officer, left Southampton for South Africa in March 1900. Of the dressers, two were recent graduates and the others were medical students of Edinburgh University. On arrival, they proceeded to Norval's Pont. They treated 343 patients in the hospital and, when they left later in the year, they gifted the building to South Africa. When the staff of the Edinburgh hospital returned they took charge of 600 sick and injured men being repatriated to Britain on a hospital ship. All this seems to have been financed by public subscription and controlled by a committee of management.[83]

Insights into to the work of a Scots doctor at the Cape in the early twentieth century are provided by memoirs compiled by his daughter.[84] James Rutherford Mackenzie (1864–1917) was the son of John Mackenzie, merchant, of Macduff, in Banffshire. He was apprenticed to a druggist in Aberdeen and qualified as a pharmacist in 1887. His parents emigrated to the Cape some time in the late 1880s and eventually he joined them, taking up a job in a pharmacy in Cape Town. He married an Afrikaans woman and in 1899 secured a Carnegie grant of £1,000 to enable him to achieve his ambition of training to be a doctor at the University of Aberdeen, Having completed his degree in 1905, they returned to the Cape, where he took up a practice at Salt River on the northern edge of Cape Town. Here there were a railway junction, railway workshops and a mixed population of working-class whites and Coloureds, the whites including many immigrant ethnicities such as Greeks and Italians. There was also a small Chinese community. In those pre-apartheid days Mackenzie's surgery was thronged with different races. He was additionally doctor to the hospital in the African location at Ndabeni, where a Scottish woman called Nurse Middleton was in charge. He combined his practice with dispensing medicines, remaining active in his first profession.[85] Mackenzie travelled extensively in Scotland after he had finished his degree. He was photographed in Highland dress, but according to his daughter 'he never spoke to me of Scotland or his youth there. South Africa was our home now . . .'[86] Yet she included a nostalgic poem to suggest that, though silent, his heart remained in the Highlands. But Dodds, on the other hand, certainly wrote of his desire to see Scotland again in his letters back to Sunnyside.

While Dr Mackenzie cared for the mixture of races at Salt River

[222]

and Ndabeni, one of the first Coloured doctors was being trained in Scotland. Dr Abdullah Abdurahman, later the president of the African People's Organisation, received his medical training in Glasgow, graduating in 1893.[87] He married a Scottish woman, Nellie James, and returned to Cape Town with her in 1895. He was elected to the Cape Town municipal council and the Cape Provincial Council and conducted an extensive medical practice in the centre of the city. He developed a considerable interest in training nurses, in public health issues and in the provision of housing for the poor. In the 1920s, in league with Indian associates, he bought Schotsche Kloof farm and developed a community improvement and educational scheme known as the Schotsche Kloof Institution. It may well be that his interests in medical training and in environmental public health matters were at least partly influenced by his experience in Glasgow, where both the university and the city pioneered the social approach to medicine.

Business

The rest of this chapter will deal with two contrasting groups, the Scottish businessmen who dominated many aspects of colonial economic life and the radical trade unionists who came to oppose them in the later nineteenth century. Prominent Scots businessmen in the early decades of British rule at the Cape have been noticed in earlier chapters. Others, such as the Mackenzie brothers of Fochabers, will appear in Chapter 8. The Mackenzies were part of the major migration to South Africa attendant upon the minerals boom of the last decades of the nineteenth century. They moved into accounting, and it is clear that Scots came to be prominent in various branches of financial services. A survey of some of the biographical works which became a feature of South African publishing in the period reveals the extent to which Scots seem to have penetrated the worlds of insurance and banking.[88] Many had training in Scotland before leaving for South Africa.[89] There were other areas of specialism too, and the examples that follow constitute only a selection of the most prominent figures who moved there in the 1880s and 1890s. They demonstrate the manner in which the region offered opportunities for advancing careers and making considerable fortunes. What is also striking is the extent to which so many Scots seem to have translated their success in business into involvement with public life.

An interesting case of an upwardly mobile colonial who brought influences from one colony to another is William McLarty (1858–1940). Born on the island of Arran, he trained as a carpenter. Between 1886 and 1896 he worked in both building contracting and insurance in

New Zealand and New South Wales. In 1896 his company, the National Mutual Life of Australasia, sent him to South Africa to open branches there. He set up a company presence in Cape Town and then moved on to Durban; he was South African manager of the company until 1900. He started his own business as an estate agent and insurance broker and from there took off into other businesses including coal mining. He became active on the Durban stock exchange and was later manager of the Southern Life Association. In 1903 he was elected to the Natal legislative assembly, served as deputy speaker, and concerned himself with social welfare and industrial legislation (for whites). He considered himself to be a Labour member (though he never joined the Labour Party) and was dedicated to bringing the more advanced social legislation of New Zealand and Australia to South Africa. He sponsored an Early Closing Act in 1904 (designed to reduce the hours of shop workers) and attempted, unsuccessfully, to promote compulsory arbitration and conciliation in industrial disputes. He was active in the YMCA, becoming the Natal president, as a lay preacher, and in a parliamentary debating society. Thus, from a relatively humble background, trained only as an artisan, he became a successful businessman and an active provincial parliamentarian with a social conscience, if only in respect of white colonists.

Scots were also active in retail and mercantile trades. As in the early period at the Cape, they were storekeepers, merchants and agents. William Arbuckle (1839–1915) was born in Stirlingshire and arrived in Natal as a Byrne settler. He opened a retail and wholesale grocery and was soon successful enough to be able to enter local politics. He was mayor of Durban three times, entered the Natal legislature in 1884 and moved to the upper House in 1893. In 1902 he was chairman of the Natal legislative council and in 1905 became the Natal Agent General in London. By then he had secured the customary knighthood. William Duncan Baxter (1868–1960) from Dundee (where his father was in jute) emigrated to South Africa in 1886 and took a job in his uncle's drapery business in Cape Town. By 1895 he was proprietor of the firm and was a leading figure in the chamber of commerce. He sat on the Cape Town City Council, was mayor of the city and entered the Cape Assembly in 1908. He had a major interest in botany, theatre and music, became chairman of the Kirstenbosch botanical garden and president of the Botanical Society of South Africa. He left a bequest to found the Baxter Theatre. James Henderson (1878–1932), from Whitburn, arrived in Natal in 1890 and joined a firm of wholesale merchants and shipping agents, of which he later became manager. He entered the Union parliament in 1910 as a Unionist and became something of a specialist in railway policy.

Many Scots immigrants moved from job to job in search of fortune and influence. A good example was John Laing (1842–1903), from Kirkcudbright, whose uncle James Laing was a frontier missionary at Burnshill earlier in the century. Laing arrived at the Cape in 1861 to be a teacher in Fort Beaufort, but by 1864 he had opened a store. He tried his luck on the diamond fields, but was unsuccessful, and turned to farming at Stockenstroom. In 1874 he was elected to the Cape legislative assembly and was Commissioner of Crown Lands in Sprigg's Ministry between 1878 and 1881. He was strongly imperialist in sentiment, which led him to be highly critical of Rhodes, whom he considered to have a serious conflict of interest in attempting to combine his power in the British South Africa Company with the premiership of the Cape.[90] Subsequent events, not least the Jameson Raid, were certainly to prove Laing right. He had the town of Laingsburg named after him in 1881.

South Africa was a region in which there were many opportunities for engineers, both because of the development of mining as a lead sector in the economy and because of the consequent growth in the building of railway lines. Harold Ross Skinner (1867–1943) was a son of the manse in Tarland, Aberdeenshire, who studied civil engineering and surveying in Aberdeen. In 1889 he emigrated to South Africa to become assistant manager and surveyor of the North East Bultfontein & Gordon Diamond Mining Company in Kimberley. His subsequent career took him to a number of Rand gold mines. After the Anglo-Boer War he went on an international mission to consider the practicality of introducing Chinese labourers. His positive report was accepted and he has to bear some of the responsibility for this ultimately disastrous policy. Nevertheless, through his membership of international associations he brought many international engineering and geological connections to bear in South Africa, and eventually became president of the South African Association of Mine Managers. He served in the Anglo-Boer War as a captain in the Rand Rifles and was second-in-command of the Transvaal Scottish Volunteers until 1909. He returned to Britain at the time of the First World War and worked in the Ministry of Munitions, which earned him a knighthood. Although he returned to South Africa after the war, he retired to Scotland and died in Aberdeen.[91]

William (later Sir William) Dalrymple (1864–1941) used accounting as a route into mine management. Born in Stirlingshire he was educated in Scotland, London and Dresden, arriving at the Klerksdorp goldfields early in 1888. He swiftly rose to hold managing directorships and became prominent in the Chamber of Mines. He was a member of the Uitlander Council between 1897–99, thus identifying himself with the English-speaking, imperialist faction. He served on the Johannesburg municipal council, on the Transvaal legislative council (1907–10) and, after the First World War, was chairman of the council of the University of Witwatersrand. He was a leading figure in military, sporting, educational and Scottish organisations. He commanded the Scots Horse Volunteers (1902–07) and was a prominent member of Caledonian societies. He was also interested in the development of a museum in Johannesburg. But he was almost brutally anti-trade union (see below) and refused to countenance any negotiations with trades organisations, thus contributing to the violent worker resistance of the period before and after the First World War.

James Mackenzie (1862–1941) was born in Blairgowrie, served his time with various chartered engineers, and migrated to South Africa in 1889 to join the Cape Government Railways. In 1890 he moved to the Natal Government Railways and was responsible for the building of a number of lines before returning to the Cape in 1901. He subsequently specialised in bridge building and strengthening: a paper he wrote on the subject won him the Telford Gold Medal of the Institution of Civil Engineers in London. From 1910 he was Union bridge engineer to the South African Railways. After retirement he became a consultant to Rhodesia Railways and died in Southern Rhodesia. John Roy (1856–1941) joined the Natal railways in 1880 and later started a railway contracting firm. But he moved on to work in finance and then in coal mining, supplying coal for the railways. He also went into farming and became president of the Witwatersrand Agricultural Society. Daniel Macfarlane Davidson (1881–1957), from Stirling, studied engineering in the Technical College in Glasgow, where he lectured for a period. He went to South Africa in 1901 to join the staff of the military railways, moving on after the war to be a mechanical engineer with the East Rand Proprietary Mines. He was later manager and chairman of a major engineering company and was prominent in various engineering institutes. He travelled extensively, became internationally known, and was also active in sporting and Caledonian associations.

One of the most celebrated Scots railway workers in South Africa was Sir William Wilson Hoy (1868–1930). Hoy was the son of a farmer in Kinross and had a very limited education. He joined the North British Railway in Edinburgh as a clerk at the age of twelve and migrated to the Cape in 1889. He moved rapidly up the clerical hierarchy and became a local manager. His real opportunity came with the Anglo-Boer War, when he supervised the British military railway network in the Orange Free State and the Transvaal. By 1910 he was general manager of the entire South African Railways network, and developed a considerable interest in electrification (the line from Glencoe to Pietermaritzburg was electrified in 1926). Work on military railways in the First World War earned him his knighthood and he was chairman of the South African section of the British Empire Exhibition at Wembley, 1924–25. He was involved in the establishment of the South African Electricity Supply Commission.

Few Scots in South Africa were more controversial than James Sivewright (1848–1916). Even in a freewheeling, barely regulated age Sivewright stands out for his naked pursuit of wealth at all costs. A biographer of Rhodes has considered him 'clever, ambitious, unscrupulous, and conservative in terms of the role of Africans'.[92] Indeed, he shared with Rhodes a belief that the end justified almost any means, whether in financial or imperial matters. Perhaps it is unfortunate that he himself suggested that his success was due to his parental upbringing and his Scottish education, since those influences run the risk of training him as a crook. He was born in Fochabers and educated there and at Aberdeen University. Although he took an arts degree, his main interest was in telegraphy, and he became a notable practitioner in this field, rising to the top of the profession at a young age. He co-authored the *Textbook in Telegraphy* (1876) with the Postmaster General, William Preece, and in the following year was invited to South Africa to report on Cape telegraphy. Over the next few years he reorganised the telegraph systems of all four South African territories and planned telegraphic communications during the Zulu War. He co-founded the South African Philosophical Society with John X. Merriman and used it as a vehicle to propose telegraphic projects. He became a close associate of Cecil Rhodes and was able to use the extraordinary networks he had established throughout South Africa to further Rhodes's schemes, including the utilisation of rather shady concessions in Central Africa, the creation of the British South Africa Company and the plan for a trans-Africa telegraph. He was also significant in securing railway agreements (this won him a knighthood in 1891) and, through his friendship with Kruger, was instrumental in the supply of water and gas street lighting to Johannesburg.[93] Ever opportunist, he had joined the Afrikaner Bond and entered the Cape legislature in 1888, serving as Commissioner of Crown Lands and Public Works in both Rhodes and Sprigg Ministries. But he was mired in corruption and, although he survived the award of a major railway catering contract to a friend (later repudiated),[94] he returned to Britain, with his fortune, in 1898. He invested heavily in South America and satisfied his interests in restoring and developing estates. He had already done this at the Dutch residence Vergelegen on the Lourensford estate at the Cape, and bought Tulliallan Castle and its estate in Fife for the same purpose.[95] He bequeathed £10,000 to the University of Aberdeen to endow scholarships for students from Morayshire.[96]

Radicals

The radical figures of the 1820s and after might almost be described as Establishment radicals. Though Fairbairn, Philip and their associates seemed to resist the colonial authorities, paradoxically they stood for social stability and the assertion of liberal and economic values that would become the new orthodoxy. Though often of humble origins, their education and their professional and economic activities took them up the social scale at the Cape. Moreover, as time went on, their apparent radicalism in the social field became blunted. As the racial fissures opened wider – and coincidentally as the original figures like Pringle and Philip departed or died – this tradition began to identify with at least some aspects of the settler cause. It was inescapable that they were bourgeois and evangelical, with the first progressively blunting the second. But the new group of radicals who emerged later in the nineteenth century were of a very different breed. They had usually emerged from depressed working-class spaces and strata within Scotland. They exported their discontents, their rage at capitalism and big business, and their sense that something needed to be done in South Africa. Though generally artisans by trade, they professionalised themselves by becoming trade union organisers, journalists and politicians.

We know most about James Thompson Bain (1860–1919) because of Jonathan Hyslop's excellent biography, the first major work in South African history to deal adequately with the setting of Scottish contexts and the interaction between Scotland and South Africa in the period.[97] Bain is unknown in Scotland, yet his career trajectory casts light on Scottish society in ways that might not have happened had he stayed at home. He was born in the Hill Town of Dundee and his life and attitudes were in many respects formed in that gritty, socially deprived city of jute. A child worker himself, he came to loathe exploitative capitalists. As a teenager he made the escape open to many young men of his generation. He joined the army. He subsequently served in South Africa in the Zulu War and then in the Kiplingesque imperial military setting in India. He returned to Scotland, to Edinburgh, in the 1880s and became a classic autodidact, seizing all the hours and light available to him after his day job as a fitter. Self-educated and radicalised, he immersed himself in the writings of Carlyle, and the sage of Ecclefechan and Chelsea became his greatest hero. (This was an interest he kept alive in South Africa.⁹⁸) He also joined a socialist study group that gathered around the extraordinary Rev. John Glasse of Greyfriars Kirk, and attended his meetings at the manse in Tantallon Place. There Bain may well have met William Morris, Prince Peter Kropotkin, Annie Besant and other luminaries of the left. When Bain set out for South Africa again, this time as an emigrant, he had educated himself and had become thoroughly politically and socially aware.

Bain may have spent some time in Argentina before moving on to the Cape. He had been a member of the Amalgamated Society of Engineers in Scotland and he was soon embroiled in trade union activity in Cape Town. He helped to revive the ASE there as well as the trades council. He also sought to disseminate the ideas and publications of the socialist Robert Blatchford. He soon moved on from the Cape, spent a little time in Kimberley, where the immense power of De Beers helped to confirm his hatred of large-scale capitalism. But, almost inevitably, he reached the Rand, a major destination for Scots in the boom years of the late 1880s and 1890s. Bain was radicalised yet further. He was soon involved in the foundation (1892) of the Witwatersrand Mine Employees' and Mechanics' Union, and his trade union, socialist and editing activities now became legion. He frequently chaired key meetings and became a noted orator. He also became a republican, a sympathiser with the Boer Republic and, indeed, acted as its spy in the fraught period surrounding the Jameson Raid of 1896. He provided Kruger's government with information on weapons smuggling (travelling extensively as he did so, on one occasion spying in the northern Transvaal upon the family of a Scots farmer called Pittendrigh). For these reasons he was influential in ensuring that the trade union movement broke with the *uitlander* Transvaal National Union, which was fighting for the franchise and other rights of immigrant white workers, which was too closely associated with the imperial power. He also provided the government with information on illegal drinking dens and brothels, often testifying against black efforts in these fields. In short, he married his radical politics to a Presbyterian sense of social morality.

With the outbreak of the Anglo-Boer War he became, once more, a soldier, though this time against the British Empire. He acted as a leading organiser and recruiter for John McBride's Irish Brigade[99] along with several other Scots and saw action early in the war at the battle of Talana Hill, near Dundee, Natal, named, as we have seen, by immigrants from Bain's Scottish birthplace.[100] When caught by the British in 1900 he survived execution as a traitor only because he had prudently taken out Transvaal citizenship and was therefore an enemy alien.

Along with many other prisoners, including four other Scots, he was sent to a PoW camp in Ceylon, Diyatalawa. There he became one of the leaders of the inmates and was influential in the production of a camp newspaper. Throwing himself back into radical politics after the war, he endured a precarious existence as organiser and polemicist, securing work as a fitter whenever employers would have him. He was involved in the founding of a Rand branch of the ASE and became closely involved with an international set of socialists and trade unionists, including several fellow Scots such as Archie Crawford, from Glasgow, John Campbell,[101] raised on Clydeside, James Davidson from Montrose, John Reid, yet another Glaswegian, David McKerrel and Andrew Watson. All these were active as trade union organisers or as activists and candidates for the nascent Labour Party.[102] Another striking feature of this activism was the close involvement of women. These included the Glasgow-born Christina Barnet, who, with her husband, Robert (also a Scot), was involved in left-wing journalism and energetically organised the Women's Labour League at Benoni on the East Rand.

Bain helped to welcome James Keir Hardie (1856–1915) to the Rand in 1908, chairing meetings at which the visiting Labour leader spoke. It might be thought that Keir Hardie, a former miner from Ayrshire, founder of the Scottish Miners' Federation, journalist and editor of *The Labour Leader*, first Labour MP, and prominent 'Pro-Boer', would have had much in common with Bain. Bain certainly admired him, but Keir Hardie (though often ambivalent) had views on socialism, racial equality and equal pay for different races that Bain may well not have agreed with.[103] (On the other hand, Hardie believed that equal pay would ensure an advantage for white men, and he was certainly opposed to imperial Chinese labour policies.) Hardie was on a tour of the world that was intended to be a health cure. He had already visited Canada, Japan, India, New Zealand and Australia. In India he was accused of seditious sentiments in showing some sympathy for the nationalist movement. In South Africa he visited Durban, Pietermaritzburg, Ladysmith, Johannesburg, Bloemfontein and Cape Town, and was received with enormous hostility in most places. In Natal he was vilified for his anti-imperial views on the Zulu Bambatha rebellion and everywhere else for his alleged support for Indians and for black workers. A good deal of rowdyism and violence attended his meetings, particularly one in the Caledonian Hall in Johannesburg. (He was rather better received in Bloemfontein and Cape Town, perhaps because he avoided South African issues.) Interestingly, Hardie frequently had his Scottishness (presumably as a badge of radicalism) thrown at him by the South African press. A cartoon in the *Sunday*

Times depicted him as a Zulu *sangoma*, or traditional healer (witch doctor, in the parlance of the time), with horns sprouting from a deerstalker hat and his skirt of tails looking somewhat like a kilt. At the Johannesburg meeting the Cornishman Tom Matthews blamed the rowdy behaviour and violent disruption of the audience on English immigrants, an interesting case of Celtic solidarity.

By the time of Hardie's visit, racial, labour and political relations had become a minefield with intermittent explosions. Chinese labour had been introduced to the Rand in 1904; the Witwatersrand Native Labour Association was extending its recruiting operations deep into Central and East Africa; there had already been marches and strikes of white labour in 1907; and the attitudes of employers to union activity had become almost pathological in their violent antipathy. Bain was in the thick of all of this. Bain co-ordinated much of the resistance as agitation grew against the employment policies of the Premier Mine in Cullinan and the New Kleinfontein Company in Benoni. It is striking that Scots were on both sides in these disputes. Many of the supervisors, as well as the artisans, at the Premier Mine were Scots, while the chairman of the New Kleinfontein Company was none other than William Dalrymple, to whom Bain inevitably became anathema. Bain thus positioned himself to be the major leader of the great Rand strike of 1913–14, and was now abominated alike by the mining magnates and the politicians of the Union, already in unholy alliance. Moreover, the Royal Scots Fusiliers were sent in to suppress the strike. Bain was imprisoned and deported without warning and in great secrecy by the Botha/Smuts government. With eight other trade unionists (at least three of them Scots), he was forcibly placed on board the SS *Umgeni* and sent back to Britain. When this ship arrived in the Thames he was met by Arthur Henderson and other Labour leaders and was astonished to find himself hailed as a hero. He was received by all the leading Labour figures of the day, spoke at a Hyde Park demonstration, and set off on an extensive speaking tour of Britain which took him back to his native Scotland. This was of course a time of considerable disruption in the imperial metropole, characterised by major strikes, Irish rebellion and the suffragette movement, but the impact of Bain's activities was inevitably blunted by the outbreak of the First World War. He returned to South Africa and threw himself into trade union activism once more. He was involved in a power workers' stoppage, led by the Scot A. B. Dunbar, and then in another major Rand strike before his death in 1919.

Bain thus symbolises an extraordinary constellation of often conflicting forces in the period. His life history demonstrates the possibility of radicalisation in Edinburgh in the period, even the opportunities to meet major international figures. He reflects the extraordinary complexities of the Anglo-Boer War and the major tensions between international socialism and imperial sentiment, particularly during the First World War; and he suffered from the oppression and violence of the large-scale capitalism of the Rand, incited by the problems of low-grade ores, the need for intensive capitalisation and the expectation of major profitable returns to both magnates and international investors. But he also symbolises the efforts of white workers to protect themselves against black and Chinese labour. He contributed to the new alliance of a postwar South Africa: imperial/internationalist Afrikaners with capitalists aligned against Nationalist Boers with white labour. Bain's primary concern was with the fortunes of white workers and for him black labour was a threatening force rather than a brotherhood of the oppressed.

But Scots took many different routes towards their radical goal. A contrasting figure to Bain is Alexander Seaton Raitt (1867–1907). Born in Renfrew, Raitt was apprenticed to an engineering firm in Blairgowrie and emigrated to South Africa in 1890. There he worked on Rand mines and made enough money to return to Dundee to take a mechanical engineering degree. He became an important figure in the ASE in the Transvaal and served in the Anglo-Boer War on the imperial side. He came to the notice of Milner, who nominated him to the Johannesburg municipal council in 1902 and to the Transvaal legislative council in 1903, on which he was the sole Labour representative. He developed a considerable concern for the welfare of black workers, particularly the high mortality and death rates on the mines, and was fiercely opposed to Chinese labour, though he argued against the extension of the franchise to blacks. The High Commissioner, Selborne, again nominated him to the legislative council in 1907 to represent workers' and black rights, but he died three months after being appointed the first Transvaal inspector of white labour. His attempt to secure workmen's compensation in 1904 failed, but he led delegations to government during the Transvaal miners' strike of 1907. Mainly concerned with the interests of white labour, he nonetheless involved himself in a paternalist way with the fortunes of black workers. But he was always seen as a safe radical, in contrast to Bain.

Given the predilections of the time, Robert Cruickshank Graham (1869–1950) was a trade unionist who was strongly opposed to the operations of the colour bar in trade unionism. Graham was born in Aberdeen, was a child worker both on a farm and in a factory, and was apprenticed as a monumental mason. He emigrated to the United States and then to Canada before moving on to South Africa in 1901, where he worked as a mason on important government buildings. He became full-time secretary of his union (the Operative Stone Masons'

Society) and was also active in the confederation of trade unions and the Cape Federation of Trades. He served on the minimum wage board for artisans and labourers and continued to be active in South African and international trade unionism until the 1940s.

Raitt, Graham, Bain and his associates would no doubt have allied their Scottish identity and their childhood experience to a sense of a radical fight against injustice. Raitt and Graham were unusual in considering black workers' rights. Bain, who was in some respects more radical than either, did not. He worked with other Scots, often representatives of a prototype 'Red Clydeside', as well as with figures of an international movement that embraced Ireland, Canada, the United States, Australia and the various parts of the United Kingdom. His experiences in Ceylon and his encounter with Keir Hardie gave him an awareness of wider imperial struggles. Not for him the kitsch Scottishness of the Caledonian Societies, which boasted many of his capitalist opponents in their membership (see Chapter 8). But Hyslop has argued that at the time of the deportation and the major speaking tour of Britain imperial sentiment was more powerful than international socialist solidarity. Ramsay MacDonald thundered that the treatment of Bain and his associates constituted 'a disgrace to the British Empire'. Bain himself was sucked into belief in the 'rightness of the British way' and to the conviction that reform within the British Empire was more practical than international revolutionary aspirations.[104] Thus, according to Hyslop, 'the power of this identification with empire' kept the campaign within the bounds of the racially exclusive working-class trade union diaspora in Canada, Australia and South Africa.[105] Raitt and Graham were certainly 'imperially minded'. For many such Scots the British Empire could mean a higher and hopefully more noble authority in the face of local injustice. It was a strangely optimistic, but ultimately illusory, standpoint which was shared by many other whites and blacks in South Africa.

Notes

1 For a further discussion of these phenomena see John M. MacKenzie, 'Missionaries, science, and the environment in nineteenth-century Africa' in Andrew Porter (ed.), *The Imperial Horizons of British Protestant Missions, 1880–1914* (Grand Rapids MI and Cambridge 2003), pp. 106–30.
2 Richard H. Grove, 'Scottish missionaries, evangelical discourses and the origins of conservation thinking in southern Africa, 1820–1900', *Journal of Southern African Studies*, 15: 2 (1989), pp. 163–87, reprinted in Grove, *Ecology, Climate and Empire: Colonialism and Global Environmental History, 1400–1940* (Knapwell 1997), pp. 86–123. See also Grove, 'Early themes in African conservation: the Cape in the nineteenth century' in David Anderson and Richard Grove (eds), *Conservation in Africa: People, Policies and Practice* (Cambridge 1987), pp. 21–40.
3 Robert Moffat, *Missionary Labours and Scenes in Southern Africa* (London, 1846),

pp. 87 and 153. In the first he cites two sources, including Lyell, on desiccation theory. In the second he refers to the scientific achievements of the Smith expedition.
4 Ibid., p. 147.
5 John M. MacKenzie, *Empires of Nature and the Nature of Empires: Imperialism, Scotland and the Environment* (Phantassie 1997), p. 38 and *passim*. See also MacKenzie, 'The iconography of the exemplary life: the case of David Livingstone' in Geoffrey Cubitt and Allen Warren (eds), *Heroic Reputations and Exemplary Lives* (Manchester 2000), pp. 84–104.
6 A more extended discussion of these concepts of environmental taming and training can be found in MacKenzie, 'Missionaries, science and the environment', pp. 109–12, and in MacKenzie, *Empires of Nature and the Nature of Empires*, pp. 37–42.
7 Richard H. Grove, 'Scotland in South Africa: John Croumbie Brown and the roots of settler environmentalism' in Tom Griffiths and Libby Robin (eds), *Ecology and Empire: Environmental History of Settler Societies* (Keele 1997), pp. 139–53.
8 The Rev. John Brown (1722–87), the author of the 'self-interpreting' Bible, which was an extraordinary best-seller, running to fifty-one editions.
9 For a brief biography of Brown see P. J. Venter, 'An early botanist and conservationist at the Cape: the Rev. John Croumbie Brown, LLD, FRGS, FLS', *AYBSAH* (1952), II, pp. 279–93.
10 Grove, *Ecology*, p. 2.
11 Among Brown's publications are *The Truth and Truths of Christianity* (Cape Town 1845), *Pastoral Discourses* (Cape Town 1847), his extensive reports of the 1860s, *The Hydrology of South Africa, or, Details of the former Hydrographic Condition of the Cape of Good Hope, and of Causes of its present Aridity* (Edinburgh 1875), *Réboisement in France, or, Records of the Replanting of the Alps, the Cevennes and the Pyrenees with Trees* (London 1876), *Forests and Moisture, or Effects of Forests on Humidity of Climates* (Edinburgh 1877), *The Schools of Forestry in Europe: a Plea for the Creation of a School of Forestry* (Edinburgh 1877), *Water Supply in South Africa and Facilities for the Storage of it* (Edinburgh 1877), and at least fifteen other books, published down to 1892, on forests in France, England, Russia, Finland, Norway, Poland, Lithuania and the Ukraine, and on forestry schools (for which he campaigned indefatigably) in Germany and Spain. He also wrote a family history of the Browns and a work on prehistoric and mythic Finland (the myths of the *Kalevala*).
12 John Croumbie Brown, *Management of Crown Forests at the Cape of Good Hope under the Old Regime and the New* (Edinburgh 1887), p. iii.
13 The first forest conservator appointed in Natal was James Archbell, English-born of Scots descent, in 1867 (to the Swartkop forests), though it was another twenty years before a forestry department was established. Bev Ellis, 'Pietermaritzburg and its environs: the early decades of white settlement' in John Laband and Robert Haswell (eds), *Pietermaritzburg, 1838–1988: a new Portrait of an African City* (Pietermaritzburg 1988), p. 31.
14 Grove, *Ecology*, p. 114.
15 The desiccation discourse is analysed at some length in Richard H. Grove, *Green Imperialism: Colonial Expansion, Tropical Island Edens and the Origins of Environmentalism, 1600–1860* (Cambridge 1995). See also Grove, 'Imperialism and the discourse of desiccation: the institutionalisation of global environmental concerns and the role of the Royal Geographical Society, 1860–1880' in Morag Bell, Robin Butlin and Michael Heffernan (eds), *Geography and Imperialism, 1820–1940* (Manchester 1995), pp. 36–52.
16 Grove, *Ecology*, p. 27.
17 William Beinart, *The Rise of Conservation in South Africa: Settlers, Livestock, and the Environment, 1770–1950* (Oxford 2003), pp. 113–14.
18 Margaret Hermina Lister (ed.), *Journals of Andrew Geddes Bain: Trader, Explorer, Road Engineer and Geologist* (Cape Town 1949), pp. xii–xiii.
19 He had already been concerned with the planning of a pass across the Oudeberg

from Graaff Reinet in the late 1820s. Lister, *Journals*, pp. xiii–xvi.
20 As a reward for his war services (which were not without controversy) he received a 3,000 morgen farm in the new Queen Adelaide Province but lost it when London reversed Sir Benjamin D'Urban's annexation. This farm included land where Lovedale and the town of Alice were established.
21 An article in *Looking Back*, 13: 4 (1973), p. 109, 'Andrew Geddes Bain and the Ecca pass', deals with the building of this road.
22 These passes remain among the most dramatic road routes in the world. He also worked on improving other passes.
23 A. G. Bain to John Montagu, secretary to the government of Cape Colony. Lister, *Journals*, pp. 210–13. This includes a sketch map of his alternative routes.
24 A. G. Bain, 'Geology of South Africa: reminiscences and anecdotes', *The Eastern Province Monthly Magazine (EPMM)* (1857), pp. 7–20; Bain, 'Geology of the Western Province', *EPMM* (1857), pp. 396–407; Bain, 'Geology of the Eastern Province', *EPMM* (1857), pp. 456–65. His results were also published in the *Transactions of the London Geological Society* in 1856. As a result of his efforts, geological societies were founded in Grahamstown and Graaff Reinet. Bain met the luminaries of the Geological Society of London only on his sole leave visit to England, in 1864, shortly before his death.
25 A memorial to Bain was erected at the top of the Bain's Kloof Pass in 1953 (renewed on a further anniversary in 2003) and at the summit of the Ecca Pass in 1964. These passes were built mainly with convict labour in what must have been terrible conditions.
26 S. H. Houghton, 'The father of South African geology', *South African Notes and News*, September 1964. See also A. W. Roger, 'The pioneers in South African geology and their work', *Transactions of the Geological Society of South Africa*, 39 (1937), annexure.
27 *Report of the Association for the Advancement of Science meeting in South Africa* (1905), pp. 145–81.
28 Beinart, *Rise of Conservation*, p. 170. A list of passes that T. C. J. Bain worked on can be found in Lister, *Journals*, p. xxxv.
29 He designed the church on Robben Island.
30 Phillida Brooke Simons, *The Life and Work of Charles Bell* (Vlaeberg 1998), p. 58. Details of Bell's career and artistic activities are to be found in this work.
31 There were also 'stationer's shop artists' who produced prints mainly for sale to visitors and passengers on ships calling at the Cape.
32 This included representations of fossils to celebrate Bain's interest.
33 Charles Piazzi Smyth, obituary of Charles Davidson Bell in *Proceedings of the Royal Society of Edinburgh*, XII (1886–87), quoted in Simons, *Life and Work*, pp. 128 and 150.
34 All three were painted in 1850 and were exhibited at the first fine arts exhibition in Cape Town in 1851. They continued to be exhibited at a succession of such exhibitions which took place in 1852, 1858 and 1866 and were reproduced (particularly 'The landing of Van Riebeeck') in many school texts and other illustrated works. Thus Bell made a considerable contribution to the iconic imaging of Cape history. Michael Godby, 'The art of Charles Bell: an appraisal' in Simons, *Life and Work*, p. 157. This article, pp. 140–60, provides a valuable assessment of the surviving work of Bell.
35 In a letter to his parents quoted in Simons, *Life and Work*, p. 35.
36 He drew up an extensive account of his own Bell ancestors and, having become fascinated by heraldry, also set about compiling an inventory of the arms of all the old Cape families – illustrating yet again his double affiliation.
37 Godby, 'The art of Charles Bell', p. 150.
38 'George William Smith, architect and surveyor', *Looking Back*, 16: 1 (1976), pp. 7–8.
39 The phrase comes from Hutcheon's *Report of the Colonial Veterinary Surgeon* (1881–82).

40 For a detailed account of the veterinary and environmental theories and applications of Branford and Hutcheon see Beinart, *Rise of Conservation*, pp. 132–57. This was published earlier as 'Vets, viruses and environmentalism at the Cape' in Griffiths and Robin, *Ecology and Empire*, pp. 87–101.
41 A more detailed account of his work can be found in John M. MacKenzie, 'Experts and amateurs: tsetse, nagana and sleeping sickness in East and Central Africa' in MacKenzie (ed.), *Imperialism and the Natural World* (Manchester 1990), pp. 187–212.
42 As we have seen, Andrew Smith and Charles Bell were inevitably involved in hunting in southern Africa, often claiming scientific research – as well as the imperative of survival upon the frontier – as justification.
43 John M. MacKenzie, *The Empire of Nature: Hunting, Conservation and British Imperialism* (Manchester 1988).
44 Roualeyn Gordon Cumming, *Five Years of a Hunter's Life in the far Interior of South Africa* (two volumes, London 1870). For an account of Cumming's activities see MacKenzie, *Empire of Nature*, pp. 96–103 and *passim*.
45 Cumming claimed, perhaps with some exaggeration, that the entire town turned out to marvel at them. Cumming, *Hunter's Life*, I, p. 215.
46 The resulting book, *Prince Alfred's Progress through South Africa* (Cape Town 1861), detailed this slaughter in gory detail. The elaborate cover of this book was designed by Charles Davidson Bell.
47 For a sensitive biography see Jane Carruthers, *Wildlife and Warfare: the Life of James Stevenson-Hamilton* (Pietermaritzburg 2001).
48 Jane Carruthers, *The Kruger National Park: a Social and Political History* (Pietermaritzburg 1995).
49 Stevenson-Hamilton was a prolific writer. See, for example, his *Animal Life in Africa* (London 1912), *The Kruger National Park* (Pretoria 1928), *The Low Veld: its Wildlife and its Peoples* (London 1929), *South African Eden* (London 1937), *Our South African National Parks* (Cape Town 1940). For a more extensive bibliography of his many publications see Carruthers, *Wildlife and Warfare*.
50 For various considerations of the relationship between white identity, southern Africa's landscapes and its faunal resources see several of the contributions to William Beinart and Joann McGregor (eds), *Social History and African Environments* (Oxford, Athens OH and Cape Town 2003).
51 For this question of multiple identities see John M. MacKenzie, foreword to Carruthers, *Wildlife and Warfare*, pp. xi–xii.
52 Grove, 'Scotland in South Africa', p. 139.
53 See Christine E. Jackson and Peter Davis, *Sir William Jardine: a Life in Natural History* (Leicester 2001), for an example of the intellectual and international networks of a Scottish landowner in the Borders. Jardine (1800–74) had a brother in Australia and a son who went on extensive world travels, including South Africa, in pursuit of natural history specimens. Sir William also formed a connection with Sir Andrew Smith.
54 AWC: Boonzaier Collection, A 2039.
55 J. Forbes Munro, 'Glasgow University and Africa', unpublished paper.
56 Between 1860 and 1920 over 16 per cent of all Aberdeen graduates who went overseas emigrated to South Africa (311 in all). If only the empire figures are used, the South African proportion rises to more than 20 per cent. The South African figure is higher than that of Australia (243), Canada (157) or New Zealand (107). Only the Indian figure surpasses that of South Africa (407). Of these 311 graduates, a high proportion became ministers, missionaries, teachers and doctors. The dynamic of the flow is also interesting: between 1860 and 1880 the percentage (of all overseas migrants) was over 16; 1880–1900, over 21 (the highest percentage to any colony or region) and 1901–20 15.3. It would be interesting to see similar figures for other Scottish universities. John D. Hargreaves, *Academe and Empire: Some Overseas Connections of Aberdeen University, 1860–1970* (Aberdeen 1994), p. 125.

MEDICINE, BUSINESS AND RADICALS

57 The most sophisticated survey of these processes can be found in Harriet Deacon, Howard Phillips and Elizabeth van Heyningen (eds), *The Cape Doctor in the Nineteenth Century: a Social History* (Amsterdam 2004). The Cape doctor is also the name given to the healthy south-easterly wind.
58 This dominance continued well into the twentieth century. Dr Isaac Marks has informed me that he was trained almost entirely by Scottish professors at the University of Cape Town after the Second World War.
59 Joy B. Brain, 'Health and disease among white settlers in colonial Natal', *Natalia*, 15 (1985), pp. 64–77, especially p. 72.
60 Grey's Hospital was founded in 1855 with a £1,000 grant from Sir George Grey. Its site was chosen by Dr Peter Sutherland (1822–1900), who was a doctor as well as first Surveyor General of Natal. One of its first matrons was Elizabeth Macdonald. Angus Rose, 'Grey's Hospital' in Laband and Haswell (eds), *Pietermaritzburg*, p. 182.
61 Some of the biographical information that follows is derived from the *DSAB*. It is of course true that the doctors included in this reference work are, by definition, those who achieved prominence in other fields.
62 A. H. Tonkin, 'The doctors who came to the Cape', *Coelacanth*, 15: 1 (1977), pp. 2–8.
63 Ian Colvin, *The Life of Jameson* (two volumes, London 1922).
64 See also Harriet Deacon, Elizabeth van Heyningen, Sally Swartz and Felicity Swanson, 'Mineral wealth and medical opportunity' in Deacon *et al.*, *Cape Doctor*.
65 Peter Allan, *Report of the Tuberculosis Survey of the Union of South Africa* (Cape Town 1924). This is an impressive report dealing with the incidence of TB among whites and Africans in different parts of the Union.
66 There is an inadequate account of this in P. W. Laidler and M. Gelfand, *South Africa – its Medical History, 1652–1898: a Medical and Social Study* (Cape Town 1971), p. 435.
67 Dr A. S. Presley, *A Sunnyside Chronicle, 1781–1981: a History of Sunnyside Royal Hospital, produced for its Bi-centenary* (Montrose 1981). Presley was the principal psychologist at the hospital. One of its superintendents, Dr W. A. F. Browne, had written as early as 1834 that his intention was 'to treat the insane as if they were sane' (p. 8).
68 Ibid., p. 10.
69 Copies of *The Sunnyside Chronicle* can be found in the Montrose Museum. It is an impressively printed and professionally produced journal. The archives of Sunnyside were deposited, after its closure, in the archives of the University of Dundee.
70 *The Sunnyside Chronicle*, 3: 2 (July 1889), p. 18.
71 Ibid., 3: 4 (September 1889), pp. 58–61.
72 Ibid., 6: 2 (July 1892), p. 17.
73 Ibid., 3: 3 (August 1889), pp. 33–6; also 3: 5 (September 1889), p. 74. Dodds was said to have been active in cricket, curling, amateur dramatics, the local literary society and much else.
74 An account of Collie's voyage and arrival appeared in the *Chronicle*, 4: 1 (June 1890), pp. 1–5.
75 This is recounted in a letter, *Chronicle*, 5: 4 (September 1891), pp. 49–52. Collie later became district surgeon at Lady Frere, Queenstown, on the Eastern Cape.
76 *Chronicle*, 4: 7 (December 1890), p. 93.
77 Ibid., 4: 10 (March 1891), p. 141.
78 Ibid., 7: 1 (July 1904), pp. 10–11.
79 Dodds to H. W. Pearson, Colonial Secretary, 16 January 1890, considering the merits of various potential sites. AWC: CO 4270/D5.
80 As inspector-general of psychiatric hospitals at the Cape, Dodds was frequently on tours of inspection. See for example AWC: T1045/1706 and T978/1615.
81 *Chronicle*, 7: 10 (April 1905), pp. 155–6. Later in the year, in November (7: 5), it was apparent that Dr Dodds was still in touch with Sunnyside, sending an invitation

for the (unnamed) editor to come out with the British Association for the Advancement of Science for its forthcoming meeting in South Africa.
82 Conan Doyle was in South Africa for a few months in 1900, paying his own way and receiving no salary. His mother fiercely opposed the war and was distressed by his decision to go. Martin Booth, *The Doctor and the Detective: a Biography of Sir Arthur Conan Doyle* (New York 1997), pp. 226–33. He subsequently wrote a book about the war.
83 David Wallace and Francis D. Boyd (eds), *Report of the Edinburgh and East of Scotland South African Hospital* (Edinburgh 1901). Wallace was a surgeon and Boyd a physician who had been involved with the scheme.
84 Barbara Mackenzie, *Salt River Doctor* (Cape Town 1981)
85 He charged 2s 6d for a visit to the surgery, 3s 6d for a house call, 2s for a bottle of medicine and 30s for a confinement. There were many debtors.
86 Mackenzie, *Salt River Doctor*, p. 56.
87 Mogamed Ajam, 'Dr Abdullah Abdurahman – benefactor of the Bo-Kaap', *Kronos*, 17 (1990), pp. 48–58. See also Nigel Worden, Elizabeth van Heyningen and Vivian Bickford-Smith, *Cape Town: the Making of a City* (Cape Town 1999), II, pp. 29, 65 and 86.
88 Examples of these would include *Men of the Times: Pioneers of the Transvaal and Glimpses of South Africa* (Johannesburg, Cape Town and London 1905), *Men of the Times: Old Colonists of the Cape Colony and Orange River Colony* (Johannesburg, Cape Town and London 1906), and the *South African Who's Who* (which started in the nineteenth century, but I used the 1908 edition).
89 Examples would include Colin MacIntyre (b. Greenock 1862), who went to the Cape in 1897 and became a manager of the South African Mutual Life Assurance Company; Donald MacKenzie (b. Ullapool 1866), arrived in the Transvaal in 1896 and, after a period with the Bank of Africa, became Secretary of the Alliance Permanent Mutual Building Society and Savings Bank; Alfred MacLeod (b. Aberdeen 1880), arr. Cape Town 1903 and became Resident Manager of the Central Insurance Company; John MacRae (b. Rossshire 1881), arr. Transvaal in 1903 to work for the National Bank of South Africa and later moved to Cape Town as Resident Secretary of the African Life Assurance Society; and Alexander Aiken (b. Old Meldrum 1861), arr. South Africa 1890, worked for South African Loan, Mortgage and Mercantile Agency in Pretoria and for the South African National Bank before starting his own accountancy practice, later financial adviser to Lord Roberts in the war and treasurer of the Johannesburg municipality. These instances could be multiplied many times.
90 Robert I. Rotberg, *The Founder: Cecil Rhodes and the Pursuit of Power* (Oxford 1988), p. 346.
91 William Alexander MacKenzie (1881–1947) moved from banking into mines. Born in Aberdeen, he went to Johannesburg in 1902 to work in the Johannesburg African Banking Corporation, subsequently becoming manager. After the First World War he worked for Consolidated Gold Fields and became vice-president of the Transvaal Chamber of Mines. He also retired to Scotland.
92 Rotberg, *The Founder*, p. 344.
93 Sivewright became commander-in-chief of the Cape Town Highlanders in the 1890s. This reflects the extent to which Scottish cultural and military icons became fused with supposed Establishment success (see chapter 8).
94 Colleagues in the Rhodes Ministry were so concerned about his corrupt practices that they declined to serve with him, but Rhodes refused to dismiss him and dissolved the Ministry instead. A good contemporary account of these events can be found in Lewis Michell, *The Life and Times of Cecil John Rhodes* (London 1912), pp. 227, 231–4.
95 The modern house at Tulliallan (there is also a fourteenth-century castle) was built by Admiral George Keith Elphinstone, the commander-in-chief of the fleet that took the Cape in 1895, between 1817 and 1820. Sivewright must have been well aware of this intriguing South African connection. Glen L. Pride, *The*

Kingdom of Fife: an Illustrated Architectural Guide (Edinburgh 1990), pp. 22–3.
96 Hargreaves, *Academe and Empire*, p. 82.
97 Jonathan Hyslop, *The Notorious Syndicalist: J. T. Bain, a Scottish Rebel in Colonial South Africa* (Johannesburg 2004). The following account of Bain is based mainly on Hyslop.
98 Jonathan Hylsop, 'A Scottish socialist reads Carlyle in Johannesburg prison, June 1900: reflections on the literary culture of the imperial working class', *Journal of Southern African Studies*, 29: 3 (2003), pp. 639–55. For another instance (in this case the Irish-born Robert Noonan) of radicalisation in South Africa see Jonathan Hyslop, 'A ragged trousered philanthropist and the empire: Robert Tressell in South Africa', *History Workshop Journal*, 51 (2001), pp. 65–86.
99 Donal P. McCracken, *MacBride's Brigade: Irish Commandos in the Anglo-Boer War* (Dublin 1999). For Bain see pp. 25, 119, 170. See also the full account in Hyslop, *Notorious Syndicalist*, chapter 13. Other Scots in the brigade were Oliver John (Jack) Hindon, J. Baird Kidd, a Glaswegian, and John Murray, also from Glasgow. The brigade included Americans, Australians, Afrikaners, an Italian, a Norwegian, a Belgian. But not all the members can be identified as to their origins. See also Donal P. McCracken, *The Irish pro-Boers, 1877–1902* (Johannesburg and Cape Town 1989).
100 The battlefield site on the edge of Dundee is now a notable museum.
101 Campbell was a follower of the syndicalism of the American Daniel De Leon.
102 More detail about these figures can be found in Hyslop, *Notorious Syndicalist*, passim. Archie Crawford and John Campbell were unusual in that they had some interest in the unionisation of blacks.
103 Frederick Hale, 'British Labourite James Keir Hardie in South Africa: the politics of race in a working-class colonial setting', *Quarterly Bulletin of the National Library of South Africa*, 56: 4 (2002), pp. 142–72. This account is based mainly on (often hostile) press descriptions of Hardie's travels and attempts to get a hearing.
104 Hyslop, *Notorious Syndicalist*, p. 253.
105 Ibid., pp. 253–4. All of this casts a very curious light upon the claims of Bernard Porter in *The Absent-minded Imperialists* (Oxford 2005) that British society in general, and its workers in particular, had no interest in imperialism in any form. Like it or not, their radicalism was deeply affected by it.

CHAPTER EIGHT

Maintaining Scots identity

In his most celebrated poem, 'Afar in the desert', Thomas Pringle recounted a ride across the Karoo, evoking the landscape and the fauna while pessimistically ruminating on 'My high aims abandoned – my good acts undone'. But his bitterness is assuaged by memories of:

> My Native Land – whose magical name
> Thrills to the heart like electric flame;
> The home of my childhood; the haunts of my prime;
> All the passions and scenes of that rapturous time
> When the feelings were young and the world was new,
> Like the fresh bowers of Eden unfolding to view;
> All – all now forsaken – forgotten – forgone!
> And I – a lone exile remembered of none.[1]

Romantic nostalgia for Scotland somehow overlaid the mix of ambitions, hopelessness and fear which had taken the Pringle family to southern Africa, where they had encountered a harsh environment and the inevitable hostility of the dispossessed. Yet something of this yearning runs through a great deal of the Scottish cultural activity which developed some decades after Pringle's death and continued – often losing all sense of genuine ethnic relationships – for the next 150 years. Many Scots, whether prospering or failing, seem to have been unwilling to let go of an idealised vision of their origins.

Certainly, with increasing numbers of Scots, the opportunities for cultural and other forms of association grew. This chapter will examine the various ways in which Scots declared their identity in the second half of the nineteenth and early years of the twentieth centuries. Caledonian Societies emerged throughout southern Africa. The totemic days of the Scottish calendar were widely celebrated. Highland games were instituted as major sporting and cultural events, matching their counterparts in the United States, Canada, Australia and New Zealand.[2]

These societies also produced magazines for their members. Another glossy journal, *The South African Scot*, was founded which was designed to celebrate the achievements of Scots in the subcontinent and emphasise both their supposedly distinctive contribution and their allegedly constructive relations with other ethnicities. The Presbyterian Church expanded its operations, notably into the Orange Free State and the South African Republic in the decades before the Anglo-Boer War of 1899–1902. Various military units were founded which adhered to Scottish regimental forms. Schools adopted kilts and pipe bands as cultural signifiers even when they were not necessarily Scottish in their pupil constituency.

These developments raise a number of questions which shed some light on parallel activities elsewhere in the British Empire. Caledonian Societies were not designed merely for social and recreational purposes. They had deeper instrumental significance which helps to explain their apparent success. Moreover, Scots seem to have had a particularly strong desire to cling to their origins through the naming of places, farms, companies and individuals. The Presbyterian Church was, at one and the same time, enthralled with what was seen as a heroic missionary past, with its relationship with colonists and with the Dutch Reformed Church. Yet, as the racial order became more intensely separated, these two streams flowed in many respects in different directions. Moreover, the two Churches, Presbyterian and Dutch, were distinct in their theologies. Though they had many personnel in common, it was in some respects the myth of their association – and therefore of the allegedly sympathetic relationship between their two congregations – which became more potent than the reality. It was a myth which was repeated so often that it came to have some kind of propagandist value. And that helps to explain why the supposedly Scottish regiments and the schools which displayed outwardly Scots forms in aspects of their cultural and sporting activities came to appeal to an Afrikaans community which presumably saw them as a means of striking some kind of cultural blow against the English and Anglicisation.[3] For it is indeed the case that in the twentieth century many Afrikaners seemed to adopt Scottish emblems, just as they took up rugby (admittedly an English sport, but one with some Scottish resonances) as their distinctive sporting activity.[4]

But the Scots, whether first, second, third or even further generations, seemed to use their cultural forms as a means of constantly shifting their allegiances. Their societies and publications were invariably respectful towards the imperial power. During the First and Second Boer Wars they were open in their allegiance to the British authorities. Yet in the aftermath of conflict they were loud in their protestations of affinity with the Afrikaners. Moreover, although they had appeared to be prominent in the humanitarian and missionary activities in the nineteenth century, the influx of colonists into Natal, the Orange Free State and the South African Republic, later the Transvaal, had ensured a close identity with white interests. This was readily transferred to loyalty to the new Union after 1910. While Scottish associations of one sort or another appeared to adhere to what were seen to be the geographical and cultural affinities of alleged ethnic origins, they never swam against a developing racial and political tide. They also invariably took an Establishment position in opposition to more radical Scots who often confronted them in trade union activity or, occasionally, in the adoption of anti-white positions.

Caledonian and other Scottish societies

The first Caledonian Society appears to have been founded on the Eastern Cape frontier. This is significant, both because of settler nerves over the frontier wars (and it was in existence before the final conflict with the Xhosa) and also because settlers were in greatest need of mutual support there. Known as the Kaffrarian Caledonian Society, it was founded in King William's Town in 1870. Two Scots, Alexander Duncan and Thomas Henderson, sent out a printed notice inviting Scots 'to revive national sympathies and recollections, inspire patriotic sentiments, and perpetuate Caledonian good-fellowship'. They proposed that a meeting of 'leal-hearted' Scots would be held on the 2 January 1871 for the purpose of indulging in 'reminiscences of the land o' cakes, recitations of national poetry, and other information that may be of interest to Scotchmen in exile'.[5] Future meetings would take place on St Andrew's Night. But the society soon had more practical objectives: it was concerned to help immigrants find lodgings and work, provide indigent widows with financial support, assist in schemes of welfare for the young and old, as well as support the education of the children of poorer or deceased members.

The best documented of the early societies is that of East London, only thirty-five miles from King William's Town. It was founded in 1876 and it was said that the original members wished to celebrate St Andrew's Night together. It was also concerned with social support systems. Its centennial history describes the manner in which its members participated in both of the Anglo-Boer conflicts, and the First and Second World Wars. Another clue is offered in the suggestion that the society was always closely involved in welcoming distinguished visitors to East London, such as the Duke and Duchess of York, Prince and Princess Arthur of Connaught, Earl and Countess Haig, as well as being instrumental in bringing celebrated performers such as Harry Lauder and Joseph Hislop, the then celebrated Scottish tenor, to the city.[6] These societies combined their devotion to the tartan image of Scotland with fierce loyalty to King and Empire. They were also a significant source of socialisation, 'networking' and entertainment in towns that were far from being oversupplied with 'things to do'.[7]

Caledonian Societies spread to Cape Town, Port Elizabeth, Pietermaritzburg and Durban in the course of the 1880s and to Bloemfontein and other centres of Afrikanerdom only slightly later.[8] A Scottish Association was founded in Port Elizabeth in 1882, shortly after the first Burns Night gathering had been held in January that year.[9] Scots had, however, been celebrating St Andrew's Night there since November 1851. Leading lights included Robert Black, a merchant from Haddington, David Brown, a chartered accountant and law agent, originally from Glasgow, and the Association's chief, Alexander Fettes, from Laurencekirk, who was piper to the Scottish company of the Prince Alfred Guard in the town. Fettes was also a town councillor, mayor and a member of the Provincial Council.[10] The Durban society was founded in 1883 with Sir David Hunter of the Natal Railways as its first chief. It went through a bad patch in the 1890s but was revived in 1897, and was said to pursue a 'progressive policy' of 'philanthropy, music and sport'. Its influential secretary was A. M. Hay, a successful jeweller and watchmaker, born in Banffshire and apprenticed in Aberdeen, who migrated to South Africa in 1889 and opened his business in Durban in 1894.[11] Meanwhile the extraordinary growth in the population of the gold diggings on the Witwatersrand, and the arrival of many Scots, were reflected in the fact that a society was founded in Johannesburg in early 1892.[12] In a matter of months it had established a sports day, including the traditional Highland Gathering events of tossing the caber, throwing the hammer and putting the shot.[13] Musical, literary and dancing competitions also became a central aspect of the gathering, and the Johannesburg Caledonian Society formed its own pipe band. In 1895 Kruger's government gave permission for the pipes and drums of the Black Watch, then at the Cape, to come to the games to enhance the atmosphere of Scottishness. But the Caledonian Society sometimes flirted with scandal. In that year its acting chief was John Stroyan, known to be a lecher and a financial swindler, attracting investments to useless mining propositions.[14] Stroyan returned to Scotland, where his activities seem to have done him no harm: he was returned to Parliament in the 'khaki election' of 1900 as Liberal Unionist MP for West Perthshire, but was defeated in the Liberal landslide of 1906.

Before the end of the same year a number of Scots had met in the St Andrew's Hall in Pretoria to found another society. As we have seen, the foundation stone of this hall had been laid, with due Masonic ceremony, by President Kruger in 1890, the Presbyterian minister the Rev. James Gray officiating.[15] It subsequently became, as its name implies, the centre of all Scottish cultural activity in the republic's capital. The charter of the Pretoria society carried the signatures of no fewer than 118 founder members and its first chief was the proprietor and editor of the *Transvaal Advertiser*, John Keith. Yet again Scots seemed to be at the centre of journalistic activity. In 1898 the society acquired Caledonian Park as a central recreation ground and soon opened the first bowling green in the Transvaal there.[16] The park retains this name to this day.

With the outbreak of the Anglo-Boer War the Caledonian Societies suspended their activities. In Johannesburg the membership turned their minds to more serious imperial patriotism. They suggested to Kitchener the formation of a unit to be known as the Scottish Horse (see below). In 1904 a memorial to these cavalry regiments was unveiled on Caledonia Hill, Kensington, Johannesburg. The archives in Pretoria retain many documents relating to these societies that are indicative of their activities and the significance their members sought to carve out for them. The documents include charters of incorporation,[17] land grants, legal cases, addresses of loyalty to Queen Victoria on the occasions of her jubilees, the granting of honorary membership to Establishment figures such as Milner,[18] as well as invitations to senior officials to attend Burns Suppers[19] and St Andrew's Night dinners,[20] not to mention Hallowe'en and Hogmanay. These were sufficiently important events in the colonial calendar that figures with no Scottish connections at all seem to have been eager to participate. In 1905 the foundation stone of a new Caledonian Hall was laid on the corner of Jeppe and End Streets in Johannesburg. Many of the members were people of substance, and the societies seem to have had little difficulty in going into property. The society soon set up a bowling club in the city, and the annual Highland Games became a significant social, cultural and sporting fixture each September. (Caledonian football teams were also founded and, even if not associated with Caledonian Societies, they were often encouraged and patronised by leading society members.[21]) But by 1914 the Caledonian Society's property activities in Johannesburg had come unstuck. The society went into liquidation. When in a sound financial position it had bought stands 1209 and 1210 in the city as a source of income, but property in the area had declined in quality; the tram line which passed the society's hall was diverted, and shops on the ground floor could no longer be let.

The property depreciated so rapidly that its liabilities soon far exceeded its assets.[22]

The significant number of Scots in the Orange River Colony (later the Free State once again), the Transvaal and Natal is well attested by the manner in which Caledonian Societies spread to relatively small centres such as Kroonstad, Ficksburg, Vryheid, Eshowe, Kokstad, as well as Dundee, Newcastle and Alexandra, together with places that are now suburbs of the vast Johannesburg conurbation, Benoni, Boksburg, Germiston, Randfontein, Standerton and Witbank. There was also a society at Ermelo, close to the 'New Scotland' settlement of the 1860s.[23] The first capital of the South African Republic, Potchefstroom, boasted a society, dating from before the Anglo-Boer War. In 1904 this society began to interest itself in 'heritage'. Potchefstroom had an old fort which had been a significant centre of conflict during the first Anglo-Boer War. British troops (notably a contingent of about 150 of the Royal Scots Fusiliers) were located in this fort while the town was under siege by an Afrikaner commando.[24] After the war a transport company drew attention to the fort when it applied to extend its business into it. The Caledonian Society responded by suggesting that it would take the fort over, fence it, restore it and create a monument to the memory of those who had fallen in its defence. The Potchefstroom municipality accepted this proposal on condition that no offence were caused to the 'Dutch' inhabitants of the town. The Caledonian Society's proposal was duly carried out, at a cost of under £21, in 1905.[25]

But South African Scots did not concentrate their efforts into Caledonian Societies alone. Various other Scottish societies were founded offering a mixture of cultural interests and sometimes social support systems. These included the Aberdeen, Banff and Kincardine Society of Cape Town, the Highland Society of the Cape, the Cape Edinburgh Society, the St Andrew's Society of Simonstown, the Scottish Associations of Oudtshoorn, Cradock and Port Elizabeth, the 'Umvioti Scots' at Greytown and the Natal Highland Society. In Johannesburg a Burns Society was founded in 1904 by leading members of the Caledonian Society: it was described as being virtually the literary branch of the latter body.[26] In Natal the Highland Society organised a Mod to celebrate Scottish poetry, music and dance, although it cannot have been dedicated to Gaelic in the manner of the Scottish Mods. Some Gaelic was spoken, and Natal boasted a Comunn Gaidhealaich (Gaelic Association), but it is clear that the Scots and English languages were mainly deployed.[27] All these societies held dinners and some offered support to members and other Scots who were in difficulties. It was said of the Natal

Highland Association that it adhered to the 'historical hospitality of the Gael':

> Some fellows, who, as a result of the want of employment and adverse fate, were feeling the pinch of want, have been assisted by the Association both financially and otherwise, while others have been placed in comfortable employment.[28]

Meanwhile, it was said that the membership of the Pietermaritzburg Caledonia Society exceeded 200, that:

> It is financially in a very enviable position, and its record of work is praiseworthy in the extreme. For instance, during the past twelvemonth no less than £50 was dispensed in assistance to indigent Scots people, including the cost of no less than 377 meals and beds and the payment of railway fares on behalf of many who were stranded in pecuniary difficulty.[29]

At this same period, societies noted that the depression was causing many bankruptcies on the Rand and that Scots were able to help each other. Moreover, it is noticeable that there were connections between the Caledonian Societies and the Scottish Masonic lodges. For example, it was emphasised that A. J. McGibbon, the president of the Pietermarizburg Caledonian Society, was an active Scottish Mason, holding high office in the St Andrew's and Maritzburg county lodges, as well as in the District Grand Lodge of Natal, Scottish Constitution.[30]

Something of the elite flavour of these organisations can be derived from accounts of the St Andrew's Day banquets in 1905. In Johannesburg the event was attended by the High Commissioner, Lord Selborne, and his staff, as well as the colonial secretary and the Commissioner for Lands. After the haggis, verses and songs, the chief of the society proposed the toast of the High Commissioner, who replied by dilating upon the importance of Scots around the empire. He also deprecated provincialism and held the Scots up as a model, holding to their own ethnicity while working for the interests of the empire as a whole. No fewer than 420 members and guests of the society sat down to this banquet.[31] On the same day a gathering of about eighty met for a similar celebration in Bloemfontein, with the Lieutenant-governor of the Orange River Colony, Sir John George Fraser, present. In his speech he pointed out that the society had a membership of 300 out of a 'Scotch population' in the city of 2,000, men, women and children. His implication was that more should support the society, but, given that they tended to be men-only in this period, 300 seems a high proportion. Two ministers also attended the dinner, the Revs James Craig and S. Thomson, a reminder that in many of these societies the local Presbyterian ministers, guardians as it were of the patron saint, offered a sanctification of these ethnic organisations.

At any rate, so great was the proliferation of Caledonian Societies in the decades before and after the Anglo-Boer War that by the time of the First World War there were no fewer than forty Caledonian Societies in southern Africa (including Southern and Northern Rhodesia). Each had its 'chief' as though it were a clan. There were attempts to create a federation of these societies as early as 1905, as recounted in *The South African Scot*.[32] The writer, William Mirrlees (who had been chief of the Durban society), recounted that he had proposed such a federation when delegates from all over South Africa met in Johannesburg to honour the Scots of the Scottish Horse who had been killed in the Anglo-Boer War. Scots being highly peripatetic, he proposed that membership of one society should mean membership of them all. Scots would also become much more acquainted with what was going on in other towns. But, he suggested, his ideas had foundered on that other propensity of the Scot, to be independent and freedom-loving. Such a federation did come into being in 1918 (presumably the advantages of co-operation had become more obvious with the exigencies of the war), when all the societies joined in the Federated Caledonian Society of Southern Africa, which was described as 'the strongest and most active of all the British patriotic societies in southern Africa'.[33]

A powerful hierarchy was now established, with a chief presiding over each of the then four provinces of South Africa (and two in the Rhodesias), with an overall federal chief elected at the annual congress each year. In the course of the inter-war years Queen Elizabeth, later the Queen Mother, became the patron and the society was always eager to emphasise its significance by claiming leading figures in its membership. But there is plenty of evidence that the Caledonian Societies were something more than just an opportunity for tartan socialisation. Members used the meetings to make business contacts, to advance their interests (particularly in the fast-growing capitalist hotbed of Johannesburg) and to 'network' in highly effective ways. An excellent example of this comes from a family of Mackenzies who emigrated from north-east Scotland (Fochabers) to South Africa. In particular, three brothers, William, George, and John Mackenzie, all educated in Aberdeen, arrived in Johannesburg just after the Boer War. All three became very successful businessmen, in banking, accountancy and eventually lucrative company directorships. The author of the family history was quite clear about the importance of Caledonian Society membership:

George Mackenzie now had a fairly shrewd idea of what he would do in life. He had come in contact with auditors and accountants and he liked what he saw of their work. He had met them socially as well. His brother John took him to a reception the Caledonian Society gave in August, 1905, in honour of the Scottish members of the visiting British Association. [The British Association for the Advancement of Science met in South Africa in 1905.[34]] John was a member of the committee of the Society and George had joined also. There were no fewer than 1,000 members of the Caledonian Society in Johannesburg in 1905 [but see note 36, below], a remarkable total: and this led the guest of honour, Dr. (later Sir) James Murray, the great lexicographer and editor of the Oxford English Dictionary, to comment on how there were Scotsmen everywhere – there would be one sitting on the top of the South Pole if ever you went there, he said. At this reception George was introduced to the honorary chief of the Society, Mr James Fraser, with whom he was soon to have important associations. He also met Mr Charles Stuart. Both were prominent accountants.[35]

This was just a start. The three young brothers (all only in their twenties at this point) continued to meet influential Scottish businessmen at the society, and the connections they made there unquestionably helped them to build successful careers and considerable fortunes. William Alexander Mackenzie was later to become chairman of Consolidated Gold Fields. This offers the impression that such a society was particularly valuable to members of an ambitious elite, although the smaller-scale societies of King William's Town and East London – together with others – clearly tapped into the needs of Scots and their descendents of more modest social status.

The proliferation of a variety of Scots societies in the years after the Anglo-Boer War seemed evidence of extraordinary energy in the desire for Scottish associations. As the years passed there was a tendency for some of these to come under the umbrella of the Federation of Caledonian Societies, but it is certainly the case that no English, Welsh or Irish society seems to have aspired to the activism of the Scots. This may be testimony to the numbers of educated, elite and business Scots who recognised that the Caledonian Societies could not only maintain contacts with their homeland and people of a supposed fellow ethnicity but also benefit them in a variety of ways.

The South African Scot

In 1908 J. H. Gray, of the Thistle Printing Works, of Pritchard Street in Johannesburg (normally legal and commercial printers), applied to the Registrar of Deeds in Pretoria to register an 'unpretentious little magazine of 24 pages' to be distributed to the members of the Caledonian Societies in South Africa. The print run was to be 1,500, which indicates a rather small figure for the whole territory, but, as with most things to do with Scots, numbers were seldom an indication of significance or influence.[36] And, as we have seen from the example of the Mackenzie brothers, this was a society in search of cohesiveness and mutual business support. The journal was clearly designed to facilitate this further. The 'unpretentious little magazine' eventually became an organ of the entire Caledonian Federation and continued to be produced for many decades after its founding.

This Caledonian Society magazine may have been substitute for a more impressive journal, *The South African Scot*, which first appeared in November 1905. This first issue trumpeted its loyalty by offering a portrait of Edward VII as its frontispiece, although the caption duly annexed him as 'King of Scots'. (On other occasions the King was referred to as Edward I, since the other six were of course only Kings of England.) In its opening editorial it proclaimed its objects as being:

(1) To foster and preserve amongst Scots in South Africa, Scottish sentiment, traditions, literature, music – in short all that is worth preserving in the heritage of the Scottish people; (2) To bring the Scottish societies in South Africa into close, friendly relations with each other by providing an effective medium wherein their interests, aims and work may be recorded and intelligently discussed; and (3) To discuss current events and thought, moderately and without partisanship, from the standpoint of Scottish experience and ideals.[37]

The *South African Scot* was ambitious, both in its format and in its aims. The first issue carried endorsements from Scottish aristocrats and distinguished Scots from around the empire. Clearly dedicated to Scottish exceptionalism, it suggested that Scots could make a distinctive contribution to South African politics and society. Thereafter the *South African Scot* settled into a fairly standard format. Each issue carried articles on Scottish heroes of the past, famous South African Scots of the present, obituaries of notable Scots, letters from Scotland, news and gossip from the Presbyterian Church, the Caledonian Societies, St Andrew's Night celebrations, Burns Clubs (including the major one in Johannesburg), with reports on balls, Scottish concerts, as well as sporting events. An early issue carried an article on the 'Aims and ideals of Caledonian and Highland Societies'.[38] The occasional piece appeared on Scottish regiments and their South African counterparts. Sometimes it branched out into political controversy, as with an article on 'Tariff tinkering in Cape Colony' in the January 1906 issue, and another on Joseph Chamberlain's tariff reform proposals in March, when it seemed to be quite clear about its own free-trade credentials (no doubt viewed as a Scottish-inspired policy). It was on safer ground with its insistence that the South African education system wished to emulate that of Scotland.

Prominent South African Scots were impressively profiled. The list included Sir John George Fraser, son of the minister the Rev. Colin McKenzie Fraser, who was in fact born in South Africa (already encountered as Lieutenant-governor of the Orange River Colony), Sir David Hunter, James Stewart of Lovedale, Sir David Gill, Thomas Muir, Sir E. J. Buchanan (chief of the Caledonian Society in Cape Town), Sir William Bisset Berry, Mr Justice Graham, and – the only woman – Dr Jane Waterston. As with most such publications, the advertisements are particularly interesting. It is clear that a fair number of companies wished to emphasise their Scottish connections, either through their personnel, the products on offer (such as tartan goods, whisky and tobacco[39]) or their adherence to Scottish origins through naming policies.[40]

One enduring theme was the alleged, and oft-repeated, sympathy between Scots and Afrikaners. This was alluded to in the very first editorial. The next issue carried a two-page article on 'Scots and Dutch affinities', in which it was suggested that both had a 'passion for independence', that they had a similar 'mental and moral make-up', that as societies there was a 'structural resemblance and spiritual relationship', that both were deeply imbued with a sense of an environmental context, that they shared 'the unadorned sanctities of religion' and a feeling for epic, heroic pasts and iconic (my word) heroes, and that they were incurably democratic, with the Church (itself representing the demos) at the centre of their lives.[41] In several places, interestingly, a contrast was drawn with the English and the Anglican Church. As we have seen, this was an enduring theme of Scots 'cultural acclimatisation' in South Africa, clearly designed, in the aftermath of the Anglo-Boer War, to position the Scots (so many of whom lived in Afrikaner communities) in an intermediate and reconciliatory role.[42] What it also did, of course, was serve to harden the racial boundaries. A people who professed such affinities with Afrikaners were unlikely to take a stand on the acts of violence and dispossession that were increasingly the lot of the black population of the country, and which were wrought by whites in general.

A year after its first publication the *South African Scot* moved into a rather more modest format. The last copy in the holdings of the South African Library in Cape Town dates from May 1907. It may be that the library has an incomplete run, but it is also possible that it ceased publication on that date and that the 1908 'unpretentious little magazine' was designed to replace it. In the libraries I have used in South Africa I have not been able to find further copies. Its dates are certainly significant. This is clearly a time, in the post-war reconstruction era, when ethnic solidarity may have been seen as being at a premium. These were also years when more Scots were migrating to South Africa, when ambitions (illusory, as it turned out) were being laid to build up the English-speaking component of the population. If it did 'run out of steam' there could be a number of reasons for its failure. It may have been too ambitious in its format, and consequently too expensive for the potential readership, effectively catering only for an elite. It may be that Scots identity and solidarity worked better on a local level than in a 'national' context. It is also possible that Scots were becoming sufficiently integrated into the white population that the objectives laid out by the *South African Scot* did not particularly appeal. But the existence and growth of societies and clubs would seem to run counter to this, though such organisations clearly offered social, cultural and business opportunities in more urban and regional contexts. In other words, those of Scots descent were interested in various forms of real and tangible utility. The role of the *South African Scot* was altogether more intangible. Historians often warn against writing of Scots – or for that any other ethnicity – along the lines of 'Here's tae us; wha's like us?'[43] While that is transparently true, nonetheless historians have to understand why it is that such a self-regarding appeal has apparently had some potency in the past. The founding, content and apparent failure of the *South African Scot* offers some clues. Scots seem to have been more eager than other ethnicities to maintain a connection with 'home'. There are probably at least three reasons for this. Scots unquestionably had a high opinion of themselves and imagined that they brought special qualities to the colonial situation. Scotland had developed an international romantic lustre celebrated almost everywhere, not least in the musical and literary forms of nineteenth-century continental Europe.[44] Given the marginality of Scotland and the strikingly high proportion of its emigrants, Scots, like many diasporic peoples, regarded themselves as a people apart. This also led them to stress their educational attainments, their spiritual values and their alleged role as high achievers in the British Empire in general and the South African colonies in particular. But it is probable that such ideas were much more potent in maintaining the cohesion of an elite than in influencing Scots further down the social scale.

The South African 'Scottish' regiments

The almost paradoxical origins of the Scottish regiments in the aftermath of the Jacobite revolt of 1745–46, often connected with the efforts of Highland aristocrats (in some cases) to expiate their disloyalty and ingratiate themselves with the Hanoverian dynasty, are well known. These regiments immediately became highly prominent in the imperial wars of the second half of the eighteenth century as well as in the Napoleonic Wars. The Highland soldier became central to the mythic creation of the Highlands as a cultural entity, as well as in the take-over of Scottish Lowland culture by the symbols and forms of the new 'Highlandism'.[45] In 1881 even Lowland regiments were prompted to adopt tartan symbols as a badge of their Scottish origins. In these respects the Highland regiments have been seen as resolving the conflicts of Scottish history.[46] There can also be little doubt that the image and reputation of Scots regiments in the British Empire had an effect upon the national self-image of Scotland, even if recruitment was so often a badge of economic problems and unemployment. Some Scots soldiers remained overseas as settlers, but the returning soldier invariably brought back images of death, injury and despair that cannot have encouraged migration.

Nevertheless, the ideological construction of the Highlands had significant colonial repercussions. At the Cape, as we have seen, Scottish regiments arrived from the earliest days of British rule in 1795, constituting a certain degree of continuity with the mercenary Scotch Brigade of the Dutch.[47] As we saw in Chapter 1, these regiments were significant in the spread of both Presbyterianism and Freemasonry,[48] as well as helping to encourage Scots settlement. 'Highland' regiments (often recruited from the cities of the Lowlands) were involved in the frontier wars of the nineteenth century[49] and in the first Anglo-Boer War in 1880–81. The disaster of the battle of Majuba Hill in 1881 was recycled as 'a tale of Highland Heroism' in a pamphlet published by James Cromb in 1891 and reprinted in a longer version on the eve of the Second Boer War.[50] By this time, as Heather Streets has convincingly demonstrated, the Scots had been elevated to 'martial race' status in countless writings of officers and military commentators dealing with colonial wars.[51] They shared this alleged racial propensity for warfare, rooted in a supposed mountain environment and pastoral lifestyle, with peoples like the Punjabi Sikhs and the Nepalese Gurkhas. They were often bracketed with these Asian 'martial races' and frequently shared campaigns with them on the frontiers of the Indian subcontinent. This sometimes even received artistic expression.⁵² Indeed, they became by far the most notable source of military images to war artists, both those working in military theatres, sending their sketches back for the British illustrated press, and those who worked on the new genre of colonial military painting in Britain.⁵³ Scottish soldiers were exotic, colourful and 'painterly'.

This was a tradition which began to take root in colonial contexts. The Scots had become celebrated for their military exploits; there were Scottish settlers throughout the empire. It seemed obvious that the creation of similar fighting units in the colonies might ensure that some of this martial reputation might rub off on them, particularly if they adopted the symbols of Scottish uniforms and the stirring outdoor music of pipe bands. And in doing so they would not only make a military statement, they would also establish a key role in civil society. On the lighter side, they would form a superb accompaniment to civic and imperial ceremony. They would entertain in bandstands and at sporting and other events. On the darker, their intimidating reputation could be used in the control of civil disturbance. The Scots, after all, had a (now unenviable) renown in this respect too.⁵⁴

As Jonathan Hyslop has put it, sections of South African society now 'became part of a global politics of military Scottishness'.⁵⁵ Town guards and volunteer frontier forces often had a strong Scottish component. For example, the rifle corps in Port Elizabeth was founded in 1856. It guarded Prince Alfred on his visit in 1860 and then took the name of Prince Alfred's Guard. A Scottish company was formed which had its own piper.⁵⁶ A number of the Scots founders of Dundee, Natal, were members of the Buffalo Border Guard.⁵⁷ But the first convincing example of the adoption of Highlandism in southern Africa took place at the Cape in 1885. The volunteer movement had spread to the Cape in the 1850s with the founding of the Duke of Edinburgh's Own Volunteer Rifles (also known as the Cape Town Rifles) in 1855, and the creation of Scottish companies of this corps in 1859 and 1882.⁵⁸ At the time it was decided that this Scottish company, consisting of sixty men, should not wear the kilt, but a Rifle Green jacket with Campbell tartan trews and tartan on the cap. But sufficient pipers were forthcoming to create a band. Interestingly, it was a later dispute over uniform that prompted officers in this company to think about a separate Scottish regiment. The resulting Cape Town Highlanders started from small beginnings. A meeting of these local Scots, no doubt also mindful of the various colonial and imperial problems of the decade, the gathering conflicts of the Partition of Africa, and the final conquest of southern African black kingdoms, decided to found a Scottish unit. Only three officers and sixteen men turned up for its first parade, but their impact upon watching crowds was sufficiently great that the numbers grew rapidly. It received an additional infusion when the Scottish company of the Cape Town Rifles was transferred to it. The Gordon tartan was soon adopted, and by the end of 1887 the ladies of Cape Town had presented the company with bagpipes for the band, an essential component of their image, their recruitment efforts and their role in Cape Town society. Officers aspired to enhanced social status (like their counterparts in Scottish regiments, who often came from the higher echelons of Scottish society). And ambitious schemes were got up to emphasise the Scottishness of the project.[59] A stag was imported to be the regimental mascot and there were even classes in Gaelic offered to the men. How many took them up is not known. By 1906 the men were sporting the full Gordon Highlanders outfit and in that year the regiment became known as the Duke of Connaught and Strathearn's Own Cape Town Highlanders. In all its subsequent histories it has boasted of being the oldest kilted regiment in the southern hemisphere.[60]

It was soon involved in the control of civil disorder (a valuable function of the volunteers, since it released regular troops for other conflicts). In 1886 the Cape Town Highlanders were active in the suppression of a demonstration by Cape Muslims, protesting at the closure of a cemetery which they had traditionally used. But, as Jonathan Hyslop has pointed out, this event represented the manner in which Scots, and descendants of Scots, could so often find themselves on opposite sides. The protest was led by Abdol Burns, the son of a Scottish soldier and a Muslim woman, who was proud of his ancestry.[61] The Cape Town Highlanders developed a prominent public visibility in the years before the Anglo-Boer War, for example in forming the guard of honour at the unveiling of Queen Victoria's statue in 1890. Their band established a considerable reputation (it was to perform at Rhodes's funeral in 1902), as did officers and men in shooting competitions. Although the numbers fluctuated between six companies in 1892 and only four in 1895, it was despatched, with the Cape Mounted Riflemen, to Bechuanaland in 1897. Various detachments were in action in the Anglo-Boer War and it was sent to help in the suppression of the Bambatha Zulu revolt in 1906, though it saw no action. It continued to be used in support of the civil authority and in 1914 became part of the South African Scottish, the fourth South African Infantry Regiment, seeing service in Egypt and France.

This desire to adopt the regalia of military Scottishness spread to Kimberley. In 1890 one William Ross wrote to J. W. Sauer, the colonial secretary in Cape Town, 'on behalf of Scotchmen of Kimberley who intend forming a Highland Volunteer Corps of several hundreds strong'. He went on to seek government approval and the opportunity to participate in the parliamentary grant available for such a body 'the details of which I have verbally placed before you'. If Sauer would but agree, he would receive the gratitude of 'not only Scotchmen but of the whole population of Griqualand West'.[62] The Kimberley Scots were duly founded, also wearing Gordon tartan kilts and with an original strength of 110, but they lasted only until 1893, when they amalgamated with the Kimberley Regiment.[63]

During the Anglo-Boer War a number of further Scottish units were raised.[64] In 1900 the Marquess of Tullibardine,[65] heir to the Duke of Atholl, who was stationed in Newcastle, Natal, heard of a proposal to found a corps to be known as the Scottish Horse. He immediately wrote to Kitchener, under whom he had served in the Sudan, making various suggestions. Kitchener took the hint and appointed Tullibardine as the commanding officer.[66] The first regiment was raised in Johannesburg (a newspaper report called on men who could 'ride and shoot' to join up), and also in Cape Town and Pietermaritzburg, with some recruits from Scotland. But it was accepted from the start that it was impossible to constitute the regiment only of Scots (half were to be Scots or of Scots descent). In 1901 the second regiment was raised from a combination of Australians, Scots and Natalians, with regular officers. No fewer than 3,500 men were recruited. The Scottish Horse took part in various engagements of the war and were laid down only in 1906. They wore the Atholl Murray tartan, with a St Andrew's cross on their badge.[67]

At the end of the war, faced with the prospect of the breaking up of the Scottish Horse (by then there were three regiments), Tullibardine proposed the creation of volunteer units, authorised by the Volunteer Ordinance of 1902, to continue the tradition. These became known as the Transvaal Scottish, partly connected with the Rand Rifles, an *uitlander* corps with many Scots members, whose function was to defend the gold mines against Boer raids. The Johannesburg and other Caledonian Societies had maintained an interest in the Scottish Horse and were now implicated in the formation of the new regiment. The societies 'spared no effort to help attract recruits'. Illustrations of this included recruiting drives which were held in late 1902 and early 1903 at Caledonian Society 'smoking concerts' at the Durban–Roodepoort gold mine, at Germiston and another at Jeppestown. At each of these, officers were present, including Lieutenant-colonel Dalrymple, Lieutenant-colonel Sandilands, Major Grant and Pipe-major Macleod. The pipes were used as an incentive, and a doctor was present to examine recruits as they presented themselves. It was even suggested that each recruit was expected to produce a letter of recommendation from the secretary of a Caledonian Society branch.[68]

The societies and the recruiting officers were perhaps helped by what was described as a 'wave of military enthusiasm over the Rand', by the fact the Volunteers were exempt from poll tax, from jury service, and were able to travel by rail at special rates when in uniform.[69] A number of Scots who had fought in the war and decided to stay in the country signed up, although one disincentive must have been that the drills were invariably held at 6.30 a.m. before work. It was also claimed that 'the lure of the kilt' had an effect. At any rate, by the end of 1903 no fewer than 10 per cent of the eligible male population of the Rand had become Volunteers. In 1904 another company, with its own headquarters, was established in Krugersdorp. In the same year both the Transvaal Scottish and the Scottish Horse paraded for the unveiling of the Scottish war memorial on the Kensington estate in Johannesburg. There were a number of other ceremonial appearances, often associated with visits of members of the royal family, governors-general, and so on. During this period the first serious action took place, during the Bambatha rebellion in Zululand, when the Transvaal Scottish took part in a massacre of Zulus at the Mome Gorge.[70] In 1910, after the death of Edward VII, who had been colonel-in-chief of the regiment, the Duke of Atholl took his place.[71]

The affiliations of the Transvaal Scottish were clear. The regiment was associated with St George's Presbyterian Church, whose minister was its chaplain. It was also virtually the private force of the mine managements. William (later Sir William) Dalrymple, whom we have already encountered as chairman of the New Kleinfontein mine, was instrumental in its founding and was its honorary colonel from 1908 to 1943. Gordon Sandilands, the first colonel, was also involved in mining, as was his successor in 1908, Colonel Boyd, an executive with the Central Mining & Investment Corporation. It is not surprising, then, that in the Rand strikes of 1913–14 the regiment should have been involved in helping to suppress the disturbances and round up the leading labour activists. These included J. T. Bain, from Dundee, David McKerrell, formerly a miner in Kilmarnock, Archie Crawford and Andrew Watson, from Glasgow.[72] This turbulent time on the Rand had something of the flavour of an ethnic civil war, with Scots equally involved at the leading edge of radical resistance and hegemonic control.

But 'ethnicism' (as Hyslop has called it) was in retreat. Throughout these years the Transvaal Scottish struggled to maintain its Scots character, but this was inevitably to be a losing battle. In 1906 Sandilands had argued before a government commission that Scottish national identity was an essential characteristic of the unit. In the years before the First World War a further fillip to recruitment, which was also to undermine the supposed Scottish character of the regiment, came with the Union Defence Act of 1913, under which all young men had to spend a compulsory four years in these citizen forces.[73] Sandilands had already permitted some non-Scots to be recruited into the Transvaal Scottish cycle unit,[74] stimulating complaints from Scottish members. By the time of the First World War, and the sweeping up of the Scottish regiments into recruitment for the new regular forces, it was no longer possible to maintain the alleged ethnic purity of these regiments. When the South Africa Scottish Regiment was established in 1914, 595 of its recruits were South African-born and 337 were Scottish-born. In addition, 301 of the men were born in England, Wales or Ireland, with forty-nine coming from a variety of other countries. John Buchan compiled the history of the South African forces in France and attempted to claim that the Scottish regiments maintained their Caledonian character while providing the statistics to the contrary.[75] It may be that he was suggesting that the Scottish cultural affiliations were more powerful than mere ethnic composition. The demographic shift represented in Buchan's figures was obviously inevitable, particularly as migration was tailing off and would come to a complete halt after the First World War. But by the time of the Second, the Scottish regiments were becoming strongly Afrikaans in their character. In 1939 a new regiment was raised which was known as the Pretoria Highlanders, with a cap badge bearing a shield and with thistles and a protea intertwined. Thus was the 'South Africanisation' of the Scottish regiment expressed in botanical form.[76] Hyslop has charted this 'dilution' and the curious and ambivalent role played by the Scottish regiments in the apartheid era.[77] Yet all the outward symbols of the regiment were maintained – the Gaelic motto 'Alba nam buadh',[78] the thistle, the cross of St Andrew and, of course, the Murray tartan.[79]

H. C. Juta, an advocate at the Supreme Court, who had been a captain in the Transvaal Scottish, ended his history of the regiment by stressing the relationship between the Scots and the Dutch. He claimed that the Murrays of Atholl were of Flemish origin, that their followers had fought for the Prince of Orange at Malplaquet, and (very dubiously) 'that the very tartan worn by the Transvaal Scottish was known in Holland many centuries ago'. The Afrikaans take-over of the regiment was therefore entirely natural. The religious affinity was stressed yet again, and he claimed that men with Dutch names sang Scottish ballads 'with a fervour unsurpassed north of the Tweed', while men with Scots names equally sang 'Sarie Marais', virtually a popular anthem of the Boers.[80] Indeed, teenage boys (often Afrikaners) were trained into this tradition in the independent schools of South Africa. Pretoria Boys' High School, St Andrew's College in Grahamstown and a number of other schools adopted pipe bands and competed in national competitions.[81] This development (which later spread to girls' schools) constituted a weird amalgam of a transplanted English tradition of the 'public' school,[82] Scottish musical forms and the education of elite Afrikaners.

Scotland and South African 'Scottishness'

It should be remembered that all these developments were taking place in an era when Scots in Scotland were apparently rediscovering their histories, their cultural and literary traditions, their Churches and the significance of their environmental contexts. All this was bound up with a new sense of cultural and political nationalism, arising in the 1870s and finding particularly powerful expression in the 1880s and 1890s. The first form of devolution occurred in 1885 with the founding of a Scottish Office, headed by a Secretary of State for Scotland, and with a variety of functions transferred from various Ministries in London. Some nationalist organisations emerged at this time, notably the Scottish Home Rule Association of 1886. Moreover, the Royal Scottish Geographical Society had been founded in 1884 and a number of other intellectual and educational developments confirmed a sense of a supposedly unique Scottish contribution to the global geopolitics of the nineteenth century.[83] These developments were also reflected in the monuments to heroes (for example, the Wallace monument near Stirling);[84] the significant exhibitions in Glasgow and Edinburgh between 1888 and 1911, all of which emphasised Scottish history in an international context; the status of the Scots as a 'martial race' supposedly famed for their exploits in imperial campaigns overseas; the appearance of new museums and other intellectual institutions; and the international popularity of the much abused 'kailyard' school of literature as well as misty mountains, lochs, deer and Highland cattle of the 'ben and glen' school of Scottish art.

To a certain extent, therefore, South Africa was experiencing the backwash of what became a matter of international Scottish political, social and cultural revival. This constituted a potent mix of the 'invention of tradition' and a renewal of Scottish identity that ultimately led to devolution at the end of the twentieth century. Yet this 'Scottish identity' does not lend itself readily to definition. It was possible to maintain a regional identity – as in societies relating to the northeast of Scotland or Edinburgh, as we have seen – or a supposedly integrated Caledonian cultural ethnicity, or again a supranational conception of being Scottish. Those who felt themselves to be Scots, within the communities of multiple affiliation in South Africa, could therefore identify themselves with those who came from a common area of origin, with those who professed outward forms of Scottishness, and with those who constituted an international diaspora in other colonies of settlement or imperial territories. But they must also have identified themselves as white or male and female or bourgeois or working-class, categories which connected them with other white middle-class or working people whose ethnicity, even their language, was different. Or again they might align themselves with other members of their profession or social and religious milieu. A doctor probably felt an affinity with other doctors who were not Scots. Clergymen and others, men and women, who worked in missions clearly felt themselves to be part of a greater religious community of missionary activity. Women created a community of needs and aspirations with other women. A few people at least began to sense some kind of community across ethnic and even racial lines. And most progressively came to feel that they were South African.

But not many of these multiple affiliations were expressed in poetry. The soft-focused cultural reinvocation of Scotland found poetic dimensions which have a special relevance to South Africa. We have already seen how Thomas Pringle created a romantic amalgam out of Scottish forms and Cape contexts. Eighty years on, the *South African Scot* published poetry in almost every edition. In November 1905 it carried a poem by Fiona MacLeod which hymned 'the old race strong and proud'. 'The clans of the north and the west are scattered the wide world round,' while in South Africa Scots were 'forging a new great nation in beauty and hope and might'. Given the poet's name, it is perhaps not surprising that she should equate Scots with 'clans' or with a sense that those clans now spanned the globe. In identifying with settlers in 'white dominions' the growing racial tragedy of South Africa clearly passed her by. Other issues included poems by Archibald Campbell. It may even be the case that the *South African Scot* carried poetry by Charles Murray (1864–1941), who, though living in South Africa, became one of the most celebrated Scots poets of the age.[85] Murray's reputation was at its peak between the time of the creation of the Union and the years after the First World War. As it happens, he was Secretary of Public Works of the Union of South Africa, although his writings were accepted as though he were a poet living in Scotland. Born near Alford, in Aberdeenshire, he wrote in a north-eastern Scots dialect and, significantly, his major collection of poetry was published in 1929 under the title of *Hamewith* (Homeward, with a subsidiary meaning of 'self-interest'). But he used this form to create a powerful blend of Scots and imperial patriotism, particularly when dealing with what he saw as the necessity of volunteering during the First World War.[86] Yet he also stressed the distinctive character of Scottish military, linguistic and poetic traditions. Hugh McDiarmid even included one of Murray's poems in his *Golden Treasury of Scottish Poetry*, a poem about a herd boy who neglected his duties because of his love of music, which he played on a whistle made by himself.[87] This was a poem which gave no indication that Murray was an exile in South Africa, but it helps to reveal the manner in which a Scots identity was equally forged at the colonial periphery.[88]

It was also a time when Scots had become touchy about national nomenclature. A neat example of this turns up even in the Kwazulu Natal archives in Pietermaritzburg. In July 1902 James Findlay, a member of the Scottish Patriotic Association (a society well reflecting this sense of ethnic revivalism) wrote to the Premier of Natal, Sir Albert Hime, complaining that the latter had been reported in the *Glasgow Herald* as using the term 'England' in an imperial sense to mean Britain when responding (clearly undiplomatically) to a toast at Edinburgh University. Findlay drew the Premier's attention to the fact that Lord Balfour of Burleigh had made a strong protest about 'a similar error' to the editor of the London *Spectator*, thus demonstrating that 'Scottish feeling against the misuse of the national names is not confined to any particular section of the community'.[89] The enclosed sheet, an impressively printed 'Personal Appeal to your Sense of Justice and Honour from the Scottish Patriotic Association', protested about the use of 'England' and 'English' when 'Britain' and 'British' were meant. It reminded its readers that 'so keenly is the injustice felt in Scotland of having the terms that stand for Union set aside' that in 1897 a petition signed by 100,000 Scots, including MPs, principals of Scottish universities, provosts and magistrates, as well as many Scots 'of all ranks and classes', as well as 'thousands of Scottish people in the Colonies', had been presented to and accepted by Queen Victoria. It went on to suggest that it was still necessary to take action against officials who had failed to note these concerns. South African Scots were thus asserting their links with Scotland in more ways than one. Yet in a curious way they were using Scottishness to assert their status as white South Africans, appropriately distanced from the Anglicisation project. To a certain extent they were also anaesthetising themselves from the oppression, dispossession and racial conflict that could scarcely be ignored by the time of the Union and the iniquitous Natives Land Act of 1913.

But in both Scotland and South Africa these phenomena clearly had differing resonances in different social and economic settings. It is hard to judge how far the cultural and political developments in Scotland influenced attitudes among the working class. Yet working-class men certainly went to South Africa to fight, and others went to settle. They came from a reasonably well educated community and they cannot have been unaware of stirrings in the character and intensity of Scottish identity. Within South Africa, the cleavage which developed between radical trade union leaders,[90] their followers, mine owners and other Scots cannot be seen purely in class terms. It also constituted the opening of a chasm between white and black labour which few white trade unionists attempted to bridge. In this society Scots organisations constituted a form of cultural *laager*, in which the spatial distinctions of class and status were as clear as those outside.

Nevertheless, while an elite certainly ran the Caledonian Societies, some of the membership came from lower down the social scale. If they did not participate in the bourgeois pleasures of St Andrew's and other 'nichts', they at least benefited from some of the support systems associated with them. The South African Scottish regiments were also raised and run by an elite, but ordinary 'Scots', both born in Scotland and born in South Africa, joined up in large numbers. They surely cannot be seen as the victims of hegemonic processes, as that would deny them any modicum of free will. Some must have been enthused by the outward symbols of Scottishness that societies, magazines and regiments offered them. They also participated with obvious pleasure in the games and sports which the Caledonian Societies encouraged. Yet they were entrammelled in a range of conflicting relationships – against the Afrikaners and sometimes with them; against some of their more radical countrymen; and above all against the Coloured and African populations of their adopted country. They were involved in class and ethnic negotiation and contestation at the same time. In all this they were playing an imperial game which increasingly became a colonial one. It is perhaps only now that these multi-directional trajectories of apparently attractive activities, with their Scottish affiliations and symbolic appeals, can be partially disentangled. For so long they have been hidden by a sort of romantic Caledonian mist which obscured the true nature of the complexities of a cultural revival in African territories with multiple populations of white, coloured and black people.

Notes

1 This, together with 'The nameless stream' and 'The lion hunt', is printed in Jane Meiring, *Thomas Pringle: His Life and Times* (Cape Town 1968).
2 Michael Brander, *The World Directory of Scottish Associations* (Glasgow n.d. but 1990s) offers a listing of many hundreds of such Scottish societies active in the

contemporary period but often with long histories, including almost 400 in the United States, well over 100 in Canada, 200 in Australia and over sixty in New Zealand. He also lists some twenty-one in South Africa. However, Brander was reliant on voluntary returns and it is clear that his listing is very conservative in its figures. From my own knowledge of the MacKenzie and MacPherson clan societies, there are many more internationally than Brander acknowledges.

3   On a visit to the Voortrekker monument in Pretoria in April 2005 a wedding party was seen to arrive for a photo opportunity. The men were all dressed in kilts; the women had tartan sashes across their dresses. They were accompanied by a piper who played on the ramparts of the monument. Yet the party were all speaking Afrikaans. Thus the central historical place of memory of the Afrikaans community was being interpenetrated by Scots forms. It may be that this was one of the many Afrikaans families that enjoyed a Scottish background through the migration of ministers and teachers in the nineteenth century. It is even possible that the groom may have had a Scots name. But it is also conceivable, as inhabitants of Pretoria explained, that they simply found this an intriguing and attractive way of dressing distinctively for a wedding party. As this chapter will demonstrate, South African schools and army regiments could also have contributed to this apparent ethnic 'cross-over'.

4   Douglas Booth, *The Race Game: Sport and Politics in South Africa* (London 1998), pp. 37–8 and *passim*.

5   A copy of this notice was in the papers of the Rev. John Ross of Pirie, CLG MS 8729.

6   *East London Caledonian Society, 1876–1976* (East London 1976). The foreword to this booklet was written by Professor Hugh Chapman, whose great-grandfather was the first chief of the society.

7   Helen Bosworth-Smith, 'The things they did', *The Coelacanth: Journal of the Border Historical Society*, 13: 2 (1975), p. 24. In East London (and presumably elsewhere) other societies included the Sons of England, the Reading Union, the Benevolent Society and the Choral Society, but of these the Caledonian seems to have been the most visible and the most successful.

8   W. D. Maxwell-Mahon, 'A century of Scottish gatherings in South Africa', *Lantern*, 41: 4 (1992), pp. 14–19.

9   Margaret Harradine, *Port Elizabeth: a Social Chronicle to the End of 1945* (Port Elizabeth 1994), p. 77. Harradine includes many potted biographies of early Scots inhabitants of Port Elizabeth. The extent to which they became prominent in settler public life, as JPs, town councillors, mayors and members of the provincial council, is striking.

10 Harradine, *Social Chronicle*, pp. 254, 260.

11 *South African Scot*, April 1907, p. 131. This article about the Durban Caledonian Society featured portraits of Sir David Hunter and also of A. M. Hay dressed in full Highland kit and resting his hand upon what appears to be an antler chair.

12 Charles Wilson, *The First Hundred Years* (Johannesburg 1992).

13 The first Highland gathering took place at St Fillan's in Perthshire, Scotland, in the late eighteenth century. The 'tradition' soon spread to other parts of Scotland and eventually, with the Scots, to the British Empire and beyond. It continues to this day in some very unlikely places, for example Djakarta in Indonesia.

14 Jonathan Hyslop, *The Notorious Syndicalist: J. T. Bain, a Scottish Rebel in Colonial South Africa* (Johannesburg 2004), pp. 96–7.

15 A photograph of this ceremony can be seen in Kruger's House, Church Street, Pretoria.

16 Harry Inglis, *Fifty Years Ago* (Pretoria 1942).

17 For example, the society's solicitors (inevitably Scots) sought incorporation under a new ordinance of 1903. NAP: LD 980 AG163/05.

18 Secretary, Caledonian Society (David Scott), to Milner, 30 January 1904, indicating that Milner had been re-elected to honorary membership. NAP: Gov. 750, vol. 12, PS45/04.

19 The first Burns supper seems to have taken place only five years after the death of the poet in 1796. It was celebrated by some of his friends and associates in Burns's cottage, Alloway, which at that time had become an inn. James Mackay, *Burns* (Edinburgh 1992), p. 688. See also Nancy Marshall, *Chambers Companion to the Burns Supper* (Edinburgh 1992). Burns Clubs were founded soon afterwards and spread throughout the British imperial territories, in both formal and informal empire. Later in the century Burns statues were also erected throughout the world. It is an interesting fact that some educated Afrikaners had a considerable admiration for Burns and his poetry. President Reitz of the Free State, for example, enjoyed Burns's work and wrote a parody of *Tam O'Shanter* called *Klaas Geswind en sy perd*, not at all politically correct, since it is about a speedy 'Hottentot' on his horse. The poet Boerneef, I. W. van der Merwe, wrote a paraphrase of 'To a louse' (private information from Elizabeth van Heyningen). It is interesting that claims have also been made for affinities between Burns and African poets. See, for example, Hilary Semple '"Brother mortals": Robert Burns and Es'kia Mphahlele', *Contrast*, 68 (17: 4, December 1989), pp. 25–41.
20 Caledonian Society to Major General Maxwell, Military Governor, 15 November 1900, invitation to attend the St Andrew's Nicht (*sic*) event on 30 November at the Caledonian Hall. £25 profit from this event was handed over to the Military Governor for the benefit of the Pretoria garrison for some 'Christmas cheer' for the troops. NAP: MAP51 7457/00.
21 For example, A. J. McGibbon, president of the Pietermaritzburg Caledonian Society, was also vice-president of the Caledonian Football Club as well as president of the Bowling Club.
22 NAP: TPD 0 714/1914.
23 Active societies were also founded in Delagoa Bay (Lourenço Marques, now Maputo), Bulawayo and other centres in Central Africa.
24 Joseph Lehmann, *The First Boer War* (London 1972), p. 100.
25 The papers relating to Potchefstroom old fort are to be found in NAP: MPO, 2/1/44 685.
26 *South African Scot*, November 1905, p. 20; December 1905, pp. 26–7, 42, 44; January 1906, p. 66; March 1906, p. 107, contain details of all these societies.
27 Ibid., April 1907, p. 131 and May 1907, pp. 153–5. The *South African Scot* did print one Gaelic poem.
28 Ibid., May 1907, p. 153.
29 Ibid., May 1907, p. 155.
30 Ibid., May 1907, p. 153.
31 Ibid., December 1905, p. 43.
32 Ibid., January 1906, p. 63. This article even appended a list of draft rules for the affiliated society.
33 *SESA* (Cape Town 1973), p. 659. Soon after the post-First World War federation of the societies an appeal was made for the erection of a statue of David Livingstone at the Victoria Falls. A pamphlet was issued calling for £15,000, with a list of trustees including many of the most prominent Scots in South Africa. CLG: South African Pamphlets, vol. 18.
34 Saul Dubow, 'A commonwealth of science: the British Association in South Africa, 1905 and 1929' in Saul Dubow (ed.), *Science and Society in Southern Africa* (Manchester 2000), pp. 66–99.
35 A. N. Wilson, *Mackenzie Saga: the Story of the Mackenzie Family of Fochabers, Scotland, and of their Contribution to the Development of Southern Africa* (Johannesburg 1977), particularly pp. 61 and 93–5. George Mackenzie eventually built a house in the Parktown district which he called 'Strathspey'.
36 It is unclear where Wilson gets his figure of 1,000 members from. Certainly the meetings of the society would indicate a considerably smaller membership. The figure of 1,000 may be a vague memory of one of his Mackenzie informants. But there is no reason to doubt the significance of the contacts they made there. On the other hand, the fact that 420 members and guests sat down to the St Andrew's Night

banquet in 1905 (see above and note 23) could imply a much wider membership.
37 *South African Scot*, 1: 1, November 1905, p. 2.
38 Ibid., November 1905.
39 'Smith's Glasgow mixture' seems to have been a favourite.
40 In addition to the examples in the *South African Scot*, the database of the South African archives throws up such examples as the Scottish Wine & Spirit Company, the Scottish Tube Company of South Africa, the African Scottish Electric Cable & Construction Company, the Scottish & African Finance Corporation and many others.
41 *South African Scot*, December 1905, pp. 26–7.
42 John Buchan, when a member of the Milner 'kindergarten', reflected on the affinity he felt for the Afrikaner farmer (with whom, as he said, Milner had no sympathy whatsoever). 'He had many of the traits of my Lowland Scots ... When I spent the night at a farm and at family worship listened to Dutch psalms sung to familiar Scottish psalm-tunes, I might have fancied myself in Tweedsmuir ... I was a Scot, a Presbyterian, and a countryman, and therefore was half-way to being a kinsman.' Buchan, *Memory Hold-the-door* (London 1940), pp. 114–15. And p. 99 for the Milner reference. Buchan also (p. 120) described the intense environmental exhilaration he felt in South Africa, which reminded him of his childhood in Scotland.
43 Most recently Ewen Cameron in *The Times Higher*, 1 April 2005, p. 28.
44 See, for example, Robert Fiske, *Scotland in Music* (Cambridge 1983), which charts the considerable influence of Scottish popular musical forms, of Burns and, above all, Scott on European music.
45 Charles Withers, 'The historical creation of the Scottish Highlands' in Ian Donnachie and Christopher Whatley, *The Manufacture of Scottish History* (Edinburgh 1992), pp. 142–56, particularly pp. 149–50.
46 Stuart Allan and Allan Carswell, *The Thin Red Line: War, Empire and Visions of Scotland* (Edinburgh 2004), p. 32.
47 There are countless regimental histories, but for a popular account of the actions of the 98th (later the 91st) Highland Regiment at the Cape see William McElwee, *Argyll and Sutherland Highlanders* (London 1972).
48 For example, the Highland Light Infantry almost certainly had a travelling Masonic lodge which operated in Cape Town in early 1806. K. J. Wilson, 'To Buenos Aires via Melkbosstrand, Blouberg and Cape Town with the Highland Light Infantry in 1806', *Quarterly Bulletin of the South African Library*, 40: 4 (1986), p. 154.
49 J. B. Scott, 'Scottish regiments in the Eighth Frontier War', *Looking Back*, 17 (1977), p. 18. This deals with the 74th (Highland Light Infantry) and 91st (Argyll) regiments in actions in 1851. The 74th wore the Lamont tartan.
50 Allan and Carswell, *Thin Red Line*, pp. 37–8.
51 Heather Streets, *Martial Races: The Military, Race and Masculinity in British Imperial Culture, 1857–1914* (Manchester 2004).
52 For example in W. Hall's 'After the battle of Dargai: Gordon Highlanders carrying down killed and wounded Gurkhas from the scene of action', National Army Museum, London.
53 John Springhall, '"Up Guards and at them!" British imperialism and popular art, 1880–1914' in John M. MacKenzie (ed.), *Imperialism and Popular Culture* (Manchester 1986), pp. 49–72; J. W. M. Hichberger, *Images of the Army: the Military in British Art, 1815–1914* (Manchester 1988); Allan and Carswell, *Thin Red Line*.
54 Within the British Isles, Scottish fencible regiments had been used to help suppress the Irish rebellion of 1798.
55 Jonathan Hyslop, 'Cape Town Highlanders, Transvaal Scottish: military "Scottishness" and social power in nineteenth and twentieth-century South Africa', *South African Historical Journal*, 47 (November 2002), pp. 96–114.
56 Harradine, *Social Chronicle*, lists a number of Scots members of Prince Alfred's Guard.
57 Sheila Henderson, 'Colonial Coalopolis: the establishment and growth of Dundee', *Natalia*, 12 (1982), pp. 16 ff.

58 Major G. Tylden, *The Armed Forces of South Africa* (Johannesburg 1954, reprinted 1982), p. 75; C. Graham Botha, *The Cape Royal Rifles and other Volunteer Units, 1855–1881* (Cape Town 2001), p. 70.
59 The Cape Town Irish were also founded in 1881 but lasted only until 1891, when they were absorbed into the Volunteer Rifles. Nonetheless, South African Irish regiments were raised in both 1914 and 1939. Tylden, *Armed Forces*, pp. 65, 168.
60 Neil Orpen, *The Cape Town Highlanders* (Cape Town 1986). Also W. S. Douglas, *Regimental History of the Cape Town Highlanders* (Cairo 1944).
61 Hyslop, 'Cape Town Highlanders', p. 114. On Abdol Burns see also Nigel Worden, Elizabeth van Heyningen and Vivian Bickford-Smith, *Cape Town: the Making of a City* (Cape Town 1999), p. 243.
62 Ross to Sauer, 23 August 1890, AWC: CO 4272/57.
63 Tylden, *Armed Forces*, p. 104.
64 In 1900 Lieutenant-colonel R. G. Scott raised Scott's Railway Guards, with a strong Scottish element in its 500 strength, to guard the railway between the Orange River bridge and Kimberley.
65 John George Murray, Marquess of Tullibardine, later eighth Duke of Atholl (1871–1942). Tullibardine came from a military family which remains the only one in Britain permitted to keep a private army. Educated at Eton, he served in the Black Watch and the Royal Horse Guards. He was seconded to the Egyptian army with the rank of Bimbashi in 1898 and served in the Sudan campaign. In the Boer War he was a captain in the Royal Dragoons and took part in the relief of Ladysmith, the battles of Colenso, Spion Kop, Vaal Krantz, Tugela Heights and Pieter's Hill. Founding the Scottish Horse offered him the chance of rapid promotion. He returned to Scotland in 1903 and in the First World War commanded the Scottish Horse Brigade.
66 Peter K. A. Digby, *Transvaal Scottish, 1902–2002* (Johannesburg 2002), p. 8.
67 Tylden, *Armed Forces*, pp. 156–7.
68 J. C. Juta, *The History of the Transvaal Scottish* (Johannesburg 1933), p. 6.
69 Ibid. See the introduction by the Duke of Atholl and p. 4.
70 So fashionable did the Scottish military format become in Edwardian times that various other units adopted forms of Highlandism. The First City Volunteers had been founded in Grahamstown in 1875, without any Scottish accoutrements. In the years after the Anglo-Boer War, however, they adopted Graham of Montrose tartan, forming a Highland company and establishing a pipe band. This was supposedly because Grahamstown had been founded by Colonel John Graham of Fintry and of the 93rd Regiment, which wore Montrose tartan. A photograph of the pipe band outside the Grahamstown drill hall can be seen in the collection of the Albany Museum. Other units in South Africa also considered pipe bands and other supposedly Highland symbols as being crucial to their image. Hyslop, 'Cape Town Highlanders', p. 104.
71 Interestingly, the present Duke of Atholl and his heir the Marquess of Tullibardine are South Africans and live in the Limpopo Province.
72 Hyslop, 'Cape Town Highlanders', p. 108.
73 Juta, *Transvaal Scottish*, p. 17.
74 The original Scottish Horse had included fifty special scouts and fifty picked cyclists. This tradition was continued into the Transvaal Scottish. Digby, *Transvaal Scottish*, pp. 8–9.
75 John Buchan, *The History of the South African Forces in France* (London 1920), pp. 16–17. Hyslop, 'Cape Town Highlanders', pp. 105–6.
76 Tylden, *Armed Forces*, p. 141.
77 Hyslop, 'Cape Town Highlanders', pp. 105–14.
78 This means 'Scotland in my [or of the] victories [or triumphs]'. More colloquially it might be rendered simply as 'Victorious Scotland'. The continuing use of such a motto into the twenty-first century provides an interesting insight into the entwining of Afrikaans and Scots identity – either that or forgetfulness about Gaelic meanings!

79 Tylden, *Armed Forces*, pp. 194–5.
80 Juta, *Transvaal Scottish*, epilogue.
81 Maxwell-Mahon, 'A century of Scottish gatherings', pp. 26–9.
82 Peter Randall, *Little England on the Veld: the English Private School System in South Africa* (Johannesburg 1982).
83 John M. MacKenzie, 'The provincial geographical societies in Britain, 1884–1914' in Morag Bell, Robin Butlin and Michael Heffernan (eds), *Geography and Imperialism* (Manchester 1995), pp. 93–124.
84 A later South African example of this devotion to the statuary of heroes was the unveiling of a statue to David Livingstone at the Victoria Falls in 1934.
85 *South African Scot*, December 1905, p. 26, printed a poem which carried some of Murray's hallmarks.
86 Hyslop, 'Cape Town Highlanders', pp. 106–7.
87 Hugh MacDiarmid (ed.), *Golden Treasury of Scottish Poetry* (London 1940, reprinted 1948), pp. 265–8. The poem was reprinted in John MacQueen and Tom Scott (eds), *The Oxford Book of Scottish Verse* (Oxford 1989), pp. 462–4.
88 As I argued in my inaugural lecture at Lancaster University, 13 May 1992, 'Scotland and the Empire'.
89 KZNA: PM 32 1902/2484. James Findlay seems to have had some effect, at least in the short term, since his letter was circulated among some Natal officials. In his minute to the letter the secretary to the Prime Minister indicated that 'In reply to this, I tendered an apology for injuring the susceptibilities of the Scot'!
90 Hyslop, *Notorious Syndicalist*.

CHAPTER NINE

Conclusion

One of the enduring themes of South African history in the British imperial period is Anglicisation. Lord Charles Somerset set out to Anglicise the administrative, legal and educational systems. The British sought to Anglicise the frontier, with military force and by settlement. They took over Natal from the Boer Trekkers. They made repeated and unsuccessful attempts to Anglicise the interior between the 1840s and 1870s, always foundering on the resistance of Boers and the environment, as well as upon their own hesitation or incompetence. Helped by diamonds, they extended and partially Anglicised the north-western Cape frontier, though gold had the effect of internationalising the Boer interior. The climactic effort at Anglicisation came with the Anglo-Boer War of 1899–1902 and its aftermath, when Milner indulged in a final ambitious push towards what we might call imperialisation. But ambitions were seldom realised and Anglicisation, at the very least, remained only partial. There were several reasons for this. Afrikaners effectively resisted. Africans may have welcomed some aspects of Englishness, but their cultural integrity ensured that they tended to assimilate and modify rather than adapt. And Anglicisation was dissipated by the presence of other metropolitan ethnicities, notably the Scots.

Anglicisation has too often been treated as though it were some kind of undifferentiated phenomenon.[1] The term has been used indiscriminately, even when dealing with the developments which were most strongly influenced by the Scots.[2] Vivian Bickford-Smith has rightly argued that we need to understand how the British world was constructed and maintained, in order to recognise the ways in which hegemony (here quoting Raymond Williams) is a 'lived system of meanings and values'. But then he indulges in a rather transparent let-out. He refers to 'English values and customs, derived from Englishness itself, which was the dominant influence within

Britishness'. Next he cites the English language, English education and other aspects of the political, economic, social and cultural transformations that are part of Anglicisation. When he turns to Kirsten McKenzie's 'rational public sphere' in which middle-class identities are formed, he seems to assume that the founding of the *South African Commercial Advertiser*, the South African Museum and the South African Library were all part of a process of Anglicisation that expressed this dominant Englishness.[3] Yet all three of these were founded by Scots, often against the opposition of the English political elite, and largely in league with the Dutch educated middle class. Suddenly the word Anglicisation seems just a little threadbare. In other words, there are significant non-English elements in it that we really should be at more pains to understand. In doing this we would be transferring the calls of J. G. A. Pocock, Laurence Brockliss, David Eastwood and Hugh Kearney for a four-nation approach to British history to South Africa, and elsewhere in the empire.[4] The 'imperial metropole' is too often seen as some kind of undifferentiated whole, the powerful monolithic force which operates upon highly complex colonial contexts. It was nothing of the sort: the metropole needs to be deconstructed as much as the periphery.

Thus the imperial power interacts with a complex of forces within southern Africa – different white and black groups; various political systems, colonial, republican and African; a range of economies, if progressively converging through the operations of large-scale capitalism with its technological, infrastructural, financial, commercial and labour needs; and a variety of urban, rural and environmental contexts. But the imperial metropole is seen as a single entity, reflected in the politics, administration and pressure groups of London. But it too represented a complex of peoples with different histories, group identities, religions (in the sense of Christian denominations), educational systems and ethnic loyalties. It is only when we 'complicate' the metropole that we can begin to understand the complex of forces that were brought to bear upon southern Africa and its peoples. We need, in short, to remember that the systems and values of empire, its ideologies and its cultural and religious manifestations were made up of a combination of elements of four metropolitan ethnicities, other settlers such as Afrikaners, as well as indigenous peoples. Sometimes these elements operated in conjunction to form compounds, at other times there was a distinctive catalyst which produced new combinations, and then again they occasionally produced combustible reactions, as in the Anglo-Scots controversies of the 1820s at the Cape, the missionary responses to the frontier, the alliances that seemed to form between Scots and Dutch at various periods, and the Anglo-Boer

CONCLUSION

War when Irish and Scots fought on both sides. Such multiple identities are not fixed but are constantly fluid: some Scots after all actually became Afrikaners.

We should also note that the status of ethnic minority, as in the case of the Scots at the Cape, does not necessarily lead to marginalisation. White ethnicity in the British Empire was invariably made up of a consciousness of what it meant to be different as well as some sense of the ways in which communities contributed to the dominant yet elusive forms of Anglicisation. Thus Anglicisation was made up of endless and complex negotiations, repeated stand-offs and *rapprochements* in which, as time passed, memory and reconnections with a home culture played a significant role. The cultural amalgam that in reality constituted the British world came to be reconstituted and overlaid with the distinctive memories and celebrations of heroic and exemplary figures who had helped to form their 'peripheral' as well as their metropolitan identities. Through multilateral processes of mediation the ethnicities of the dominant fraction of the population of the British Empire mutually constituted, or at least modified, each other while also invariably seeking to emphasise difference.

Despite the relatively small number of Scots in South Africa, they were there in larger numbers than their proportion within the United Kingdom warranted. And their experience and their alleged capacities, as well as their 'pushiness', ensured that they always 'punched above their weight'. Whether justified or not, they had a high reputation as people who could cope with the environment, as agriculturalists, as artisans in the construction industry and as engineers. They were highly influential in the Church, in education, in medical, scientific and environmental professions, as well as in the military, in business and in trade union activity. There may be a number of explanations for this: while there were a fair number of agricultural and working-class migrants, it was always apparent that it was mainly a destination for the middle classes. Many of those who did decide to take the bold decision to go there seem to have come from a relatively enterprising segment of Scottish society. Then there were the perceived affinities between Scots and Afrikaners which so influenced religious and educational recruitment. By the end of the nineteenth century tremendous opportunities had opened up in mining, engineering, railway and urban construction, all occupations in which Scots were supposed to excel. This occurred at all levels, as is witnessed by the major efforts to recruit construction workers, and the resulting voluble complaints of non-Scots.

But, as we have seen, Scots were far from being monolithic in their affinities. They seem to have been particularly active in the liberal/humanitarian faction at the Cape in the early nineteenth century. But they were also voluble as settlers in the colony and on the Eastern Cape, where white–black conflicts in the frontier wars contributed to the rapid decline of liberalism. As that frontier closed, the missionaries themselves rapidly became less liberal in their ideas. The original ideals, however modified, of a multi-racial mission society, reflected in educational, industrial and medical policies, had been wiped out by the 1890s, with racial segregation becoming the order of the day. While the missionaries had been highly influential in the creation of a new black bourgeoisie, some of whom would be leaders of early nationalist movements, they also created the tensions that arose from relatively autocratic and exclusivist administrative policies. Such tensions may, however, have added to the powerful black sense of injustice, economic, social and political, which was to be suppressed for much of the twentieth century but was to secure a victory in the great transformation of the 1990s. In the white sector, Scots also exported their class divisions, their mixture of privilege and deprivation which was to engender the deep cleavage between Benjamin Moodie's feudal vision and the freedoms sought by his settlers, and between Scots-born businessmen and white trade union leadership.

It may be that this powerful class distinction also operated in the significant area of ethnic identity. Dr Johnson was not quite right when he said that, in moving about, 'Scots change nothing but their place of abode'. Inevitably, Scots – like all other people – are modified by migration. If Johnson was hostile, a Scots sentimental saying that 'you can take the Scot out of Scotland, but not Scotland out of the Scot' is intended to have a positive ring. And Scots did seem to cling to the signs and symbols, the literature and landscape, the culture and alleged conviviality of their Caledonian origins.[5] However much these may have been invented traditions, they seem to have been no less potent as markers of difference and of a sense of ethnic unity. The middle class may well have been particularly keen to socialise in Caledonian and St Andrew's Societies, Masonic lodges and regional associations: the 'Here's tae us; wha's like us?' tendency. But other social groups were unquestionably sucked into sport, the Presbyterian Church and the Scots volunteers and regiments, replete with kilts and pipes. Working-class figures like John McPherson, fiddler, clearly kept Scottish musical traditions alive in early Natal. These markers of identity, strangely based on a sense of misplaced superiority, were prominent throughout the nineteenth century, but they seem to have reached a particular climax in the late nineteenth and early twentieth centuries. This was partly for international reasons: it was, after all, the era of the creation of carefully organised and regulated

CONCLUSION

societies and organisations; it was also a time of renewed cultural revival in Scotland and therefore throughout the British Empire. The more local explanations can be based on the manner in which Scots continued to distance themselves from English or Irish, partly in order to stress their alleged sympathies with Afrikaners and even, at least in the missionary context, with Africans.

But it may also have originated in a growing sense of anxiety. The notion that southern Africa, in terms of its indigenous population, was just like any other colony of white settlement, was already unsustainable by the end of the nineteenth century. Whereas in Canada, Australia and New Zealand (and of course in the United States) white migration had placed 'native peoples' in a more or less minority position, that was far from being the case in South Africa. Indeed, as the territories were rounded off in the additional acquisitions of the final partitioning of the subcontinent in the last years of the century, the statistical imperative moved further against the whites. Such apprehensions were partly masked by the intermittently booming economy, by the major conflicts within white society and the colonial-republican-imperial tensions that disastrously worked themselves out in the Jameson Raid and the Anglo-Boer War. Throughout all this, Scots kept up their propaganda about their capacity to conciliate the Afrikaners and perhaps in the process forgot their older protestations of affinities with, and obligation to the protection of, the various black peoples of the region, however patronising those may have been.

To what extent was the experience of the migratory Scot to South Africa different from those who went to North America or Australasia? Such a question may demand another book to answer it, but there were both similarities and differences. It would be too glib to see southern Africa as a destination for the slightly better-off or for professionals and people with technical expertise related to mining and the provision of infrastructure. Such people also went to the United States, Canada, Australia and New Zealand. Many of those who went to the Cape or Natal were poor: some dropped off on the way to Australasia; some chose southern Africa because they knew it had a more appealing climate than Canada; some also found the prospect of employing African servants at cheap wages appealing. But it is also true that by late Victorian and Edwardian times the mining revolution, war and reconstruction, urbanisation, the expansion of education and the building of harbours and railway lines set up an insatiable demand for middle-class migrants. Moreover, because of the existence of black labour and the development of a colour bar in the workplace, working-class migrants almost automatically joined a white 'aristocracy of labour' in ways that did not necessarily happen elsewhere. There was thus a greater opportunity for rising up the social scale in South Africa. We are inevitably left with a great irony. Scots so often left situations of economic and social deprivation (and this could be true, in different ways, of the gentry as well as the ordinary folk) in order to 'improve themselves'. In the context of South Africa their efforts to do so invariably led to the spreading of that very economic and social deprivation to African peoples, whether on the land or in the cities.

In deconstructing forms of migration and their effects, we can perhaps divide the 'long nineteenth century' in the history of Scots in South Africa into four major (and overlapping) periods. The first is the time of military and commercial activity, when Scots were closely involved in the conquest and occupation of the Cape, including the violence of the frontier. The second is the era of so-called 'Anglicisation', a very important one in the history of Scots at the Cape. The third is the counterpoint to that, the period of the closing of the frontier in the final wars, the development of further migration, the expansion of economic activity, and the climax of missionary and educational endeavour. The fourth was the time of unbridled capitalist activity, in which Scots were enthusiastically engaged as much as, or more than, others. In this period, Scots class rivalries and the conflict between Tory establishment and radical trade unionism had its manifestations in South Africa. It was also a period when on the one hand Scotland was to be used as an analogy for white race conciliation in the post-war period after 1902 while on the other Africans were forced into increasingly restricted spatial, economic and social conditions.

It has also become common to see white colonial society as a fragmentary phenomenon which replicates the metropolitan in ways that are regarded as inferior. Thus the colonial society exists in an uneasy liminal space in which it lacks the cultural autonomy and self-confidence of the metropolis while not achieving the assertiveness of modern nationalist identity. An examination of the activities of Scots in South Africa seems to refute this, at least in certain key ways. In the 'public sphere' of the Cape, Scots were able to achieve a prominence and make political and cultural contributions that would have been quite impossible for them at home. In the missionary setting, too, individuals who might have served (as husbands and wives) in some obscure Scottish parish aspired to heroic endeavour, as constructed by themselves and by some of their supporters and followers, in the missionary context. A few became genuine celebrities; others hung on the coat tails of their celebrity. They were featured in magazines, lectures, sermons and books. Other Scots achieved land holdings, businesses, wealth that would have been unheard of in

CONCLUSION

Britain. As a result, they often had high opinions of themselves and, as travel became easier, they were able to lord it at home in ways that entirely belied their often humble origins. As they formed identities that were a combination of the colonial and the Scottish, their self-perceptions seem often to have been almost superior in tone. The minority that achieved major successes, professionally, financially, commercially, were certainly assertive enough to see themselves as having the capacity to influence home society.

This was also the case in scientific and environmental endeavours, which so many historians leave out of account. Far from seeing themselves as some kind of inferior colonial group, articulate Scots in South Africa indulged in major 'entryism' into legislative assemblies as well as into educational, scientific, religious and cultural institutions. They also portrayed themselves as possessors of an identity which had apparently insignificant geographical origins but which had developed major international overtones. Scots, their culture and their institutions, were everywhere. Scotland had become, in this perception, some kind of major force in the world. Though Arthur Herman often indulges in hyperbole, perhaps he was not too far off the mark when he remarked that 'being Scottish turns out to be more than just a nationality or place of origin or clan or even culture. It is also a state of mind, a way of viewing the world and our place in it.'[6] He goes on to assert that 'it is a self-consciously modern view'. The irony here, of course, is that though the Scots certainly saw themselves as apostles of modernism, they expressed their national affiliation in invented traditions which purported to be antique. As they touted social and economic modernism they blunted the message with cultural atavism.

Thus, as the Scots exported their social tensions, they were also exporting their cultural and environmental dilemmas. Many of the Scots, including ministers and professionals as well as working-class people, came from urban settings, yet it was so often a romantic rural image which was projected. During his relatively brief period in post-bellum South Africa, John Buchan played heavily on this paradox. As Peter Henshaw has demonstrated, Buchan saw Scots as having a major role to play in South Africa, both as exemplars and as agents.[7] His construction of the South African landscape was inseparably bound up with his romantic memories of Scotland. His admiration for Afrikaner rural society lay in the connections he saw between it and Scots agriculturalists of the Lowlands and Borders. Impractically, he saw Scots as somehow timelessly rural rather than urban and industrial. Yet, for him, the Scots had reconciled their Scottish cultural nationalism with membership of the United Kingdom, and beyond that with a larger imperial entity. This could act as a model for white society in southern Africa. If Scots could be Scottish, British and imperial at once, then Boers could be Afrikaners, South Africans and even citizens of the empire. And the religious and cultural affinities of the Scots made them the ideal bridgehead between English- and Afrikaans-speakers. It was the kind of vision that seems to have reached the journal, *The South African Scot.*

What Buchan failed to see (apart from the fact that Scots were primarily an industrial people) was that Scots in Scotland were also being modified by their role in South Africa. Scottish Presbyterianism became something new and different through its experience of missions, missionary education and medicine, and through the heroisation of figures such as David Livingstone, John Philip, James Stewart and Jane Waterston. The position of women in some areas of Scottish society was transformed by opportunities afforded by the Church and the heroic images created by the roles of women at the mission stations. It was not only African women who found their destinies influenced by missionary endeavour. Thus Scots were participating in interactive processes with blacks as well as whites. Moreover, the Scots' experience in South Africa had its effects upon the fabric of Scotland. It was not just Indian nabobs who reinvested fortunes: South African money also came back. Tulliallan Castle in Fife would be one example among many. The Scottish built environment reflects the association with the subcontinent in other ways, not least in Boer War memorials to be found in many towns, kirk yards and other places. A grand tower dominating Glen Prosen in Angus commemorates the death of the Earl of Airlie in that war, an event still invoked by the present Earl.[8] The small town hall in Inverness contains at least two plaques relating to South Africa.[9] Some professionals returned to apply their experience within Scotland – as the distinguished historian W. M. Macmillan did when he taught at St Andrews University after the Second World War.

'Black Scotsmen' seems on the face of it like a piece of self-flattery, a wished-for but ultimately chimerical condition. In so far as it was used by the black products of mission stations, it was symbolic of forms of religious and educational clientage. But perhaps it should not be so hastily rejected. It need not suggest a denial of black consciousness and pride in history and culture. Tiyo Soga, with his Scottish education, his marriage and adherence to a Scottish Church, still stressed forms of negritude and sought to record and highlight his own traditions. Yet his children, offspring of a Scots mother and educated in Scotland, recognised a hybrid condition that was more than genetic. They were perhaps a relatively unusual case (although a fair number of Coloured people have black, Khoi and Scots ancestors), but the many products of Scottish-influenced schools, missions and colleges

CONCLUSION

carried some cultural traces. And, perhaps even more potently, they were also influenced by radical journalism and trade union activity, even if they sometimes operated within supposedly white contexts and were not always directed at them. The history of both blacks and whites in South Africa can be strongly illuminated by the exposure of the Scottish social and cultural strand. The rainbow spectrum is more complex and colourful than has hitherto been recognised.

Notes

1 James Sturgis, 'Anglicisation at the Cape of Good Hope in the early nineteenth century', *Journal of Imperial and Commonwealth History*, 11 (1982), pp. 5–32.
2 Vivian Bickford-Smith, 'Revisiting Anglicisation in the nineteenth-century Cape Colony', *Journal of Imperial and Commonwealth History* (special issue, *The British World: Diaspora, Culture and Identity*, ed. Carl Bridge and Kent Fedorowich), 31: 2 (2003), pp. 82–95.
3 Kirsten McKenzie, 'The *South African Commercial Advertiser* and Middle-class Identity in early Nineteenth-century Cape Town', M.A. thesis, University of Cape Town (1993), and 'Gender and Honour in Middle-class Cape Town: the Making of Colonial Identity, 1828–1850', D.Phil. thesis, University of Cape Town, 1997.
4 J. G. A. Pocock, 'British history: a plea for a new subject', *Journal of Modern History*, 47 (1975), pp. 601–21; Laurence Brockliss and David Eastwood (eds), *A Union of Multiple Identities: the British Isles, c. 1750–1850* (Manchester 1997); Hugh Kearney, *The British Isles: a History of Four Nations* (Cambridge 1989), and Kearney, 'Four nations in one?' in Bernard Crick (ed.), *National Identities: the Constitution of the United Kingdom* (Oxford 1991).
5 Zine Magubane's construction of the Scots in her *Bringing the Empire Home: Race, Class, and Gender in Britain and Colonial South Africa* (Chicago 2004) largely fails to cohere with my analysis. She views the Scots as victims of English imperialism (accepting Michael Hechter's disputed *Internal Colonialism* as gospel) and ingeniously connects eighteenth-century descriptions of Scots Highlanders and Islanders with parallel constructions of Khoi and other black people in South Africa. Thus images of British Others were inseparably bound up with those of colonial Others. While there is something to this (and she makes interesting connections with the Scots humanitarians), it says nothing about the vast majority of non-Highland Scots and their willingness to accept aspects of Highland culture. Moreover, in her analysis, commercial and industrial capitalism are conflated in disabling ways.
6 Arthur Herman, *The Scottish Enlightenment: the Scots' Invention of the Modern World* (London 2002), p. vii. He goes on to paraphrase Andrew Carnegie, that without Scotland the world would be a very poor show.
7 Peter Henshaw, 'John Buchan from the "Borders" to the "Berg": nature, empire and white South African identity, 1901–1910', *African Studies*, 62: 1 (2003), pp. 3–32.
8 He gave a speech about it at a ceremony commemorating the sixtieth anniversary of VE Day in Alyth, Perthshire, in July 2005.
9 One relates to Robert Carruthers of the *Inverness Courier*, who went to Natal. The other refers to an extraordinary incident when a Scot removed the flag of the South African Republic from the office of the Magistrate of Pretoria at the time of the occupation of the city in June 1900. The flag was brought back to the Highlands as a souvenir and was given to Inverness Town Council. It was returned to the Transvaal Province (it is not clear whether it was in the Union or Republic period) and a grand plaque in gratitude was duly installed at the head of the stairs in Inverness town hall!

INDEX

Note: 'n.' after a page reference indicates the number of a note on that page

Abdurahman, Dr Abdullah 223
Abercrombie, Dr James 43, 44, 175, 193, 198n.26, 218
Adamson, Rev. James 39, 78, 85, 87–8, 176–8, 193
Afrikaner (Boer) 17, 19, 20, 34–5, 45, 55, 56, 62n.83, 80, 81, 83, 95–9 *passim*, 125n.7, 125n.8, 125n.14, 129n.62, 135–6, 137, 150, 152, 153, 158–63 *passim*, 173, 180, 184, 188, 190, 191, 192, 200n.70, 207–8, 211, 213, 215, 216, 227, 229, 232, 241–2, 245, 250, 255, 257–8, 261, 263n.19, 264n.42, 267–74 *passim*
America vii, 2, 5, 14–21 *passim*, 25n.34, 38, 41, 51, 66, 85, 92n.57, 94, 112, 138, 139, 147, 161, 166n.57, 179, 187, 227, 229, 232, 233, 239n.99, 240, 261n.2, 271
American Independence, War of 31, 34, 35, 57n.3, 82
Anderson, Rev. William 103, 127n.36
'Anglicisation' vii, 52, 64–5, 162, 173, 184, 189, 192, 193, 241, 260, 267–9, 272
Anglo-Boer War (1880–1) 172, 241, 242, 245, 252
Anglo-Boer War (1899–1902) 17, 19, 22, 112, 115, 153, 155, 160, 162, 173, 182, 189–92, 199n.58, 214, 215–16, 221–2, 225, 226, 229, 232, 241–55 *passim*, 265n.70, 267, 268, 271, 274
Anglo-Zulu War 121, 153, 227, 228
Arbuckle, Sir William 179, 224
Arbuthnot, James and Jane 139–40, 144, 149, 164n.21, 197n.19
Australia 2, 3, 7, 8, 18–21 *passim*, 24n.23, 31, 35, 38, 39, 41, 66, 82, 85, 137, 138, 144, 146, 147, 151, 152, 156, 161, 162, 166n.57, 175,
190, 192, 201n.90, 207, 213, 214, 224, 230, 233, 236n.53, 236n.56, 239n.99, 240, 255, 261n.2, 271

Bain, Andrew Geddes 208–9, 211
Bain, James Thompson 228–33, 256
Baird, General Sir David 4, 36, 38
Banks, Sir Joseph 4, 25n.36, 32, 33
Barnard, Lady Anne 35, 38, 58n.29, 58n.31–2, 59n.42
Barry, Dr James 44, 72, 91n.32, 218
Bathurst, Lord 41, 42, 51, 65, 71, 73–4, 91n.37, 175
Beattie, Sir Jock Carruthers 194
Bell, Charles 86, 93n.75, 235n.34, 236n.42
Bell, Charles Davidson 46, 209–12
Bell, Colonel John 86, 105, 209–10
Bennie, Rev. John 104, 105, 115, 128n.45, 128n.50, 130n.65
Berry, Dr Sir William Bisset 218–19, 250
Bloemfontein 131n.82, 161, 171, 172, 179, 187–8, 192, 193, 199n.47, 230, 243, 246
Blythswood (Mfengu) mission 112, 114–15, 123, 132n.93, 132n.104
Boers *see* Afrikaners
Borders, Scottish 6, 13, 15, 42, 54, 56, 67, 85, 236n.53, 273
botanic gardens 31–3, 67, 88, 110, 207, 224
Botha, Louis 195, 231
Brand, President 187
Brebner, John 183, 187–8
British South Africa Company 225, 227
Brown, John Croumbie 193, 206–8
Brown, Archibald 184, 197n.8
Brownlee, Rev. John 104, 105, 106, 107, 119, 128n.47, 129n.57, 129n.64
Bruce, Sir David 214

[276]

INDEX

Bruce, Rev. John 180
Brunton, Walter 145, 165n.28
Buchan, John 163, 257, 264n.42, 273–4
Buchanan, David Dale 75, 83, 146, 183
Buchanan family 146, 183–4
Buchanan, Sir E. John 194, 250
Burns, Robert 13, 16, 18, 118, 128n.48, 167n.79, 243, 244, 245, 249, 263n.19, 264n.44
Bushmen *see* Khoisan
Byrne, Joseph Charles 138–40, 143, 150–1, 164n.16–17, 179, 180, 224
Byrne settlers *see* Byrne, Joseph Charles

Calderwood, Rev. Henry 109, 116, 130n.73
Caledonian Societies 24n.23, 153, 182, 188, 226, 233, 240, 241–50, 255–6, 261, 262n.7, 263n.20–1, 263n.33, 263n.36, 266n.84, 270
Campbell, General Charles 51, 61n.80, 218
Campbell, Sir Marshall 155, 167n.67
Campbell, Rev. William 179–80
Canada vii, 3, 8, 18, 19, 20, 21, 23n.11, 28n.78, 35, 60n.68, 66, 82, 85, 141, 145, 161, 163, 179, 190, 192, 201n.90, 213, 230, 232, 233, 236n.56, 240, 261n.2, 271
see also America
Cape Town 14, 29, 32–9 *passim*, 43, 44, 51, 53, 61n.80, 64–75 *passim*, 78, 80, 81, 82, 85, 87, 88, 91n.39, 92n.59, 96, 120, 127n.36, 131n.82, 148, 151, 156, 170–8 *passim*, 181–5 *passim*, 193, 194, 198n.34, 200n.67, 201n.76, 210, 212, 217, 219–24 *passim*, 229, 230, 235n.34, 237n.58, 238n.89, 243, 245, 250, 253–4, 255, 264n.48, 265n.59
Cape Town Highlanders 238n.93, 253–4
Carlyle, Thomas 92n.67, 202n.105, 228
Chalmers, Rev. John 108, 117, 189
Chalmers, Rev. William 105, 117, 118, 122
churches
    Anglican 65, 132n.93, 134n.130, 174, 175, 190, 199n.52, 211, 250
    Baptist 17, 174
    Catholic 4, 13, 26n.51, 149, 174, 175, 197n.13, 197n.18, 211
    Church of Scotland 6, 48, 55, 67, 71, 101, 102, 120, 121, 128n.45, 134n.136, 139, 156, 170, 174, 175, 177, 178, 188, 198n.25, 198n.31

Congregationalist 17, 69, 102, 145, 146, 174, 175, 179, 185, 197n.20, 206
Dutch Reformed Church 9, 17, 48, 91n.39, 97, 156, 170–9, 184, 187, 190, 192, 193, 198n.36, 202n.101, 211, 241
Episcopalian 156, 174, 197n.19
Free Church of Scotland 101, 108, 111, 114, 120–1, 123–4, 128n.43, 128n.45, 130n.65, 131n.82, 133n.121, 139, 156, 174, 178, 179–80, 187, 198n.31, 201n.76
Methodist 52, 62n.86, 120, 126n.20, 130n.74, 164n.16, 174, 198n.33
Presbyterian Church of South Africa 65, 123–4, 134n.135–6, 181, 199n.55
United Presbyterian 101, 116, 128n.43, 128n.45, 130n.67, 131n.88
see also missions; Presbyterian
coal 115, 120, 143, 147, 153, 156, 166n.50, 224, 226
Cole, Sir Lowry 47, 64, 74, 80, 82, 83, 90n.17, 210
Coloured, Cape 1, 10, 83–4, 117, 177, 195, 222, 223, 261, 274
convicts 75, 81, 83, 235n.25
Cook, Captain James 32
Cradock 52, 56, 95, 97, 170, 245
Cradock, Sir John 53, 98, 103
Craig, General Sir James Henry 4, 35, 37, 58n.31, 217
Cumming, Roualeyn Gordon 215, 216
Currie, Sir Donald 213

Dalrymple, Sir William 225–6, 231, 255, 256
Dalzell, Dr James 120, 121, 125, 133n.125
Dawson, William 184, 197n.8
diamonds 131n.82, 147, 151, 157, 219, 225, 267
Dobie, John Shedden 147
Dodds, Dr William 220–1, 222, 237n.73, 237n.80–1
Donkin, Sir Rufane 47, 52, 53, 75, 127n.39
Doyle, Arthur Conan 216, 221, 238n.82
Duff, Thomas 141–2
Dundas, General Francis 4, 35
Dundas, Henry 35, 58n.29, 58n.32
Dundee (Natal) 120, 121, 134n.136, 152, 156, 166n.51, 166n.53, 229, 245, 253

[277]

D'Urban, Sir Benjamin 83, 125n.5, 235n.20
Durban 46, 88, 136, 137, 139, 140–9 passim, 151, 153–4, 156, 165n.28, 165n.33, 166n.63, 167n.67, 179, 182, 188, 193, 221, 224, 230, 243, 247, 255, 262n.11
Dutch 1, 2, 9, 17, 27n.54, 29, 30, 31, 33, 34, 35, 36, 38, 41, 45, 56, 57n.3, 58n.33, 64, 67–78 passim, 82, 88, 89, 95, 96, 102, 104, 106, 140, 184, 187, 197n.14, 217, 227, 252, 257, 268
    see also Afrikaner; churches, Dutch Reformed Church
Dutch East India Company (VOC) 29, 31, 32, 34, 57n.8, 76, 95, 96, 125n.7

East India Company 22n.4, 37–8, 58n.32, 59n.40, 137
East London 95, 97, 129n.64, 134, 157, 179, 195, 198n.38, 218, 242, 248, 262n.7
Ellis, James 144–5, 197n.20
Elphinstone, Admiral George Keith 35, 37, 238n.95
Enlightenment, the 11, 14, 25n.34, 31, 33, 55, 58n.32, 64, 82
    see also Scots and intellectual life
Exhibitions 5–6, 23n.11, 23n.15, 215, 227, 258

Fairbairn, John 46, 48, 67–8, 71–5, 77, 78–85, 87, 91n.39, 185, 193, 211, 228
Faure, Rev. Abraham 71, 171, 197n.9
Findlay, Captain John 39, 72
Fingo, Fingoland see Mfengu
First World War 163, 225, 226, 227, 231, 232, 242, 247, 257, 260
Forbes, Alexander 148–9, 197n.20
Fort Hare (University College) 108, 110, 111, 112, 116, 134n.136, 195–6
Fraser, Rev. Colin 171–2, 197n.8
Fraser, Rev. Colin McKenzie 171, 173, 250
Freemasonry 36, 144, 176, 210, 244, 246, 252, 264n.48, 270
frontier ('Kaffir') wars 53, 56, 63n.104, 81, 84, 97, 99, 106–8, 109, 111, 114, 116, 119, 125n.16, 129n.57, 130n.68, 143, 157, 208, 212, 252, 272

Gaelic 13, 31, 128n.51, 245, 254, 257
Gcaleka, chief 95, 99
Gill, Sir David 93n.82, 194, 202n.108, 250

Gill College 187, 194
Godlonton, Robert 75, 218
gold, South African 2, 9, 15, 18, 47, 66, 115, 145, 147, 151, 153, 158, 160, 161, 162, 181, 199, 213, 225, 238n.91, 243, 248, 255, 267
Gordon Memorial Mission 112, 120–1, 133n.121, 133n.125
Gordon, Colonel Robert J. 30–1, 32, 33, 35
Govan, Rev. William 111, 131n.80
Graaff Reinet 52, 74, 86, 97, 171, 172, 174, 200n.67, 208, 218, 235n.24
Graham, Colonel John 41, 53, 97, 98, 99, 125n.13, 209
Graham, Robert Cruikshank 232–3
Grahamstown 19, 46, 47, 52, 53, 61n.73, 74, 75, 95, 97, 98, 107, 131n.82, 132n.99, 179, 181, 189, 193, 194, 209, 218, 235n.24, 258, 265n.70
Gray, Rev. James 181, 199n.55
'Great Trek' 28n.73, 172, 173, 177, 197n.13
Greig, George 70, 71–5, 85, 91n.46
Grey, Sir George 85, 111, 237n.60
Griqua 14, 96, 103, 127n.36

Hardie, James Keir 230–1, 233
Hart, Robert 97, 200n.70
Herschel, Sir John 81, 185, 200n.67, 211
Highland games 240, 243, 244, 262n.13
Highland Scots 13, 15, 25n.32, 41, 42, 50–1, 52, 54, 55, 123, 139, 140, 147, 245–6, 249, 252, 275n.5
    see also Scots and the military
Highlands, Scottish 6, 7, 12, 13, 42, 129n.64, 137, 222, 252, 258
'Hottentot' see Khoisan
Hoy, Sir William Wilson 226–7
hunting 55, 59n.46, 86, 87, 96, 135, 136, 139, 140, 146, 158, 163n.5, 204, 208, 210, 212, 214–16, 236n.42, 236n.46
Hutcheon, Duncan 213
Hyslop, Jonathan 18, 19, 169, 228, 233, 253–7 passim

Innes family 185, 187, 200n.70
Innes, James Rose 80, 105, 183, 184–5, 188, 193, 197n.8
intermarriage 7–8, 17, 24n.22, 30, 31, 45, 51, 97, 101, 116, 117, 127n.30, 136, 172, 173, 182, 208, 222, 223, 254, 274
Irish 1, 3, 4, 6, 7, 8, 16, 19, 22n.4, 36, 51–2, 65–6, 137, 139, 149, 155–6,

INDEX

161–2, 178, 229, 231, 248, 265n.59, 269, 270

Jameson, Dr Leander Starr 219
Jameson Raid 187, 225, 229, 271
Jardine, Alexander Johnstone 85, 89, 175
Johannesburg 151, 154, 181, 189, 191, 194, 226, 227, 230, 231, 232, 238n.89, 238n.91, 243–9 *passim*, 255, 256

'Kaffir Wars' *see* frontier wars
Kaffraria 95, 107, 108, 109, 112–13, 114, 118, 121, 123, 126n.24, 126n.25, 181, 200n.61, 242
Kat River 99, 106, 107, 125n.16, 127n.30
Kerr, Alexander 195–6
Kew Gardens 32, 33, 35, 88, 207
Khoisan 1, 25n.36, 31, 32, 33, 34, 45, 54–5, 70, 77, 78, 86, 95–106 *passim*, 125n.7, 125n.8, 125n.13, 125n.14, 127n.33, 133n.109, 212, 274, 275n.5
Kimberley 131n.82, 179, 194, 219, 221, 225, 229, 254–5, 265n.64
King William's Town 95, 105, 107, 129n.57, 179, 182, 242, 248
Kitchener, Lord Horatio Herbert 244, 255
Knox, Dr Robert 84, 86, 130n.65, 218
Kruger, President 170, 227, 229, 243, 244

Ladysmith 143, 144, 151, 153, 156, 179, 199n.44, 214, 230, 265
Laing, Rev. James 105, 107, 118, 130n.65, 225
Laing, John 225
Lesotho *see* Sotho
libraries 67, 73, 80, 84–5, 88, 93n.71, 93n.72, 167n.67, 181, 186, 199n.57, 219, 268
Livingstone, David vii, 5, 23n.8, 25n.35, 55, 100, 105, 111, 173, 181, 205–6, 263n.33, 266n.84, 274
LMS *see* missions
Love, Rev. John 102–5 *passim*
Lovedale mission 97, 101, 104–8 *passim*, 109–13, 114, 115–16, 120, 121, 123, 124, 126n.25, 129n.64, 130n.65, 130n.74, 131n.82, 134n.130, 134n.136, 189, 195
Lowlands, Scottish 13, 15, 42, 56, 137, 252, 264n.42, 273
Lyell (Forbes), Margaret Stewart 148–9

McCorkindale, Alexander *see* New Scotland
McDiarmid, Alexander 105, 108

Macdonald, Alexander 38, 175, 198n.24
Macfarlane, John and Walter 147, 150
McIntosh, Helen and James 151
MacKay, William Don 97–8
Mackenzie brothers (George, John, William) 223, 247–8, 249
Mackenzie, Dr James Rutherford 222–3
Mackenzie, Rev. John 127
McKidd, Rev. Alex 173
McLaren, Rev. James 114–15
McLarty, William 223–4
MacLeod, Adam Gordon 186, 201n.76
Macvicar, Dr Neil 115–16
Mann, Dr Robert James 150, 201n.79
Maqoma, chief 106–7, 116, 129n.62
Masson, Francis 30, 31–3, 34, 35, 58n.21, 58n.28
Menzies, Judge William 92n.52, 176
merino sheep 30, 79, 80, 92n.62, 97, 153, 194
Mfengu (Fingo) 99, 108, 109, 112, 114, 117, 120, 123, 125n.17, 131n.88
see also Blythswood mission
migration schemes 15–16, 42, 46, 47, 50, 135, 137, 142, 147, 148, 150–1, 154, 156–7, 162–3, 164n.16, 168n.90–1, 170–2
see also Byrne, J. C.; Moodie settlement; settlement of 1820
Milner, Alfred 112, 163, 168n.91, 189, 190, 191, 192, 232, 244, 264n.42, 267
missions, missionaries 4, 9, 14, 15, 17, 18, 19, 21, 22, 55, 56, 84, 92n.57, 94–134, 173, 176–9, 181, 185, 195, 196.2, 198n.28, 198n.36, 199n.42, 205, 208, 215, 241, 242, 259, 270, 272, 274
Glasgow Missionary Society 102, 103, 104, 105, 111, 118, 128n.41, 128n.43–5
London Missionary Society 48, 72, 101, 102, 103, 106, 109, 127n.36, 130n.68, 130n.73, 170, 197n.20, 206
see also churches
Moffat, Robert 70, 86, 90n.18, 103, 127n.30, 127n.35, 205–8
Moodie, Benjamin *see* Moodie settlement
Moodie, Donald 40, 43, 60n.68, 138, 147, 164n.14
Moodie family 47–8, 59n.45, 60n.68
Moodie, John 40, 45–6, 59n.46, 60n.68, 105–6, 129n.59
Moodie settlement (1817) 36, 39–48, 49, 51, 60n.57, 60n.59, 60n.61, 60n.68, 79, 81, 97, 105, 138, 218, 270

[279]

Moodie, Thomas 47, 60n.68
Muir, Dr John 219–20
Muir, Sir Thomas 114, 183, 186, 188, 250
Murray, Rev. Dr Andrew (snr) 171, 172, 197n.8
Murray, Rev. Dr Andrew (jnr) 170, 187–8
Murray, Charles 259–60
Murray family 170–2, 173
museums 5, 28n.73, 62n.83, 67, 85–7, 88, 166n.63, 207, 226, 258, 268

Namaqualand 33, 44, 103, 209, 210, 212
Napoleonic Wars 37, 40, 58n.32, 59n.46, 61n.82, 64, 98, 136, 209, 252
Natal 18, 19, 47, 60n.68, 74, 75, 86, 96, 97, 120, 121, 123, 135–156, 158, 159, 160, 161, 172, 179, 180, 181, 183, 188, 189, 194, 195, 197n.19–20, 213, 214, 217, 221, 224, 230, 237n.60, 242–6 passim, 255, 260, 267, 271
Natal Government Railways 143, 154–5, 166n.53, 226, 243
Ndlambe, chief 97, 98, 103, 127n.38
New Glasgow (Natal) 141, 148, 164n.16
New Scotland (Transvaal) 147, 148, 157–61, 163n.5, 245
New Zealand 2, 3, 7, 8, 18, 19, 20, 21, 23n.11, 24n.23, 66, 85, 137, 138, 162, 183, 184, 190, 192, 224, 230, 240, 271
Ngqika (Gaika), chief 95, 102, 103, 105, 106, 107, 116, 125n.8, 127n.38
Nguni, northern 86, 95, 99, 135, 139, 141, 152, 153, 159, 167n.87, 218, 230, 231, 254, 256
  see also Anglo-Zulu War; Zululand
Nguni, southern 1, 41, 53, 54, 55–6, 84, 95–108 passim, 114–20 passim, 122, 125n.7, 125n.16, 126n.25, 127n.31, 129n.57, 208, 242
  see also Gcaleka; Maqoma; Ndlambe; Ngqika (chiefs)
Niven, Rev. Robert 108, 112

Orange Free State 18, 47, 146, 151, 158, 161, 171, 182, 183, 187–8, 189, 195, 219, 226, 241, 242, 245
Orange River Colony 189, 190, 245, 246, 250

Paterson, Francis 30, 32, 33–5, 58n.28
Paterson, John 75, 185, 200n.68, 201n.71
Philip, Dr John 26n.53, 48, 69–70, 72, 75–9, 81, 83, 87, 91n.34, 91n.39, 97–8, 102, 103, 106, 129n.59, 129n.62, 175, 193, 228, 274

Pietermaritzburg 139, 143, 146–9 passim, 153, 154, 156, 159, 165n.20, 165n.23, 165n.25, 165n.33, 165n.35, 166n.63, 179–80, 193, 199n.52, 217, 230, 243, 246, 255, 260, 263n.21
Pillans, Charles Stuart 73, 92n.55, 175, 198n.24
Pine, Lieutenant-governor Benjamin 75, 139, 140, 143, 146, 165n.33
police 113, 157
population 2, 12, 20, 36, 48, 65–6, 149–50, 155–6, 161–2, 165n.40, 178, 205
Port Elizabeth (Algoa Bay) 32, 39, 52, 54, 65, 74, 75, 79, 81, 88, 93, 95, 102, 131n.82, 132n.99, 156, 157, 167n.70, 179, 180, 185, 186, 187, 197n.18, 198n.37, 200n.67–8, 213, 218, 243, 245, 253, 262n.9
Presbyterian 9, 17, 26n.51, 36, 39, 56–7, 57n.6, 65, 73, 78–9, 85, 87, 89, 91n.37, 97, 102, 103, 120, 124, 128n.44, 132n.99, 146, 153, 156, 162, 169–72 passim, 174–83, 188, 189, 190, 195, 197n.21, 198n.25, 198n.36, 198n.38, 199n.42, 199n.46–7, 199n.52, 199, 211, 218, 229, 241, 244, 246, 249, 252, 256, 264n.42, 270, 274
  see also churches; missions
Pretoria 19, 160–1, 179, 181, 189, 190, 191, 193, 199n.46, 199n.58, 214, 244, 248, 257, 258, 275n.9
Pretorius, President 158–9
Pringle, John 37–8, 198n.36
Pringle, Thomas 44, 48–57, 59n.43, 61n.82, 62n.93, 63n.101–2, 64, 67–75, 78–9, 85, 87, 91n.37, 91n.38, 92n.57, 228, 240, 259
Proudfoot family 136–7

racial politics 20–1, 48–9, 62n.86, 75, 77, 83–4, 89, 94, 112, 113–14, 115, 150, 177–8, 200n.70, 204, 228, 230–3, 241–2, 250, 257, 259, 260–1, 270, 271–2
railways 137, 141, 143, 150, 153–5, 165n.34, 166n.53, 166n.64, 210, 213, 221–7 passim, 246, 256, 265n.64, 269
  see also Natal Government Railways
Raitt, Alexander Seaton 232–3
Rattray, James 184, 197n.8, 200n.67
Read, James 69, 106
Reid, Joseph 185–6, 200n.67–8
Reitz, President 187, 263n.19

INDEX

Rhodes, Cecil 47, 109, 112, 114, 219, 225, 227, 238n.94, 254
Robertson, Rev. William 170, 171, 173, 184, 187, 197n.8
Romantic movement 12, 52, 55, 64, 68, 206, 251
Ross, Rev. David 171, 173
Ross, Rev. John 104, 105, 106–7, 108, 114, 119, 126n.21, 128n.50–1, 129n.64
Ross, Rev. Richard 108, 109, 114, 116, 129n.64
Russell, Rev. John Munro 178, 198n.38
Russell, Robert 183, 188
Rutherfoord, H. E. 70, 88

San *see* Khoisan
Sandilands, Gordon 256–7
Sandile, chief 117, 118, 132n.100
Scotch Education Department 190, 191
Scotch Irish (Northern Irish or Ulster Scots) 3–4, 36, 65, 89
Scots and
   agriculture 6, 11, 14, 38–53 *passim*, 55, 63n.102, 79, 80, 88, 95, 97, 100, 103, 109, 110, 111, 115, 121, 137, 140–8 *passim*, 151–3, 157, 158, 163, 186, 205–6, 207, 213–14, 216, 225, 226, 269
   business 5, 9, 14, 17, 20, 21, 29, 36, 37–9, 44, 45–7, 59n.43, 64, 66, 67, 70, 77–81, 122, 136–7, 140–8 *passim*, 149, 151, 152–5, 160–1, 164n.20, 165 n.23–5, 185, 204, 223–8, 247–8, 250–1, 264n.40, 270, 272
   culture 4, 5, 13, 14, 16, 17, 20, 21, 24n.23, 45, 54, 67, 80, 142, 162, 177, 179, 186, 187, 197n.22, 201n.76, 210–11, 213, 224, 226, 235n.34, 237n.73, 238n.93, 240–51, 253, 257–61, 262n.3, 264n.44, 270–3 *passim*
   see also Burns, Robert; Caledonian Societies; Highland games
   education 4–5, 9, 11, 13, 38, 67–9, 79, 80, 87, 91n.39, 100, 101, 102, 105–6, 109–16, 120, 123, 126n.24, 126n.25, 132n.93, 133n.124, 141, 142, 155, 160, 169–203, 218, 219, 220, 227, 228, 241, 250, 251, 269, 272
   engineering, civil 15, 44, 81, 142, 154, 161, 166n.63, 194, 204, 208, 210, 218, 225, 226, 232, 269
   environment, the 9, 12, 14, 15, 18, 21, 26n.38, 26n.53, 52–6, 103, 111, 204–16, 250, 258, 264n.42, 273
   exploration 15, 30, 31, 32, 33–4, 54, 86, 103, 105, 208–9, 211, 218
   finance 80, 143, 144, 146, 148, 159, 165n.26, 167n.67, 187–8, 200n.67–8, 210, 211, 223–4, 225–6, 238n.89, 243, 247–8
   forestry 9, 193, 204–8 *passim*, 216, 234n.11, 234n.13
   frontiers 13, 14, 18, 41, 45, 47, 48–9, 51–6, 60n.57, 62n.83, 63n.101, 63n.104, 69, 70, 73, 77, 79, 81, 86, 94–134, 136, 148, 208, 210, 211, 219, 236n.42, 242, 270, 272
   intellectual life 9, 13, 14, 17, 45, 56, 64, 66–7, 68, 70, 73, 84–8, 193, 210, 212, 218, 219, 227, 258
   law, the 30, 36–7, 43–6, 61n.73, 76, 81, 92n.52, 143, 144, 145, 146, 147, 148, 169, 184, 200n.67, 201n.87, 211
   medicine 4, 9, 22n.4, 29–30, 43, 44, 68, 72, 80, 85–6, 97–8, 113, 115–16, 120, 121, 122, 129n.64, 130n.65, 145, 202n.108, 204, 210, 213–14, 216–23, 237n.60, 237n.75
   military, the 5, 9, 18, 19, 22, 25n.32, 29–30, 31, 35–6, 37, 39, 40, 44, 52, 57n.1, 57n.3, 58n.33, 58n.34, 59n.35, 59n.38, 59n.46, 60n.68, 61n.80, 61n.82, 86, 97–9, 106–7, 136, 140, 142–3, 144, 149, 160, 163, 165n.34, 175, 176, 181, 197n.18, 208, 209–10, 214, 215, 225, 226, 229, 231, 238n.93, 241–5 *passim*, 249, 252–8, 260, 261, 263n.19, 265n.64–5, 265n.70, 272
   see also Anglo-Boer War; Cape Town Highlanders; Transvaal Scottish Volunteers
   mining 153, 162, 194, 219, 224, 225–6, 231, 232, 238n.91, 243, 256, 261, 269
   'networks' 11, 14, 16–17, 26n.38, 26n.42, 39, 67–8, 89, 120, 143–4, 145, 154–5, 194, 209, 221, 236n.53, 243, 247–8, 249, 261
   politics 21, 44, 47, 51, 64, 69–75, 81, 85, 90n.17, 90n.18, 92n.52, 103, 106–7, 134n.136,

[281]

143–7 *passim*, 149, 152, 155, 161, 169, 185, 197n.18, 200n.68, 218, 219, 223–7 *passim*, 228–33, 243, 249–50, 256, 258, 261, 262n.9, 268, 273
press, the 9, 12–13, 15, 16–17, 26n.39, 66–81 *passim*, 83, 85, 91n.46, 92n.60, 102, 103, 104, 110, 112, 131n.79, 134n.136, 140, 141, 145, 146, 153, 155, 166n.47, 167n.67, 176, 185, 186, 200n.68, 209, 212, 214, 215, 218, 220–1, 228, 229–30, 231, 244, 248–51, 253, 275
religion 9, 13, 15, 17, 26n.51, 27n.54, 64, 67, 68, 70, 76, 78, 147, 156, 169–203, 204–8, 218, 228, 246–7, 250, 258, 264n.42, 269, 272, 274
representative government 44, 81–4, 89, 140
science and engineering 9, 11, 12, 14, 15, 30, 33, 35, 38, 67, 68, 81, 84–8, 93n.82, 122, 141, 143, 145, 147, 154–5, 162, 166n.63, 194, 196, 202n.106, 204–9, 212–14, 216, 219–20, 226, 227, 229, 232, 248, 269, 273
social mobility 11, 12, 33, 34, 38, 46, 56, 60n.61, 73, 85–6, 88, 123, 144, 169, 208, 223, 228, 248, 254, 272–3
surveying, land 4, 9, 15, 39, 46, 76, 86, 141, 145, 152, 160, 163n.5, 194, 208–9, 210, 213, 225
trades union 18, 155, 169, 186, 223–4, 226–33 *passim*, 239n.102, 242, 261, 270, 275
universities 11, 13, 25n.35, 66–7, 101, 110, 178, 186, 192–6, 202n.106, 202n.108, 202n.111, 216–17, 228, 236n.56
urban society 6, 9, 11, 14, 42, 56, 69, 76, 79, 139, 152–3, 160, 205, 269, 273–4
'Scotsmen, black' 123, 134n.129, 274
Scott, Rev. Charles 139, 179
Scott, Sir Walter 12, 16, 51, 54, 55, 64, 264n.44
settlement of 1820 36, 48–57, 61n.77, 61n.82, 62n.83, 93n.71, 99, 139, 159, 160, 200n.70, 218
Shepstone, Sir Theophilus 146, 150, 165n.40
Sivewright, Sir James 227–8, 238n.93
Skinner, Sir Harold Ross 225

slaves 8, 45, 54, 55, 70, 73, 74, 77–9, 82, 83, 92n.55, 92n.56, 115, 176–7
Smith, Rev. Alexander 105, 197n.8
Smith, Dr Sir Andrew 85–7, 89, 218, 236n.42
Smith, Sir Charles Abercrombie 194
Smith, Sir Harry 83, 109, 129n.57
Smith, Thomas Paterson 152–3
Smuts, Jan 155, 231
Smyth, Charles Piazzi 211, 212
Smythe, Charles John 151–2
Socialism 229–32 *passim*
Soga family 116–18, 132n.102–6, 181, 214
Soga, Rev. Tiyo 116–18, 119, 122, 132n.98, 132n.101, 274
Somerset, Lord Charles 42, 43, 47, 51, 53, 64, 66–74, 82, 87, 91n.32, 91n.34, 91n.39, 91n.42, 98, 104, 170, 173, 184, 267
Somerville, Dr William 217–18
Sotho 86, 96, 116, 125n.3, 146, 152, 215
South African College 38, 67, 80, 87, 88, 178, 185, 192–3, 194, 202n.106, 206, 211, 219
South African Republic 144, 153, 201n.84, 241, 242, 245, 275n.9
South African Scot, The 241, 247–51, 259, 274
Stellenbosch 14, 16, 17, 170–3 *passim*, 184, 193, 194, 197n.10, 202n.111
Stevenson-Hamilton, James 215–16
Stewart, Rev. James 101, 110, 111–12, 114, 115, 116, 120, 121, 124, 127n.29, 131n.81, 195, 250, 274
Steyn, President 171
Stockenstroom, Sir Andries 83
sugar 140, 142, 143, 144, 147, 149, 150, 151, 155, 156, 210
Sutherland, Dr Peter Cormac 145, 165n.35, 237n.60
Swazi 147, 152, 158, 159, 160, 167n.87
Swellendam 14, 44, 47, 48, 171, 172, 186, 200n.67

Templeton, Robert 189, 200n.70, 201n.87
Tennant, Sir David 193
Thom, Rev. George 170–1, 175, 177, 184, 197n.8
Thomson, Rev. William Ritchie 104, 107, 116, 118, 197n.8
Transkei 95, 96, 97, 108, 109, 115, 117, 123, 195
Transvaal 9, 18, 44, 47, 86, 109, 145, 148, 151, 153, 158–63 *passim*, 167n.84, 173, 185, 189, 190, 191, 195, 200n.67, 216, 219, 226, 229,

232, 238n.89, 238n.91, 242, 244, 245, 275n.9
Transvaal Scottish (Volunteers) 225, 255–7
Tswana 1, 86, 96, 103, 134n.130, 205, 208
Tullibardine, John George Murray, Marquess of 255, 265n.65
Tyumie (Chumie) mission 102, 104–9 passim, 119, 122, 126n.25, 195

Uitenhage 105, 184, 185, 189, 200n.70
uitlander 181, 225, 229, 255
Union (of South Africa, 1910) 8, 10, 17–20 passim, 66, 152, 161, 163, 183, 185, 195, 201n.87, 219, 224, 226, 231, 237n.65, 242, 257, 259, 260, 275
Union, Act of (1707) 10, 11, 260
University of Cape Town (formerly Cape of Good Hope) 178, 188, 193–4, 202n.111, 217, 219, 237n.58

van der Kemp, Johannes T. 69, 102–4
VOC see Dutch East India Company

Waterston, Dr Jane 113, 119–20, 133n.119–20, 250, 274
Witwatersrand (Rand) 66, 126, 162, 163, 169, 180, 181, 193, 194, 213, 225, 226, 229–32 passim, 243, 246, 255–6
Wodehouse, Sir Philip 114
women 11, 17, 39, 43, 49, 67, 69, 85, 100–2, 105, 106, 109–10, 111–13, 115, 118–21, 123, 126n.24, 126n.25, 127n.30, 127n.31, 131n.86, 132n.102, 133n.116, 133n.119–20, 133n.124, 134n.131, 140, 144, 148–9, 152, 157, 162–3, 168n.90–1, 181–3, 186, 189–92, 195, 220, 222, 230, 259, 274

Xhosa see Nguni, southern

Yonge, Sir George 35, 70, 102, 218

Zulu see Nguni, northern
Zululand 112, 136, 142, 144, 149–50, 152, 159, 165n.40
Zuurveld 41, 95, 97, 98, 187

EU authorised representative for GPSR:
Easy Access System Europe, Mustamäe tee 50,
10621 Tallinn, Estonia
gpsr.requests@easproject.com